Microsoft® Office
Excel® 2007

The L Line,™
The Express Line to Learning

Microsoft® Office Excel® 2007

The L Line,™
The Express Line to Learning

Kathy Jacobs

Wiley Publishing, Inc.

Microsoft® Office Excel® 2007: The L Line™ The Express Line to Learning

Published by
Wiley Publishing, Inc.
111 River Street
Hoboken, NJ 07030-5774
www.wiley.com

Copyright © 2007 by Wiley Publishing, Inc., Indianapolis, Indiana

Published by Wiley Publishing, Inc., Indianapolis, Indiana

Published simultaneously in Canada

For general information on our other products and services, please contact our Customer Care Department within the U.S. at 800-762-2974, outside the U.S. at 317-572-3993, or fax 317-572-4002.

For technical support, please visit www.wiley.com/techsupport.

Wiley also publishes its books in a variety of electronic formats. Some content that appears in print may not be available in electronic books.

Library of Congress Control Number: 2006939424

ISBN: 978-0-470-10788-1

Manufactured in the United States of America

10 9 8 7 6 5 4 3 2 1

WILEY

About the Author

When did you start using Office? **Kathy Jacobs**, Microsoft MVP in PowerPoint and OneNote, has been using Office since its earliest days. She started out using Word for newsletters, letters, books, and other documents in the late 1980s. She added PowerPoint to her areas of expertise in the early 1990s, when she first moved to Office on the PC while developing training at Honeywell. At that same training job, she started using Excel to create budgets, track students, and perform a wide variety of other tasks. In truth, she couldn't live without any of the major Office products. She has been an active Office beta tester since its 2002 release and has been working with Office 2007 for many months.

Kathy specializes in helping people from all backgrounds and all walks of life learn to use Office to make their lives easier. As a PowerPoint and OneNote consultant, trainer, and writer, she has written about Office topics for her own site (www.onppt.com), her blog (Vitamin CH — The cure for all computer ailments), Office Online, Lockergnome, IndeZine, and the PowerPoint FAQ. She presents regularly on a variety of subjects at the Phoenix PC User Group, where she is vice president. She has given the AZ Association of Computer Clubs User Group tour twice, including a tour of Office 2007.

Actively involved in PPT Live (the PowerPoint conference for users) since its inception, Kathy has written *Kathy Jacobs on PowerPoint* and co-written *Unleash the Power of OneNote*. She is the creator of KeyStone Learning's OneNote 2003 training DVD. Right now, she specializes in helping people solve their Office emergencies through her service, Call Kathy Solutions.

Publisher's Acknowledgments

Acquisitions, Editorial, and Media Development

Project Editor
Kim Darosett

Executive Editor
Greg Croy

Copy Editor
Rebecca Whitney

Technical Editor
Damir Bersinic

Supplements Writer
Peo Sjoblom

Editorial Manager
Leah Cameron

Media Development and Quality Assurance
Angela Denny, Kate Jenkins, Steven Kudirka, Kit Malone

Media Development Coordinator
Jenny Swisher

Media Project Supervisor
Laura Moss-Hollister

Editorial Assistant
Amanda Foxworth

Sr. Editorial Assistant
Cherie Case

Composition Services

Project Coordinator
Erin Smith

Layout and Graphics
Denny Hager, Heather Ryan

Proofreaders
Christy Pingleton, Ethel M. Winslow

Indexer
Joan Griffitts

Anniversary Logo Design
Richard Pacifico

Publishing and Editorial for General User Technology

Richard Swadley, *Vice President and Executive Group Publisher*

Andy Cummings, *Vice President and Publisher*

Mary Bednarek, *Executive Acquisitions Director*

Mary C. Corder, *Editorial Director*

Composition Services

Gerry Fahey, *Vice President of Production Services*

Debbie Stailey, *Director of Composition Services*

Author's Acknowledgments

The author would like to acknowledge the assistance and support of the following people during the development of this book:

Bruce Jacobs, for helping out in all phases of the book and for keeping it moving whenever I got stuck

Austin Myers, for support during the writing of the macro and add-ins chapters

Kim Darosett, for doing a great job of editing and making my words look good

Neil Salkind, for believing

Dedication

To Hannah — and she knows why

To Bruce — 23 years and counting

Contents at a Glance

Contents

Preface

From the Publisher

Welcome to *Excel 2007: The L Line, The Express Line to Learning.* This book belongs to a new tutorial series from Wiley Publishing created for independent learners, students, and teachers alike. Whether you are learning (or teaching) in a classroom setting or wanting to learn how to use Excel 2007, this book is for you. As rigorous and replete as any college course or seminar, *Excel 2007: The L Line* offers instruction for understanding not just how to use Excel but also how to use it in the real world.

Like all titles in *The L Line, The Express Line to Learning* series, this book's design reflects the concept of learning as a journey — a trip on a subway system — with navigational tools and real-world stops along the way. The destination, of course, is mastery of Excel 2007.

From the Author

Excel. Say the word, and many people blanch. Excel is associated with number crunching, data analysis, accounting, charting — anything to do with numbers and math. It is not many people's favorite subject.

It's unfortunate that Excel has this reputation. Yes, Excel is used for number crunching, formulas, and data analysis, but it is also used to sort and filter data of all kinds, to show data graphically, and to help you learn all you can from the data your business generates.

I have written this book to help you learn how to use Excel to make your life easier. I am not a number cruncher; I am a trainer and a writer. In fact, I train people to use PowerPoint and OneNote more frequently than I train them to use Excel. I look at Excel from the same viewpoint as you do: Have Excel do as much of the work as possible so that I can spend time on the tasks that it can't do. (I don't spend my hours playing around with data just for fun.)

I don't want to be Excel's slave, and neither should you. Excel exists to make it easier to work with and understand your data. It doesn't exist to make your life harder.

This book is for users who know that they should use Excel but don't know how. If you have some knowledge of previous versions of Excel, you will find this book useful in understanding which features in Excel 2007 have changed. If you are an Excel novice, this book will help you step though its intricate processes in a clear, concise manner.

The exercises and the data used in this book are based on real-life situations and problems. This approach will help you see how Excel 2007 can help you navigate the world of data and come out on the other side with a real understanding of how to apply the concepts to your life. The sample files that you need to perform the exercises in the book are available for downloading at the book's Web site.

What Will You Learn?

By working through the exercises in this book, you will become proficient in using Excel to learn everything your data can tell you. The first few chapters in this book describe the basics of moving around in Excel. Later chapters get progressively more involved, ending with chapters about writing macros and add-ins.

The 16 chapters in this book cover everything you need to know in order to use Excel. Each chapter also uses independent scenarios to help you learn.

- Chapters 1 through 4 introduce you to the Excel 2007 interface and the basics of creating your first few spreadsheets. Even if you have used previous versions of Excel, check out these chapters. Excel 2007 uses an entirely new interface, which may take you some time to get used to. By the time you finish the exercises in Chapter 4, you will know the basics of using Excel 2007.

- Chapters 5 through 9 describe other ways to look at your data. You will learn all about Excel charting, using pivot tables, printing, and sharing data with other applications.

- Chapters 10 through 12 help you extend your Excel skills beyond the basics by learning about filtering and sorting your data, validating your data, analyzing your data, and customizing the way you use Excel.

- Chapters 13 through 16 walk you through the final step in your Excel journey. In these four chapters, you will learn how to use other programs available to extend Excel, how to create your own macros (which are programs), and how to make your macros available no matter which spreadsheet you are using.

When you reach the last stop on the Excel 2007 L-Line, you will be an Excel expert!

What Will You Need?

To complete all the exercises in this book, you need the following items, including hardware and software:

- A computer running Windows Vista or Windows XP Service Pack 2

- A basic understanding of how to use Windows

- Reliable Internet access
- An installed version of Excel 2007
- (Optional) A full installation of Office 2007

What's in Each Chapter?

This book is not written for you to just read — it is written to help you learn. As you go through each chapter, you will find these elements:

- **Stations Along the Way:** A quick list of what you will learn in this chapter.

- **Enter the Station:** A list of questions to get you thinking about the topics covered in the chapter. As you read the questions, try to answer them. I don't expect that you will be able to answer most of them before starting to read the chapter. Instead, use the questions to help you target the parts of the chapter where you need to pay closer attention.

- **Step-by-step exercises:** A series of step-by-step exercises to help you work with Excel while you learn to use it. You can get by with just reading the chapter content. However, by doing the exercises whenever possible, you cement the knowledge in your brain and your fingers. Each exercise has been tested to ensure that the information you are working with reinforces the topics covered.

- **Screen shots:** Provided wherever possible to show you what you should see on your screen and to explain the resulting changes to your data. Text alone is not the best way to learn about a topic!

- **Street Jargon:** A mini glossary, at the end of each chapter, that reviews key technical terms.

- **Practice Exam:** Your last stop before finishing a chapter. The Practice Exam tests you on the concepts you learn in each chapter. All answers are in Appendix A.

Icons Used in This Book

The following margin icons are used in this book to assist with your understanding of the material and indicate points of particular interest:

Information Kiosk

These tip icons use the international symbol for information to point you to content of special interest.

Watch Your Step

Warning icons are placed next to information that can help you avoid making common mistakes.

Transfer

These cross-reference icons direct you to related information found in another section or chapter.

Step Into the Real World

These icons are in sidebars that provide you with real-life scenarios where the information in the chapter makes an impact. The information in the scenarios should help you determine how to apply your knowledge to a real-life situation.

Using the Web Site

I truly hope that you enjoy reading this book. If that's all you do, however, you'll miss out on the real joy of this enterprise. For many of the tasks outlined in this book, you can find free sample files on the companion Web site (www.wiley.com/go/thelline) so that you can follow along. You won't learn this stuff by just reading about it. You really have to get in there and do it yourself. Jump in, make some mistakes, and keep working away at the tasks outlined in this book. That's how learning really happens.

For Instructors and Students

Excel 2007: The L Line, The Express Line to Learning has a rich set of supplemental resources for students and instructors:

- **Instructors:** You can find a test bank, PowerPoint presentations with course and book outlines, and an instructor's manual and sample syllabi online. Please contact Wiley for access to these resources.

- **Students and independent learners:** You can find resources such as chapter outlines and sample test questions at www.wiley.com/go/thelline.

CHAPTER

1

Exploring Excel

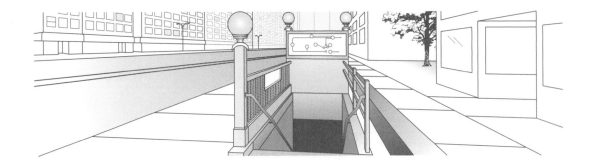

Enter the Station

Questions

1. What are some advantages to using Excel to manage your data?

2. How do you access the commands for opening and saving files?

3. What is the Ribbon?

4. How many tabs are always on the Ribbon?

5. What is a contextual tab?

6. What is the difference between a task pane and a dialog box?

7. Are Excel files stored as binary code or as XML?

8. What is the difference between a file with the extension .xlsx and one with the extension .xlsm?

9. How do you access the Excel Help system?

Express Line

If you already understand why you would use Excel 2007, how to do basic navigation in Excel, and how to get help in Excel, skip ahead to the next chapter.

Welcome to the world of Excel. In today's world of constant information and change, everyone needs a way to organize, process, and handle data of all types. Excel is one of the best programs around for doing just that.

Excel lets you learn from data of all kinds. You can:

- Sort data to see it in a different order.
- Filter data to see just pieces of it.
- Use data in formulas to create new data.
- Chart data to learn what happened in the past and forecast what may happen in the future.
- Build applications and interfaces that let you verify, correct, and change the data.

While working through the exercises in this book, you learn about real tasks that people do with Excel every day, such as the ones in the following list:

- Remove duplicates from e-mail lists.
- Generate automated time cards.
- Chart the changes in inventory and sales over time.
- Create and manage budgets.
- Generate, track, and print invoices.

To start the process, you need to understand the basics of using Excel. In this chapter, you learn more about what Excel is, how the parts of the interface fit together, how data is stored using Excel, and how to get help as you go along.

What Is Excel and Why Use It?

The original purpose behind Excel was to crunch numbers. People knew that a computer could do complex data analysis and number crunching faster than they could do those tasks manually. To facilitate that, in the early 1980s, a number of programs were created that helped users move to their desktops some of the number crunching that was done on mainframe computers. Microsoft released Excel in 1985 as a replacement for Multiplan, its original spreadsheet (number-crunching) program.

Excel has always been good at making calculations. One of the best ways to learn from information you have is to use a formula or series of formulas to expand what that data is telling you. Originally, formulas created by Excel were clumsy and complicated. Now, formulas are better organized and much easier to understand. Many formulas can even be nested to create complicated computations.

Over the years, Excel has been used to work with larger and larger amounts of data at a single time. In addition, Excel users have moved from having all the data stored on their local machines to working with data from huge SQL Server 2005 and other relational databases in Excel. This situation may seem like a throwback to the early days of computers, where all the data was stored on mainframes. However, with the power of today's machines, far more computational and storage power is inside your desktop computer than was available on any mainframe when Excel was first released.

Why use Excel? Excel 2007 makes it easy to track, understand, and work with the data you come in contact with every day at home or at work. The program lets you organize your data into groups of information. You can then chart that information so that you can see trends in the data. You can combine the data by using a wide variety of formulas to create more data and to learn from it.

In short, you can use Excel to help you understand what your data can do for you.

Information Kiosk

Until recently, workbooks were limited to sheets of 256 columns and 16,384 rows. In Excel 2007, you can have more than 16,000 columns and 1 million rows on as many sheets as your computer can handle. With these larger spreadsheet sizes, you can now store more data in a single Excel file than many mainframe machines could handle when Excel was originally developed.

The Excel 2007 Ribbon Interface

If you have used previous versions of Excel, you may know that every time you upgraded, you had to relearn where existing functionality was hidden and reread the documentation to learn how to access and use new features. As Excel has grown, the number of items on the menus and the number of features available have grown exponentially. If Excel 2007 had continued with the menu-driven approach, it would have been virtually impossible to find everything you needed.

Excel 2007 doesn't work like anything you have ever used. In Office 2007, Microsoft replaced the menus and toolbars with a new interface: the *Ribbon*. The Ribbon is designed to help you more easily find elements within the interface and work with your data overall. In addition, the Ribbon can easily be expanded in future versions without adding more complexity.

If you have used a previous version of Excel, you may find the Ribbon confusing at first glance. Give yourself some time to get adjusted to it. Microsoft put a good deal of work into making sure that the content of the Ribbon is organized in a work-friendly manner.

The vast majority of your work is done by using buttons of one kind or another. These buttons reside in groups, which in turn reside on tabs. The available tabs make up your Ribbon. Figure 1-1 shows you the Ribbon, which is at the top of your Excel interface.

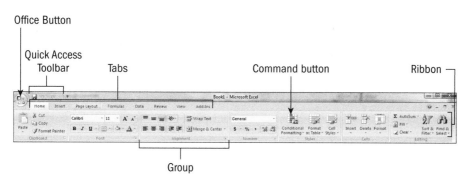

Figure 1-1: Various parts of the new Ribbon interface.

The Ribbon, which is designed to help you do your work, is organized so that the functions used most often are on the far left side. The least used and most specialized functions are on the far right side.

Office Button: On the far left side of the Ribbon, the Office Button lets you perform tasks that are common across many Office applications, such as opening, saving, and closing files. The right side of the list shows the documents most recently accessed from Excel. The options you can access from the Office Button are shown in Figure 1-2.

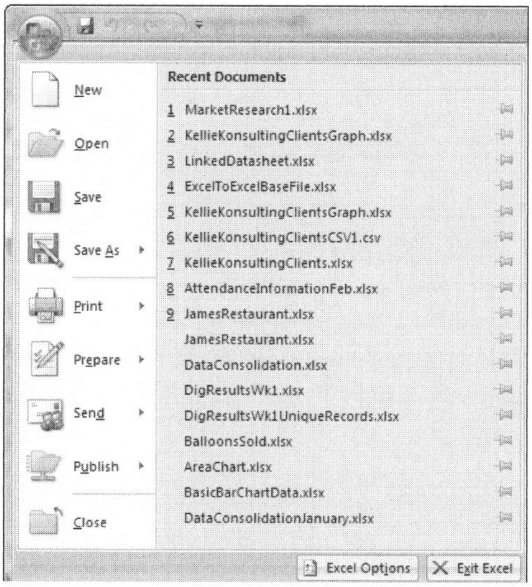

Figure 1-2: Options and functions that are accessible from the Office Button.

Quick Access Toolbar: The top half of the Office Button sits on the Quick Access Toolbar (QAT), where you can place buttons for actions you perform frequently. Although the term QAT is technically an acronym, you seldom hear it called by its full name. It is generally referred to as the QAT (pronounced "kwaht"). Chapter 13 explains how to customize your QAT.

Tabs: Just below the QAT is the row of tabs. Clicking a tab name once activates the tab. Clicking any tab twice collapses the Ribbon under the tabs so that it disappears. The Ribbon is still accessible by clicking the tabs, but it shrinks out of your way when not in use.

On the far right side of the Excel interface are the Minimize, Restore, and Close buttons for Excel (on the top row) and the Help, Minimize, Restore, and Close buttons for the active document (on the second row).

Tabs

At most times, your Ribbon has eight tabs on it. If you are working with certain items within Excel, you will have extra tabs known as contextual tabs. Each tab name indicates the type of task you can do with the buttons grouped within that tab. This list describes the type of task you can perform on each tab:

Home tab: Format the contents of your Excel file, from the cell level to the sheet level. You spend most of your time working from this tab. The Home tab is selected in Figure 1-1. If you are using other Office 2007 applications, notice that the buttons and groups on the Home tab look somewhat similar across all ribboned applications.

Insert tab: Add content to your Excel spreadsheet. As shown in Figure 1-3, this tab gives you one-click access to new tables, illustrations, charts, links, and text items.

Figure 1-3: Use the Insert tab to add content to your worksheet.

Page Layout tab: Prepare your Excel sheets for printing. As shown in Figure 1-4, this tab gives you one-click access to your worksheet's theme, page setup, scaling, and options and to the arrangement of visible sheets.

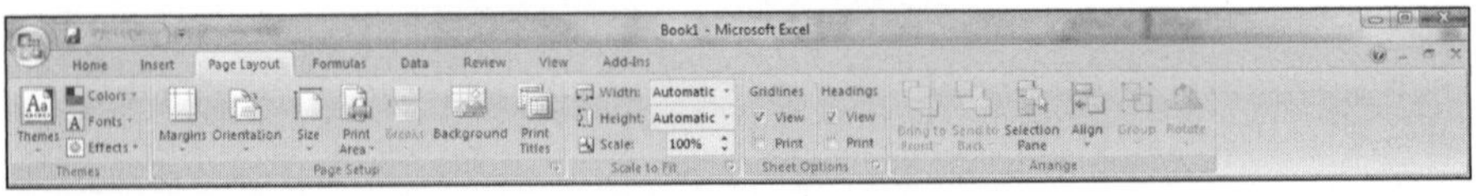

Figure 1-4: Use the Page Layout tab to fine-tune your worksheet for printing.

Formulas tab: Work with the data in your sheet by adding formulas to the data. As shown in Figure 1-5, this tab gives you one-click access to all formulas, which have been categorized for your ease of use. In addition, you use the Formulas tab for creating names for your cells and tables, checking formulas, and defining the calculations of your sheet values.

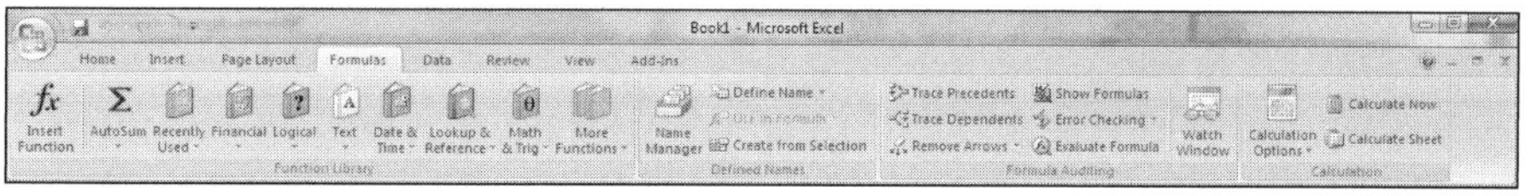

Figure 1-5: Use the Formulas tab to add formulas to your document.

Data tab: Add data to your sheet from other sources, merge data within sheets, and sort and filter visible data. As shown in Figure 1-6, this tab gives you one-click access to external data sources, the sort and filter functions, and the outlining and data tools.

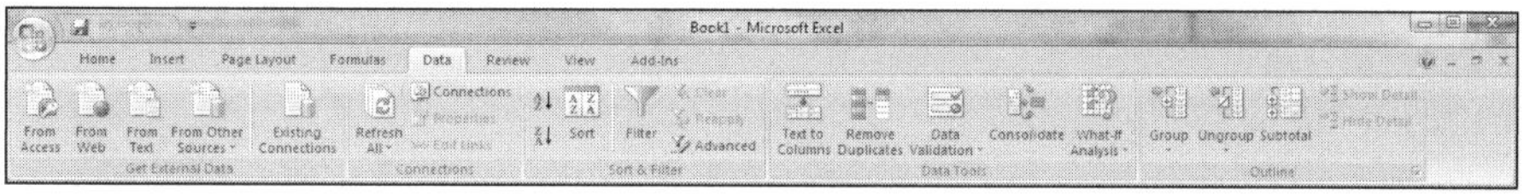

Figure 1-6: The Data tab enables you to add existing data to your worksheet.

Review tab: Proofread, comment on, and protect the contents of the active Excel sheet, as shown in Figure 1-7. These functions are most useful when you are sharing your work with other users.

Figure 1-7: The Review tab comes in handy when you're working collaboratively.

View tab: Define exactly how, and how much of, your work is shown on-screen. As shown in Figure 1-8, this tab gives you one-click access to the various views that Excel supports and to the window and zoom functions. From this tab, you can turn on and off various parts of the Excel interface. In addition, the far right side of the tab shows the interface to the macro environment, which you learn about in Chapter 15.

Figure 1-8: Use the View tab to change the look of the Excel interface.

Add-Ins tab: Access any add-ins you may have installed. *Add-ins* are like macros, but are attached to your Excel environment rather than to individual files. The Add-Ins tab is blank by default. If it is not blank, you have installed additional software to support or enhance your use of Excel.

Transfer

If you want, you can turn on one more tab: the Developer tab, where you work with macros and add-ins in a more concentrated manner. This tab is discussed in Chapter 15.

As you work in the ribboned environment, sometimes additional tabs are visible. These *contextual* tabs are related to specific functionality within Excel. For example, the Table tab is shown only when the active cell is inside a defined table. The charting tabs are visible only when you are working with a chart, as shown in Figure 1-9.

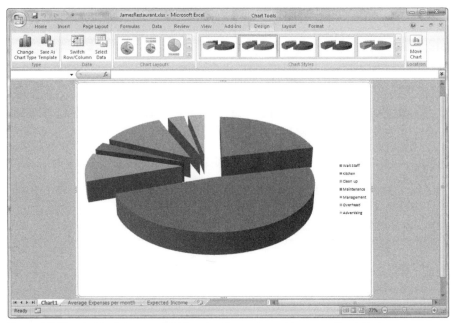

Figure 1-9: The charting tabs are available only when you're working on an Excel chart.

Contextual tabs are an attempt by Microsoft to guess what you want to do and when you want to do it. Because the interface for Excel has gotten so complex, it makes sense to offer certain parts of the interface only when the objects that use those parts are selected. For example, you can format a table only if the active cell is within a table. As another example, although the basic functionality of adding a chart is always accessible, the functionality related to just charting is visible only when a chart is active. You can always add a chart by using the buttons on the Insert tab, but you can see and use the chart formatting tab only when a chart is selected.

You are likely to find that you either love or hate contextual tabs. If you are used to having every option visible at all times, it takes some time to get used to the fact that some tabs just aren't available sometimes. However, the implementation of contextual tabs is fairly smooth. You eventually get adjusted to the availability of extra tabs and don't miss "missing" tabs.

Buttons

When you click a button that appears in the new Ribbon interface, it performs one of the following actions:

- **Carries out an immediate change:** These buttons are just like your old toolbar buttons — you click the button, and something in your sheet changes.

- **Opens a drop-down list that contains additional options:** Every time you click a button that displays a drop-down list, a predefined action is taken, and you can choose from a separate group of actions on the drop-down list.

- **Opens a gallery:** *Galleries* are buttons with multiple choices available. Each choice does something different to your data. You will find that most galleries are associated with the formatting of your data and charts. The closest thing to a gallery in the older versions of Excel were some of the formatting-oriented task panes.

The Ribbon interface has one big drawback: You cannot move buttons from one tab to another, and you cannot add buttons to, or remove buttons from, the Ribbon itself. As you learn in Chapter 13, you can add buttons to the QAT, but you cannot, as a casual user, change the contents of a tab or group. You need either some knowledge of XML or an outside tool to make the changes for you.

Task panes

Some buttons on the Ribbon bring up the task panes you may have seen in previous versions of Office. *Task panes* are similar to dialog boxes, except that task panes are permanently attached to either the side or top of your work area. You can open or close task panes at the click of a button. An example of a task pane in Excel is the clip art interface, shown in Figure 1-10.

As you can see, task panes open vertically by default, usually on the right side of the Excel interface. You can drag around the task pane by clicking and dragging on the pane's title bar. When a task pane is open, you can use it, move it to one of the other locations, change its size, or close it.

Figure 1-10: The Clip Art task pane.

You find only a few task panes within Excel. The PivotTable task pane is useful as you learn more about your data. You use the Data Management task pane if you are working with documents on a SharePoint or Office Live server. You are not likely to run into other task panes during your regular work.

Dialog boxes

In contrast to task panes, many buttons open dialog boxes. *Dialog boxes* are the windows that open to allow you to change properties or provide extra information from within Excel. You're probably most familiar with the Open dialog box, where you open new files, and the Close dialog box, where you save and close your work.

There are two basic types of dialog boxes:

- **Modal:** You indicate changes you want to make to your information, and the changes are made when you click either OK or Close (depending on the dialog box). The Open and Save dialog boxes are modal dialog boxes.

- **Nonmodal:** You see your changes immediately. For example, when you open the Find and Replace dialog box, shown in Figure 1-11, the dialog box stays open while you make changes to the cells in your sheet. Each change is applied automatically as you work rather than after you close the dialog box.

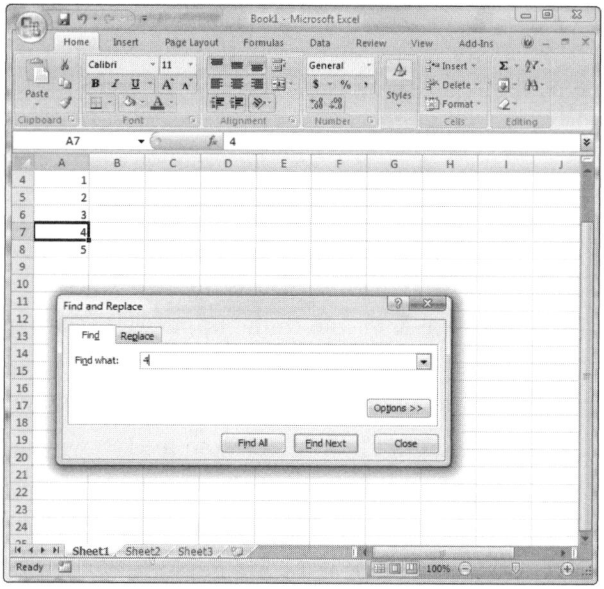

Figure 1-11: The Find and Replace dialog box is one of the few nonmodal dialog boxes in Excel 2007.

Excel Document Types and the New File Format

Historically, Excel files have been stored as binary files on the hard drive. These files have the `.xls` extension. Excel data stored as a binary file is stored in a proprietary format. One disadvantage of this format is that the only way that data can be changed is by using Excel.

With Office 2007, Microsoft started storing Word, Excel, and PowerPoint data in a more open format. The new format is based on Extensible Markup Language (XML). In addition to being a more open format, XML files tend to be smaller than the older, binary formats.

As an average user, therefore, you have several different formats in which to save your Excel data. In this section, you learn about each of those formats and when you should or should not use them.

XLSX

XLSX is the default format for files created in Excel 2007. You use this file format throughout the majority of this book. An *XLSX* file is a special kind of compressed file that contains all the data, document formatting, and formulas in one compressed file.

One interesting thing about the new format is that what appears to be a single file is actually a compressed set of files. You can uncompress this file with Windows XP or Windows Vista to see what the internal structure of the file looks like. In the following exercise, you look at a small sample Excel file in a number of different formats. The data in the file is all the same — the only difference between the files is the way they have been saved. Follow these steps:

1. **Open Excel. Click the Office Button and choose Open to open the file `SampleXLSXFile.xlsx`. Look at the data on the first sheet.**

2. **Close Excel by clicking the X button in the upper-right corner.**

3. **In Windows Explorer, right-click `SampleXLSX.zip` and choose Extract All from the menu. Accept the defaults for the extraction process.**

   This file is an exact copy of the file you just examined. Now you will expand this file from one compressed file to the uncompressed files that comprise it.

4. **In the Extraction Wizard, accept all the defaults to extract the files.**

   When the extraction is done, a new Windows Explorer window opens that contains the extracted files, as shown in Figure 1-12.

Name	Date modified	Type	Size
_rels	12/1/2006 2:34 PM	File Folder	
docProps	12/1/2006 2:34 PM	File Folder	
xl	12/1/2006 2:34 PM	File Folder	
[Content_Types].xml		XML Document	2 KB

Figure 1-12: The extracted files from the XLSX file.

Your list of files will look different if your default file view is set to anything other than Details.

Each of the folders contains a part of the Excel document. If you want to see the actual XML that makes up this Excel document, you can open any of the XML files with either Notepad or Internet Explorer.

5. **Double-click the xl folder icon to view the contents of that folder. Double-click the tables folder icon to view the contents of that folder.**

   You are looking at the folder that contains your actual Excel data, and you are ready to open the XML file in your Internet browser.

6. **Double-click the file `table1.xml`.**

   The XML code that defines the table appears in your browser. The first few lines tell Excel what the table looks like:

```
<?xml version="1.0" encoding="UTF-8" standalone="yes" ?>
- <table xmlns="http://schemas.openxmlformats.org/spreadsheetml/2006/main"
```

```
id="1" name="Table1" displayName="Table1" ref="A1:E16" totalsRowCount="1">
 <autoFilter ref="A1:E15" />
- <tableColumns count="5">
```

The next few lines contain the definition of the table columns. You can see that the column names from the original file match what is shown in these lines:

```
<tableColumn id="1" name="Store" totalsRowLabel="Total" />
<tableColumn id="2" name="Color" />
<tableColumn id="3" name="Inventory" totalsRowFunction="sum" />
<tableColumn id="4" name="Sold" totalsRowFunction="sum" />
- <tableColumn id="5" name="Total" totalsRowFunction="sum" dataDxfId="0">
<calculatedColumnFormula>SUM(B2:D2)</calculatedColumnFormula>
```

The final lines end the definition of the table and define the style information for the table:

```
</tableColumn>
</tableColumns>
<tableStyleInfo name="TableStyleMedium9" showFirstColumn="0" showLastColumn="1"
showRowStripes="1" showColumnStripes="0" />
</table>
```

Although you do not work with the XML directly while learning to use Excel, it is useful to be familiar with the pieces of the files that are stored within the XLSX compressed file. Spend a few minutes browsing through the folder with the uncompressed file information.

 **Information Kiosk**

To learn more about XML and how Excel uses it, search the Web for either **XML** or **Excel XML**. The documentation that describes how Microsoft uses XML and how to write your own is readily available.

XLSM

Another change Microsoft made with Excel 2007 is to split the basic format of files into two types. You just explored the first type, the data file. Another type, *XLSM,* is used to store any Excel spreadsheet that has macros. *Macros* are programs that help you do work better, cleaner, and more efficiently.

A file with the extension .xlsx cannot have any code attached to it. If you are storing a file with code in Excel 2007 format, the code must go into a file whose extension ends with the letter *m* rather than the letter *x.*

Why make this differentiation? For security reasons. In the past, lots of viruses were distributed as macros hidden in seemingly harmless documents. Merely opening the document would run the virus code and spread it to all other documents on the computer. With this new setup, the potential for spreading viruses through regular Excel files is minimized.

If you receive an XLSX file by e-mail, you know that the file does not have any code included. If you receive an XLSM file, you know that code may be attached to the file and you need to decide whether to trust the code. If you receive a file with the .xlsm extension from someone you do not know, you can tell Excel not to enable the macros.

The file you use in the following exercise appears to be an exact duplicate of the file you just worked with. However, this new file has a macro hidden in it. In the following steps, you open this file twice — once with the macro enabled and once with it disabled:

1. **Open Excel. Click the Office Button and choose Open to open the file SampleXLSMFile.xlsm.**

   When you open the file, you see a new line below the Ribbon. The new line contains the security warning shown in Figure 1-13.

   ![Security Warning Macros have been disabled. Options...]

   Figure 1-13: A security warning.

   ## Watch Your Step

   Because of the split between Excel data files and Excel data files with macros in them, companies can now restrict employees from opening any file whose extension indicates that it may have macros in it. If you attempt to open an Excel file when your computer is set up this way, the file does not open.

2. **Click the Options button.**

   As shown in Figure 1-14, the Microsoft Office Security Options dialog box appears.

   Figure 1-14: The Microsoft Office Security Options dialog box.

3. **Click the Enable This Content radio button and then click OK.**

When you click the OK button, the Security Warning dialog box and the security warning itself disappear.

4. **Choose View ➜ Macros ➜ Macros.**

You navigate the Ribbon by finding the buttons in a specific group on a specific tab. For the remainder of this book, all Ribbon elements are referenced this way. When you click the Macros button, the Macro dialog box appears, as shown in Figure 1-15.

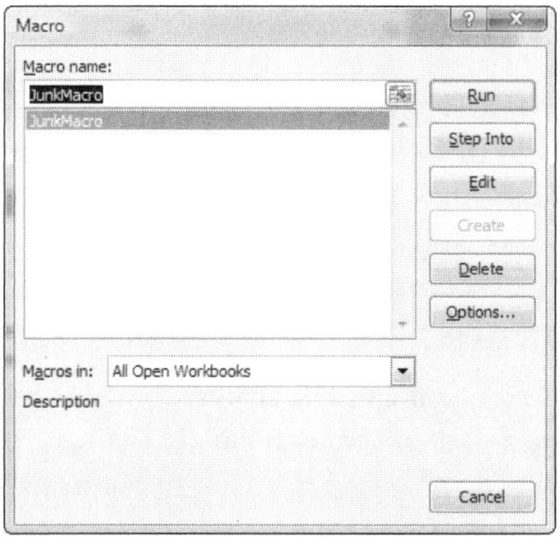

Figure 1-15: The Macro dialog box.

5. **Click the Run button.**

A new line of text appears on the spreadsheet, showing that the macro has run.

6. **Close the Excel file.**

Next, you open the file a second time. This time, you will attempt to run the macro without enabling the macro content.

7. **Double-click the file to open it in Excel.**

The file opens, and the security warning appears again.

8. **Choose View ➜ Macros ➜ Macros.**

The Macro dialog box appears again.

9. **Click the Run button.**

Rather than run the macro, Excel displays the error message shown in Figure 1-16.

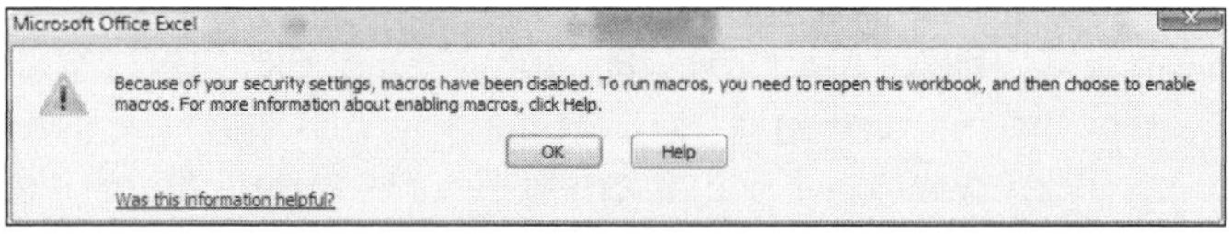

Figure 1-16: This message indicates that macros have been disabled.

Because you have not enabled the macros, Excel does not run the code. The program protects you from accidentally destroying your work by opening an Excel file containing hidden code.

10. **Click OK to clear the message, and then close Excel to continue.**

Transfer

To learn more about macros and Excel, see Chapter 15.

XLS

Files created in previous versions of Excel have an `.xls` extension. When these files are opened in Excel 2007, Excel opens in Compatibility mode. In this mode, you can make changes to documents and use the new features. When you save a file in this format, the Compatibility Checker runs, and a list of incompatible features is shown. An example of this report is shown in Figure 1-17. This report shows that the tables set up in the active file are not displayed in the previous version.

After the Compatibility Checker has run, you can either save the file anyway, in which case the incompatible features are disabled, or you can cancel the save operation and use the Save As command to save the file as an XLSX file, to retain its full format and function.

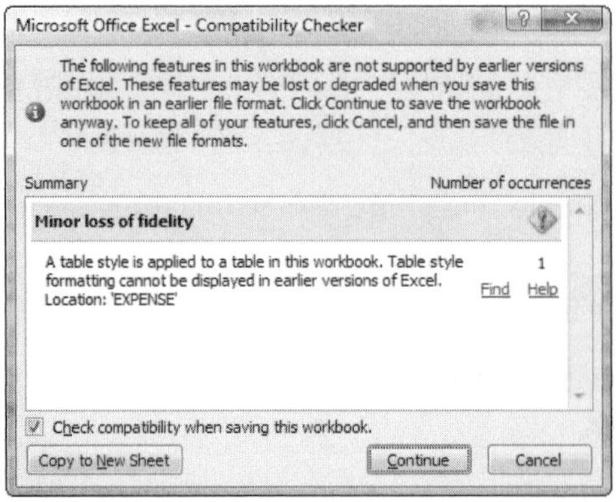

![Microsoft Office Excel - Compatibility Checker dialog box. The following features in this workbook are not supported by earlier versions of Excel. These features may be lost or degraded when you save this workbook in an earlier file format. Click Continue to save the workbook anyway. To keep all of your features, click Cancel, and then save the file in one of the new file formats. Summary / Number of occurrences. Minor loss of fidelity. A table style is applied to a table in this workbook. Table style formatting cannot be displayed in earlier versions of Excel. Location: 'EXPENSE' — 1, Find, Help. Check compatibility when saving this workbook. Copy to New Sheet / Continue / Cancel.]

Figure 1-17: A simple compatibility report.

XLSB

In addition to the XML-based file types developed for Excel 2007, Microsoft created a new binary format for this version. The new binary format, whose extension is `.xlsb`, was created to provide a way for Excel users to store extremely large files. *XLSB* files are set up to be slightly smaller and considerably more efficient to open and run. Unless you are creating very large files, you are not likely to create XLSB files.

Other file types

Excel can access several other file types. As you progress through this book, you come in contact with a few other formats:

- **XLTX and XLTM:** Excel template files, without macros (.xltx) and with macros (.xltm). Template files make it easier to create new files from a common starting point.

- **CSV and TXT:** Nonformatted text files that contain only data. CSV files separate the data into columns by using commas; TXT files use a variety of different delimiters to separate data into columns.

- **PDF:** With an additional add-in available from the Microsoft site, you can use Excel to create PDF files that are compatible with Adobe Acrobat.

Getting Help

The Excel 2007 Help system shows itself in a number of ways that you may or may not expect from working with other programs. Most of the time, you access Help by clicking the Help button in the upper-right corner of your Ribbon. (The Help button contains the image of a question mark with a circle around it.) This action brings up the default Help page, as shown in Figure 1-18.

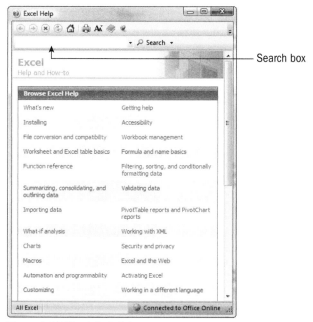

— Search box

Figure 1-18: The default Help page.

On this page, Excel provides a series of links to the topics that Microsoft believes users will need to access most often. To access any of the topics, you click the blue linked text. Follow these steps to use the Help system to find out what's new in Excel 2007:

1. **Open Excel. Click the Help button.**

Notice the online indicator in the lower-right area of the Help page.

2. **Click the What's New link.**

The Help page displays the list of links for the new information topics, as shown in Figure 1-19.

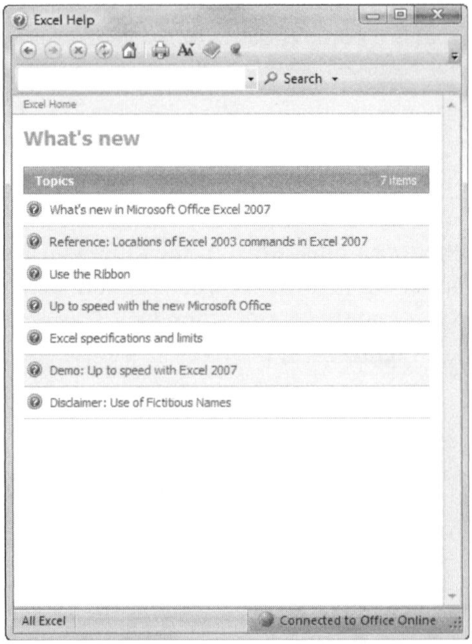

Figure 1-19: The What's New Topics Help page.

3. **Click the What's New in Microsoft Excel 2007 link.**

The first part of the page for this Help topic appears. As you read through the page, you can change the font size, and you change the size of the page by clicking and dragging its edges.

4. **Use the Back arrow button or the Home button to return to the main Help page.**

You navigate Help pages the same way you navigate in your browser. You can use the Forward, Back, and Home buttons to move between the Help topics you have seen.

5. **Click the Getting Help link.**

This Help page displays a list of Help subcategories as well as a list of topics for getting help.

6. **Read through the list of available Help categories. Click and read any that you think are useful.**

In addition to navigating the Help topics by using the established links, you can find help about topics by typing a phrase into the Search box and searching for help.

7. **Find the Search box at the top of the Excel Help window. Type the word** pivot **into the search box and either click Search or press Enter.**

A page that flashes on-screen tells you that Excel is searching the Help system for your topics. Then it lists the 20 results it found. Each item listed is a link to a Help item that references the word *pivot*. To see all topics, use the scroll bar to the right to scroll through the topics.

Step Into the Real World

As you work in Excel, you will need to find answers to questions that are beyond the scope of this book. Unlike previous versions of Microsoft products, the Office 2007 suite provides excellent help. Unfortunately, you may or may not have access to it.

In Excel 2007, only a small portion of the available Help resources are stored on your machine. The bare basics are stored locally so that you can find answers in your time of need. However, because the product has become so complex, Microsoft has moved to a centralized Help system. The help you need is centralized on the Microsoft Web site servers rather than distributed to your machine (and everyone else's machines).

If you are connected to the Internet, you won't notice any problem with accessing Help — the connection between local Help and online Help is smooth and instantaneous. You may not even realize when your information is coming from the Microsoft site. Sometimes, the information you are viewing is obviously coming from the Microsoft site, though, because the information is shown in your browser rather than in the Help window.

If you are not connected to the Web at the time you need help, you know it. Some Help information is not accessible and does not even show up in your search results. In addition, most of the templates, code examples, formula examples, clip art, and other elements come to you from the Web site. If you are not online, you do not have access to these items.

compress: To encode data to take up less space on your hard drive.

contextual: The display of an element based on whether the selected object needs it.

default setting: The normal choice, taken when no specific preference is shown.

dialog box: A window that contains choices and information for users.

gallery: A large window that has numerous icons you can use to specify a graphical choice.

interface: The system by which a user communicates with and uses a software program.

modal dialog box: A type of dialog box displayed by an application that asks a question or a series of questions that must be answered before the user can continue.

nonmodal dialog box: A type of dialog box displayed by an application that allows the user to continue to interact with the application in other ways.

Office Button: The round button with the Office logo on it by which Office 2007 users access file-level commands, such as printing, saving, or opening files.

open format: A public file format that allows users to access data within a file without having to use the program.

proprietary format: A type of file format that a single company creates and uses to store its documents. No documentation is publicly available for accessing the contents of the file. The program used to create proprietary files must be used to access the data within them.

Quick Access Toolbar (QAT): The customizable toolbar within Excel that is located just to the right of the Office Button either above or below the Ribbon.

Ribbon: The collection of tabs at the top of the Excel interface by which users select functions to be performed in an organized manner. The Ribbon replaces earlier menu-driven interfaces.

spreadsheet: The logical grouping of cells within an Excel file.

tab: The part of the Ribbon that contains a group of related functions.

task pane: A dockable window used to interact with a program or find more information than can fit easily on a tab.

worksheet: See spreadsheet.

Last Stop

Practice Exam

1. **Before Excel 2007 was released, the number of rows that spreadsheets allowed was**

a. smaller than the number of columns now allowed.

b. fixed.

c. 26.

d. There was no limit, just as there is none now.

2. **You use the _____ Button to perform tasks such as opening and saving files.**

3. **The Ribbon is made up of which of the following:**

a. Tabs

b. Groups

c. Buttons

d. All of the above

4. **Which tab contains the commands for adding content to your worksheet?**

_____

5. **True or False: You can collapse the Ribbon by double-clicking a tab.**

6. **If you look for the Table Tools tab and it isn't showing, what should you check first?**

_____

_____

7. **XLSX files**

   a. are compressed XML and formatting files.

   b. are binary files.

   c. are files in a proprietary format.

   d. can be opened only by Excel.

8. **True or False: XLSX files can contain macro code.**

9. **True or False: Splitting the file format for Excel files into a macro-enabled format and non-macro-enabled format was done to allow greater security and protection against viruses.**

10. **Which of these file formats can Excel open?**

    a. XLSX

    b. XLS

    c. XLSB

    d. All of the above

11. **True or False: All of the Help information for Excel 2007 is stored locally on your computer.**

2

Creating Your First Excel Worksheet

STATIONS ALONG THE WAY

- O Identifying the different parts of a worksheet
- O Navigating a worksheet
- O Selecting cell ranges
- O Using a predesigned template to create a worksheet
- O Creating a worksheet from scratch
- O Saving your worksheet

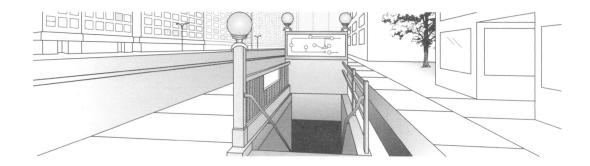

Enter the Station

Questions

1. What is the relationship between a cell, a row, and a worksheet?

2. Where do you find the name of the active worksheet?

3. What are some advantages of using a template over creating your file from scratch?

4. What is the quickest way to select a block of data with the keyboard?

5. How do you know whether you are replacing or editing the contents of a cell?

6. What is the difference between choosing Save from the Office Button menu and clicking the Save icon on the Quick Access Toolbar?

Express Line

If you are already familiar with the basics of creating worksheets in Excel 2007, skip ahead to the next chapter.

Now that you have explored Excel, it is time to start understanding how to use it. In this chapter, you start with the basics of getting around in your worksheets and then move on to the various ways you can select data within a sheet.

After you understand how to navigate your data, you discover how to create a worksheet the easy way, from a template, and then the more labor-intensive way, from scratch. After you have mastered the basics of creating the worksheets, you save your data for use at another time.

Getting to Know the Elements in a Worksheet

Now that you understand what Excel 2007 is and how to navigate around ribbons, tabs, groups, and buttons, it is time to add data to your worksheets. The first step in this process is to open Excel 2007 and check out how to move around and get acquainted with the pieces of your worksheet.

Excel 2007 stores data in individual cells. Each cell has a specific location, which you can use to reference the contents of the cell. The following list explains the various elements that make up a worksheet, as shown in Figure 2-1.

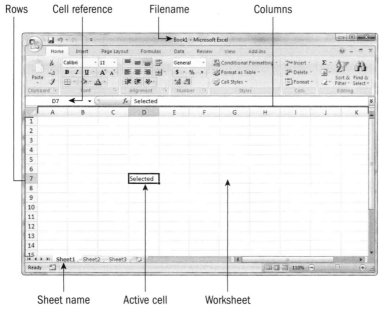

Figure 2-1: All these elements are part of the Excel worksheet.

Cell: Individual elements of data, results of functions, and other types of information are stored in cells. You can tell which cell is selected because it's outlined with a solid black line. (Refer to Figure 2-1.) Cells can contain

- Numbers
- Text
- Formulas

Cells might appear to contain other types of content, as you will see, but all the other types are based on one of these three elements.

Row: Each cell is located in a row, which is referenced by a number. That number starts at 1 and increases sequentially. You can tell which row contains the selected cell because the row number is highlighted in yellow.

Column: Each cell is also located in a column. Columns are referenced by either a letter name or column name. If you are referencing the columns by letter names, the letters run alphabetically from A to Z, and then from AA to AZ, and then to BA, and so on. When you exceed column ZZ, a third letter is added, and the naming process continues. You can tell which column contains the selected cell because the column letter is highlighted in yellow. By the way, the order of the letters is important: AB is a different column than BA.

Worksheet: Rows and columns make up worksheets. You use sheet names to reference the worksheets. When you open a new, blank workbook, you see three new worksheets at the bottom, named Sheet 1, Sheet 2, and so on. (Refer to Figure 2-1.) Sheets can contain either data or charts. Sheets created with the charting tool are named Chart 1, Chart 2, and so on. These sheets contain only charts (also known as *graphs*), not rows and columns of data. You can tell which sheet you are working on because the active sheet tab has a white background, and the other sheet tabs have a blue background.

Excel file: Multiple worksheets make up Excel 2007 files. A file can have only one sheet or a number of sheets. What is the maximum number of sheets per file? That depends on your computer. You can tell which file you are working on by looking at the title bar at the top of your Excel 2007 window. If you have not yet saved your file, this line reads Book1 - Microsoft Excel 2007. If you have saved your file, Book1 is replaced by a filename.

 Information Kiosk

If the filename says Book2 or some other number, it just means that you have opened more than one Excel 2007 file during this session of Excel 2007. You might have opened and closed them earlier, or you might still have them open.

Cell reference: When you are working in Excel 2007, each cell has a *reference,* which tells you where this cell is located. In a simple worksheet, the cell reference is the column indicator followed by the row indicator. For example, the selected cell in Figure 2-1 is in column D and row 7, so the cell reference is D7.

If your file contains more than one worksheet and you want to distinguish between cell C22 on Sheet 1 and cell C22 on Sheet 3, you add the sheet name to the cell reference. In this case, Sheet 1's C22 is Sheet1!C22, and Sheet 2's C22 is Sheet2!C22. (The exclamation point tells Excel where the sheet name ends and the cell reference begins. The exclamation point is merely a separator between the two pieces of the cell reference.)

Using sheet names is a good way to differentiate which cell on which sheet you are referencing. However, the default names are not descriptive. To change the name of a sheet, double-click the sheet tab and type a descriptive name. Don't worry about changing sheet names after you have referenced them — Excel 2007 keeps track of which sheet has which name and updates any formulas or references you create.

You can take this convention one step further. If you want to reference a cell that is in another Excel 2007 file, you can add the filename to the front of the reference. After the filename is added, the reference for Sheet 2's C22 looks like this: `[filename.xlsx]Sheet2!C22`.

Finding Your Way around a Worksheet

Before you can add data to a worksheet, you need to know how to move around in the worksheet. Although you can do all your selection and navigation with the mouse, sometimes you don't want to take your hands off the keyboard. In these cases, you should understand how to move around without your mouse.

Moving from cell to cell

How do you move from cell C22 to cell A5 within the same worksheet? The easiest way to move the cursor from cell C22 to cell A5 is by clicking. What if you want to move from cell A5 to cell GGG390? How do you do it?

You could scroll your mouse over to the right until you get to column GGG and then down to row 390, but you can use an easier way.

The cell reference box (refer to Figure 2-1) tells you where you are on the active worksheet. In addition, it can allow you to quickly navigate from one place in your Excel 2007 worksheet to another.

Follow these steps to use the cell reference box to move from cell A5 to cell GGG390:

1. **Click in cell A5.**

The cell reference says A5, as shown in Figure 2-2.

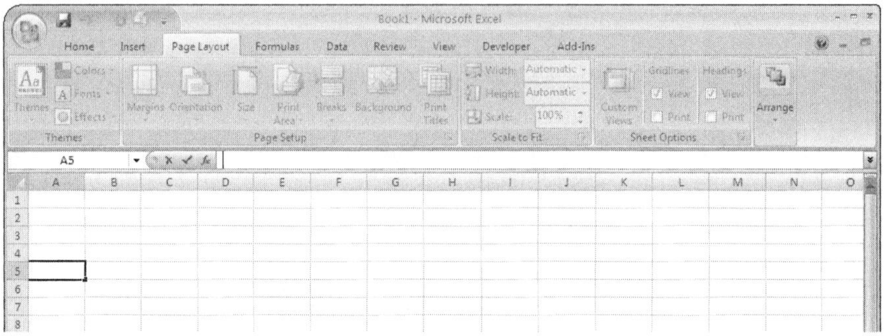

Figure 2-2: The Navigation Bar contains the cell reference box and the current value for the cell.

2. **Click in the cell reference box.**

The current cell reference is highlighted.

3. **Type GGG390 and press Enter.**

The cursor moves to cell GGG390.

This technique is helpful, but you might not see why you would need it. As you use Excel more and more, you will use formulas to do much of your work. When you click in a cell that has a formula in it, you are given the cell references that make up the formula rather than the actual data. In these cases, you want to be able to quickly navigate to the cells to see what their values are when you are error checking.

Moving from sheet to sheet

The next step is to move from one sheet to another. To do this, click another sheet name at the bottom of the Excel 2007 window. You are now looking at another sheet.

Did you notice which cell you ended up in? If you have not already selected a cell in this sheet, you end up in cell A1. If you have already selected a cell in this sheet, you end up in that cell.

Using keyboard shortcuts to move around

You can use other ways to move around in your worksheet. If you moved off Sheet1, go back there. Make sure that cell GGG390 is selected. To make it easier to follow along, type anything you want in this cell. Try out the keystrokes in Table 2-1 in order, and note what happens.

Table 2-1   Shortcut Keys for Moving Around in a Worksheet

Keystroke	Where the Cursor Moves	Cell Moved To in the Example
↑	One cell above.	GGG389
→	One cell to the right.	GGH389
↓	One cell down.	GGH390
←	One cell to the left.	GGG390
Ctrl+→	To the last cell in row 390.	XFD390
Ctrl+←	To the next cell to the left that has data in it. If nothing is in any cell in the row, the cursor moves to the first cell in the row.	GGG390
Home key	To the first cell in the row.	A390
Ctrl+→	To the next cell to the right that has data in it. If nothing is in any cell in the row, it moves to the last cell in the row.	GGG390
Ctrl+↑	To the next cell up in the column that has data in it. Because none of the cells above contain data, the cursor moves to the first row of this column.	GGG1
Ctrl+↓	To the next cell down that has data in it. If no cell has data in it, the cursor moves to the last cell in the column.	GGG390
Ctrl+↓ (again)	To the last cell in the column. Again, if a cell has data in it, the cursor moves there.	GGG1048576
Ctrl+Home	To the first cell in the sheet.	A1

Using the Ctrl+arrow keys allows you to move around in your worksheet much more easily than just moving cell by cell. You have to remember two rules when you use the Ctrl+arrow keys to move around:

- If the next cell in the direction you want to move doesn't have data in it, the Ctrl+arrow key takes you to the next cell that does have data in it.

- If the next cell has data in it, the Ctrl+arrow key moves you to the last consecutive cell with data in it.

Selecting a Range of Cells

If you want to work with more than one cell at a time, you need to select a range of cells. You can do this in a number of ways, as described in this section.

Selecting a small group of cells

To select a small group of cells, click in one of the cells and drag across, up, or down to select the others. You can tell when a group of cells is selected because they have slightly changed color and the row and column indicators change to orange.

Follow these steps to select all the data in cells G3 through G9 quickly:

1. Click in cell G3. Do not release the mouse button.

2. Drag the mouse down until you reach cell G9.

3. Release the mouse button.

Cells G3 through G9 are highlighted and selected.

Selecting all the cells in a row

To select all the cells in a row, click the row number. All the cells in that row are then selected, whether they contain data or not. For example, to select all the cells in row 3, click the number 3 on the left side of the screen. The entire row is highlighted and selected.

To quickly select all the data in rows 4 through 7, follow these steps:

1. Click the number 4 on the left side of the screen, and then drag down to the number 7.

2. Release the mouse button.

Rows 4 through 7 are highlighted and selected.

Step Into the Real World

Understanding the difference between worksheets and chart sheets So far, you have looked only at the worksheet style of sheet. You can also create a second sheet style, a *chart sheet,* in Excel 2007. A chart sheet does not contain cells with data. Instead, each chart sheet contains a single graph. That graph is powered by a set of data, formatted the way you want and shown on-screen or in print. A sample chart is shown in the following figure:

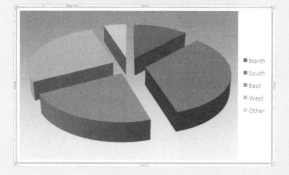

You can place an Excel 2007 chart on either a regular worksheet or its own chart sheet. When you place the chart on its own sheet, Excel 2007 gives the sheet the default name `Chart 1`. You can change this name when you create the chart sheet or afterward. To do it afterward, click the sheet name and type the new name (just as you do with a regular worksheet).

Why put a chart on its own sheet rather than on a data sheet? Because when it is on its own sheet, it is easier to print, easier to reference, and easier to work with. You don't have to worry about the chart overlapping the data on the worksheet. If you need to embed the chart in a Word or PowerPoint document, you can do it by merely referencing the chart sheet rather than by having to know where the chart is on the page so that you can select it.

You find out how to do much more with charts in Chapter 5.

Selecting all the cells in a column

To select all the cells in a column, click the column letter or letters. All the cells in that column or columns are selected, whether they contain data or not. For example, to select all the cells in column C, move the cursor over the letter *C* at the top of the worksheet and click once. The entire column is highlighted and selected.

Follow these steps to select all the data in columns D through G:

1. **Move the cursor over the letter *D* at the top of the worksheet.**

2. **Click and drag right to the letter *G*. Release the mouse button.**

Columns D through G are highlighted and selected.

Selecting a large group of cells

Hold down the Shift key as you use the Ctrl+arrow key sequences, and all the cells you move past are selected. You are most likely to use this technique when you need to select a range of cells with data in them. For example, if your worksheet has data, as shown in Figure 2-3, you may want to change the formatting on all the cells at one time.

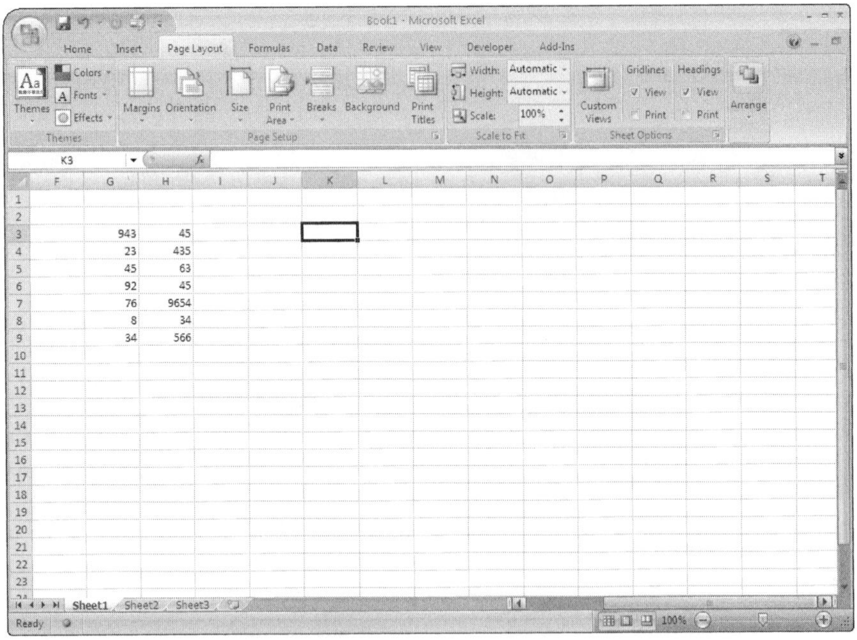

Figure 2-3: Consecutive data to be selected.

To quickly select all the data in cells G3 through H9, follow these steps:

1. Click in cell G3.

2. Press Shift+Ctrl+↓ once.

Cells G3 through G9 are selected.

3. Press Shift+Ctrl+→ once.

Cells G3 through H9 are selected, as shown in Figure 2-4.

If any empty cells are in the data range, you do not get the same result. In that case, using the mouse to select the cells is easier.

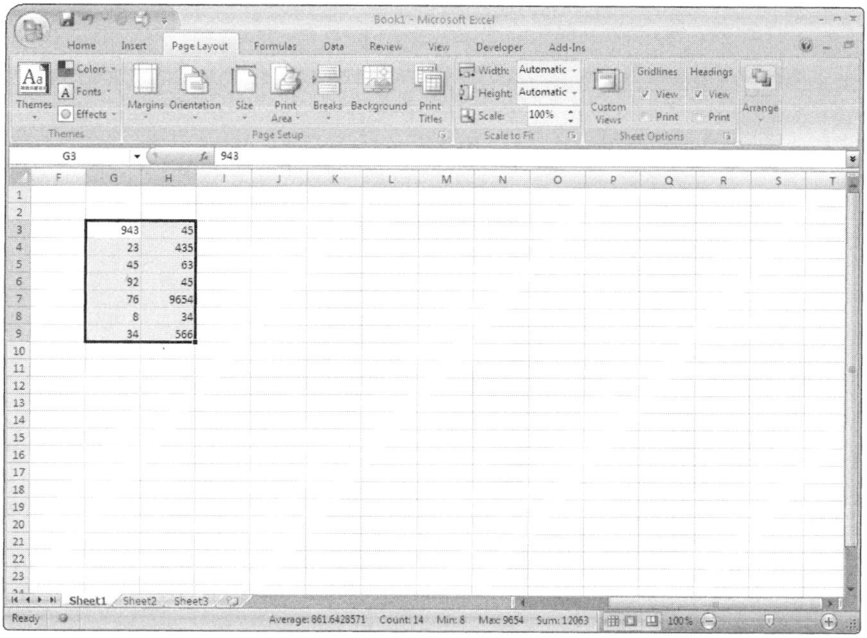

Figure 2-4: The consecutive data is selected.

Creating a Worksheet from a Template

When you open Excel 2007, you see a blank worksheet. While you are learning to use Excel 2007, looking at all those empty cells can be a little daunting. You know that you need to create an invoice, a time card, a calendar, a budget, or some other seemingly simple project, but you don't know quite where to begin. Microsoft provides a way to get a jump-start on these documents: a template.

A *template* is an Excel 2007 file that someone has already created that contains formatting, formulas, and data-entry areas. By using a template to start a project, you start with what someone else has created rather than start from scratch. Several templates are delivered with Excel 2007. Even more are available for your use from Office Online.

Finding the templates installed on your computer

To see which Excel templates are installed on your machine, click the Office Button and choose New. The New Workbook window appears, as shown in Figure 2-5.

Figure 2-5: The New Workbook window.

Although your list of featured templates is likely to be different from the ones shown in Figure 2-5, the functionality of the window is the same. In the left pane, you select the category of workbook you want to create. The pane on the right offers you places to find templates and files on which you can base your new workbook. The right side of this window changes as you move through the template categories.

Information Kiosk

Why would your list of featured templates look different from the one shown in Figure 2-5? Because if you are connected to the Web, Excel 2007 grabs the list of featured templates from Office Online. This list is expected to change regularly.

When Featuring is selected in the left pane, the right pane is split into two horizontal sections:

- **New Blank:** The three options in the New Blank section of the window — Blank Workbook, My Templates, and New from Existing — let you create a new workbook from the templates or files on your computer.

- **Microsoft Office Online:** This section allows you to see the featured templates and access the other templates available from Office Online. (*Note:* You can download the Office Online templates only if you are connected to the Internet.)

In this chapter, you work with some of the installed templates and the templates available from Office Online.

When any of the other categories are selected on the left, the pane on the right generally shows previews of the templates available in that category. The exception is the Installed Templates choice. Although templates available from Office Online are required to have a preview, those installed with Excel 2007 are not. The reason is that many of the installed templates are based on templates created for older Excel versions and do not have current previews.

On my installation of Excel 2007, I have 11 installed templates. I have a range of personal and business templates, including templates for time cards, to-do lists, budgets, expense trackers, and more. In the next section, you take a detailed look at the Billing Statement template and work through adapting it for a company named Juniper Flowers.

Entering data in the Billing Statement template

The best way to learn how to use a template is to create a file from a template and fill it in. In this section, you create a new billing statement, based on the Billing Statement template delivered with Excel 2007.

Suppose, for example, that you are the owner of a company named Juniper Flowers, and you need to complete a billing statement for Hart's Hotel, one of your customers. You decide that it would be much easier to create the billing statement from the template that is provided, so you open the template and complete it as covered in the exercises that complete this section.

First, you need to create a new file from the Billing Statement template. Follow these steps:

1. **Click the Office Button and choose New.**
2. **Select Installed Templates from the left pane of the New Workbook window.**
3. **Select Billing Statement from the right pane of the New Workbook window.**
4. **Click the Create button.**

   A new billing statement opens, as shown in Figure 2-6.

A workbook based on this template and a blank workbook have several differences between them:

The view of the worksheet is different. This template shows a new worksheet in Page Layout view rather than Normal view, enabling you to see how each page of the billing statement will look when printed.

Some cells have been filled in for you. These are the cells you look at next.

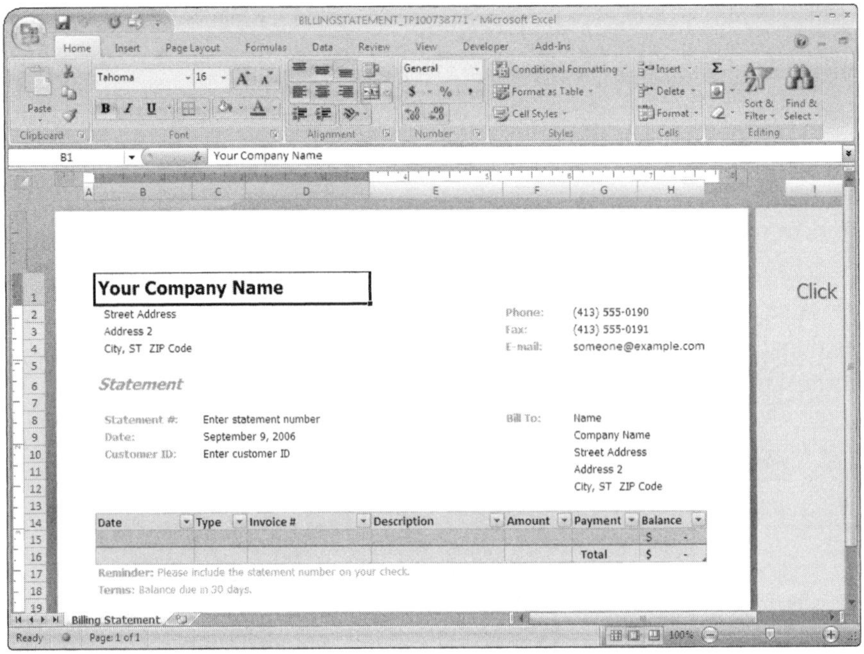

Figure 2-6: A new billing statement.

This template is an excellent example of the kind of head start you can get by using a template. Some areas of the worksheet are already completed for you, a table has been created for your billing information, and the page is formatted for printing. That is helpful, but how do you use this template for your work? The answer: Just as you would use any other worksheet. Click in a cell and change its contents. Work through filling in this billing statement to see how it works:

1. Click in Cell B1.

Notice that you are changing cells B1, C1, and D1.

2. Type Juniper Flowers **and press Enter.**

3. Fill in the other cells in rows 2 through 12 by entering the following values:

- *Juniper Flowers address:* 128 Pleasant Valley Road, Suite 202; Story City, IA 50248

- *Phone:* (123) 555-6789

- *Fax:* (123) 555-8901

- *E-mail:* johndoe@local.com

- *Statement #:* 987

- *Date:* Today's date
- *Bill To:* John Doe, Hart's Hotel; 234 Bumpy Road; Blue Rock, IA 56789

You have now updated the generic billing statement to contain the static information for the Juniper Flowers bill to Hart's Hotel, as shown in Figure 2-7. The next step is to complete the invoice table for this bill. The table has been predefined to contain a heading row, data rows, and a total row. Even though only one data row is now shown in the table, as you add data to the table, it expands to hold those rows.

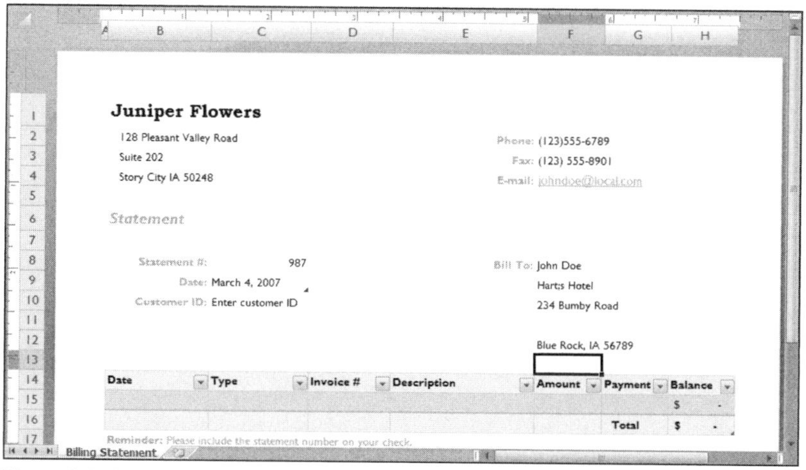

Figure 2-7: Completed company and billing information.

4. **Click in cell B15. Fill in row 15 with the following values by entering the values and then pressing Tab to move to the next column:**

Date: June 15, 2006

Type: Lobby Floral Displays

Invoice #: C16360

Description: 3 daily floral displays for lobby

Amount: 360

Payment: 0

When you press the Tab key to move from the Amount column to the Payment column, the amount reformats itself in dollars and cents. Also, the number is reflected in the Balance column and the Total Balance cell because these two areas are cells where you will not enter data. Instead, the data is filled in by using a formula.

5. From the Payment column, press the Tab key twice on your keyboard.

The cursor temporarily changes to an hourglass. When the cursor changes back to a plus sign (+), a new row will have been added to the table.

6. Complete the new row 16 and the next four as shown in Figure 2-8.

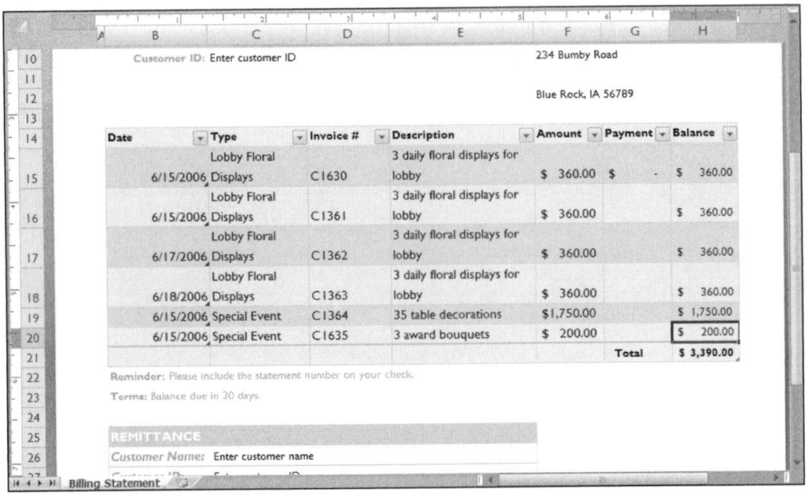

Figure 2-8: The completed invoice section of a billing statement.

7. Press the down-arrow key to move the cursor down to the remittance area. Type Hart's Hotel in cell D26 and the customer ID (19911) in cell D27. Notice that the statement ID, the date, and the amount due are all filled in from the information you have already provided.

This step completes the billing statement. Your final billing statement should be the same as the file `JuniperFlowersBillingStatement.xlsx`.

Notice that as you updated the invoice table, cell D30 was given the same value as the total balance due for this invoice. Again, this cell is filled in by using a formula. The formula this time is based directly on the data you entered in the table.

Creating a Basic Worksheet from Scratch

Now that you have created a worksheet from a template, the next step in learning to use Excel 2007 is to create a worksheet from scratch.

As you have seen, when you open Excel 2007, it automatically opens a new file for you (refer to Figure 2-1). That file has a default of three blank worksheets, each of which has the full complement of rows and columns. The active cell defaults to cell A1 in the first worksheet.

Adding data by using the keyboard

The most basic way to add data to a cell is to click in the cell and type either the number or the text you want the cell to contain. You already know how to move from cell to cell, so you now know the basics of creating your first worksheet. In this section, you create a worksheet that contains quarterly sales data for Juniper Flowers. Follow these steps:

1. Open Excel 2007.
2. Starting in cell A1, fill in cells A1 through H1 and cells C2 through G8 with the data shown in Figure 2-9.

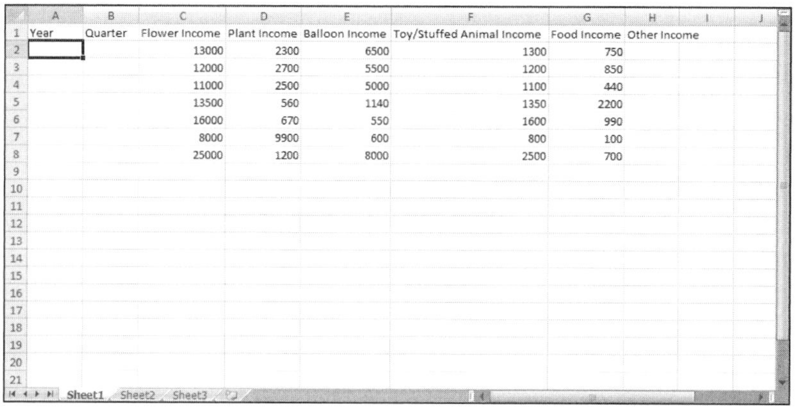

	A	B	C	D	E	F	G	H	I	J
1	Year	Quarter	Flower Income	Plant Income	Balloon Income	Toy/Stuffed Animal Income	Food Income	Other Income		
2			13000	2300	6500	1300	750			
3			12000	2700	5500	1200	850			
4			11000	2500	5000	1100	440			
5			13500	560	1140	1350	2200			
6			16000	670	550	1600	990			
7			8000	9900	600	800	100			
8			25000	1200	8000	2500	700			

Figure 2-9: Some sample data to enter.

You enter the year and quarter information in the next section.

Information Kiosk

To move from cell to cell, did you click in each cell or use the mouse? When you are entering blocks of data into a worksheet, you can use an easier method: Select the block of cells you want to complete (cells C2 through G8 in the example.) Notice that the whole block becomes highlighted, but the active cell is not. The cell that is not highlighted tells you where you are, and the highlighted cells tell Excel 2007 which cells you are working with. Click in cell C2. Press the Tab key seven times. Where did you end up? Did you notice that Excel 2007 kept you within the bounds of your selected cells and knew where you wanted to go when you reached the end of the selection? Play around with the Enter key, and you will see that it moves you through the columns in the same manner.

If you make a mistake while typing, you can correct cell values in two ways: Select the cell by clicking it and just retype the new value, or use the Formula Bar to make your corrections, as detailed in these steps:

1. Click cell H1.

Notice that Other Income is also shown on the Formula Bar, just above your worksheet, as shown in the top image in Figure 2-10.

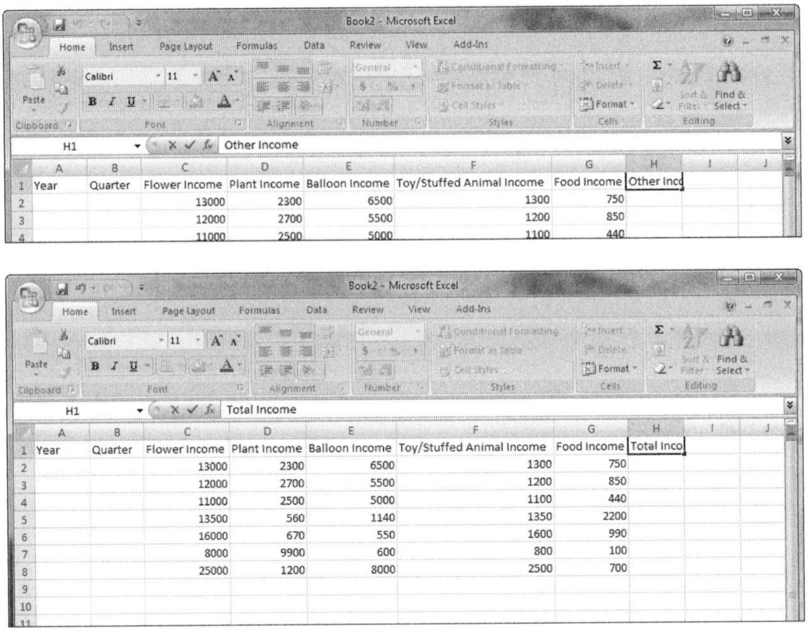

Figure 2-10: The Formula Bar shows both the original column label and the new column label.

2. Click just after the word Other on the Formula Bar.

3. Backspace over the word Other and replace it with the word Total.

4. Press Enter to apply the change to the cell.

The result is shown in the bottom image in Figure 2-10.

You can use this method to change numbers, text, or formulas in cells. If you don't want to make the change, click the X button on the Formula Bar to cancel your changes. If you have already applied the change, click the Undo button on the QAT.

Typing data is just one way to add data to your worksheet. If your data follows a regular pattern, you can use an easier method to add the data: AutoFill, which is described next.

Filling in a series of entries with AutoFill

AutoFill allows you to determine the first few pieces of data and then lets Excel 2007 do the work of repeating the pattern throughout the cells you tell it to fill.

This process is one that is easier to do than to explain. Follow these steps to fill in the Quarter column in the sheet you are working with:

1. **Starting in cell B2, fill in the first set of unique values: Enter** Q1 **in cell B2,** Q2 **in cell B3,** Q3 **in cell B4, and** Q4 **in cell B5.**
2. **Click and drag to select the cells you just filled.**
3. **Move the mouse so that it hovers over the lower-right corner of the block of cells.**

   You should see a plus sign (+) just to the right and below the block of cells, as shown in Figure 2-11.

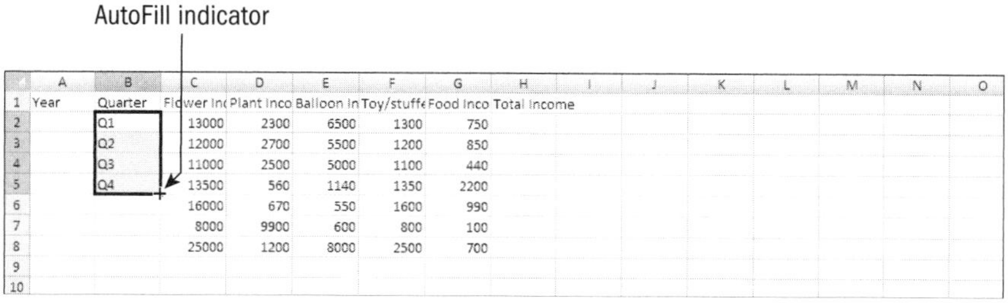

	A	B	C	D	E	F	G	H
1	Year	Quarter	Flower Inc	Plant Inco	Balloon In	Toy/stuffe	Food Inco	Total Income
2		Q1	13000	2300	6500	1300	750	
3		Q2	12000	2700	5500	1200	850	
4		Q3	11000	2500	5000	1100	440	
5		Q4	13500	560	1140	1350	2200	
6			16000	670	550	1600	990	
7			8000	9900	600	800	100	
8			25000	1200	8000	2500	700	

Figure 2-11: The AutoFill indicator.

4. **Click and hold the mouse button where the plus sign appears.**
5. **Drag slowly down to cell B8.**

   To the right of your cells, Excel 2007 tells you which value it will enter in each cell.
6. **Release the mouse button.**

   The cells get their new values, as shown in Figure 2-12.

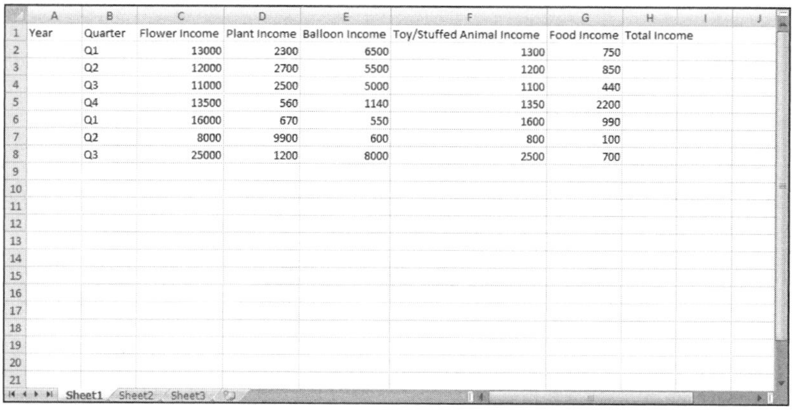

	A	B	C	D	E	F	G	H
1	Year	Quarter	Flower Income	Plant Income	Balloon Income	Toy/Stuffed Animal Income	Food Income	Total Income
2		Q1	13000	2300	6500	1300	750	
3		Q2	12000	2700	5500	1200	850	
4		Q3	11000	2500	5000	1100	440	
5		Q4	13500	560	1140	1350	2200	
6		Q1	16000	670	550	1600	990	
7		Q2	8000	9900	600	800	100	
8		Q3	25000	1200	8000	2500	700	

Figure 2-12: Using AutoFill to complete Column B.

Pretty cool, right? Try doing the same thing with the Year column. Fill in **2006** in cell A2, and use AutoFill to complete the rest of the column. Did you get what you expected?

Because the sequence was Q1 to Q4, Excel knew that you meant it to represent four quarters. If you had used A1 through A4 instead, AutoFill would have given you A1 through A8.

Because only one value is in the sequence, Excel 2007 used that value to fill all the cells you dragged across. To get the years in each of the four quarter rows, you need to fill in **2006** and the first instance of **2007** and then use AutoFill down the rest of the column. Using this method, you can set up the years for as far in the future as you want.

Step Into the Real World

Named Ranges   Many people find it easier to reference their cells by what they are rather than by their cell references. Luckily, the Excel feature *Named Ranges* allows you to do this easily. Named ranges can be anything you want, but for now you see how to name columns based on the first row of data. This method makes it easier to remember what data you are referencing. Follow these steps:

1. **On Sheet 2, select cells A1 through H9.**

2. **Click the Formulas tab on the Ribbon.**

3. **Click the Create from Selection button in the Named Cells group.**

   The Create Names from Selection dialog box appears.

4. **If the Top Row check box isn't already selected, do it now, as shown in the following figure.**

Create Names from Selection ? _ ☒

Create names from values in the:

☑ Top row
☐ Left column
☐ Bottom row
☐ Right column

OK   Cancel

5. **Select the Left Column check box.**

6. **Click the OK button.**

   It doesn't look like much has happened. However, now you can select any of the columns by typing the column name in the cell reference box. You have to watch out for one thing: If your column name had any spaces in it, every space is replaced with an underscore.

You can also name single cells or cell ranges directly from the cell reference box:

1. **Select cells A1 through H9.**

2. **Click in the cell reference box, type a name for the cells, and then press Enter.**

   Your cell is named. You can navigate to this specific cell by typing its name in the cell reference box.

Watch Your Step

Why can't you just drag the first five Year amounts and have AutoFill do the work? Try it. You will see that Excel 2007 isn't quite intelligent enough to understand what you want. Rather than fill the following cells with the next set of years, it attempts to make the numbers approach the pattern you have selected, which is not what you want.

You can also use AutoFill to complete the series for numbers, days of the week, and months. In addition, if your cell contents are letters followed by numbers, Excel 2007 tries to read your mind and figure out what you want as the AutoFill results.

If your cells contain words, names, or other character strings, Excel 2007 takes the strings you enter in the selected cells and repeats them through the cells you drag over. AutoFill doesn't just work by dragging up or down through the same column. You can select multiple columns and use AutoFill to complete both columns at one time.

Saving Your Worksheet

Now that you have created your first worksheet, it is time to save it to your hard disk. Then you can use the file again in the future.

When you save your file the first time, you need to find a place to put it on your hard disk and give it a name. Follow these steps to save the quarterly sales worksheet you created in the previous section:

1. Click the Office Button and choose Save.

The Save As dialog box appears, as shown in Figure 2-13.

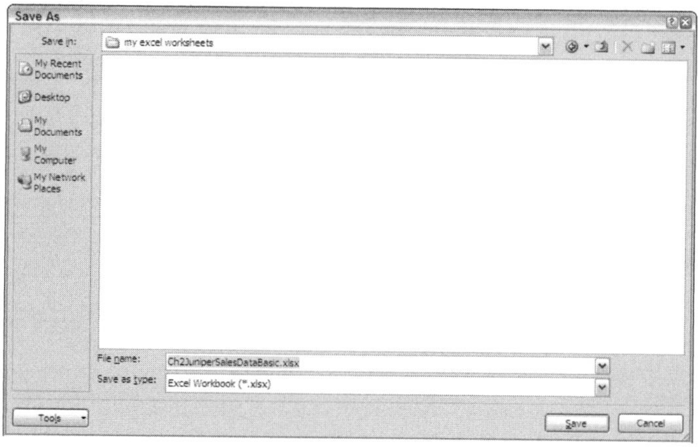

Figure 2-13: The Save As dialog box.

2. Navigate to the folder where you want to save your document.

3. In the File Name field, type JuniperQuarterlySales.

4. Click the Save button.

ℹ Information Kiosk

What if you need to share the file with someone who isn't using Excel 2007? In this case, you are likely to need to save your file as an XLS file. In the Save As dialog box, click the drop-down arrow to the right of the Save As Type list box. From the list, select Excel 2007 97–2003 Workbook (*.xls). Give the file a name and click the Save button.

Whether you save from the Office Button (as described in the preceding step list), from the keyboard by pressing Ctrl+S, or from the QAT, the process is the same as the one you just used. The difference is in how you get there:

- To save by using the keyboard, press Ctrl+S.

- To save from the QAT, click the icon shown in Figure 2-14.

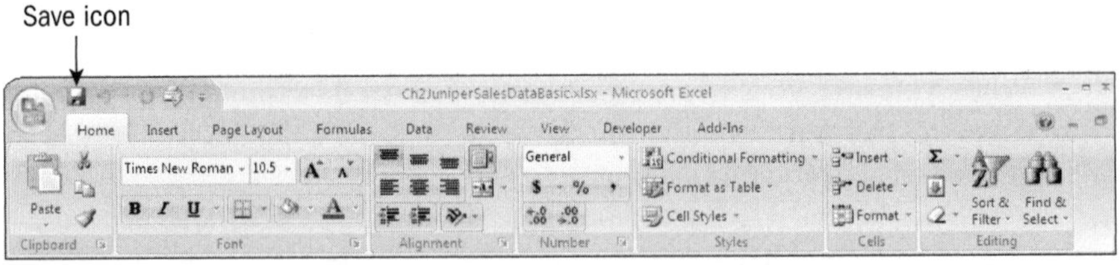

Save icon

Figure 2-14: Click the Save icon (the one that looks like a disk) on the Quick Access Toolbar.

After you save your file the first time, you can use any of the three save methods to save the file again with the same name. Be sure to save your work every 15 minutes or so, especially because you are learning to use Excel 2007.

AutoFill: An Excel feature that determines the contents of a series of cells based on the data in the first few cells.

chart: A pictorial representation of data. For more on charts, see Chapter 5.

focus: The selected cell or cells.

Formula Bar: The space between the worksheet and the Ribbon that shows the current value of the selected cell or its defined formula.

graph: *See* chart.

Navigation Bar: Located between the worksheet and the Ribbon; indicates which cell or range is selected. In addition, you can use the Navigation Bar for quickly navigating between cells or ranges.

range: A group of contiguous cells that have some relation to each other, either logically or by location. Rows and columns of cells are examples of ranges related by location. Related data, such as the answers to questions, are cells that make up a logical range of data.

template: A workbook created as a starting point for quickly creating related data for specific tasks. Templates are made up of cells that are preformatted and that might contain sample data and formulas.

Last Stop

Practice Exam

1. Name two elements of a worksheet that are used to reference a cell.

_____

_____

2. When cell G55 is selected, which of the following cells can always be reached in one keystroke?

a. Cell A1

b. The first cell with data in column G

c. Cell H56

d. Cell XFD55

3. If you are in cell Q999, what is the quickest way to get to cell B6?

_____

4. If cell A16 on Sheet1 is selected, which cell will be selected when you move to Sheet2?

_____

5. What is the quickest way to select all cells in a single row?

_____

6. Name three advantages to using templates.

_____

_____

_____

7. How do you edit the text in a cell from the Formula Bar?

_____

_____

8. When sharing files with people who are using other versions of Excel, you will need to:

    a. Send them the XLSX file, which they will be able to open.

    b. Send them a printout of the file, and tell them to mark it up and you will edit it.

    c. Save your file as an XLS file, which they will be able to open.

    d. You cannot share files with people using older versions of Excel.

CHAPTER

3

Fine-Tuning Your Worksheet

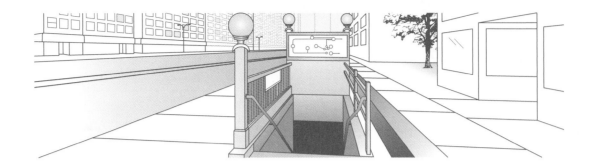

 # Enter the Station

Questions

1. When you have copied a group of cells, when can't you paste them more than once?

2. What are the advantages of grouping data?

3. What is the difference between sorting a column of data in a table and sorting a column of data that is not in a table?

4. What is the advantage of naming a table?

5. What is the difference between the conditional formatting data bar and color scale?

6. In addition to the spelling checker, what other grammar and resource tools are available in Excel 2007?

7. What is the advantage of adding a date to the footer of your worksheet?

Express Line

If you are already familiar with the basics of formatting and printing your worksheets in Excel 2007, skip ahead to the next chapter.

In this chapter, you learn more about the basics of working with data in Excel. You use the Juniper Flowers worksheet you created in Chapter 2 to learn how to fine-tune the look of your worksheet so that all the data is shown and printed and can be shared in a professional manner. You can get this file, named `Chapter3JuniperFlowers1.xlsx`, from the Web site.

In addition, you learn how to use formatting to highlight and emphasize by organizing your data into a table. After your data is organized, you can use conditional formatting to help you show what data has changed from period to period. You can then highlight areas where you need to concentrate more of your efforts.

Resizing Columns and Rows

Sometimes when you add text to a row or column in a worksheet, part of the text is cut off. For example, in the Juniper Flowers worksheet, the column labels in row 1 are not fully displayed. The words are there, but the default width for the columns is too small to show the whole title.

To fix this problem, tell Excel 2007 to adjust the width of the columns to the width of the data:

1. Open the **Chapter3JuniperFlowers1.xlsx** file.

2. Select columns A through G.

3. Move the cursor to the bar between any two column indicators.

The cursor changes to the icon shown in Figure 3-1.

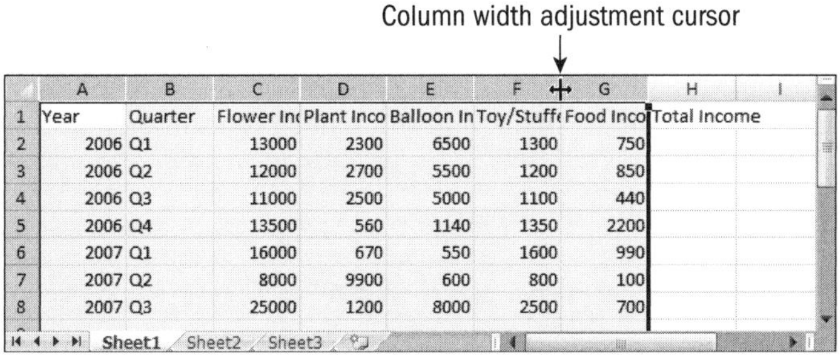

Column width adjustment cursor

	A	B	C	D	E	F	G	H	I
1	Year	Quarter	Flower Inc	Plant Inco	Balloon In	Toy/Stuff	Food Inco	Total Income	
2	2006	Q1	13000	2300	6500	1300	750		
3	2006	Q2	12000	2700	5500	1200	850		
4	2006	Q3	11000	2500	5000	1100	440		
5	2006	Q4	13500	560	1140	1350	2200		
6	2007	Q1	16000	670	550	1600	990		
7	2007	Q2	8000	9900	600	800	100		
8	2007	Q3	25000	1200	8000	2500	700		

Sheet1 / Sheet2 / Sheet3

Figure 3-1: The adjustment cursor appears between two column indicators.

4. When you see the adjustment cursor, double-click.

Each selected column automatically adjusts to the width of the data in its cells.

If the row height is causing data to not show, you can adjust the height of each row in the same manner as you can adjust the columns:

1. Select Rows 1 through 9.

2. Move the cursor to the bar between any two rows.

The cursor changes to the icon shown in Figure 3-2.

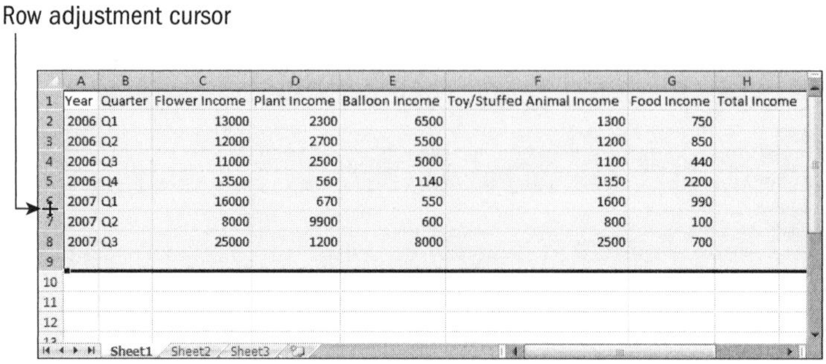

Row adjustment cursor

Figure 3-2: The adjustment cursor appears between two row indicators.

3. Double-click when you see the adjustment cursor.

Each selected row automatically adjusts to the height of the data in its cells.

If you prefer to change the height of a row or the width of a column by hand, select the row or column, position the cursor between that column and the next one, and drag the edge to make your change.

Copying and Pasting Data in Excel

When you are creating a spreadsheet, you often need the same content in more than one place. To make a copy of a cell or a series of cells, you can copy or cut the cells and then paste them in another place.

Performing basic copy and paste functions

Make sure that you open the Juniper Quarterly Sales worksheet you've been working on. (Or, you can open the Chapter3JuniperFlowers2.xlsx file from the Web site.) Then create some copies of this data as a practice exercise for copying and pasting:

1. Select cells A1 through G9 in Sheet1.

2. **Press Ctrl+C to copy the cells to the Clipboard.**

Alternatively, choose Home ➜ Clipboard ➜ Copy.

Notice that the border for the selected area becomes a moving dotted line. Figure 3-3 shows the dotted line for the area selected in the example.

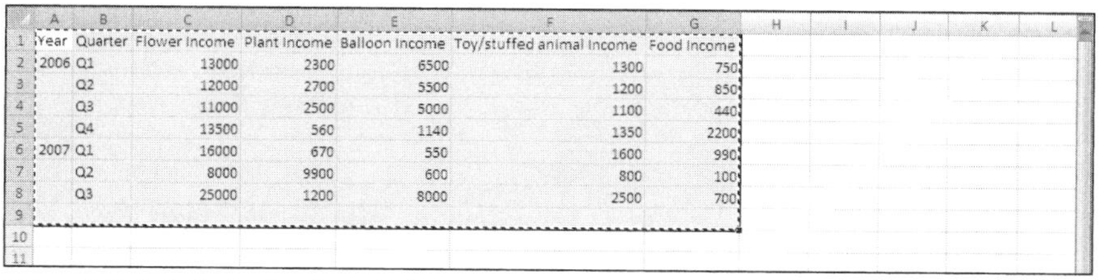

	A	B	C	D	E	F	G	H	I	J	K	L
1	Year	Quarter	Flower Income	Plant Income	Balloon Income	Toy/stuffed animal Income	Food Income					
2	2006	Q1	13000	2300	6500	1300	750					
3		Q2	12000	2700	5500	1200	850					
4		Q3	11000	2500	5000	1100	440					
5		Q4	13500	560	1140	1350	2200					
6	2007	Q1	16000	670	550	1600	990					
7		Q2	8000	9900	600	800	100					
8		Q3	25000	1200	8000	2500	700					
9												
10												
11												

Figure 3-3: Selected cells after copying.

3. **Move to Sheet2 by clicking on its name at the bottom of the worksheet.**

4. **Click in cell A1 and press Enter.**

Your table is pasted into Sheet2.

5. **Click in cell A28 on Sheet2, and press Ctrl+V to paste the data.**

Alternatively, choose Home ➜ Clipboard ➜ Paste.

Notice that the cells did not paste a second time. If you press Enter, like you did in Step 4, you can paste the content only once. To paste cell content more than once, you must either choose Home ➜ Clipboard ➜ Paste or press Ctrl+V for the first paste operation. After you paste in one of those two ways, you can repeat the paste operation.

6. **Repeat Steps 1 through 3. This time, paste the cells into Sheet3 by pressing Ctrl+V or clicking the Paste button.**

7. **After you paste the cells the second time, type Hello in cell A15 of the active sheet.**

8. **Attempt to paste the cells again.**

Nothing happens. Because you have done something else between the time you copied the data and the time you tried to paste it, Excel no longer has the data in the Clipboard. This situation, which is rather different from most Windows applications, may take some time to get used to. When you copy and paste data in Excel, you should always paste your data right after you copy it.

9. **Close the file, and don't save the changes. You use this file again in the next exercise, where you will start with just a single copy of the data.**

Watch Your Step

You may be wondering how the Paste option works in Excel 2007. You cut by either pressing Ctrl+X or choosing Home → Clipboard → Cut. The difference between copying and pasting is that copying leaves the data where it was and makes a second copy where you paste. On the other hand, cutting removes the data from where it was and pastes it where you want it to be. When you cut and paste in Excel 2007, the data is not removed from the original location until you paste. If you do anything else before you paste, the data is not cut or pasted.

Gaining more control with Paste options

Because each cell contains data, formatting information, and, possibly, formulas, when you paste the cells you need to tell Excel 2007 what you want to paste. As you discovered in the preceding section, when you just do a flat paste, everything is pasted. As you get more experience in working with Excel 2007 data, sometimes you want just the values or just the formatting or some other combinations.

When you paste data into cells in Excel 2007, a small Paste Options menu appears next to the cells you pasted, as shown in Figure 3-4. This menu is one of the two ways you can tell Excel 2007 what you want to paste. The other way is by using the drop-down arrow on the Paste button itself, as shown in Figure 3-5. You can use one of these two methods to choose from a variety of pasting options. Which method you use to control the data you paste depends on what you want to paste.

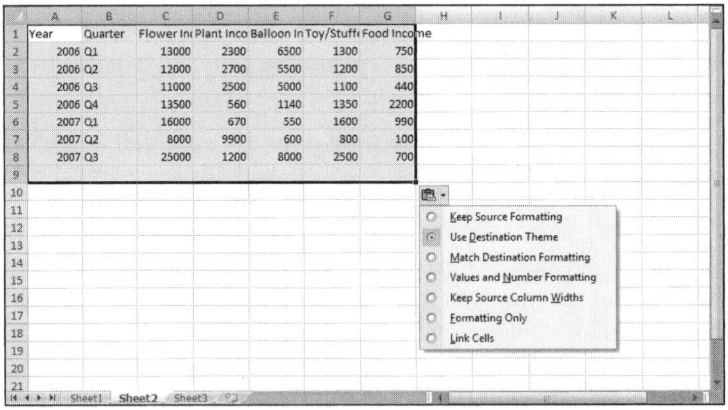

Figure 3-4: The Paste Options menu.

Table 3-1 lists the options available on the Paste Options menu, and Table 3-2 summarizes the Paste button options.

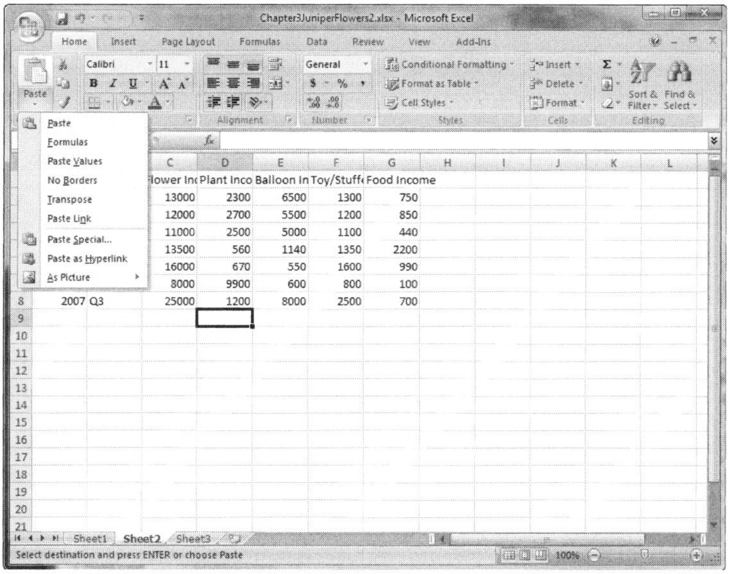

Figure 3-5: Options on the Paste button.

Table 3-1   Options on the Paste Options Menu

Option Name	When to Select This Option
Keep Source Formatting	Force the cells to keep the formatting of their original location (the source).
Use Destination Theme	Explicitly use the theme for the document you are pasting something into. (Sometimes, when you paste from one document to another, you need to choose which document's theme to use.)
Match Destination Formatting	Make the cells take on the formatting of the location you are pasting into.
Values Only	Paste the result of the formula and have it take on all the formatting of the destination. (When you are working with a formula, sometimes you need to paste just the value, not the formula that created the value.)
Values and Number Formatting	Keep the result and any number-related formatting. (This is another option for working with the result of a formula.)
Values and Source Formatting	Paste the value but keep all the formatting from the source.

continued

Table 3-1 *continued*

Option Name	When to Select This Option
Keep Source Column Widths	Paste the actual cell content (formula or result) but tell Excel 2007 that the resulting column should have the same width as in the source document. No other formatting is copied — just the column width. (This option is a little different from the others.)
Formatting Only	When you don't want to copy the contents or the formula but you want the cells to be formatted like the source cells. (You can get this result by choosing Home ➜ Clipboard ➜ Format Painter.)
Link Cells	When you want to see changes in the original cells reflected in the pasted cells, and paste everything but keep the cell linked to the source cell.

Table 3-2   Paste Button Options

Option	When to Select It
Paste	When you want to paste the data as it is, with its formatting intact. This option is the equivalent of pressing Ctrl+V.
Formulas	When you want to paste the formula, not the resulting value.
Paste Values	When you want to paste just the results of the formulas and no formatting.
No Borders	When you want to paste the cell formatting, content, and formulas but not any cell borders that might have been defined.
Transpose	When you want to swap rows for columns and vice versa. (Sometimes, when you are pasting content from one range of cells to another, you realize that the column content in the source location is row content in the destination location. This option is also useful if you need to turn a table on its side.)
Paste Link	When you want to see changes in the original cells reflected in the pasted cells, and paste everything but keep the cell linked to the source cell.
Paste Special	When you want to select (in the Paste Special dialog box) from an even wider range of formatting options. You can also perform operations on the data as Excel 2007 pastes it.
Paste Hyperlink	When you are pasting data from the Web or a similar source. (This option is available only in that instance.) Excel 2007 places *the location of the data,* rather than the actual data, in the cell.

Option	When to Select It
Paste Picture Link	When the picture is linked to the source data and you want to update both the source data and the picture. (If you don't want to edit your data, you can use one of these last three options to create a picture of your data at the location where you paste.)
Paste As Picture	When you want to paste a static picture that does not change when the source data changes. This option is the same as Paste Picture Link (see the preceding table entry) except that no link is created.
Copy As Picture	When you want to create a picture of the data (either as it looks on the screen or as it will look when printed) and then paste it anywhere you want.

As you work through the exercises in this book, you will play with some of these paste options. Some of them are quite useful to the average Excel 2007 user, and some of them are useful only in restricted circumstances.

Information Kiosk

If you want to play around with the various options for pasting, open the file `PasteSpecial.xlsx` and practice pasting that data by using the various paste options.

Grouping Data in Tables

Within a single worksheet, you can group data to create a table. *Tables* are areas of data that have a natural relationship to each other. For example, within a worksheet of inventory information, you might have tables defined that contain the data for specific groups of products or that contain inventory counts for each location.

The data isn't any different from the selected cells you are already used to working with. It is a series of cells with data, organized in rows and columns. You might have guessed that the data is related in some way because some data formatting is already done.

In Excel 2007, defining a range of cells as a table gives you the ability to add not only extra formatting but also special rows and columns that allow you to work with your data quickly and easily. Remember the rows you added to the Juniper Flowers billing statement in Chapter 2? All Excel 2007 tables can be expanded, just as that one was.

You can format tables more quickly than a group of cells because Excel knows that tables have heading rows, total rows, and other specific data. In addition, after you create a table, you can name the table and use its name to reference it in charts and other sheets.

That's all well and good, but the real power of tables becomes obvious when you work with data inside a table. As you will see in the next section, the process of filtering and sorting table data is simple and powerful. Having the data predefined as a table means that you don't need to tell Excel what the values to be sorted or filtered are, nor do you need to worry about data in one column getting organized differently from the data in the other columns. All data in a single row is connected, and the whole row is sorted or filtered at once.

Follow these steps to change the data in your file from unformatted data to an Excel table:

1. Open the **Chapter3JuniperFlowers2.xlsx** file.

2. Click and drag with your mouse to select cells A1 through G9.

3. Choose Insert → Tables → Table.

The Create Table dialog box appears, as shown in Figure 3-6. The range of cells you selected in Step 2 automatically appears in the text box. The My Table Has Headers check box tells Excel that the first row of your data isn't data, but instead consists of the names of the columns in your data. Predefining your headers makes it easier to work with your data.

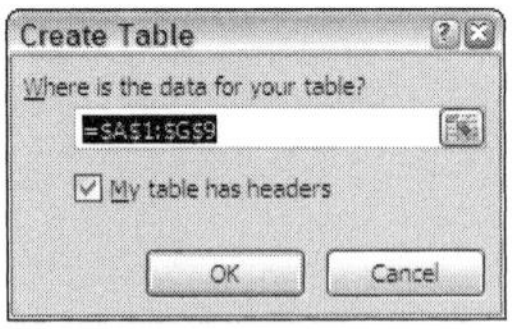

Figure 3-6: The Create Table dialog box.

4. Click the OK button to define your table.

Although the data in your table doesn't change, its *formatting* does. The resulting table should look like Figure 3-7.

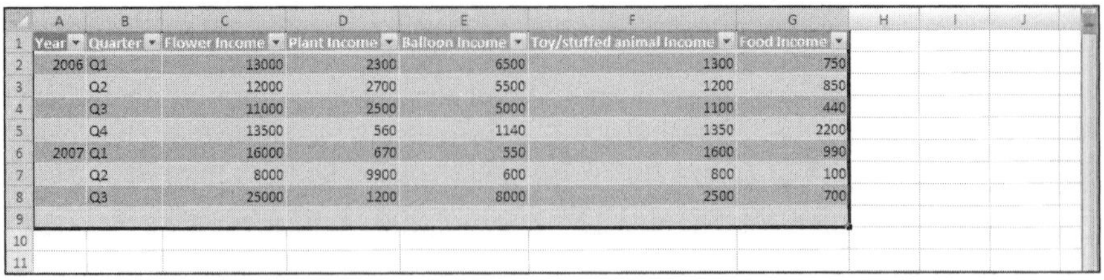

Year	Quarter	Flower Income	Plant Income	Balloon Income	Toy/stuffed animal Income	Food Income
2006	Q1	13000	2300	6500	1300	750
	Q2	12000	2700	5500	1200	850
	Q3	11000	2500	5000	1100	440
	Q4	13500	560	1140	1350	2200
2007	Q1	16000	670	550	1600	990
	Q2	8000	9900	600	800	100
	Q3	25000	1200	8000	2500	700

Figure 3-7: The Juniper Flowers sales data table.

Now look at some elements that make this group of cells a table:

- **Headings:** Notice that row 1 doesn't contain data. Instead, it contains descriptive text that comprises the title of the column, which is the *heading*. Headings tell you what data is in each column.

- **Drop-down arrows:** Did you notice the drop-down arrow next to the word Year in cell A1? That drop-down arrow lets you quickly sort and filter the data in the table by the values of the cells in that column.

One advantage of changing your data to a table is that you can now easily sort and filter the data so that you see exactly the information you want.

Filtering and sorting table data

Filtering and sorting are different ways of looking at your data without removing any of it. Think about a deck of cards. You can *sort* the cards by rank, suit, or color. All the cards are there and visible, but you see them in a specific order.

On the other hand, you can pull out some of the cards so that you can see only certain ones. You can *filter* out either color of card, any of the suits, or any of the ranks. The cards you filter out still exist — you just can't see them right now. A good example is making a pinochle deck from a regular deck: You pull out the lower-ranking cards and use only the 9 cards and higher.

In Excel 2007, sorting and filtering work the same way:

- **Sorting** lets you change the order of the rows in the table with a single mouse click.

- **Filtering** lets you decide which rows of data you want to see. You can filter in or out any of the rows of data based on the contents of the cells.

To filter or sort the data in your table, click in one of the heading cells, and then click the drop-down arrow at the right edge of the cell. Here are your sorting and filtering options, as shown in Figure 3-8:

- **Sorting options:** You can sort numbers from largest to smallest or by the color of the cell.

- **Filtering options:** You can filter in or out any of the rows of data based on the contents of the cells in this column. Just as with the sort options, Excel 2007 has a number of filters that you can turn on and off with just a couple of mouse clicks, or you create your own specialized filter by choosing Number Filters ➜ Custom Filters (or Text Filters ➜ Custom Filters, if you are working with text rather than with numbers).

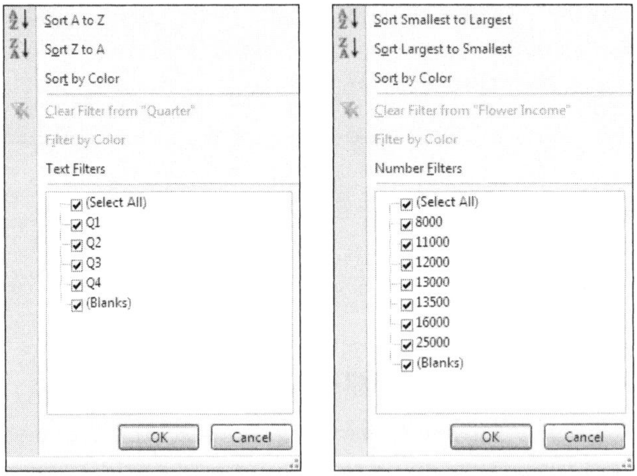

Figure 3-8: Sorting and filtering options for text data (left) and numerical data (right).

Because the data you're working with has been defined as a table, the rows of data stay together the way you want when you sort them. If you had used the sort options on data that is not in a table, you would sort only the data in the active column and leave the other columns alone. On the other hand, filters work only on entire rows of data. You cannot use a filter to prevent a single cell from being shown.

Follow these steps to learn the basics of applying a filter:

1. **Continue with the table you created in the previous section, or open the `Chapter3JuniperFlowers3.xlsx` file from the Web site.**

2. **Click the drop-down arrow to the right of the Flower Income heading (Cell C1).**

3. **From the Sort options, choose Sort Smallest to Largest.**

    The order of all data changes, not just the cells in this column.

4. **Click the drop-down arrow next to Plant Income (Cell D1).**

5. **Choose Number Filters → Above Average.**

    The only visible rows of data now are those in which the value of Plant Income is higher than the average for the column.

6. **Repeat Step 4 to disable the filter and ensure that all rows are again visible.**

Transfer

For more detailed information about filters and sorting, check out Chapter 10.

Customizing your table

By telling Excel 2007 that your data is organized in a table, you also get some awesome computational features. In just a few clicks, you can add summary rows and columns to the data in your table.

If you select any of the cells in your table, a new contextual tab header appears on the Ribbon. If this tab didn't automatically get the focus when you selected your table, click it now. The Design tab under the Table Tools contextual tab header is shown in Figure 3-9.

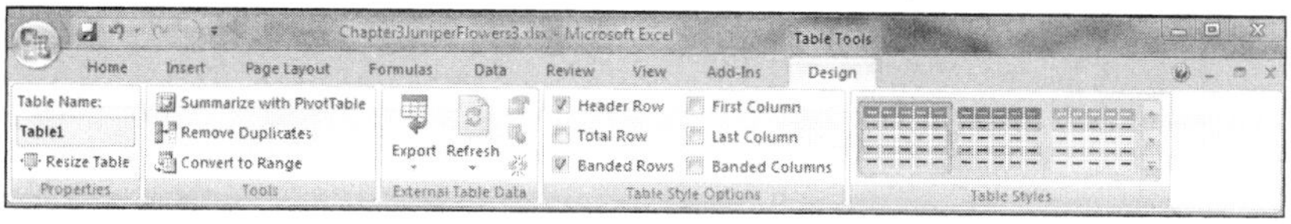

Figure 3-9: The Design tab under the Table Tools contextual tab header.

The five groups on the Table Tools Design tab let you work with your table as a whole. Three of them are described here:

Properties: This group contains two buttons that let you determine how the table is defined:

- **Table Name:** If you click below the Table Name button, you can change the name of your table from Table1 (the default) to a more descriptive name, such as Inventory June2006. Giving your table a name helps you remember which tables contain what data. If you need to move from one table to another, you can type the table name in the reference box and jump directly to the table.

- **Resize Table:** This button lets you redefine the size of your table. Clicking the button brings up the Resize Table dialog box, as shown in Figure 3-10.

  The Resize Table dialog box lets you change the starting and ending cells for your table. The notation for the cells is the same basic notation covered earlier in this chapter. To change the range, you can either edit the cell references themselves or click and drag in your worksheet to define the new size of your table.

Figure 3-10: The Resize Table dialog box.

Table Style Options: This group allows you to quickly change which specialty rows and columns in the table are visible, as well as which of these rows and columns pick up the formatting from the chosen table style.

Table Styles: The rightmost group, Table Styles, allows you to choose which table style you want to apply to your table. This group is a gallery, complete with Live Previews. As you move your mouse over the choices, the changes are reflected in the table. (Remember that gallery choices are not applied until you click to select one.)

Transfer

The options on the other two tabs are described later in this book. For details on functions and computations, see Chapter 4. If you want to know more about Pivot Tables, head to Chapter 6. External data sources are described in detail in Chapter 7.

Follow these steps to set up your table and learn the basics of formatting tables:

1. **Make sure that all the data in your table is visible.**

2. **Make sure that the Table Tools Design contextual tab is selected.**

3. **Click once in the box below the Table Name field in the Properties group.**

   Clicking in this field selects the text Table1.

4. **Type** Salesresults2006 **and press Enter.**

   The table name changes to Salesresults2006.

5. **Using the Table Styles gallery, change the table style to Table Style Medium 22.**

   Hint: Hover over the selections in the gallery to see the names of each table style.

6. **Make sure that all six check boxes in the Table Style Options group are selected.**

7. **Click in cell C10.**

   This cell is the Totals cell for column C.

8. **Click the drop-down arrow to the right of the cell.**

9. **Drag up or down to select Average from the list, and then click.**

10. **Click in cell D10.**

11. **Repeat Step 9, but select Max this time.**

12. **(Optional) Revert the row 10 cells to the total row computations by clicking the drop-down arrow for each cell and selecting Sum.**

    This step resets the table summary row to the computing totals.

    The resulting table is shown in Figure 3-11.

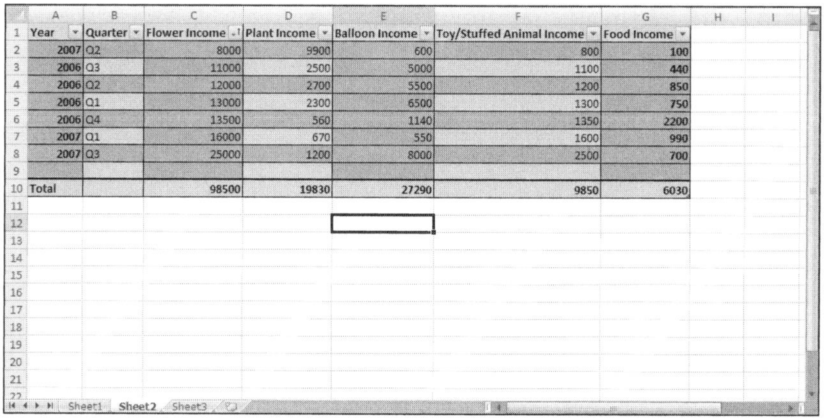

	Year	Quarter	Flower Income	Plant Income	Balloon Income	Toy/Stuffed Animal Income	Food Income		
1	Year	Quarter	Flower Income	Plant Income	Balloon Income	Toy/Stuffed Animal Income	Food Income		
2	2007	Q2	8000	9900	600	800	100		
3	2006	Q3	11000	2500	5000	1100	440		
4	2006	Q2	12000	2700	5500	1200	850		
5	2006	Q1	13000	2300	6500	1300	750		
6	2006	Q4	13500	560	1140	1350	2200		
7	2007	Q1	16000	670	550	1600	990		
8	2007	Q3	25000	1200	8000	2500	700		
9									
10	Total		98500	19830	27290	9850	6030		

Figure 3-11: The final, formatted table with the totals row.

Excel has another table feature that you are likely to find useful. After you define an area of your worksheet as a table, you add rows or columns to the table by adding the rows and columns just as you do in any other area of your worksheet. When you add the row or column, Excel 2007 realizes that you are in a table and adjusts the formatting automatically. If you have the totals row turned on, its location and values are even adjusted automatically for you.

Formatting Data for Clarity and Understanding

Sometimes, the way data looks on the screen or when it is printed helps you to understand what the data has to say. Think about the billing statement you created from a template in Chapter 2 (refer to Figure 2-6). The formatting of the page draws your eye to the most important part: the details of the current bill.

In Excel 2007, cell formatting allows you to adjust the content of a cell in many different ways. As an introduction to basic formatting, do some clean-up now on the Juniper Flowers sales table.

Formatting cells

In the previous exercise, you changed the formatting of each cell at the table level. However, you have to highlight certain data elements. To do this, you will work with some individual cells and format them.

To work with cell formatting, you use the buttons in the Font, Alignment, and Number groups on the Home tab.

Changing the alignment and fill color

The first step is to make the Year and Quarter columns look slightly different from the other columns:

1. **Open the `Chapter3JuniperFlowers4.xlsx` file.**

2. **Click the Home tab.**

3. **Select cells A1 through B9.**

4. **Click the Center button in the Alignment group.**

   This step ensures that the contents of the selected cells are centered left to right within the cells, no matter how wide the columns get.

5. **Click the Middle Align button in the Alignment group.**

   This step ensures that the contents of the selected cells are always aligned halfway between the top and bottom of the cell, no matter how tall the rows get.

6. **Choose Home → Font → Fill Color.**

   The fill color of the selected cells changes to the color of the current fill. Chances are that it doesn't look attractive with the rest of the fill colors, so you will refine it next.

7. **To change the fill color, click the drop-down arrow next to the Fill Color button and select one of colors for the background of these two rows.**

   When you finish, the table should look like the one shown in Figure 3-12.

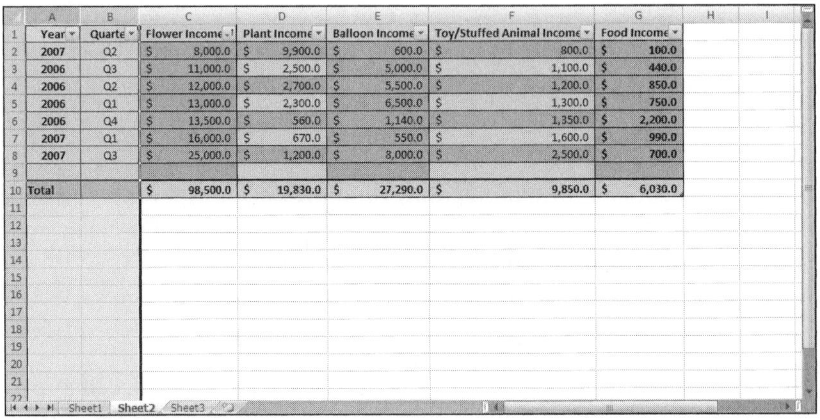

Figure 3-12: The final, formatted table with the totals row.

The Year and Quarter columns now have a more distinctive look than the other columns.

Changing the numeric format

The next step is to change the data cells so that they are formatted as currency ($1,000, for example) rather than as flat numbers (1000, for example). You do this task by using one of the special formats in the Number group on the Home tab. Follow these steps to change the numeric format of the data cells to currency:

1. **Select columns C through G.**

2. **Choose Home → Number and click the dollar sign icon.**

   This step formats each cell in these columns as dollars and cents. Because each of these numbers is a full dollar amount, you do not need to show the cents part of the number. Excel 2007 allows you to turn on and off the cents display with just a couple of button clicks.

3. **With the same cells selected, choose Home → Number → Decrease Decimal.**

   This step makes one less number visible after the decimal.

4. **Click the same button again to complete the change from dollars and cents to just dollars.**

   When you finish, the table should look like the one shown in Figure 3-13.

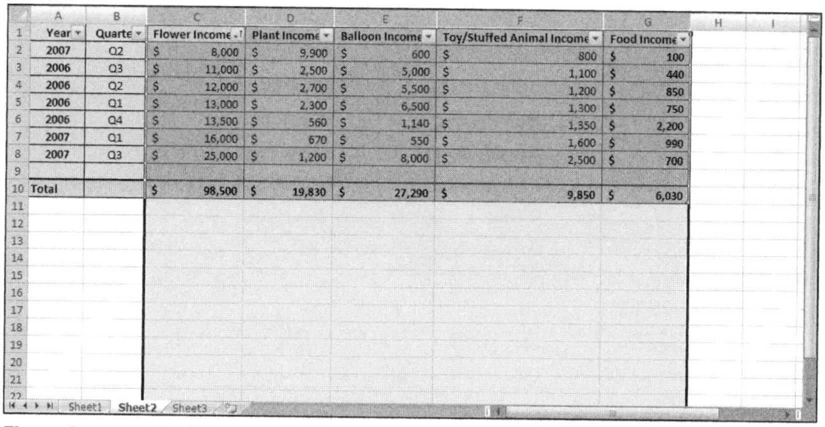

	A	B	C	D	E	F	G	H	I
1	Year	Quarter	Flower Income	Plant Income	Balloon Income	Toy/Stuffed Animal Income	Food Income		
2	2007	Q2	$ 8,000	$ 9,900	$ 600	$ 800	$ 100		
3	2006	Q3	$ 11,000	$ 2,500	$ 5,000	$ 1,100	$ 440		
4	2006	Q2	$ 12,000	$ 2,700	$ 5,500	$ 1,200	$ 850		
5	2006	Q1	$ 13,000	$ 2,300	$ 6,500	$ 1,300	$ 750		
6	2006	Q4	$ 13,500	$ 560	$ 1,140	$ 1,350	$ 2,200		
7	2007	Q1	$ 16,000	$ 670	$ 550	$ 1,600	$ 990		
8	2007	Q3	$ 25,000	$ 1,200	$ 8,000	$ 2,500	$ 700		
9									
10	Total		$ 98,500	$ 19,830	$ 27,290	$ 9,850	$ 6,030		
11									

Figure 3-13: The final, formatted table with the totals row.

Changing the numeric format is just one of the quick-formatting options available on the Home tab. Another of the formatting options that you will use regularly is date formatting, described next.

Formatting dates

Dates in Excel 2007 are stored as special numbers, but are shown to you as specially formatted text. To see just some of the date options available in Excel 2007, follow these steps to add an update date to your table:

1. Click in cell C13 and type Last Updated:.

2. Press Tab to move to cell D13, and type today's date as mm/dd/yyyy.

3. Exit cell D13 by using either the Tab or Enter key.

Notice that Excel 2007 attempts to translate the date into a dollar amount. The reason is that in Step 1 of the preceding step list, you selected the entire column for the format change. Next, you change the formatting for this cell to a date format.

4. Click back in cell D13.

5. Choose Home → Number, and click the arrow to the right of the Number Format drop-down list, which shows the General option selected.

6. From the drop-down list, select Short Date.

The content of cell D13 immediately changes to the date format you selected.

When you finish, the table should look like the one shown in Figure 3-14.

	A	B	C	D	E	F	G	H	I
1	Year	Quarter	Flower Income	Plant Income	Balloon Income	Toy/Stuffed Animal Income	Food Income		
2	2007	Q2	$ 8,000	$ 9,900	$ 600	$ 800	$ 100		
3	2006	Q3	$ 11,000	$ 2,500	$ 5,000	$ 1,100	$ 440		
4	2006	Q2	$ 12,000	$ 2,700	$ 5,500	$ 1,200	$ 850		
5	2006	Q1	$ 13,000	$ 2,300	$ 6,500	$ 1,300	$ 750		
6	2006	Q4	$ 13,500	$ 560	$ 1,140	$ 1,350	$ 2,200		
7	2007	Q1	$ 16,000	$ 670	$ 550	$ 1,600	$ 990		
8	2007	Q3	$ 25,000	$ 1,200	$ 8,000	$ 2,500	$ 700		
9									
10	Total		$ 98,500	$ 19,830	$ 27,290	$ 9,850	$ 6,030		
11									
12									
13			Last Updated	2/1/2007					
14									
15									
16									
17									
18									
19									
20									
21									
22									

Sheet1 Sheet2 Sheet3

Figure 3-14: The final, formatted table with the totals row.

You have many other formatting options for individual cells. You work with these other formatting options as you progress through this book. If you want to become familiar with the other options, click in an empty cell and experiment with the other formatting options.

Using conditional formatting

Now that you have experimented with the basics of formatting individual cells, it is time to experiment with one of the most informative Excel 2007 features: conditional formatting.

Conditional formatting allows you to select a group of cells and quickly format the data so that you can see at a glance the relationships between the data. For example, conditional formatting allows you to see at a glance which quarter had the highest and lowest sales for each category. Other conditional formats available include

- **Highlight Cells:** Apply a color highlight to cells that meet your specified criteria.
- **Top/Bottom Rules:** Highlight in some manner the top and bottom 5 or 10 elements.
- **Data Bars:** Place bars behind the data in the cells to show the relationships between the data.
- **Color Scales:** As a more advanced version of data bars, color scales allow color coding of the bars.
- **Icons:** Apply icons of various types to the end of the data to show the relationships between the data elements.

Follow these steps to format the data so that you can see the top and bottom values at a glance:

1. Select cells C2 through C8.

2. On the Styles tab, click the Conditional Formatting button, and then drag down to Top/Bottom Rules and over to Top 10 Items.

The Top 10 dialog box appears, as shown in Figure 3-15. You will change the rank so that the top four items are formatted.

Figure 3-15: The Top 10 Items dialog box.

3. Change the 10 to 4.

Either type the number or use the up- and down-arrow keys. By adding special formatting to the top four amounts for the flower income, you can now see at a glance during which quarters the stores sold the most flowers.

4. Click the drop-down arrow in the second box, and select Green Fill with Dark Green Text. Click OK.

Cells C5, C6, C7, and C8 all now have green numbers with a green background. These are the top four elements in this column.

5. Select cells D2 through D8.

6. Click the Conditional Formatting button, and then drag down to the Data Bars option and over to select the Orange Data Bar option.

Each cell now has an orange bar partway across the cell. These bars make it much easier to pick out the top and bottom values in the column.

If you want, play around with the other built-in conditional formats. Try to determine places where you would use some of the different icons and color sets.

Watch Your Step

You can apply multiple conditional formats to the same sets of cells at the same time. This procedure can be helpful, but don't go overboard. The idea behind conditional formatting is to make it easy to understand your data at a glance. If you apply too many different formats to the cells, it becomes hard to understand what your data is telling you.

Creating your own conditional formatting

In addition to customizing the conditional formats provided with Excel 2007, you can also create your own conditional formatting rules and indicators. To do this, you choose the New Rule option on the Conditional Formatting drop-down list. The New Formatting Rule dialog box opens, as shown in Figure 3-16.

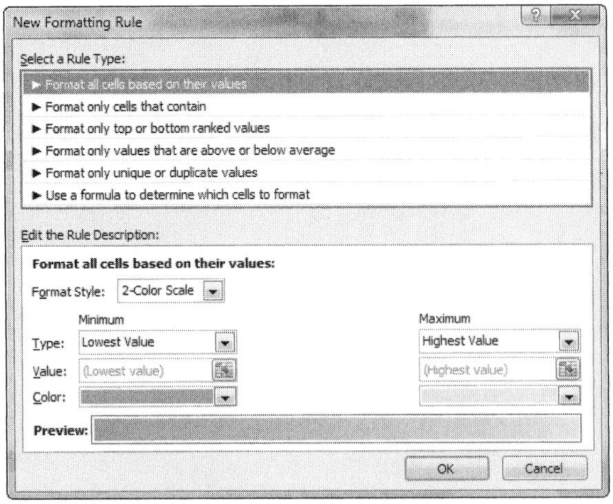

Figure 3-16: The New Formatting Rule dialog box.

The top half of this dialog box allows you to set up the type of rule you want to apply. The bottom half lets you target the rule to exactly what you want the data to show you. Follow these steps to learn first how to change which colors Excel chooses for the cell background in your conditional formatting, and then to adapt that rule so that you can easily tell which are the Top 5 values:

1. **Select cells F2 through F8.**

2. **Click the Conditional Formatting button and drag down to select New Rule.**

   The New Formatting Rule dialog box appears.

3. **From the Format Style drop-down list, select 3-Color Scale and set the Midpoint option to Number.**

   Even though you are changing the conditional formatting, the view of the data has not changed. You have to save the rule to see the change.

4. **Click OK to apply the new rule.**

   The results of your rule are shown in column F.

You can work with the rules for your table in another way: Click the Conditional Formatting button and select the Manage Rules option. The Conditional Formatting Rules Manager opens, as shown in Figure 3-17.

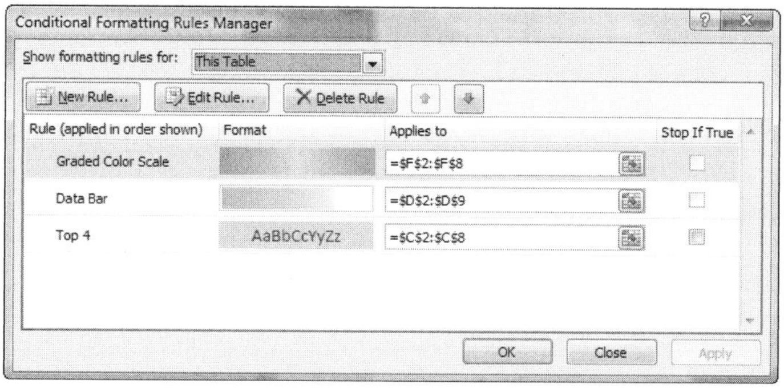

Figure 3-17: The Conditional Formatting Rules Manager dialog box.

Using this dialog box, you can see and work with all your rules at one time. To work with a rule, select the rule and click the Edit Rule button. This action brings up the same dialog box as the Create Rule option. When you finish editing the rule, clicking OK brings back the rules list so that you can work with other rules.

Applying built-in cell styles

In addition to being able to format your cells with conditional formatting, you have several built-in cell styles available. To access them, choose Home → Styles → Cell Styles. This action brings up an extensive list of built-in cell styles for you to use, as shown in Figure 3-18. These styles are similar to the ones you created in the cell formatting exercise. The difference is that because they are predefined, you can apply them in a single click.

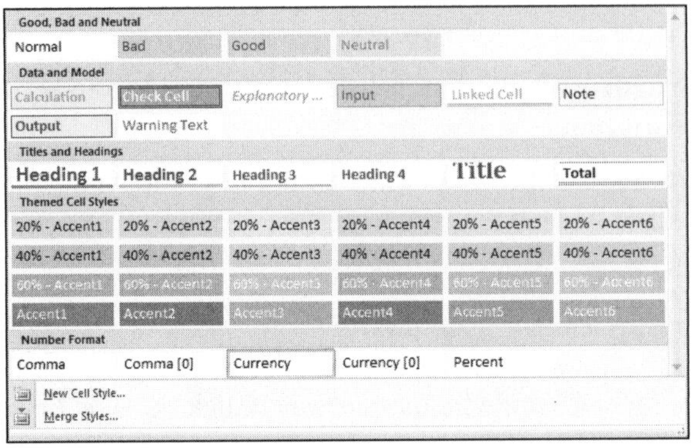

Figure 3-18: The built-in Excel cell style choices.

Cell styles can help you or others understand your data. Just as you can easily overuse conditional formatting, using too many cell styles in the same worksheet can be confusing as well.

Cell styles and the built-in conditional formats are galleries, so you can hover the cursor over the options to see what they do to the overall look of your worksheet before you apply them. Use this feature to avoid overformatting your data.

Formatting Data to Share

When formatting your data for printing and sharing, make the look of your worksheets enhance the data — not detract from it. To help you achieve this goal, Excel 2007 has built-in themes that are a quick way to define your workbook's styles and formatting.

Applying themes

You can use Office 2007 to define a common look and feel for each document you create. The look and feel of the document is defined in a theme. *Themes* contain information on document parts, fonts, colors, style sheets, and other elements. Although Excel 2007 does not interpret all the theme elements, it does allow you to apply common color schemes, font schemes, and effects for graphical elements.

The idea behind themes is to allow you to quickly apply formatting to a document so that it looks professional. Excel 2007 uses one theme per workbook. When you choose a theme for a segment of your workbook (a specific sheet, chart, or table, for example), that theme is applied to the entire workbook.

To see how themes are applied and how to change them, you return to the table before you applied the conditional formatting and then update the formatting by using themes. Follow these steps:

1. Open the `Chapter3JuniperFlowers5.xlsx` file.

2. Click in the table.

3. Choose Page Layout → Themes → Themes.

The list of themes available on your machine is displayed. The current theme is highlighted with an orange background.

4. Scroll through the available themes.

Notice that as you move across each theme, it quick-previews on your table.

Watch Your Step

If only the fonts change as you move across the available themes, the cursor isn't in the table, or your data hasn't been defined as a table. If you are not in a table, the only theme elements that appear to change are the fonts. The other theme elements haven't been applied to the data, so Excel 2007 doesn't know to preview any of them.

5. Click the Median theme icon to apply it to your workbook.

Transfer

If you want to learn more about themes, the details are in Chapter 8.

Refining your styles

In addition to being able to do quick formatting on your workbooks, you can refine the look of your data after you apply the theme. You can change the fonts and colors that are used and the look of the graphics by using the same processes discussed earlier in this chapter to apply font changes, style changes, and color changes.

Suppose that the Median theme you just applied uses the fonts and styling you want for your table, but you want to use different colors in the table. Follow these steps to change the colors used in the table:

1. Click anywhere in the table.

2. Choose Page Layout ➜ Themes ➜ Colors.

3. Move through the colors shown in the drop-down list.

The colors of the table cells and the colors of the text change, but the fonts and formatting do not.

4. Click the Concourse theme colors from the list to apply them to the table.

5. Move to cell Sheet1!A1.

6. Select cells Sheet1!A1 through Sheet1!G8.

7. Choose Insert ➜ Tables ➜ Table.

8. Click OK.

Notice that the new table has the formatting from the Median theme but has the colors from the Concourse theme, just as your original table did.

When you refine a theme, you refine the settings for your entire workbook. If you want to apply a color change to just one of the tables in your workbook, use the table formatting tools discussed earlier in this chapter.

Proofing Your Work

Part of creating a professional document is making sure that your content is correct and correctly presented. Excel 2007 has a number of built-in proofing tools that help you ensure that the data shown on your spreadsheets is correct.

Running a spell check

When most people create documents, they pay attention to what they *mean* to say, not to what they type. If all your Excel 2007 documents consist of pure numbers, you don't need to worry about the spell checker. If that's the case, though, you probably aren't living in the real world. In the real world, even spreadsheets have text for column headers, row headers, and other text elements.

Follow these steps to run a spell check:

1. Close any files you have open. Open the `Chapter3Juniper Flowers6.xls` file.

This file contains the same data you have been working with in this chapter. However, typographical errors have been added to ensure that you see the spell-check dialog boxes.

2. Click in cell Sheet1!A1.

3. Choose Review ➜ Proofing ➜ Spelling.

The Spelling dialog box appears with the first misspelled word shown in the top half of the box, and the options for correcting the misspelling in the bottom half.

4. **Select the correct word and click the Change button.**

Excel 2007 either moves directly to the next misspelled word or opens the dialog box shown in Figure 3-19.

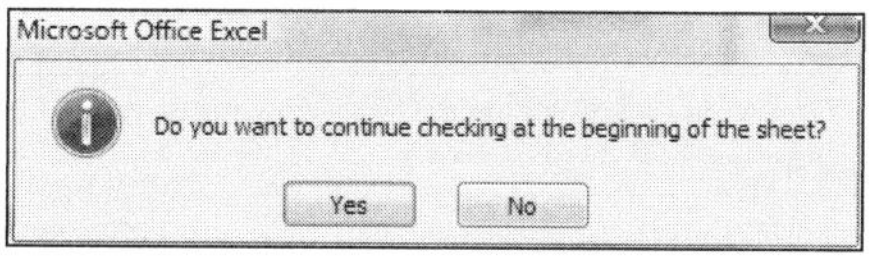

Figure 3-19: The Continue Spell Check message.

5. **No matter which option is offered, continue until you correct all the spelling errors.**

Personalizing your spelling options

You can personalize your spelling options by using one of the pages in the Excel 2007 options. To access these options, follow these steps:

1. **Click the Office button, and then find the Excel 2007 Options button and click it.**

2. **In the left column, click the word Proofing.**

The proofing options appear on the right side of the dialog box, as shown in Figure 3-20. The settings you see are the default settings for Excel 2007.

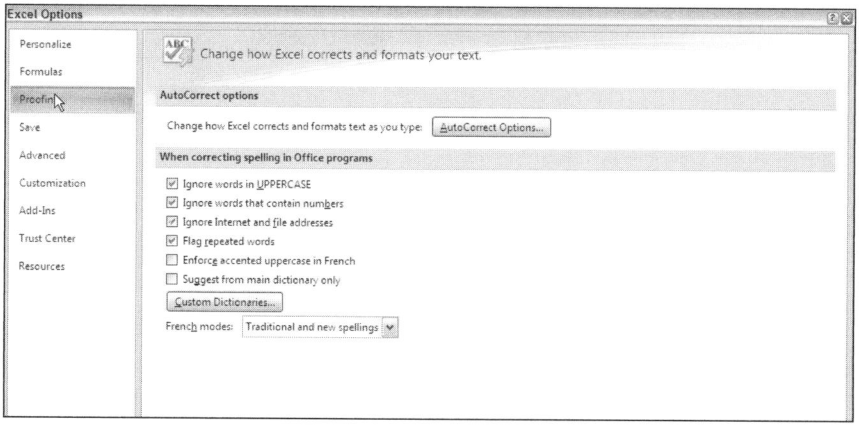

Figure 3-20: The Excel Options proofing list.

3. **If you want to change any of the settings, do so and then click OK to save your changes.**

Using the Thesaurus

Sometimes when you are creating a document, you can't think of the right word to use in a certain spot. In this situation, the Office Thesaurus comes in handy. You can activate the Thesaurus task pane this way: After selecting either a word or an entire cell, choose Review ➜ Proofing ➜ Thesaurus. In either case, Excel 2007 attempts to find options for the selected text. Follow these steps:

1. Make sure that the `Chapter3JuniperFlowers6.xls` file is open and that all the data in your table is visible.

2. Click in cell Sheet1!A1.

3. Choose Review ➜ Proofing ➜ Thesaurus.

The Research task pane appears with the Thesaurus options visible, as shown in Figure 3-21.

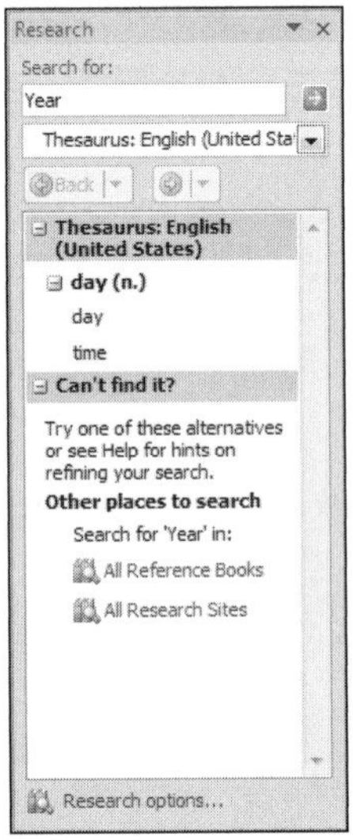

Figure 3-21: Thesaurus options in the Research task pane.

4. To replace the current word with one of the choices, double-click a selection.

Working with the Research task pane

As you just saw, when you bring up the Thesaurus, you activate the Research task pane with the Thesaurus options selected. However, several other research options are available from this task pane, ranging from the Thesaurus, translation service, and dictionary to a wide variety of online research sites of all types.

The rest of the Research task pane works just as the Thesaurus does. You select the word, phrase, or cell you want to research and choose Review → Proofing → Research. The results appear in the Research task pane.

Information Kiosk

To translate your text the easy way, select the text, and then choose Review → Proofing → Translate.

Printing Your Worksheet

When you're ready to print a table, you want to make a couple of other refinements to your spreadsheet. You are likely to want to add a header, a footer, and some other information to the sheet so that people looking at your data know when the data was collected and other important information. To add these elements in Excel 2007, you use the buttons on the Page Layout tab. However, before you add these elements, you might want to see what your table will look like when it is printed. To see it, use the View tab.

When you created the billing statement in Chapter 2, the spreadsheet was shown in page-by-page format rather than in just the rows and cells you might be used to seeing. To see the table as it will print, change to Page Layout view. Just follow these steps:

1. Open the `Chapter3JuniperFlowers7.xls` file.

2. Choose View → Workbook Views → Page Layout View.

Your view changes to a page-by-page view. Notice that the table is split across two pages, which is not what you want.

Now that you can see how the income table will look when it is printed, you need to refine the formatting to make it work for printing as well as for viewing.

Making the table fit on a single page

The first step is to make the table fit on one page. By default, pages created in Excel 2007 are created as portrait pages. *Portrait* pages are taller than they are wide. For your table, you want a *landscape* page — one that is wider than it is tall. The best way to visualize portrait mode versus landscape mode is to look at a piece of 8½-by-11-inch paper. When you hold the paper as you normally would write on it, it is in portrait mode. When you rotate the paper so that it is on its side, it is in landscape mode. These two terms come from the art world: Portraits are normally produced on taller pages, and landscapes are normally produced on wider pages.

When you change the page layout from portrait mode to landscape mode, your table fits better on a printed page. At the beginning of the following steps, your table looks like the one shown in Figure 3-22.

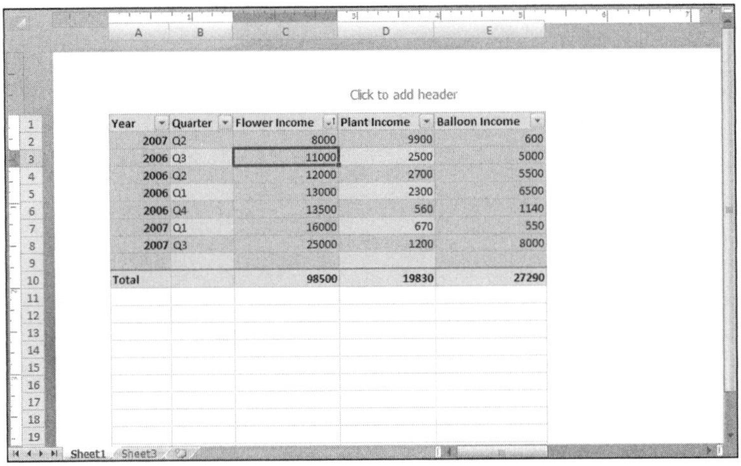

Year	Quarter	Flower Income	Plant Income	Balloon Income
2007	Q2	8000	9900	600
2006	Q3	11000	2500	5000
2006	Q2	12000	2700	5500
2006	Q1	13000	2300	6500
2006	Q4	13500	560	1140
2007	Q1	16000	670	550
2007	Q3	25000	1200	8000
Total		98500	19830	27290

Figure 3-22: The table in Page Layout view as a "portrait" page.

1. **Choose Page Layout ➜ Page Setup ➜ Orientation.**
2. **From the list that appears, select Landscape.**

   Columns A through G now appear on the first page, as shown in Figure 3-23.

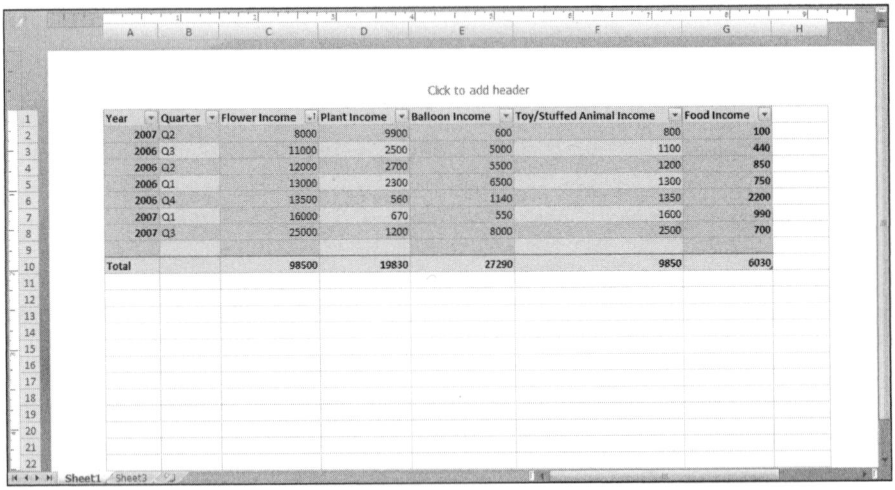

Year	Quarter	Flower Income	Plant Income	Balloon Income	Toy/Stuffed Animal Income	Food Income
2007	Q2	8000	9900	600	800	100
2006	Q3	11000	2500	5000	1100	440
2006	Q2	12000	2700	5500	1200	850
2006	Q1	13000	2300	6500	1300	750
2006	Q4	13500	560	1140	1350	2200
2007	Q1	16000	670	550	1600	990
2007	Q3	25000	1200	8000	2500	700
Total		98500	19830	27290	9850	6030

Figure 3-23: The same table in Page Layout view as a "landscape" page.

Adjusting the margins

In some cases, your data is too wide to fit on a page with regular margins, even in landscape mode. If you need to adjust the margins, use the Margins button on the Page Layout tab:

1. **Choose Page Layout → Page Setup → Margins.**

2. **From the drop-down list, select Narrow to change to smaller margins all the way around the document.**

All the columns from A to I now fit on one page, as shown in Figure 3-24.

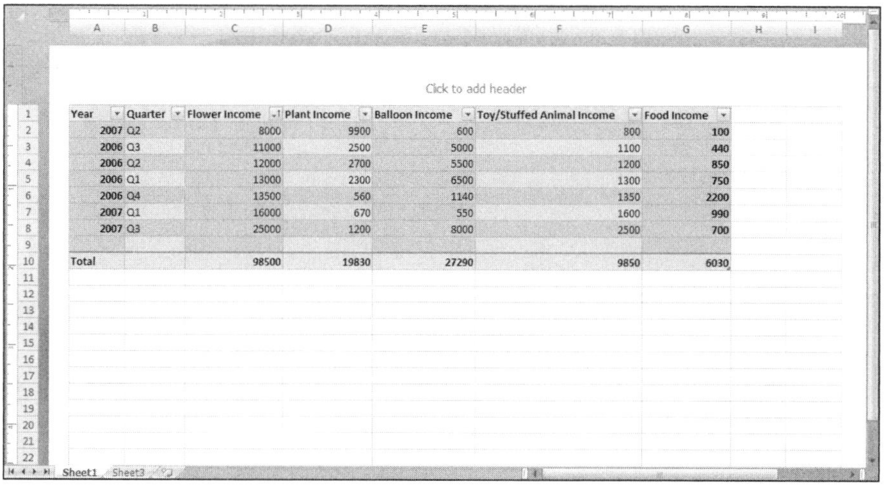

Figure 3-24: The table is adjusted for correct printing.

Adding a header and footer

You are now closer to creating an attractively formatted document. The next step is to add a descriptive header and footer that will print with the document:

1. **At the top of the sheet, just before the data lines begin, click the line that reads *Click to add header,* as shown in Figure 3-25.**

Figure 3-25: An Excel sheet in Page Layout view with no header area defined.

2. **Type** Juniper Flowers Quarterly Sales Summary.

3. **Click elsewhere in your spreadsheet.**

4. **Scroll down through your sheet until the text** *Click to add footer* **appears, in a blank area just below row 34. Click the text.**

   The Header and Footer Tools Design contextual tab should appear.

5. **Choose Header and Footer Tools Design → Header and Footer → Footer.**

6. **Select the last element on the list, the one that starts with Prepared By and ends with the current date.**

   Notice that the footer is shown at the bottom center of the page, but that the date has been replaced by [Date]. It tells Excel 2007 to insert the current date when you print the document. You can see what it should look like in Figure 3-26.

7. **Click in one of the cells of the document to ensure that the footer is no longer being edited.**

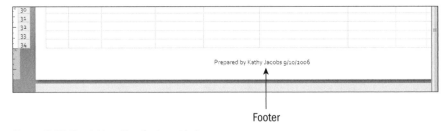

Footer

Figure 3-26: The table with a footer added.

Printing the document

After you finish refining your table, you are ready to print your document. Just follow these steps:

1. **Choose File → Print.**

   The Print dialog box appears.

2. **Accept the default print options, click the OK button, and print your document.**

Alternatively, you can print the document by using the Quick Print button on the QAT. This button accepts the default print settings and sends your document to the printer.

You can do much more formatting of your spreadsheet. You can change the background of the sheet to a picture, add a picture (such as a logo or building shot) to an area of the sheet, or even add graphical elements to the columns to show which products the columns represent. You learn more about these options in Chapter 8.

Remember that the more extras you add, the higher the possibility that the formatting will distract from the data. Extra elements can be useful as design elements, but exercise restraint when adding them.

Getting your data view back

Now that you are done printing, seeing the cells again is simple to do: Choose View → Workbook Views → Normal.

column width: The width of all cells within the column. All cells in a single column have the same width. If the data for a cell is too wide to show in the column, the data is displayed as a series of pound signs (for numeric data) or is shortened (for most instances of text).

conditional formatting: The formatting of data according to defined rules to show differences in that data. The rules you use can format the cell contents, the cell background, the cell text, or icons that are shown with the cell contents. A good example of conditional formatting is the application of data bars to show how the size of the data element relates to other elements in the range.

filter: To show only those rows of data that meet a designated criteria. Data that has been filtered out is still in the worksheet; it just is not shown when the filter is turned on. Data filtering is typically used to make large datasets more manageable for data evaluation. Data filtering is also used to find the answer to specific questions.

formatting: The look and feel of the cells within your worksheet. Formatting can also be applied to portions of the worksheet or to the entire worksheet. However, at its basic level, all formatting in Excel that affects a cell is applied at the cell level.

heading: The title of a column in your data. If no headings are defined in the first row of data, the headings for the data are the column names.

landscape: A paper orientation where the width of the paper is larger than its height.

page layout: The design of the look of your data so that it prints the way you expect. The Page Layout tab contains the buttons that facilitate the layout of your data.

portrait: A paper orientation where the height of the paper is larger than its width.

proofing: The process of verifying that your worksheet contents are spelled correctly and use the correct terms and are in the right format.

continued

 **continued**

row height: The height of each individual cell within the row. As with the column width, all cells within the row have the same height. If the data does not fit, only a shortened version of the data appears.

sort: To rearrange rows of data based on the values or formatting of a single column's cells. When data is sorted in Excel, rows of data are treated as records rather than as individual cells.

table: A defined set of rows and columns of cells that can be formatted, named, and manipulated as a single entity.

transpose: To translate data so that data in the rows is translated into columns or the data in the columns is translated into rows.

Last Stop

Practice Exam

1. List two circumstances in which you would need to adjust the size of the column or row for a cell.

_____

_____

_____

2. After you follow these steps, how many times will the data be pasted?

_____

1. Select three cells.
2. Copy the cells.
3. Move to the left three cells.
4. Paste.
5. Move to the left three more cells.
6. Type **Excel 2007**.
7. Paste.

3. Name three advantages of grouping data into tables.

_____

_____

_____

4. True or False: You can make the Table Tools tab appear at any time, regardless of whether you are working in a table.

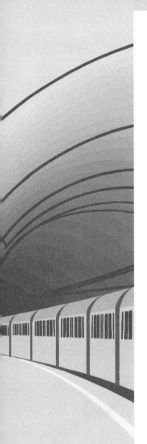

5. What are the steps to apply the stop sign conditional formatting to a series of cells?

_____

_____

6. Which tab is used to change how your worksheet will look when you print it?

_____

7. How can you tell if a word in a cell is misspelled?

_____

_____

8. List the steps to print your worksheet.

_____

_____

4

Understanding Excel Formulas

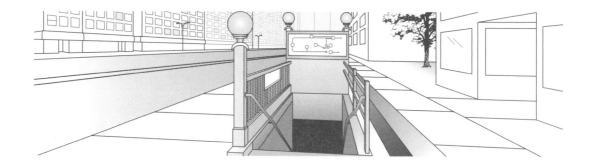

 # Enter the Station

Questions

1. What is a formula?

2. How can a formula save you time?

3. How do you determine whether a cell holds a value or a formula?

4. What is the difference between an absolute cell reference and a relative cell reference?

5. Name one instance in which you would not want your formulas to calculate automatically.

6. What error-checking rules are available in Excel 2007?

7. What is the advantage of using the Function Wizard over typing functions from scratch?

8. Which functions are available for cells containing text?

9. Beyond column names, why would you want to use a named range?

Express Line

If you are already familiar with using formulas to compute cell contents in Excel 2007, skip ahead to the next chapter.

art of the power of Excel 2007 lies in its ability to do computations for you. Rather than enter data by hand, you can enter a formula and have Excel 2007 figure out the values for some of the cells. Formulas range from the simplest summations of series of cells to the most complex business and mathematical formulas.

Formulas in Excel work on numeric data, text, and all other kinds of data. Formulas can be nested either within a single cell or by using a cell reference. As you work through this chapter, you will learn how to harness the power of the formula and make it do your work for you.

What You Need to Know About Formulas

Think about math class in elementary school. There, you probably learned your math facts by reciting "1+1=2". That is a formula. In Excel, formulas allow you to substitute cell references for the items on the left side of the equal sign and store the result in the selected cell.

When you get past that basic example, you start to see the power of formulas and why you need to understand them. For example, in the basic math fact 1+1=2, if you store the two ones in cells A1 and A2, you can store the formula in cell A3. That formula would look like this: =A1+A2. Although it reads backward from the math fact, it says the same thing: "In the current cell (A3), place the value obtained by adding the contents of A1 and the contents of A2."

Why use a formula for something this simple? Because you can change the values in A1 and A2 and let an Excel formula compute the new value for A3. After you understand this concept, you are ready to move on to the next level of formula work.

In this chapter, you work with some sample market research data. Market researchers not only need to know the overall opinions from the survey participants, but also must be able to apply a wide range of formulas to the collected data to determine how various groups of participants responded.

Creating a basic formula

The most basic way to create a formula is to select a series of cells, tell Excel 2007 which formula you want to use, and let Excel determine what the formula should be and where the answer should go.

For example, when a survey is completed, the survey results from a number of different locations need to be combined. One of the first data points to be discovered is the number of total participants. To find out, you use some simulated data and the Sum formula.

Sum allows you to select a series of cells and have Excel 2007 compute and update the total automatically. In the following steps, you use the Sum function to find the total number of respondents from several locations:

1. **Open the Excel file `MarketResearch1.xlsx`.**

   The first sheet appears, as shown in Figure 4-1.

	A	B	C	D	E	F	G	H	I	J	K	L
1		Akron	Chicago	Cleveland	Denver	Philadelphia	Phoenix	Total				
2	Expected number of participants	10	10	10	10	10	10					
3	Actual number of participants	6	7	8	10	5	9					
4												
5												
6												
7												
8												
9			Overall Average Opinion		Positive average?			Text comment Summary				
10												
11	Average Answer 1											
12	Average Answer 2											
13	Average Answer 3											
14	Average Answer 4											
15	Average Answer 5											
16	Average Answer 6											
17	Average Answer 7											
18	Average Answer 8											
19	Average Answer 9											
20	Average Answer 10											
21	Average Answer 11											
22	Average Answer 12											
23	Average Answer 13											

Figure 4-1: Respondent totals.

2. **Click in cell H2.**

   Notice that cell H3 has no value yet. You will add the formula to this cell.

3. **Select cells B2 through H2.**

4. **Choose Home → Editing → AutoSum (Σ).**

   This step places the Sum() formula in cell H2 and sets up the formula to add cells B2 through H2.

5. **AutoFill cell H3 with the Sum function.**

   When you used AutoFill in cell H3, Excel 2007 determined which cells you wanted to total, created the correct formula, and showed the computation results for you, as shown in Figure 4-2.

	A	B	C	D	E	F	G	H	I	J	K	L
1		Akron	Chicago	Cleveland	Denver	Philadelphia	Phoenix	Total				
2	Expected number of participants	10	10	10	10	10	10	60				
3	Actual number of participants	6	7	8	10	5	9	45				
4												
5												

Figure 4-2: Completed respondent totals.

This technique works well for summations, but doesn't work as well for many other types of formulas.

Creating a formula directly in a cell

The second way to add a formula to a cell is to click the cell and create the formula directly in that cell. You are more likely to use this method for computations.

Look at the market research data you're working with. You see that row 2 contains the number of responses that each location was supposed to gather. Row 3 contains the number of responses you received. In the following steps, you fill in row 4, which is now blank, with the percentage of the expected responses each location received:

Watch Your Step

Each chapter in this book uses a different scenario to show the concepts of that chapter. Within a single chapter, each exercise builds on the previous ones. With that in mind, I offer this word of warning: The world has two kinds of computer users: those who have lost data and those who will. Save your work frequently, and make backup copies of the Excel files as you move through each chapter. It makes life much easier.

1. Click in cell B4 and type an equal sign (=).

2. Click cell B3.

Notice that the formula in cell B4 changes from an equal sign to =B3. You have told Excel that the first cell in the formula is cell B3.

3. Type a right slash (/). (In Excel, the right slash means "divide by.")

Notice that even though you clicked in B3, you are still changing the formula in cell B4. It should now read =B3/, which tells Excel that you will divide B3 by a value provided later.

4. Click cell B2.

Notice that the formula in cell B4 changes to =B3/B2. This formula tells Excel that the element you want to divide by is the content of cell B2.

5. Press Enter to complete the formula.

Pressing Enter tells Excel that you have finished creating the formula. Cell B4 now shows the value 0.6 rather than the formula, but you can see the formula on the Formula Bar.

When you finish entering a formula, Excel automatically shows you the result of the formula in the cell grid, as shown in Figure 4-3.

	B4	▾		*fx*	=B3/B2						
Clipboard		Font		Alignment		Number		Styles		Cells	Editing

Ch4MarketResearchData1.xlsx

	A	B	C	D	E	F	G	H	I	J	K	L
1		Akron	Chicago	Cleveland	Denver	Philadelphia	Phoenix	Total				
2	Expected number of participants	10	10	10	10	10	10	60				
3	Actual number of participants	6	7	8	10	5	9	45				
4		0.6										
5												
6												

Figure 4-3: The worksheet looks like this after you add the first formula.

Watch Your Step

You can create this formula by merely typing in the cell references; however, this method depends on your ability to always remember the cells for your formula correctly. If anything has moved in the worksheet, your formula gives you the correct result. By clicking in the cells to add the reference to the formula, you know that the cell reference is correct. You learn how to edit the formula in the next section.

If you want that same formula in C4, you copy cell B4 and paste it in cell C3. Excel assumes that you want the formula to change to =C3/C2, which is, in this case, what you want. In general, when you copy and paste a formula, you want it to apply to cells related to the new formula. Follow these steps to copy the formula from B4 into other cells in row 4:

1. **Select cell B4.**

2. **Using AutoFill, drag this formula to the right to fill cells C4 through G4.**

   When you release the mouse button, notice that each cell now has a value. Clicking in each cell shows that each cell's value is computed by using a unique formula.

As you use AutoFill to fill the cells, you tell Excel to use the same formula for each cell, but to use the cells in this column (rather than the cells in column B) for the formula.

Because row 4 is composed of percentages, it would be useful to see the results as percentages rather than as decimal numbers. You can do that with just a few clicks. Follow these steps:

1. **Select cells B4 through G4.**

2. **Choose Home ➜ Number ➜ %.**

   All the numbers in row 4 change from decimals to percentages, which makes reading the results easier. The resulting worksheet is shown in Figure 4-4.

	A	B	C	D	E	F	G	H	I	J	K	L
		Akron	Chicago	Cleveland	Denver	Philadelphia	Phoenix	Total				
1												
2	Expected number of participants	10	10	10	10	10	10	60				
3	Actual number of participants	6	7	8	10	5	9	45				
4		60%	70%	80%	100%	50%	90%					
5												
6												

Figure 4-4: Formula results formatted as percentages.

Referencing Cells in Formulas: Relative versus Absolute Addresses

You might recall that you learned in Chapter 2 how to reference cells. That chapter covered only half the story, however. When you reference cells in formulas, you can talk about two types of addresses:

- **Absolute addresses:** When you reference a cell as an absolute address, you tell Excel that you always want to pull the data from this exact cell.

- **Relative addresses:** In relative addressing, Excel figures out the relationship between two cells and uses that rather than the absolute address of the cell.

Normally, when you reference a cell in a formula, Excel translates the address as a cell a certain distance away from you. If you move or copy the formula, Excel assumes that you want to move the reference too. You just used this idea in the preceding section to copy the percentage formulas for row 4.

By looking at the market research data, you see that each cell in row 2 contains the number of responses each location was supposed to gather. Because each location was supposed to gather 10 responses, all the cells in row 2 contain the number 10.

That is an acceptable way to set up the data, but you have to consider what happens if the data changes. What if, in order for the next survey to be able to use the worksheet, 15 responses per location are expected? Right now, you would need to change each cell in row 2 or set up a formula to make the change. However, a better option is to create one cell with the number of responses and have each of the formulas use that cell's value for the formula, as detailed in the following steps. Additionally, this exercise helps you understand the difference between relative and absolute addressing.

1. Continue with the file you used in the preceding section, or open the file **MarketResearch2.xlsx**.

2. Copy the contents of cell B2 and paste them into cell B99.

The number of responses is pasted in cell B99. Cell B99 is far enough out of the way that your data for this sheet doesn't interfere with it, but is still on the same sheet so that you can easily find it to update it.

3. Navigate back to row 2.

4. Select row 2 and delete it.

You can either right-click over the selected area and choose Delete or choose Home ➜ Cells ➜ Delete.

Notice that all the other rows moved up one row. Also notice that each cell in the new row 3 now reads #REF!, as shown in Figure 4-5.

	A	B	C	D	E	F	G	H	I	J	K	L
		Akron	Chicago	Cleveland	Denver	Philadelphia	Phoenix	Total				
1												
2	Actual number of participants	6	7	8	10	5	9	45				
3		#REF!	#REF!	#REF!	#REF!	#REF!	#REF!					
4												

Figure 4-5: Reference errors in formulas.

The #REF! message is Excel's way of telling you that you did something that made it unable to understand the formula anymore. Don't worry: You are about to fix that. Notice that Excel also put a triangular, colored flag in the upper-left corner of each cell to tell you where the errors occurred.

5. Click in cell B3.

Notice that the formula has changed and no longer shows B3 as one of the cells. Instead, it shows #REF!.

Watch Your Step

Notice that the yellow diamond next to the active cell contains a list of things you can do to address this error. The list tells you what the error is, how you can get help fixing it, and what you can do about it. In this simple example, you would merely fix the error. However, if the error occurred because the formula is a complex formula whose results depend on cells that do not have data, you might want Excel 2007 to ignore the error for now. Ignoring the error doesn't remove the error code; it just removes the highlighting on the cell. Ignoring the error can be dangerous because you might not remember later that the error occurred and therefore forget to fix it. If you are sure that you will remember to fix the error later, you can ignore it now.

6. Click the Formula Bar just in front of the pound sign, and delete **#REF!**.

7. Scroll down to cell B98 and click once.

Watch Your Step

Even though you put the value in B99, you deleted a row, so now the cell that was B99 is B98. In fact, as I wrote this chapter, I had to verify, and verify again, that my row numbers were correct so that you can keep on track. This is a good reason to use named formulas in Excel files.

8. Press Enter to complete the formula.

Notice that now the formula again computes a value.

9. Use AutoFill to fill the rest of row 3 with the formula from B3.

10. Select cell C3.

Notice that the value isn't likely what you expected. In fact, it is probably `#DIV0!`. This is another common Excel error. It means that you tried to divide by 0, which Excel cannot do.

Check out the formula on the Formula Bar. Notice that Excel changed cell B98 to C98. Because no value is in C98, Excel interprets the value as 0. Why did it change from B98 to C98?

When you copied the formulas earlier in this exercise, you might have been happy that Excel changed the cell references. That was what you wanted it to do. In that case, Excel was using *relative addressing,* which it uses (rather than the absolute address of the cell) to figure out the relationship between two cells. Usually, this is what you want.

However, when you are using a single cell to hold a value that many different formulas will use, you don't want relative addressing — you want *absolute addressing.* When you reference a cell as an absolute address, you tell Excel that you always want to pull the data from this exact cell.

To change from relative addressing to absolute addressing, you need to tell Excel which part (or parts) of the cell reference will stay the same. You can make the column reference absolute, the row reference absolute, or both references absolute. To do that, you add a dollar sign before the part of the cell reference that you want to remain absolute.

11. Select cell B3.

12. Click the Formula Bar just in front of the B in B98.

13. Change the B98 to $B$98 and press Enter.

Notice that the result is again the correct number rather than an error.

14. Use AutoFill to fill the rest of row 3 with the formula from B3.

15. Select cell C3.

Notice that each cell now computes the percentage correctly, as shown in Figure 4-6.

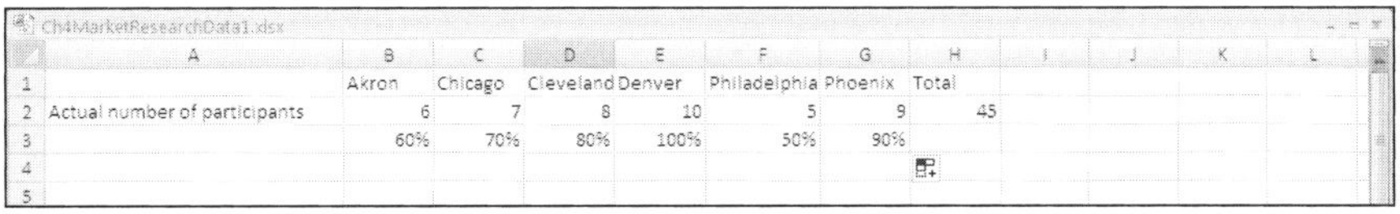

Figure 4-6: A corrected worksheet.

Exploring Formula Options for Calculation, Performance, and Error Checking

Before moving along to investigate what formulas and functions are in Excel, you need to understand some of the formula options available to you. You can find these options by clicking the Excel Options button at the bottom of the Office Button menu. Clicking the Formulas category brings up the dialog box shown in Figure 4-7. This section covers these options in detail.

Calculation Options

By default, Excel 2007 calculates the results of your formulas automatically whenever the value for a referenced cell is changed or the worksheet is opened. However, sometimes you don't want the calculation performed. To turn off automatic calculations for your entire workbook, chose one of the other options here.

If you are updating a large number of formulas, you might want to wait until you have completed the edits on the formulas in your workbook. If you turn off automatic calculations, you need to manually calculate the data in your worksheet or tables. To do this, use either of these methods:

- Press the F9 key on your keyboard.
- Choose Formulas → Calculation → Calculate Now.

If you do not have your formula results calculated automatically, you have two other choices:

- **Automatically Except for Data Tables:** This option is not one that you are likely to use now. In previous versions of Excel, data tables were used for what-if and scenario determinations. In these cases, you wouldn't want to recalculate your formula results until all the what-if data was changed. Now, tables are used for a wider variety of functionality. In fact, most of your data is likely to be stored in tables. For that reason, you are not likely to want to turn off automatic calculations for your tables unless you are turning off all automatic calculations.

- **Manually:** When you choose Manually, you tell Excel 2007 that you will initiate data calculations yourself.

If you select manual recalculation, you can pick a middle-ground calculation. When manual calculation is selected, you can also select a check box to have Excel 2007 recalculate your data before you save the file. This option, which is (in my opinion) a good idea, ensures that when you open the worksheet the next time, the data in all the cells is current and correct.

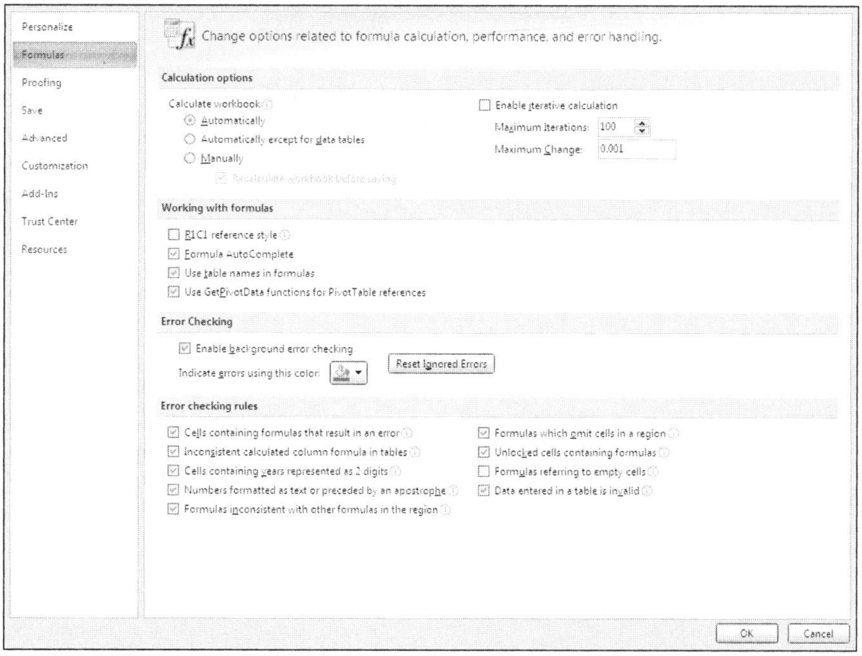

Figure 4-7: Excel formula options.

Transfer

To the right of the calculation timing options are the options for iterative calculations. Iterative calculations come into play when the result of a formula changes the result of a formula that references the original cell. Iterative calculations are most likely to come into play when you are working with Solvers and Goal Seekers. You can learn more about these options in Chapter 12.

Working with Formulas

This set of options has four check boxes. Together, they help you determine how you will reference cells when you create formulas:

R1C1 reference style: Use this option to change how you enter column references in your formulas. If you have problems tracking between the column letters and the column in the sheet, you can change to numbered columns. This check box is deselected by default, and you are unlikely to ever change it.

Formula AutoComplete: This option tells Excel 2007 that you want it to guess what you are typing and complete the formula for you. You can change the Excel 2007 suggestion by typing over it or accept it by pressing Enter.

This option is selected by default. Whether to leave it on or off is a personal choice. I leave it on because I have found it useful at times. On the other hand, many people find the AutoComplete feature annoying and turn it off.

- **Use Table Names in Formulas:** Use this option, selected by default, to reference entire tables or table contents by their table names. If you name your tables, this shortcut is useful for creating formulas. If you don't name your tables, this option doesn't change anything about how you work.

The final option in this section is related to PivotTables, which are covered in Chapter 6.

Error Checking

As you have already seen in this chapter, small changes to your worksheet can cause unexpected errors in other cells. Excel 2007 notes these errors when it becomes aware of them. Excel 2007 can perform this type of error checking in two ways:

- **Select the Enable Background Error Checking check box:** Excel checks for errors as you work and allows you to move on to do other things as it completes your error check.

- **Deselect the Enable Background Error Checking check box:** Excel checks for errors caused by changes to the active cell before it allows you to leave the cell and work with another one.

In general, your work flows better if you leave this check box selected.

You might recall learning about the error flag earlier in this chapter. If you ignored any errors, you reset the ignore flags by using the Enable Background Error Checking check box. Click the Reset Ignored Errors button to flag all errors in your document so that you can see them again.

You can change the color of your warning flags by clicking the paint bucket. For example, if the default green flag color doesn't stand out as well as you want, you can change it to red so that you can see the error more easily.

Error-Checking Rules

Excel 2007 allows you to turn on and off nine error-checking rules. You are not turning off specific calculation error messages when you deselect the check boxes for these rules; instead, you are turning off *types* of errors you want Excel 2007 to check. The default settings for these rules are the ones you are most likely to need. I don't recommend changing any of them.

Creating Formulas with the Function Wizard

Earlier in this chapter, you used Sum by clicking a button on the Ribbon to help put together your formula. A second way to create a formula is to type it by hand. However, the most efficient way to start most formulas is to use the Function Wizard.

The Function Wizard button is in the Function Library group on the Formulas tab. The best way to learn about the Function Wizard is to use it. Follow these steps to use the wizard to create a formula:

1. Open the **MarketResearch3.xlsx** file.

2. Click in cell Akron!L2.

(*Remember:* Akron!L2 is the way Excel references cell L2 on the Akron sheet.)

You will set up this cell to hold the average value for the responses to Question 1 from the Akron participants. The Akron sheet looks like the one shown in Figure 4-8.

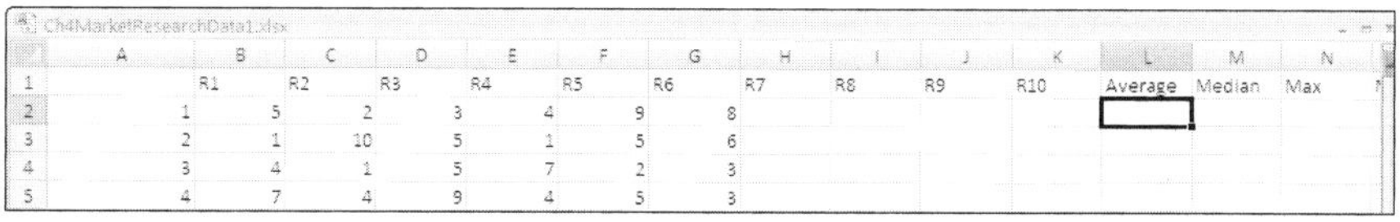

Figure 4-8: The Akron sheet at the beginning of the exercise.

3. Choose Formulas → Function Library → Insert Function.

The Insert Function dialog box appears, as shown in Figure 4-9.

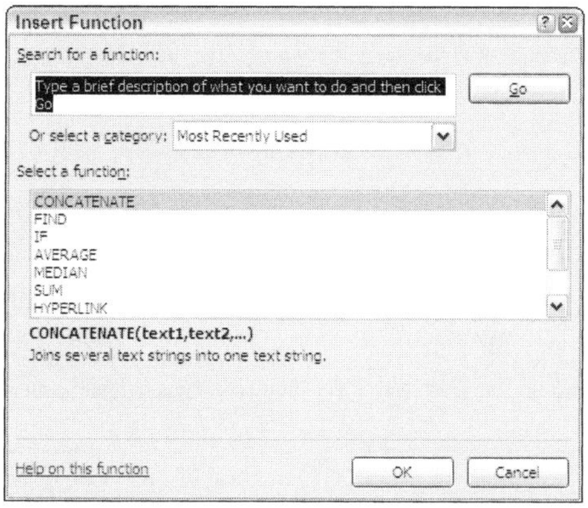

Figure 4-9: The Insert Function dialog box.

You use this dialog box to select the function you want to insert. You can select the function in either of two ways:

- *Type what you want to do into the search box, and click the Go button.* This action prompts Excel 2007 to find the function that it thinks you want.

- *Select the function from the list of functions Excel 2007 provides.* The list is divided into categories. For now, leave the category as Most Recently Used. You explore the other categories later in this section.

4. **From the Select a Function list, select AVERAGE and click OK.**

The Function Arguments dialog box appears, as shown in Figure 4-10.

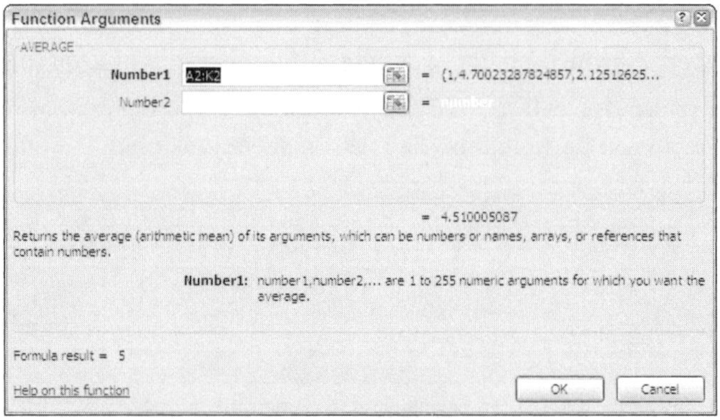

Figure 4-10: The Function Arguments dialog box.

You have two options: Directly type the cell reference in each box, or select the cells in your worksheet. (Selecting is more reliable than memory, so do it that way now.)

5. **Click the blue title bar in the Function Arguments dialog box, and drag the window so that you can see row 2 of the Akron worksheet.**

6. **Click in cell B2 and drag the cursor over to cell G2. Press Enter or click the OK button.**

Cell L2 now contains the average value for the responses to the first question. However, you should see an error flag to the left of the cell. You need to find out what the error is and whether you need to do anything about it.

7. **Click the yellow diamond to bring up the list of commands you can use to deal with the error.**

This list is shown in Figure 4-11.

The first element on this list, Formula Omits Adjacent Cells, is the most important one: It tells you what the error is. In this case, it isn't really an error (or a command), though. Rather, it's a warning that you didn't include all adjacent cells (those next to the formula cell) in your formula. There were only six respondents in Akron. If you include the empty cells in the average, the average is incorrect.

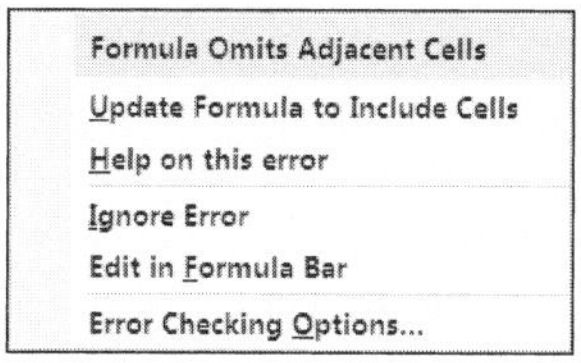

Formula Omits Adjacent Cells
Update Formula to Include Cells
Help on this error
Ignore Error
Edit in Formula Bar
Error Checking Options...

Figure 4-11: Error-handling options.

8. Ignore the error message.

This step doesn't mean that you should select Ignore Error — it means "Just don't worry about it."

Watch Your Step

You can't just tell Excel to ignore this error because, for some errors, it ignores *all* errors of that type. After you have more experience in determining which formula errors you can ignore, you can start telling Excel to ignore your errors. Until then, let it warn you whenever your formulas and calculations have errors.

9. Using the formula in cell L2, use AutoFill to fill cells L3 through L17 with the same formula.

The Average column for Akron is now complete. Next, you need to complete the Median, Max, and Min columns in the same manner. The Max function is in the Most Recently Used list; to find the other two, however, you need to look in the statistical category.

10. Select cell M2.

11. Choose Formulas → Function Library → More Functions. Choose Statistical from the first list and then Median from the sublist.

12. Complete the formula by selecting the cells B2 through G2, and then either click OK or press Enter. Use AutoFill to fill cells M3 through M16 with the formula from M2.

Notice that cells M2 through M16 are filled with the Median value for the responses for each question.

13. Repeat Steps 11 and 12 for the Max and Min columns.

This time select either Max or Min from the sublist in Step 11. When you're finished, cells N2 through O17 are filled with the appropriate values for the responses to each question. The resulting sheet should look like the one shown in Figure 4-12.

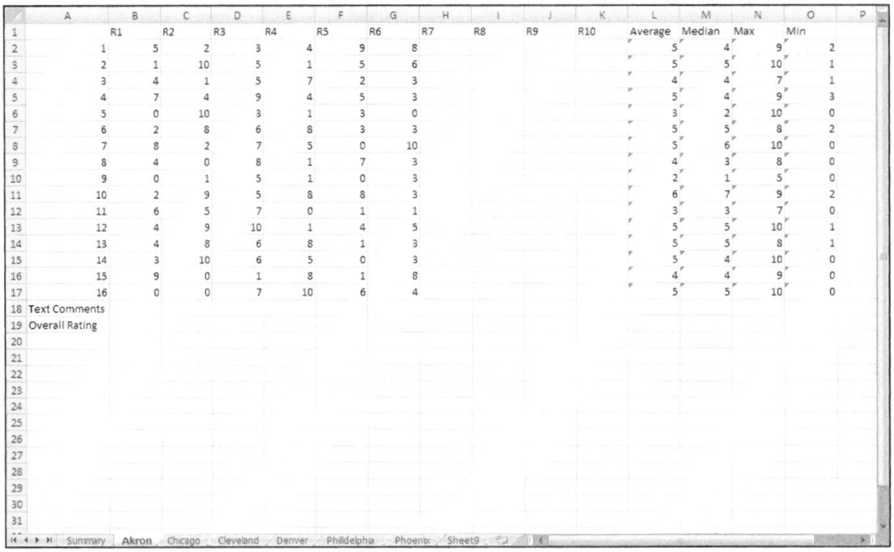

	A	B	C	D	E	F	G	H	I	J	K	L	M	N	O
1		R1	R2	R3	R4	R5	R6	R7	R8	R9	R10	Average	Median	Max	Min
2	1	5	2	3	4	9	8					5	4	9	2
3	2	1	10	5	1	5	6					5	5	10	1
4	3	4	1	5	7	2	3					4	4	7	1
5	4	7	4	9	4	5	3					5	4	9	3
6	5	0	10	3	1	3	0					3	2	10	0
7	6	2	8	6	8	3	3					5	5	8	2
8	7	8	2	7	5	0	10					5	6	10	0
9	8	4	0	8	1	7	3					4	3	8	0
10	9	0	1	5	1	0	3					2	1	5	0
11	10	2	9	5	8	8	3					6	7	9	2
12	11	6	5	7	0	1	1					3	3	7	0
13	12	4	9	10	1	4	5					5	5	10	1
14	13	4	8	6	8	1	3					5	5	8	1
15	14	3	10	6	5	0	3					5	4	10	0
16	15	9	0	1	8	1	8					4	4	9	0
17	16	0	0	7	10	6	4					5	5	10	0
18	Text Comments														
19	Overall Rating														

Summary
Akron
Chicago
Cleveland
Denver
Philadelphia
Phoenix
Sheet9

Figure 4-12: The Akron sheet at the end of the exercise.

You can complete the cells in row 19 by using the same technique but selecting each column rather than each row.

The next step is to finish the formulas for the responses for the other five cities. Although you can create the formulas for each city in turn, you can use an easier way, as described in the next section.

Adding Formulas to Multiple Worksheets at Once

One helpful shortcut within Excel 2007 lets you change multiple worksheets at the same time by having more than one sheet tab selected. In this case, you want to copy the formulas from the Akron sheet to the sheets for the other five cities by following these steps:

1. **Continue with the worksheet you used in the previous section, or open the `MarketResearch4.xlsx` file.**
2. **Select cells L2 through O17 and copy them.**
3. **Click the Chicago tab, and then Shift+click the Phoenix tab.**

   Notice that you are now looking at the Chicago worksheet. What you have just done is *group* the sheets, which means that you want Excel to do the same thing to the cells in each selected sheet.

4. Click in cell Chicago!L2. Paste the data.

Cells Chicago!L2 to Chicago!O16 are filled in with values.

5. Click each of the other selected tabs.

Notice that the values change based on the data in each sheet.

Even though the sheet looks good, don't be fooled: You aren't done yet. You have filled in the basic formulas, but if you look closely, you see that the results are not correct. You might recall that Akron had only six respondents. Well, each city has its own number of respondents. Different numbers of respondents means different numbers of columns, so your next step is to edit the formulas and correct them.

6. Click either of the unselected tabs, and then click the Chicago tab again.

Clicking an unselected tab tells Excel 2007 that you are done working with the group of tabs. You then need to move back to the sheet that you need to adjust next.

7. Select cell L2. Edit the formula on the Formula Bar to change the G to an H.

Because Chicago had a different number of respondents than Akron did, you need to adjust the ending column to match the data.

8. Repeat Step 7 for cells Chicago!M2, Chicago!N2, and Chicago!O2.

9. Use AutoFill on the remainder of columns L, M, and N to complete the update to the Chicago sheet.

When you are done, the Chicago sheet should look similar to the Akron sheet, but with different formula results, as shown in Figure 4-13.

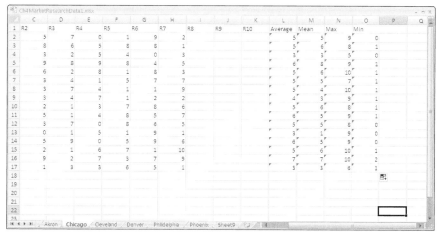

Figure 4-13: The Chicago sheet at the end of the exercise.

10. Repeat Steps 7 through 9 for the Cleveland, Denver, Philadelphia, and Phoenix sheets.

Using Data from Multiple Sheets in a Formula

Formulas within a single worksheet are quite useful. You should be ready to take the idea of formulas to a whole different dimension: cross worksheet formulas.

Part of the power of a formula is that Excel doesn't really care where the data is stored. As long as you can tell Excel where to find the data for your formula, you can compute almost anything. To start understanding this concept, you will build the overall average information for the Marketing Research worksheets:

1. Return to the Summary worksheet you used in the previous section, or open the **MarketResearch5.xlsx** file.

2. Select cell B10.

3. Choose Formulas → Function Library → Insert Function and select Average as the function to compute. Then click OK.

4. Click cell Akron!L2.

5. Click the Number2 text box in the Function Arguments dialog box.

Because you're working with nonconsecutive cells, you need to place each cell in its own entry box.

6. Repeat Steps 4 and 5 for Chicago!L2 (Number3), Cleveland!L2 (Number4), Denver!L2 (Number5), Philadelphia!L2 (Number6), and Phoenix!L2 (Number7). Click OK when all cells have been selected.

When you click OK, Summary!B2 shows the average value for the first answer.

7. Use AutoFill to fill cells Summary!B11 through Summary!B25 from the formula in Summary!B10.

When you are done, the Summary sheet looks like the one shown in Figure 4-14.

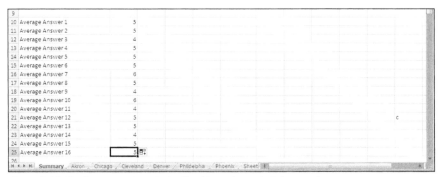

Figure 4-14: The Summary sheet looks like this at the end of the exercise.

Exploring Other Functions

As you might have noticed, a wide range of other formulas is available for you to use. Most of the formulas work with numerical data. However, before moving on, you should understand three special case sets of formulas: logical functions, text functions, and date-and-time functions. Advanced Excel users may also be interested in another category: the lookup and reference functions.

Using logical functions to compare values

Logical functions allow you to compare cell values and provide a true or false result. In addition, you can have Excel decide which values to show based on the results of logical functions. In Excel, you can use any of seven logical functions. Use the If function to find out whether the responses provided were positive or negative:

1. Open the **MarketResearch6.xlsx** file.
2. Select cell E10.
3. Choose Formulas → Function Library → Logical. Drag down to select If.

   The Function Arguments dialog box opens.
4. Click cell B10, and then type a greater-than sign (>) and the number 5.
5. Click in the Value_if_true box and type Respondents liked this part.
6. Click in the Value_if_false box and type Respondents didn't like this part.

   The resulting function box looks like the one shown in Figure 4-15.

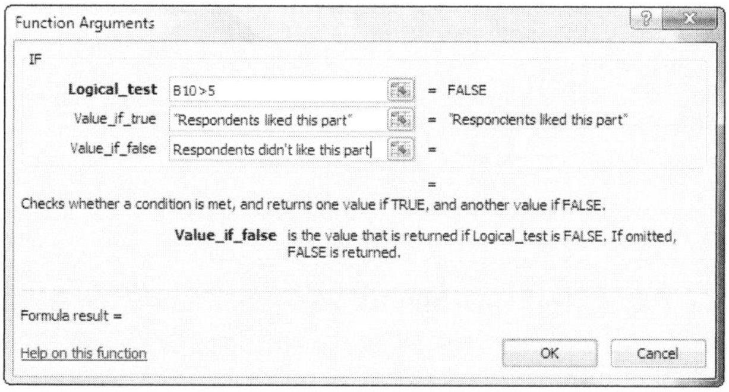

Figure 4-15: Function arguments for the If function.

7. Click OK or press Enter to apply the formula.
8. Use AutoFill to fill cells Summary!E11 through Summary!E25.

   Cells Summary!A9 through Summary E25 look like the example shown in Figure 4-16.

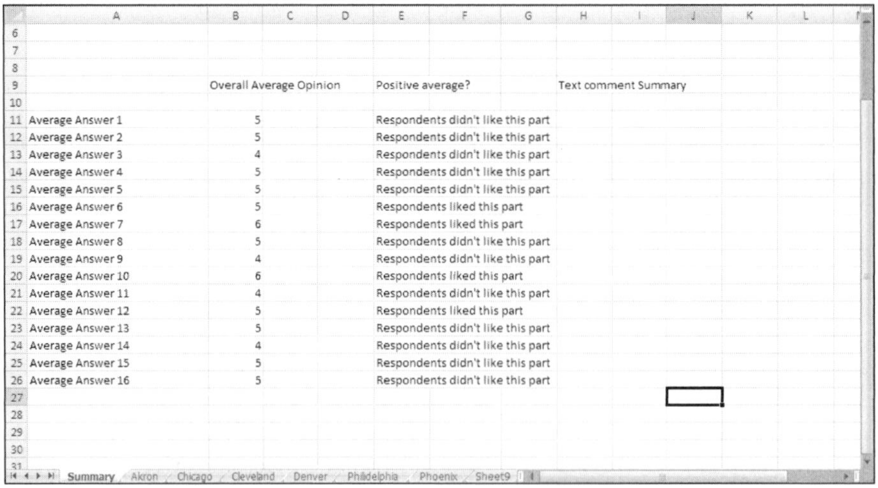

Figure 4-16: Completed summary data.

Using text functions to manipulate text strings

In addition to understanding how to work with numeric data, you need to understand how to work with text data. The text functions allow you to do string replacements, change numbers to text and back, change the case of your data, and concatenate data. (Concatenation is the placing of one string after another and putting the value into a cell.)

In this exercise, you concatenate the text responses provided by the respondents in each city. You can then take the exercise one step further and merge all comments on their own worksheet:

1. **Select cell Akron!L18.**

2. **Choose Formulas → Function Library → Text. Drag down to select Concatenate.**

   The Function Arguments dialog box appears with the fields for text concatenation, as shown in Figure 4-17.

3. **Click the blue title bar of the Function Arguments dialog box and drag the window so that you can see row 18 of the active worksheet.**

4. **Click in the box for Text1 and then in cell Akron!B18.**

5. **Click in the box for Text2 and then in cell Akron!C18.**

6. **Repeat this process for cells Akron D18 to K18. Press Enter or click the OK button when done.**

   Remember that an elevator is to the right of the dialog box. Use the elevator to move down to the other text-entry spots after you fill entry Text5.

   In this case, you don't need to worry about not having any data in some of the cells. As you can see in the result, if no text is in the cell, Concatenate ignores the cell.

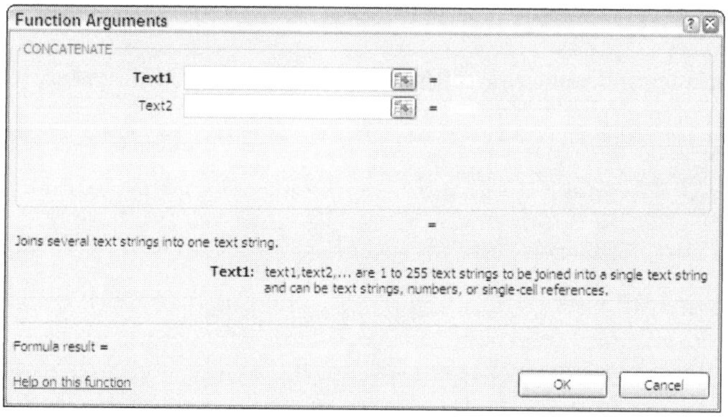

Figure 4-17: Function arguments for the Concatenate function.

7. **Copy cell Akron!L!18, group the other city sheets, and paste into cell L18 of the visible sheet.**

Each city page now has a concatenated list of the respondent's text comments, as shown in Figure 4-18. For formatting help, click the Help on This Function link at the bottom of the Function Arguments dialog box.

See how the concatenated words run together? To avoid this problem, you can either add spaces at the end of each entry or separate each entry by editing the formula.

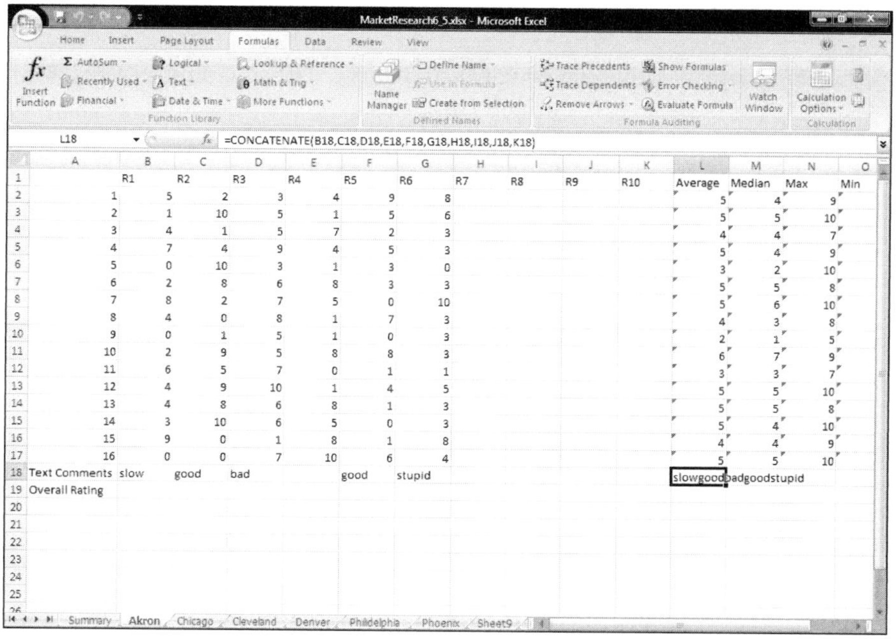

Figure 4-18: The final Akron sheet with comments concatenated.

Understanding date and time functions

The date and time functions work with any cells that are formatted as time. They allow you to:

- Get parts of the date, such as the year, the month, or the day.
- Enter the current date or time into a cell.
- Compute the differences between dates in real days or work days.

You are not likely to use the date and time functions directly in your spreadsheets. The most common use of these functions is for writing macros that deal with computing time differences, such as time sheets, date differences, or other date manipulation.

Exploring lookup and reference functions

Advanced Excel users might want to use a fourth category of data functions: lookup and reference. These functions allow you to use the data in one series of cells to determine which values and formulas to use in a different set of cells. When you are comfortable with formulas and functions, I recommend that you investigate the help information on lookup tables and reference formulas.

Naming Ranges and Formulas

You have already seen that you can name a row, a column, a table, or a group of cells. Part of the power of a named range lies in how it's used in a formula. For example, you have been working with market research data in this chapter. As you created the formulas, you selected cell ranges and used them to create the formulas. This technique works well when you are creating the formula, but what if someone else needs to use the worksheets later on? To understand which data you used for each formula, that person has to look at each referenced cell.

You can use an easier way. As you create your formulas, or after you are done and ready to put a worksheet into a production environment, you can create named ranges for the cells used in the formulas. After you create the named ranges, you can have Excel 2007 replace the cell ranges with the names of the ranges.

In the following exercise, you change some of the formulas in the market research sheets so that they use named ranges rather than cell references. You do not change the entire set of formulas, but you are welcome to change the remaining formulas on your own:

1. Open the Excel file **MarketResearchDataForNamedRanges.xlsx.**

This file is a copy of the market data that you have been working with in this chapter. By opening a fresh copy, you can be sure that your formulas are set up the same way as the ones you change in this exercise.

2. Click in cell Akron!B2. Either right-click in the cell and choose Name a Range, or choose Formulas → Defined Names → Define Name.

The New Name dialog box appears with Excel's best guess as to what you want filled in, as shown in Figure 4-19.

Figure 4-19: The New Name dialog box.

3. In the Name field, type Akron R1 Q1.

Leave the Scope and Refers To fields alone.

You are giving the field an understandable name and *scoping* it (telling Excel that the name will be accessible from anywhere within this workbook). Giving the name a scope of workbook allows formulas in other worksheets, but not formulas in other workbooks, to reference the name. In addition, you have set the range of this name to be the single cell L2.

4. Click OK.

Notice the error message shown in Figure 4-20. You cannot have spaces in the name of a range.

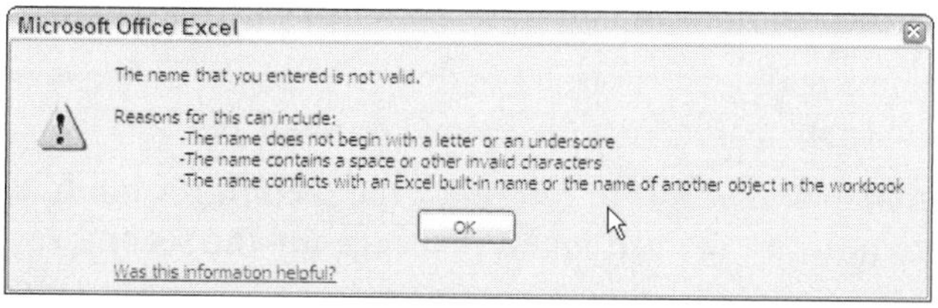

Figure 4-20: An invalid-name error message.

5. Click OK to close the error message. Delete the spaces from the name of the range so that the words run together. Click OK.

You have named cell B2 as AkronR1Q1, indicating that it is the answer to Question 1 from the first respondent. Notice that the name is shown in the cell reference box rather than in the cell reference itself.

6. Click in the cell reference box and copy the whole name.

You can now reuse this name and edit it for the remaining Akron averages. You could do this task manually for each cell by clicking the Name a Range button and editing each name individually. Instead, you use the Name Manager to create the remaining names.

7. Choose Formulas → Defined Names → Name Manager.

In the Name Manager dialog box that appears, you can work with multiple named ranges by using a single dialog box, as shown in Figure 4-21.

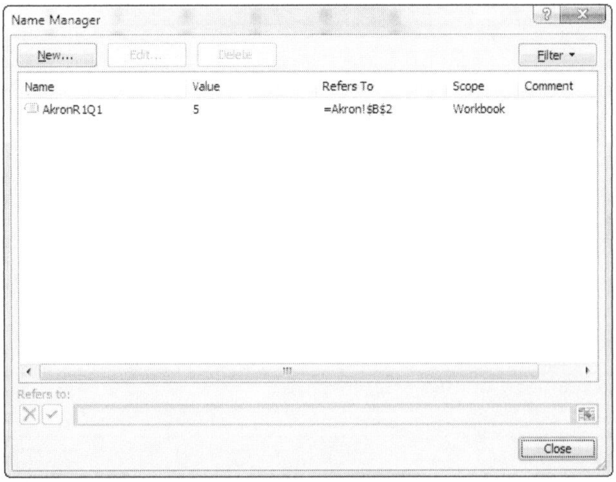

Figure 4-21: The Name Manager dialog box.

8. Click the New button in the top-left corner of the dialog box.

The New Name dialog box appears so that you can set up the new name. Next, you label the first answer from the second respondent.

9. Paste the name, and edit it to reference the second respondent. Edit the cell reference to point to the cell for the average for the second respondent. Click OK.

The name is added to the list under the first name you created.

10. Repeat Steps 8 and 9 for each of the Akron Average cells. When you finish defining all the names, close the dialog box by clicking the Close button in the lower-right corner.

Now that you have named all the Akron averages, the Name Manager list looks like the one shown in Figure 4-22. If the list of names is longer than can fit on the screen, a scroll bar appears to the right of the data.

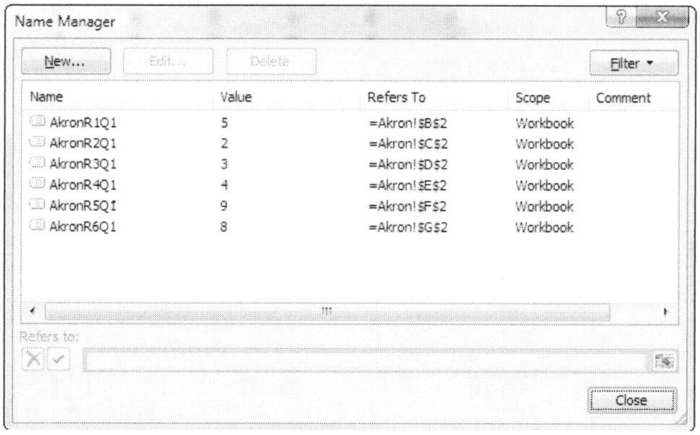

Figure 4-22: The Name Manager dialog box with multiple names defined.

Watch Your Step

If your list contains numbers greater than 10, the order of the names will be different. In this case, the list will start with the tenth item rather than with first item, as you may expect. The reason is that the names are sorted in text order rather than in numeric order. This is true whenever you sort text-based data within Excel.

You can edit and delete names in the Name Manager by using the buttons at the top of the dialog box. In addition, if you select a name, you can change its cell reference by editing the Refers To field at the bottom of the dialog box.

Just as you can select a range of cells for a formula, you can select a range of cells within a worksheet for a named range. You use the same dialog box to create the name as you use for a single cell, but select a range of cells rather than a single cell.

Now that you have created some named ranges, you are ready to tell Excel 2007 to replace the cell references with the names. You do this with the other option for the Define Name button.

11. **Choose Formulas → Defined Names → Define Name. Click the drop-down arrow and select Apply Names.**

The Apply Names dialog box appears with all your defined names listed, as shown in Figure 4-23.

You use the entries in this list to change the formulas from using the cell references to using the defined names for these cells. Using the names rather than the cell references is a clear and less error-prone method.

Figure 4-23: The Apply Names dialog box with multiple names defined.

12. **Leave the check boxes alone. Select all items on the list and click OK.**

The dialog box closes, and the names are applied. It isn't obvious that anything happened. You can see only that the warning triangle disappears from cell L2.

13. **To see the change, click in cell L2.**

Notice that the formula has changed to show the names of the cells rather than the cell addresses. This effect and the lack of warning symbols are shown in Figure 4-24.

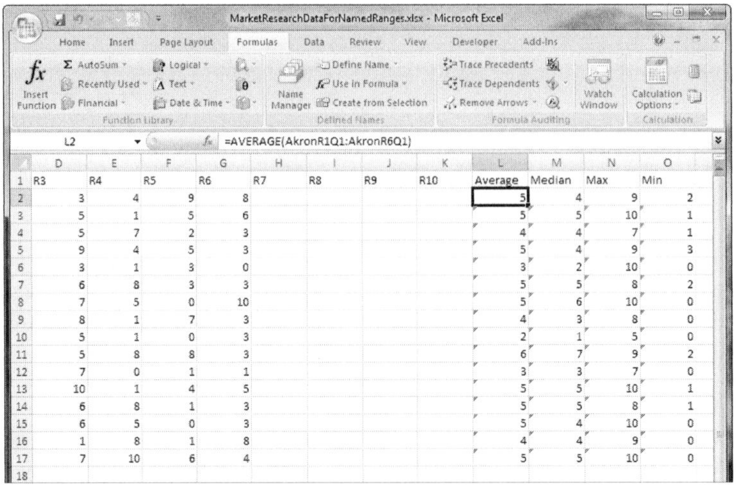

Figure 4-24: The applied names have replaced the cell references in the formula for L2.

Using names for cells and ranges helps you create more understandable formulas. By naming the cells, you remove the possibility of forgetting why you chose a certain cell for the formula. In addition, by using a named cell, you can see problems with your formulas more easily.

absolute address: The exact address of the cell within the workbook. When referenced from a formula, this type of address continues to point to the same cell, no matter where the formula is pasted.

address (or reference): The location within the workbook of a single cell. Also known as the cell reference.

AutoComplete: The function by which Excel guesses what you want to use for the value for the cell. If the cell contents consist of text, the AutoComplete suggestion is taken from other values within the column for the selected cell. When used in a formula, AutoComplete tries to guess the cells to be used in the formula based on the location of the cell.

calculation: The result of a formula or series of formulas. Automatic calculation is done in the background, and other work is done on the sheet. On the other hand, in a manual calculation, the user must wait for the calculation to complete before moving to a new cell or tab. You initiate manual calculation by pressing the F9 key or clicking the Calculate Now button.

formula (or function): The definition of the calculation to be performed to find the resulting value for a cell. A formula determines the value of a cell based on the values of other cells.

grouped sheets: Multiple selected sheets that allow work on cells across the entire set at the same time.

relative address: The address, but not the absolute address, of the cell within the workbook. When used in a formula, this type of address tells Excel how to move from the active cell to the cell to be used in the formula. When used in a formula that is pasted, this type of address changes to reflect the cell that is in the same relative location to the new cell as the address was to the original cell.

wizard: An automated method used by Excel to lead you through a step-by-step process.

Last
Stop

Practice Exam

1. Name three ways to add the Sum function to your document.

_____

_____

_____

2. Which of the following is a relative address?

a. $C16

b. C$16

c. C16

d. $C$16

3. When you create a formula that produces the result #Div, what do you need to change to fix the error?

_____

_____

4. True or False: When you use the Insert Function button, you need to know the exact function you want to use.

5. What is one danger of adding formulas to cells on multiple worksheets at once?

_____

_____

6. Open the `MarketResearch6.xlsx` file that you used in the exercises in this chapter. Describe how you would use a logical function to determine whether more than 80 percent of the needed respondents were used in this survey.

_____

_____

7. In this chapter, you learned about Date and Time functions. How can those functions prevent an AutoFill problem caused by adding years to a series of cells?

_____

_____

8. What is an advantage to naming cells and ranges to be used in formulas?

_____

_____

9. Which of the following is not a valid name for a range?

a. HappySheetResult

b. Excel!6

c. Date_Of_Ground_Breaking

d. YesOrNo

Charting: Basic Excel Chart Types and When to Use Them

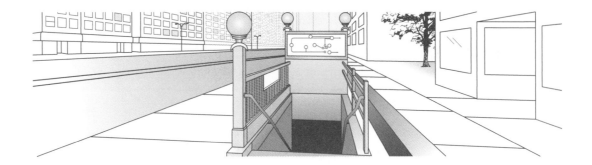

Enter the Station

Questions

1. What is an Excel chart?

2. Which three chart types are the most common?

3. What is the difference between a bar chart and a column chart?

4. Can you plot more than one series in a pie chart?

5. What is the difference between a line chart and a scatter plot with a trendline?

6. What is the difference between a line chart and an area chart?

Express Line

If you are already familiar with determining which charts to use and how to create and format them in Excel 2007, skip ahead to the next chapter.

Data is data. On its own, a single data element really can't tell you much. However, if you start combining data into groups, you can learn a lot about what has happened and what is likely to happen in the future.

Charts, or graphs, allow you to visually represent the data from a worksheet. They enable you to see trends and patterns in the data that may not be apparent by looking at the data alone. When sharing information with other people, charts enable you to present your data in a more meaningful way.

Different data needs to be shown in different ways. In this chapter, you look at how to create and use charts to help your data tell your story. In the process, you will learn not only how to set up the wide variety of charts available to you in Excel 2007, but also which charts work best for which kinds of data.

Getting to Know the Standard Chart Elements

A *chart* is a visual object made up of many parts. Although all charts have the same parts, you can decide which ones are visible and which are not, as shown in the chart in Figure 5-1.

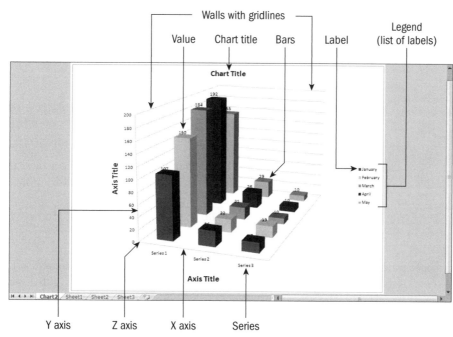

Figure 5-1: These are the standard elements of a chart.

You may or may not have every option shown in this figure displayed in your own charts. The important elements for you to know about are described in this list:

- **Chart title:** The title of the chart can describe the data in the chart, specify which conclusions you want drawn from the data, or comment on the data in the chart.

- **Walls:** The walls define the area of the chart and help to place it in space. Two-dimensional charts have one wall: the back. Three-dimensional charts have three walls: the back, the floor, and the side. (In some 3-D charts, the back is actually the front. It just depends on the viewing angle of the chart.)

- **Grid lines:** Grid lines help show the scale of the data. You generally have one set of grid lines for each axis. In more complicated charts, you can turn on more than one set of grid lines for each axis.

- **Axis:** Each axis shows the values for the data. Two-dimensional charts have two axes: X for vertical and Y for horizontal. Three-dimensional charts add a Z-axis, which shows the depth of the data.

- **Values:** The values are the data elements you are charting. In Figure 5-1, the values are the monetary values represented by each bar.

- **Series:** Each set of values within your data is referred to as a series of data. Each cell contains a value. The cells in a particular row or column comprise the series. In the chart shown in Figure 5-1, the green bars represent one series, and the blue bars represent another.

- **Bars:** Because Figure 5-1 shows a bar chart, bars are used to represent the data values. Pie charts use "pieces" to represent the data; line charts use lines and dots; and scatter charts use dots.

- **Labels:** Although the values are the actual numbers, the labels are what they represent. In Figure 5-1, the labels are the months covered by each bar.

- **Legend:** This table shows the relationship between the labels for the data and the graphical images that represent the labels. In the bar chart example, you can see that different colors (or shades of gray, on the printed page) represent different values. In a pie chart, your legend would show the correlation between the pie-piece colors and the data that is displayed.

These nine elements are the basis of every chart. You can also turn on and off the *scale* of the chart (what each blip on the axis means), trendlines, and other chart elements. You look at the other chart elements as you progress through this chapter.

Although Figure 5-1 shows a bar chart, the parts of each chart are the same, no matter which kind of chart you are using. As you continue through this chapter and learn about the different chart types, you see when and how to turn on and off the parts of a chart.

Building a Basic Column Chart

The default chart type is the 2-D column chart. At its most basic level, this chart style uses vertical bars of data to represent the data in selected cells. In the following exercise, you start by building a simple column chart from sample data. After building a basic chart, you will adjust what the chart looks like and what is shown on it.

Creating the chart

In the following steps, you create a column chart with sample data for the Brigham Balloon Corporation. The sample workbook file contains the summarized revenue, expenses, and percent profit for the company for each of its regions. You use this data for most of the charts in this chapter. Your first goal is to create a chart that shows how revenue and expenses compare for each of the five regions:

1. Open the **BasicBarChartData.xlsx** file.

2. Select a cell in the table of data. Choose Insert → Charts → Column. From the gallery that appears, select the Clustered Column chart, which is the first one in the first row.

The bar chart shown in Figure 5-2 appears. If you select a cell in a table, Excel assumes, by default, that you want all the data in the table to be used in your chart. For some charts, that is all you need to do to create your chart. However, because this particular table contains two kinds of data — dollars and percentages — you need to tell Excel which data you want it to use for the chart and then tell it how you want the data used. Because of the drastic difference in scale between dollars and percentages, the chart shown in Figure 5-2 looks off balance. Adjusting the content of the chart will fix the scale problem.

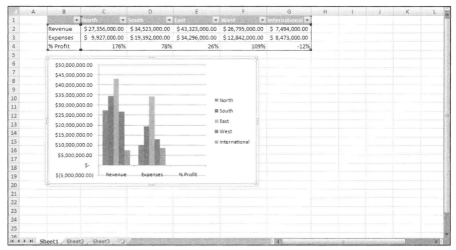

Figure 5-2: The default column chart created by Excel.

3. Press Ctrl+Z to undo the creation of the chart so that you can start over.

4. Select cells B1 through G3. Choose Insert → Charts → Column. From the gallery that appears, select the Clustered Column chart.

The chart that appears now shows only the dollar amounts for revenue and expenses. Because the bars aren't grouped logically, the chart doesn't provide useful information or tell a good story about the data. The next step is to change the chart so that the bars are better grouped to show your information. To do this, you use the Chart Tools tabs that have appeared on the Ribbon.

5. Choose Chart Tools Design → Data → Switch Row/Column.

Notice that the data shows the revenue and expenses for each region grouped together, as shown in Figure 5-3.

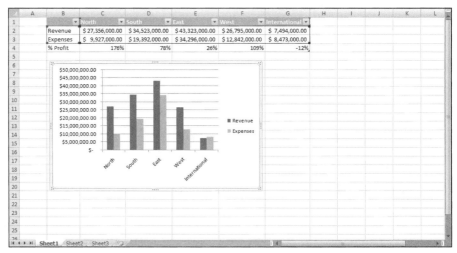

Figure 5-3: In this chart, the row and column data have been switched so that the bars are grouped logically.

This simple chart makes obvious that two different regions have problems. The East region has high expenses in relation to its revenue. The International region is even worse because its expenses are more than its revenue. In the next section, you find out how to customize the chart to further improve the presentation of the data.

Fine-tuning the design

The chart you just created gives you a visual picture of your data that you can share with others to make them aware of the problems in the East and International regions. With the graphics available in Excel 2007, you would be better served by making the chart more visually appealing before sharing it. The better the chart looks, the more information that people can get from it.

In the following steps, you change the scale of the vertical axis so that it is easier to understand; experiment with various chart styles; and make your chart three-dimensional to give it some depth:

1. Choose Chart Tools Layout → Axes → Axes to bring up the list of axes in the chart. From the list, select the Primary Vertical Axis option and then the Show Axis in Millions option.

Notice that the word *millions* appears to the left of the vertical axis and that the values are now scaled to millions of dollars, as shown in Figure 5-4. Because it is sometimes easier to see relationships between very large numbers, changing the scale makes it easier to understand the numbers that are presented. Unfortunately, with the change to millions, a number of extra zeroes are shown on each line.

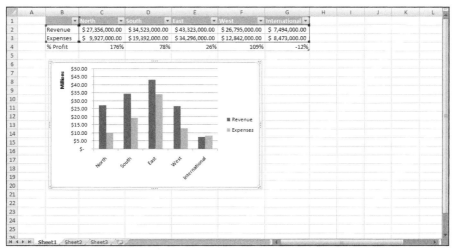

Figure 5-4: A bar graph with the scale changed so that the numbers are easier to understand.

2. Go back to the Primary Vertical Axes options, and this time select More Primary Vertical Axis Options.

The Format Axis dialog box appears.

3. Select Number on the left side of the pane, and then change the number of decimal places to 0 on the right side. Click Close.

Now that the data is more understandable, it is time to discover other chart styles that you can use for this data.

4. Choose Chart Tools Design → Chart Styles → Style 26.

Because you are using a 2-D chart, all the chart type options you have show a flat chart with nice-looking bars. One option you might want to consider is to give the chart some depth by selecting a 3-D chart.

5. **Explore other chart styles. Be sure to set the style to Style 8 before continuing.**

6. **Choose Chart Tools Design → Type → Change Chart Type.**

You can see the Change Chart Type dialog box, which shows all chart styles available for Excel 2007 (see Figure 5-5). For now, stick with the Column charts. As you progress through this chapter, you'll investigate the other chart types as well.

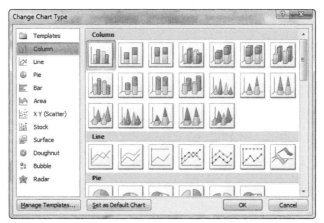

Figure 5-5: The Excel 2007 Change Chart Type dialog box shows the first sets of charts you can choose from.

7. **Select the 3-D Clustered Column chart, which is the fourth chart in the first row. Click OK.**

Your data is now shown in three dimensions rather than in only two, as shown in Figure 5-6.

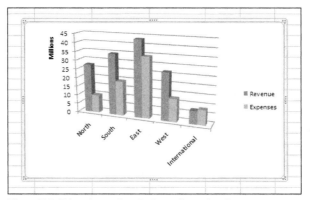

Figure 5-6: This column chart is three-dimensional.

Information Kiosk

I prefer to work with larger copies of my charts. They make it easier to see the details and to work with the chart elements. The easiest way to do that is to move the chart to its own sheet. Choose Chart Tools Design → Location → Move Chart. In the Move Chart dialog box that appears, click the New Sheet radio button and change the name to make it descriptive. Then click OK. You see a new chart sheet in your workbook, which contains only the chart. Alternatively, you can press F11 to move the chart to its own sheet. From this point on in this chapter, you can work with charts either on their own sheets or on the same sheets as your data.

Converting a Column Chart to a Bar Chart

The difference between a column chart (which you created in the preceding section) and a bar chart is the direction of the shapes in the chart. In a bar chart, the shapes run horizontally. To see the differences between the different chart types, you convert your column chart into a bar chart and change the shapes of the bars from rectangles to other shapes:

1. **Return to the chart you created in the preceding section, or open the `BasicBarChartData2.xlsx` file.**

2. **With the chart selected, choose Chart Tools Design → Type → Change Chart Type.**

   The Change Chart Type dialog box appears (refer to Figure 5-5).

3. **Click the word Bar in the left column to go directly to the bar charts. Select the Clustered Horizontal Pyramid option and click OK.**

   Your data bars now run horizontally rather than vertically, as shown in Figure 5-7.

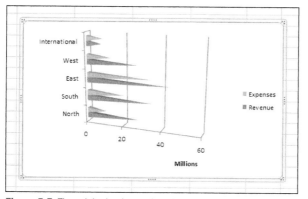

Figure 5-7: The original column chart is now a clustered 3-D bar chart.

Notice that with this change, you also change the shape of the bars from rectangles to pyramids. You can choose from several other shapes for your data bars, including pyramids, cylinders, rectangles or boxes, and cones.

4. **With the chart selected, click the Chart Tools Format tab.**

At the top of the Current Selection group, you see the drop-down list for the chart elements. Click the drop-down list to see which elements can be selected, as shown in Figure 5-8.

```
Back Wall
Chart Area
Floor
Horizontal (Value) Axis
Horizontal (Value) Axis Display Units Label
Horizontal (Value) Axis Major Gridlines
Legend
Plot Area
Side Wall
Vertical (Category) Axis
Walls
Series "Revenue"
Series "Expenses"
```

Figure 5-8: Choose the chart element you want to edit from this list.

In previous versions of Excel, to select a specific chart element, you had to click the chart element itself. You might have found it hard to select just the piece you wanted, especially if you were trying to format a specific data series or a specific wall. In Excel 2007, to select a chart element, you find it in the elements list and select it. You can still select chart elements themselves by clicking them, but the chart element drop-down list makes it easier to be sure that you have selected the right element.

5. **From the drop-down list, select the Series Revenue option. Next, choose Chart Tools Format → Current Selection → Format Selection.**

The Format Data Series dialog box appears, as shown in Figure 5-9.

This dialog box lets you format each element the way you want. In this case, you use this dialog box to change the shape and fill of the selected series.

6. **Click the word Shape in the left column. Change the shape to Partial Cone.**

Notice that the shapes on the chart change immediately, as shown in Figure 5-10. You don't need to click Close to apply the changes from this dialog box because it is a modal dialog box.

By selecting the Partial Cone option for the shape, you are adding another visual clue to your chart. By looking at the chart, you see that the only cone that ends in a full point is the revenue for the East. Partial cones convert your data to a portion of the cone shape based on the percentage of the highest value.

With this shape, it becomes even more obvious that the International region has not brought in as much revenue as the others. Each of the other cones comes closer to a point than it does.

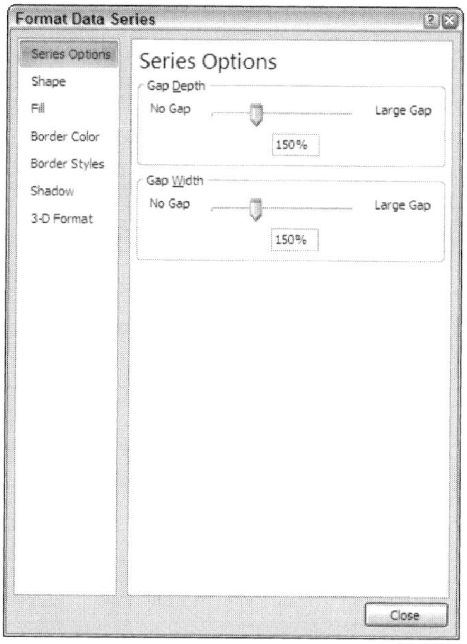

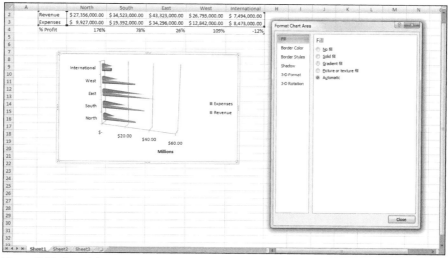

Figure 5-9: The Format Data Series dialog box.

Figure 5-10: A partial cone bar chart.

7. **Click the word Fill in the left column. Change the fill to No Fill.**

The shapes on the chart seem to disappear, but they really haven't. Although they are still there, they have no line or fill, so you can't see them. By giving them no fill, you can "see through" each bar.

8. Select the Border Color option in the left column. Change the border option to Solid Line, and click the Close button.

Your shapes are now see-through, but because they have a border around them, they still show up. Your chart should look like the one shown in Figure 5-11.

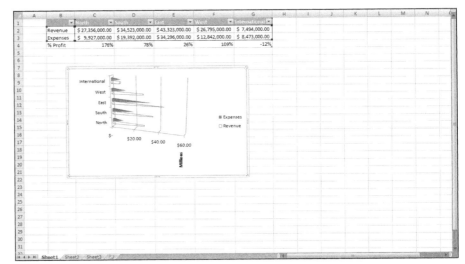

Figure 5-11: The final bar chart should look like this.

Although you may never use a bar chart that looks like the one in the figure, knowing how to change the line and fill on chart elements gives you more control over your charts.

Categorizing Data with Pie Charts

Pie charts are used to look at how the pieces of data in a single series relate to each other. Where you used the column and bar charts to see the relationship between the revenue and expenses for each region of Brigham Balloon, you will build and adapt two pie charts. The first one shows how much of the company's revenue comes from each region. The second pie chart shows how much of the company's expenses went to each of the regions.

Creating a chart to show revenue by region

Follow these steps to create a pie chart to show the revenues from each region of Brigham Balloon Corporation:

1. Open the `BasicPieChartData.xlsx` file.

You see the table of data you started with in the preceding section.

2. **Select cell C2, choose Insert → Charts → Pie, and select the Pie in 3-D option.**

The resulting chart is shown in Figure 5-12. Excel assumed that you want to compare the revenue, expenses, and % profit for North (the first column of data). However, this chart doesn't work for your purposes because you need for it to show the revenue for each region.

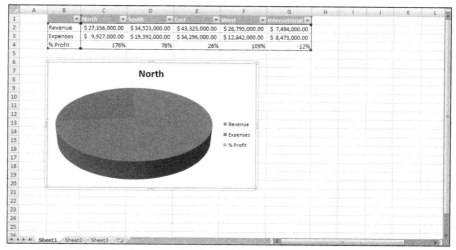

Figure 5-12: A default pie chart created by Excel 2007 from multiple column data. Because the data is not matched, the pie chart is not usable.

Watch Your Step

Because you are working with data that is in a table, Excel tried to guess what you wanted to chart. If the data had not been turned into a table, Excel would have tried to put all the data into the chart. You might have thought that you got the right data, but you wouldn't have. Always select the data that you want to chart, to avoid any problems Excel might have in guessing what you want.

3. **Choose Chart Tools Design → Data → Switch Row/Column.**

Now the chart shows the data you wanted to see: The revenue for the company is broken down by region, as shown in Figure 5-13.

Excel uses two basic types of pie charts. What you have created is a regular pie chart. The other type is Exploded Pie Chart. In an exploded pie chart, Excel moves each data piece out from the center of the chart.

Exploded charts are nice when you need to highlight each area of the pie chart. However, an unexploded chart is easier to read and work with. You can adjust the location of any given piece so that it is set off from the center, which helps maintain focus on the data values you want while still showing the overall picture.

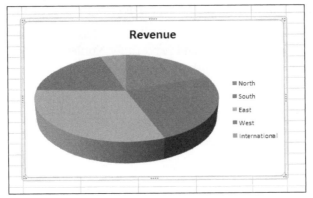

Figure 5-13: The default pie chart that is created.

4. **Click the segment for the International region's revenue. Drag it away from the rest of the chart.**

As you drag the piece, it changes to just its outline. When you release the mouse, it reverts to a full-color piece. In addition, the rest of the chart adjusts to fit the new space, as shown in Figure 5-14.

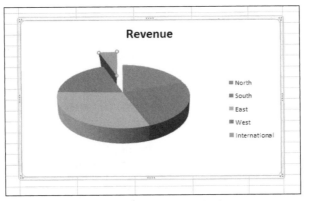

Figure 5-14: One piece is expanded in this pie chart.

This chart shows the relationships between the revenue for each region, but many people want to see the percentages when looking at a chart like this one. Your next step is change the layout to show this information.

5. **Choose Chart Tools Design ➜ Chart Layouts ➜ Layout 1.**

Quick Layouts are designed to give you a head start in formatting your charts. In this case, the layout removed the legend and turned on the labels and percentages for each pie segment. Instantly, you can see the high and low revenue generators for Brigham Balloon Corporation.

6. Click the word **Revenue. Change it to** Brigham Balloon Corporation Revenue By Region.

7. **Click on an empty part of the chart.**

This step allows Excel to resize the chart, if necessary.

You have given the chart a title that clearly describes the data within it, as shown in Figure 5-15.

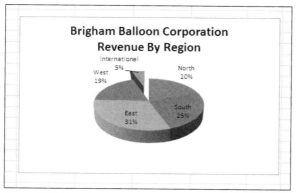

Figure 5-15: The title of this pie chart clearly describes its data.

You are now halfway to your requirement. You have a chart that is exactly what you want for the revenue, but you need an equivalent one for the expenses. Although you could go back to the beginning and create the second chart from scratch, an easier way is described next.

Creating a chart to show expense by region

Follow these steps to use the chart you just created as a basis for creating a new chart for expenses:

1. **Select the revenue chart you just created and press Ctrl+C to copy it. Click off the chart and press Ctrl+V to paste it.**

You now have two identical charts. The next step is to change the data used for this second chart.

2. **With the second chart selected, choose Chart Tools Design → Data → Select Data.**

The Select Data Source dialog box appears, as shown in Figure 5-16.

This dialog box lets you easily change the range of data used for this pie chart. You can access this dialog box for any chart to change the range of data to be charted. You can also use this dialog box to swap the rows and columns, to select specific categories of data to show or not show, and to hide cells that you don't want shown on the chart. The process for doing each of these tasks is the same. To learn that process, you will now use this dialog box to change from Revenue to Expenses.

Figure 5-16: The Select Data Source dialog box.

3. **In the Legend Entries (Series) column, click the word Expenses. Click the up arrow button to move the expenses to the top of the list. Click OK.**

Because this is a pie chart, only the first series of data is shown in the chart. By moving the expenses to the top of the list, you have now changed the chart to show the expenses rather than the revenue.

The next step is to adapt this chart so that the title is correct and the slice for the International region is highlighted.

4. **Edit the title to change the word Revenue to Expense. Click the International slice and pull it out from the main pie.**

The Expense chart is complete, as shown in Figure 5-17. Although the chart now tells the other half of the story, you can't see the previous half. You have to fix that situation.

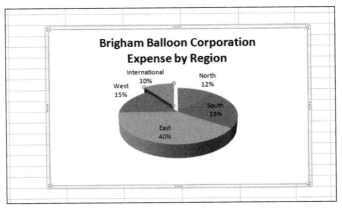

Figure 5-17: The final pie chart is formatted for best use.

Step Into the Real World

Pie charts can also be used to summarize the data for a single category and show how it relates to the other data around it. As an example, open the file `PieChart2.xlsx`. Here you see the same data, but the Western region has been expanded into the data for the individual states in this region. This data is used to create a chart known as a Bar of Pie chart.

In the sample file, change to the Bar of Pie worksheet. The chart appears, as shown in the following figure.

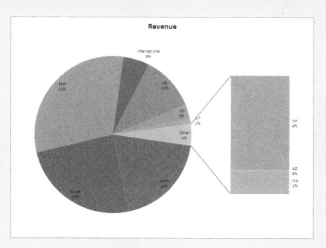

This chart had too many columns of data to make a useful pie chart. The Bar of Pie chart lets you group the smaller data items into one category named Other and then show the breakdown of Other next to it. One advantage of this chart is that it shows that the international region is bringing in less revenue than California.

By changing the type of chart, you can get better information from your data. Better information means better business decisions.

Arranging the Revenue and Expense charts side by side

Follow these steps to arrange your Revenue and Expense charts on-screen:

1. **Select each chart and arrange them to be side by side with the tops of the charts just below the table of data.**

Depending on your screen size and resolution, you might need to resize the charts to see both of them.

2. **Select the Revenue chart and then choose Chart Tools Layout → Current Selection → Format Selection.**

3. **After the Format Chart Area dialog box appears, change the border color to No Line.**

In the background, the border around the Revenue chart disappears. Because it is still the selected chart, the handles are still displayed, and the line is not.

4. **Click the Expenses chart, and then click the Format Selection button again. After the Format Chart Area dialog box reappears, change the Border Color option to No Line. Click the Close button, and then click in any cell.**

Your two charts are now both fully visible, as shown in Figure 5-18.

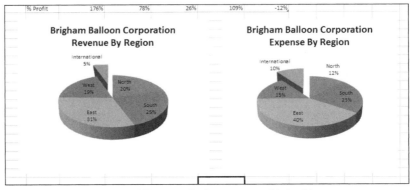

Figure 5-18: The Expenses and Revenue pie charts appear side by side.

Showing Progression with Line Charts

Line charts are used to show how data has progressed across time or other factors. For example, you might use a line chart to show how the sales across the regions were doing over a period of several quarters or even years, as detailed in these steps:

1. **Open the `BalloonsSold.xlsx` file.**

The table shows the balloons sold by color over the past few years. This data has been gathered to see whether a particular balloon color does better or worse at any given time during the year. You will build a line chart to show the answer.

2. **Select a cell in the table. Choose Insert → Charts → Line and then select the Line option under 2-D Line.**

3. **Choose Chart Tools Design → Data → Switch Row/Column to show the data by color rather than by group (see Figure 5-19).**

4. **Choose Chart Tools Design → Location → Move Chart to move the chart to its own sheet. In the Move Chart dialog box, select the New Sheet radio button, enter a name, and then click OK.**

The line chart appears, as shown in Figure 5-20.

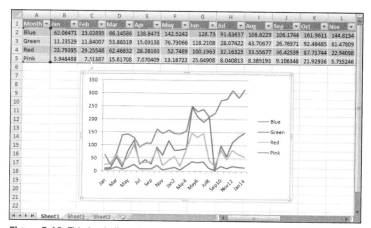

Figure 5-19: This basic line chart shows the sales for each balloon color over a 12-month period.

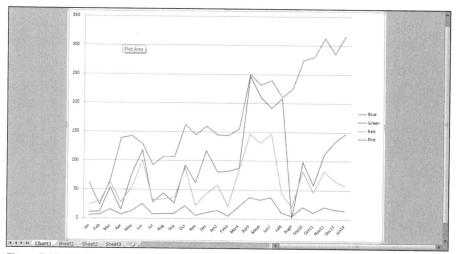

Figure 5-20: This line chart appears on its own sheet.

You need to fix two basic problems in this line chart: The pink data line is at the bottom of the chart and is hard to see because the scale for the two sets of numbers is so different, and the colors of the lines don't match the names of the balloons.

5. Choose **Chart Tools Format → Current Selection and select Series Pink from the Chart Elements list. Click the Format Selection button in the same group.**

Because you are now working with a line chart, you have some new options for formatting. You will use several of these options in this exercise. The first thing to change is the axis.

Watch Your Step

What is the difference between the primary and secondary axes? Sometimes when you are plotting data, you find that one series is in one range of numbers, and another is in a much smaller or larger range of numbers. The two series still relate to each other, so you want to show them on the same graph. If you show all the data on the same axis, the line for the smaller numbers isn't meaningful. To make the changes for this line more visible, you can plot the larger numbers on one axis and the smaller numbers on the second axis. That is what you are about to do.

6. Click the title bar on the dialog box, and use your mouse to drag the dialog box to the left so that it doesn't cover the right side of the chart. Click the Secondary Axis radio button.

Notice that the right side of the chart gets a second set of numbers on a different scale. You can see this in Figure 5-21.

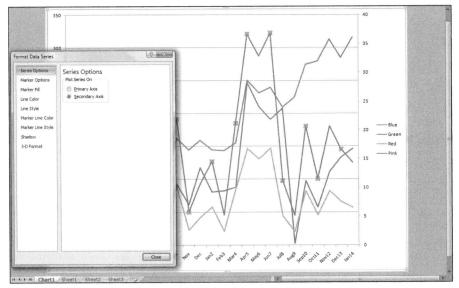

Figure 5-21: The line chart now has a secondary axis on the right.

The two scales have been calibrated so that the lines make sense, but the ranges can still be different. Although the number of pink balloons sold is much lower than the number for any other color, it still follows the same pattern as the other.

7. Select the Marker Options option in the left column, and click the Built-in radio button. From the Type drop-down list, select the last entry.

This step inserts a picture placeholder for your markers.

8. Select the Marker Fill option in the left column. Click the Picture or Texture Fill radio button.

Markers are the data points on your lines. You can format them to be anything you want, from nothing at all to a solid color, a gradient fill, or a picture. Which options you have for the marker fill depends on which fill you want to use. Because you are using a picture fill, you have the option to pick which picture and how you want it to look within your box.

9. Click the button to insert the picture from a file. Browse to the file **Balloon.tif**, select the picture of the pink balloon, and then click Insert. Deselect the Tile Picture As Texture check box.

Notice that each marker for the pink line automatically changes to a balloon, as shown in Figure 5-22.

Figure 5-22: A line chart with balloon markers.

10. Select the Line Color option in the left column. Change the line to a solid line, and then change the color to Red, Accent 2, Lighter 60% (the third swatch down, under the color red).

Notice on your screen that the line for the Pink balloons is now pink, as the change in grayscale tint shows you in Figure 5-23.

11. Click each of the other lines in succession and change them so that they show the correct line color. For the red line, use the base red color from the color selection. Change the marker for the green balloons to **Balloons 1.tif**, and the marker for the blue balloons to **Balloons2.tif**. Leave the red balloons' lines markerless.

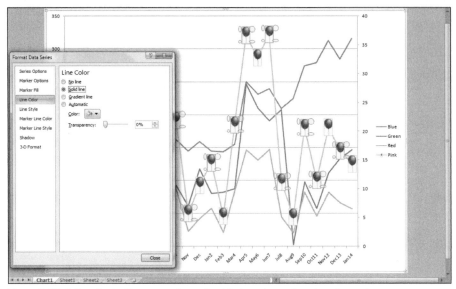

Figure 5-23: A line chart with a secondary axis with the color and marker changed.

When you finish, your chart looks like Figure 5-24.

Again, you would not create this chart in real life. You would likely use a smaller picture for the markers so that the chart is less crowded. However, if you understand how to work with markers, you can then customize your charts when you need to.

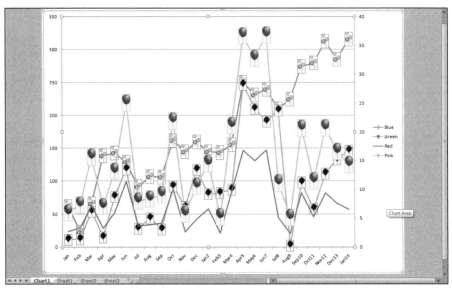

Figure 5-24: The completed line chart looks like this.

Step Into the Real World

As you can see in Figure 5-24, a correlation exists between the month the balloons were sold and the number of balloons sold. The color of the balloons doesn't seem to change, but when you look at the chart, you can see that the May/June period seems to have more balloon sales than other times of the year. Some other months have peaks as well, but the May and June peaks are always the highest.

In the real world, your next step would be to investigate what is happening in May and June around the world. Maybe a large festival or a holiday causes your sales to increase. You could then put more marketing money into those months to increase the peaks even more.

On the flip side, you can also see from this data that December and January tend to be low-selling months. With this data to back you up, you can tell the members of your marketing department that they need to find a way to increase sales in those months as well.

Finding Trends with Scatter Plot Charts

Another way to look at the balloon sales data is to look at the plot points and find the trend for each one. A line chart shows you how the data has bounced around over time, as described in the preceding section. Add too much data, though, and it becomes hard to see where the data is going overall. This is where a scatter plot comes in handy. After you have Excel create your scatter plot, you can tell it to add any of a variety of trendlines to the plot. By using the data in the chart to determine what is happening, trendlines make the data understandable to the human eye.

In this section, you use the same data as in the line chart sections: the `BalloonsSold.xlsx` file. Follow these steps to create a scatter plot chart with the data in this file:

1. **Select a cell from the table on Sheet 1. Choose Insert → Charts → Scatter. Select the first scatter plot: Scatter with Only Markers.**

2. **Choose Chart Tools Design → Data → Switch Row/Column. Then move the chart to its own sheet.**

   The resulting plot does not tell you much. As you can see in Figure 5-25, it shows all the balloon numbers across time on the same scale.

   Although each color of balloon has its own shape for a marker, the markers are mixed together. Your next step is to add trendlines to the chart so that the sales trends for each color begin to show.

3. **Choose Chart Tools Layout → Analysis → Trendline. From the list, select Linear Trendline.**

   The Add Trendline dialog box appears, as shown in Figure 5-26.

   This dialog box allows you to select the series for which you want to show the linear trendline. You will add a trendline for each color, one at a time.

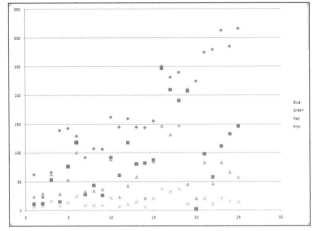

Figure 5-25: A basic scatter plot chart.

Figure 5-26: The Add Trendline dialog box.

4. **Click Blue, and then click OK.**

5. **Repeat Steps 3 and 4, but this time select Green rather than Blue. Do the same for the Red and Pink series.**

When you finish, your chart has four new lines — one for each balloon color — as shown in Figure 5-27.

With the trendlines, you can see that the sales for each color have gone up over time, but that the sales of blue balloons have gone up the fastest and are the largest. At the same time, it becomes more obvious that the pink balloons are selling much less than the other colors.

You can learn another lesson from this data, but it is hiding. Your next job is to bring it out.

6. **Choose Chart Tools Format → Current Selection, and select the Series Red Trendline from the drop-down list. Then click the Format Selection button.**

The Format Trendline dialog box opens with a new set of options, as shown in Figure 5-28.

By using these other options, you can compute the trends based on other, more sophisticated trending algorithms.

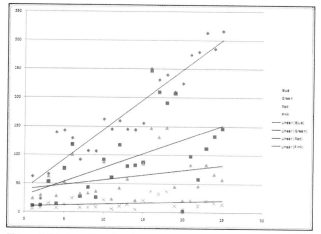

Figure 5-27: A scatter plot chart with all four trendlines.

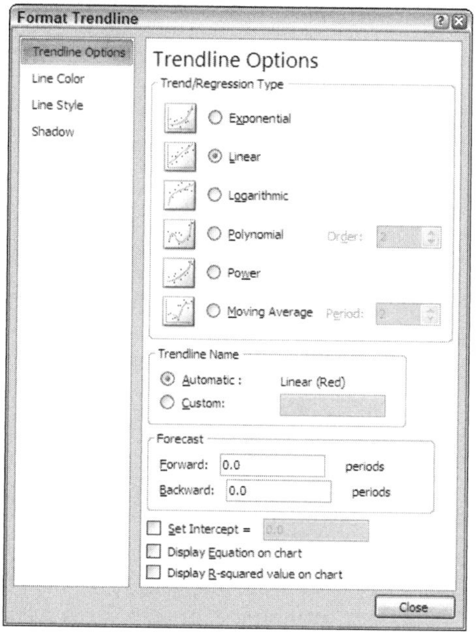

Figure 5-28: The Format Trendline dialog box.

7. **Click the other Trend/Regression Type options in the dialog box and notice the changes they make to the line.**

These other trend algorithms try to make a better path between your data, which can be useful. If you go too far, however, the lines become confusing and are not helpful. Play around with the moving average over a number of periods to see what I mean.

8. **Finish this exercise by setting up a Polynomial trendline for each of the four series.**

As shown in Figure 5-29, the polynomial trendlines show a different story than the linear ones did.

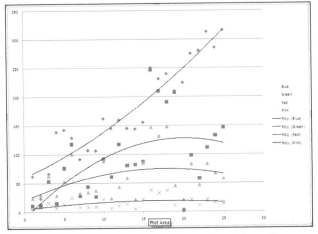

Figure 5-29: This final scatter plot has four polynomial trendlines.

From this simple change of trend algorithms, you can see that all is not well in the balloon sales world. Although the data has trended toward growth for all the balloon colors, a closer look shows that the blue balloons are still selling on an upward trend, and the green and red balloons have started to fall off their growth curves in the past few months. You might need to work with your marketing department to find out why.

Contrasting Data with Area Charts

The next way to compare your data is to create an area chart. Area charts are much like line charts, except that they overlap the data for each series so that you can find relationships more easily. One common use for area charts is to see how data elements add up to make a whole. To see this effect, you create an area chart from a small sample of the balloon data and evaluate overall balloon sales:

1. **Open the `AreaChart.xlsx` file.**

The table shows the number of balloons sold by color over a 6-month period. You will create a stacked area chart from this data to see how overall sales have progressed during the six months.

2. **Select a cell in the table. Choose Insert → Charts → Area and then select the Stacked Area in 2-D option. Move the chart to its own sheet so that it is easier to work with.**

Because of the differences in scale of the sales for the different colored balloons, the 2-D chart is not as useful as a 3-D chart might be. To see why, you will change the chart to a 3-D chart and work with it that way.

3. **Choose Chart Tools Design → Type → Change Chart Type.**

4. **Select the Stacked Area in 3-D chart type and click OK.**

By turning the chart on its side and placing it in three dimensions, you can better visualize the data. Rather than see just flat surfaces, you can see the relationship *between* the surfaces.

The chart that appears is shown in Figure 5-30. Although it looks fine as is, now you will quickly make it look fancy.

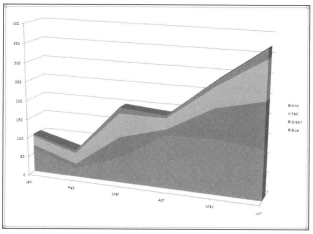

Figure 5-30: Your initial 3-D stacked area chart.

5. **From the Chart Styles gallery on the Chart Tools Design tab, select Style 39.**

You will now explore the various formatting options for this chart. You format all charts in the same way; the differences lie only in which options you have for a given chart.

6. **Choose Chart Tools Layout → Labels Chart Title → Centered Overlay Title. Change the title to** First Six Months Balloon Sales.

7. **Choose Chart Tools Layout → Labels → Axis Title → Primary Horizontal Axis Title → Title Below Axis. Change the title to** Month.

8. **Choose Chart Tools Layout → Labels → Axis Title → Primary Vertical Axis Title → Rotated Title. Change the title to** Number of Balloons Sold.

9. **Move the legend to the bottom of the chart. (Use the Legend choices in the Labels group.)**

Your chart is looking better. It should now look as shown in Figure 5-31.

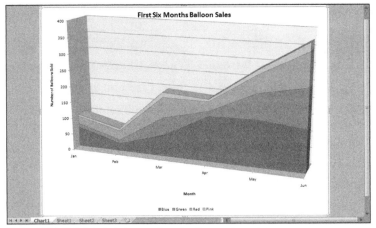

Figure 5-31: This labeled chart makes the date easier to interpret.

10. **Choose Chart Tools Layout → Background → 3-D Rotation.**

The Format Chart Area dialog box appears, with the 3-D Rotation options showing, as shown in Figure 5-32.

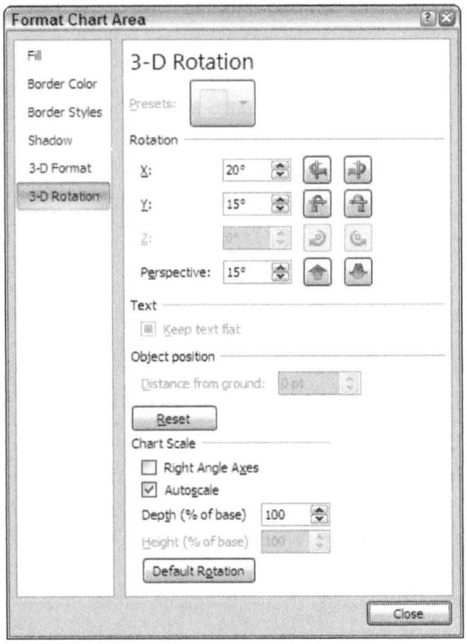

Figure 5-32: The 3-D rotation options for your area chart.

This set of options lets you change the angle of the rotation and the perspective for any 3-D chart. To adjust the x and y rotations, use the arrows in the top half of the dialog box. As you change the rotation and perspective, you see the changes reflected in your chart.

Watch Your Step

Changing the perspective and the rotation of your charts can sometimes make the data look better. But if you are not careful, you may go too far. What looks good to you might not show the story you want to tell. Keep things simple: If you need to change the 3-D rotation of your charts, for example, try to always show the chart to someone else before you use it in a document or presentation or print it.

Be careful with the Default Rotation button in the Format Chart Area dialog box. It doesn't return you to the original settings; you do that by clicking the Reset button. The Default Rotation button sets the current rotation and perspective as the default settings for this and other charts. Clicking this button unintentionally can mean that the next chart you create looks different from what you expect.

Moving On: An Overview of the Other Chart Types

The charts you have learned about in this chapter are likely to be the only ones you use. However, you might use several other specialty charts, depending on the data you are asked to chart. In this final section of this chapter, you learn about these charts.

Stock chart

A *stock* chart helps you identify how stocks perform over time. For the most basic of these charts, you provide the high, low, and close values for the stocks over the trading period. For the other charts, you add the opening values and the volume traded. The charts are then created for the stock. An example is shown in Figure 5-33.

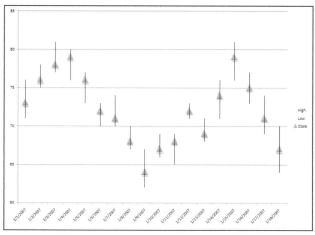

Figure 5-33: A stock chart.

Surface chart

A *surface* chart is used to correlate data when both the data categories and the data series are numeric values. These charts let you see how the data will trend in two or three dimensions. An example is shown in Figure 5-34.

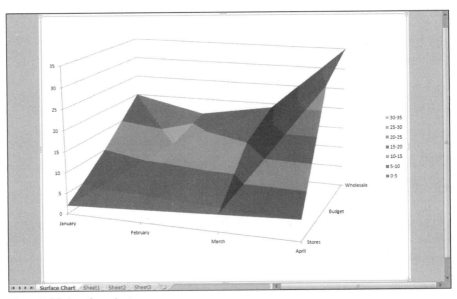

Figure 5-34: A surface chart.

Doughnut chart

A *doughnut* chart is a pie chart that tracks multiple series of data at a time. In a pie chart, you can chart only one series of data. In a doughnut chart, however, each series becomes a part of the doughnut. You can then see both the individual data elements (as colors in the doughnut) and the overall percentage of the total that the series of elements provides. An example is shown in Figure 5-35.

Bubble chart

A *bubble* chart is to a scatter chart what a doughnut is to a pie chart: You get to add a third dimension that shows how big the bubbles are. Bubbles are good for showing more detailed comparisons of the scatter chart data. An example is shown in Figure 5-36.

Radar chart

A *radar* chart allows you to chart seemingly noncomparable data. Each data point is plotted as a point from the center of the chart. Two distinct types of radar charts are used:

- Charts with one series look like an extruded area chart.
- Charts with more than one series of data look more like spider webs, with data markers serving as the intersections between the web threads.

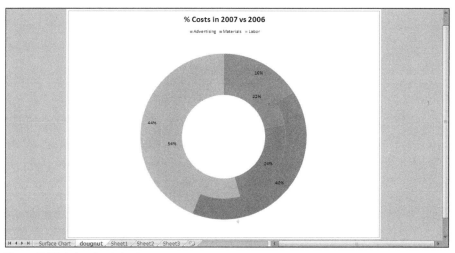

Figure 5-35: A doughnut chart.

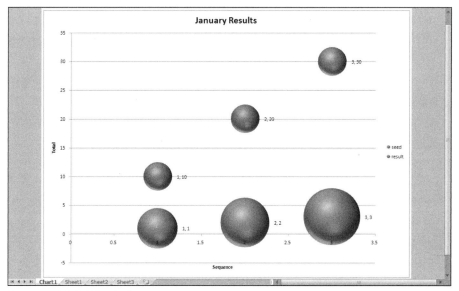

Figure 5-36: A bubble chart.

An example is shown in Figure 5-37.

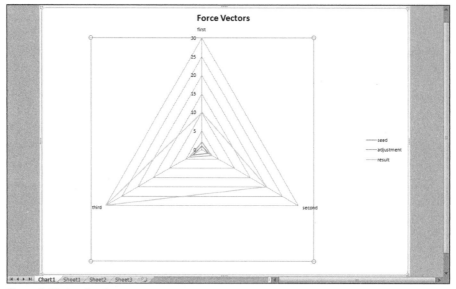

Figure 5-37: A radar chart.

2-D chart: A chart whose data is plotted in the x and y coordinate plane (often known as "along the horizontal and vertical axes").

3-D chart: A chart whose data is plotted in all three dimensions: x, y, and z (commonly known as width, height, and depth).

axis: The vertical and horizontal lines representing the walls and floors of your chart.

bar: A horizontal or vertical element used to represent a data value in a bar or column chart. Pie charts use "pieces" to represent the data; line charts use lines and dots; and scatter charts use dots.

chart: A pictorial representation of selected data in a spreadsheet.

 **continued**

chart title: A label that can describe the data in a chart, specify which conclusions you want drawn from the data, or comment on the data in the chart.

grid lines: A set of vertical and horizontal lines on a chart used to show scale. Used in bar, column, line, scatter, and area charts.

label: A word or phrase that describes what the data in the chart represents.

legend: Shows the relationship between the labels for the data and the graphical images that represent the labels.

marker: The dot on a line or scatter chart that represents the data value being charted.

scale: The relationship of the data shown by one of the axes in a chart.

segment: A pie-shaped section of the entire area in a pie chart. Each piece of the pie represents the percentage or part of the whole specified by the data in that cell.

series: Each set of values within your data.

trend: The general direction that the data in a scatter or line chart is heading.

value: A data element you are charting.

wall: The shading added to the sides or back of a chart to provide a sense of perspective or to provide a background for the visual information in the chart.

Last Stop

Practice Exam

1. Which of the following elements is the only one you should never make invisible?

   a. Title.

   b. Grid lines.

   c. Values.

   d. Legend.

2. True or False: To change from one chart type to another, you must rebuild the chart from scratch.

3. To move a chart to its own sheet, use the _____ button in the _____ group on the _____ tab.

4. Bar charts are to column charts as horizontal is to _____.

5. When you need to see percentages of a whole, the best kind of chart to use is

   a. Pie chart.

   b. Bar chart.

   c. Line chart.

   d. Bubble chart.

6. How many series of data are charted with a pie chart?

7. True or False: The order of data in the legend is fixed and cannot be changed.

8. Name one situation in which you would use a line chart with two axes.

9. True or False: Markers on line charts are always boxes.

10. Trendlines can be used with which type of chart?

    a. Bar chart.

    b. Scatter chart.

    c. Pie chart.

    d. Area chart.

11. What happens when you click the Default Rotation button while formatting the perspective and rotation of a 3-D area chart?

Pivoting Data: Looking at Your Data in a Different Way

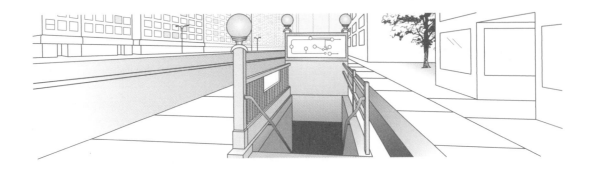

Enter the Station

Questions

1. When should you use a PivotTable?

2. What is the relationship between a PivotTable and a regular table?

3. What are the three rules for organizing data to be used in a PivotTable?

4. What is a data cube?

5. What is the relationship between value cells and header cells in a PivotTable?

6. What is the easiest way to add fields to a PivotTable?

7. How do you change the row and column headers in a PivotTable?

8. What are the most common formulas used in PivotTables?

9. What is a PivotChart?

10. Can all chart types be used to create a PivotChart?

Express Line

If you already fully understand what a PivotTable is, how to create one in Excel 2007, how to chart your pivoted data, and why you would want to use either a PivotChart or a PivotTable, skip ahead to the next chapter.

Research has shown that the human mind can handle only so many unique pieces of data at a time. If you try to summarize the data in a significantly large spreadsheet, chances are good that someone viewing the table will suffer from information overload, making it difficult to interpret the data in a meaningful way.

How should you work with large amounts of data? You can do a number of things: Manually create a number of summarization sheets that attempt to compute the data; create an outline to group the data elements into useable pieces and then summarize them; or look at the data from a higher level so that you can see the bigger picture.

Although you can manually create a higher-level view by creating a series of formulas for each type of calculation, that process is time-consuming and error-prone. Instead, in this chapter, you learn how to have Excel summarize your data quite flexibly by using the pivoting features.

PivotTables allow you to look at Excel data in a more compressed and understandable manner. They help you more quickly and easily combine the data and see the relationships between the values. PivotTables enable you to manipulate your data in a new way without your having to do a large amount of work.

Excel has two pivoting features:

- **PivotTables:** Create data groupings so that you can see data in the form of tables.
- **PivotCharts:** Use PivotTables results to create a chart directly from the pivoted data.

In this chapter, you start by learning about some common applications of pivoted data. Then after you understand how you might use a PivotTable, you create a basic PivotTable, enhance it, and graph it in a PivotChart.

Introducing PivotTables

One common question you hear when you are given data to analyze is "What does this data mean?" If the amount of data you have is small enough, you can summarize the data manually and create a chart to answer the question. However, when you work with large amounts of data, the amount of data can overwhelm you. In many cases, there is so much data that summarizing it in a meaningful manner is impossible.

One solution is to build an Excel PivotTable for your data. When you change your data from a flat file to a PivotTable, you can then quickly summarize the data in any of a number of ways.

When you *pivot* your data, you don't turn it on its side; instead, you change the angle from which you look at the data. You "step back" from it. Rather than look at what each piece of data has to say, you put the pieces of data together and let Excel analyze what the combinations of data can tell you.

Data that will be used in a PivotTable is organized so that Excel can easily understand which data is related. Suppose that you're working with inventory data for a pet store and you have the following table of data:

Item Name	Date Sold	Customer Name	Cost of Item
Cat	1-Jan	Jane	45
Dog	1-Feb	Jane	33
Bird	1-Mar	Jane	46
Cat	1-Jan	Joe	45
Dog	1-Feb	Joe	33
Bird	1-Mar	Joe	46
Cat	1-Jan	Mike	45
Dog	1-Feb	Mike	33
Bird	1-Mar	Mike	46
Cat	1-Jan	Harry	45
Dog	1-Feb	Harry	33
Bird	1-Mar	Harry	46
Cat	1-Jan	Sam	45
Dog	1-Feb	Sam	33
Bird	1-Mar	Sam	46

Each row contains the information for a specific item sold to a specific customer on a specific day. The actual list of records would be very large, with duplicate values in some of the columns. For now, you'll work with only these 15 records.

In this case, you can pivot the data to learn when each item was sold, to whom it was sold, and how much you made from the sale. To do that, use the Excel PivotTable feature to create several different tables from the same data.

The first table might list the item names in a column and the customer names in a row across the top. In the individual cells, you could place a calculation for the total amount of money a customer spent for that item over a specific period. That table is shown in Figure 6-1.

The power of the PivotTable is that after you create a single PivotTable, you can easily adapt it to find the number of items bought each day. To do this for the pet store example, you change the rows to contain the dates; the columns to contain the names of the items; and the cells to contain the item count, producing the table shown in Figure 6-2.

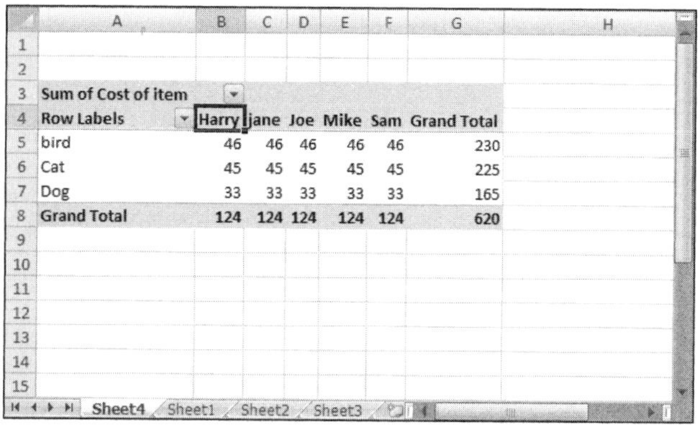

Figure 6-1: A simple PivotTable example.

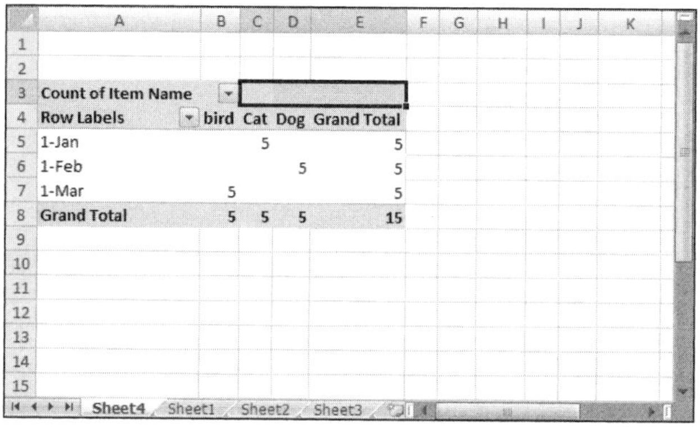

	A	B	C	D	E	F	G	H
1								
2								
3	Sum of Cost of item							
4	Row Labels	Harry	jane	Joe	Mike	Sam	Grand Total	
5	bird	46	46	46	46	46	230	
6	Cat	45	45	45	45	45	225	
7	Dog	33	33	33	33	33	165	
8	Grand Total	124	124	124	124	124	620	

Figure 6-2: The PivotTable should look like this after you make changes.

	A	B	C	D	E	F	G	H	I	J	K
1											
2											
3	Count of Item Name										
4	Row Labels	bird	Cat	Dog	Grand Total						
5	1-Jan		5		5						
6	1-Feb			5	5						
7	1-Mar	5			5						
8	Grand Total	5	5	5	15						

If you were to create these two tables from scratch, the process would be time-consuming and you'd end up duplicating some of your work. By allowing Excel to create the PivotTable for you, you spend just a few moments creating the table and only a few seconds changing it.

One useful feature of a PivotTable is that you can set it up with a small sample of data, such as in the pet store example, and then expand the records in the table. As long as you keep all the records within the table, Excel automatically updates the PivotTables to match the records in the data table.

You can also use PivotTables to create expandable summaries of combinations of data. For example, if you want to know both the items sold per day and who bought them, you can add the customer information to the rows. If the date is shown first, the data is totaled by date and then subtotaled by customer. If the customer information is listed first, the data is totaled the other way around.

Creating a Basic PivotTable

In this chapter, you'll be working with historical data from a hotel chain. The chain has three hotel properties: Jackson Hotel, Miguel Ranch, and Pengueno Place. Each property has four departments: rooms, restaurants, catering, and conference facilities. As you might guess, trying to get an overall historical picture of the chain's financial information can be overwhelming. You have been given the quarterly income and expense data for the years 2002 through 2006 in one sheet, and that sheet has 300 records of data in it.

You could create the formulas to find and summarize the spending amounts in each category and in each year, but that would take a while. Instead, create a PivotTable to learn everything you need to know.

Getting your data in the right format

The first step in creating the PivotTable is to make sure that your data is in a format that the PivotTable feature can understand. In this case, you have to follow a few basic rules:

- **No blank lines can appear in the data.** If you have a blank line, the PivotTable does not use the data after the blank line.

- **Each column must have a header.** Headers help you place data in the rows and columns of the PivotTable.

🔵 **Your data must be consistent.** For example, if you name your quarters Q 1, Q 2, and so on, you must always reference them that way. Excel doesn't know that Q 1 is the same as Q1 or Quarter 1.

Refer to the pet store table used in the examples in the preceding section. Notice that all the results you received are numerical. If you're working with numerical data, you can perform a wide variety of operations on the data to analyze it. However, if you're working with textual data, the only operation you can perform on the data is to count the number of times that a piece of data appears.

Creating the PivotTable

After you get your data in the right format for a PivotTable, creating the PivotTable is fairly easy. You use Excel's drag-and-drop features to manipulate the pieces of data and summarize them in many different ways.

In this exercise, you create a basic PivotTable from the data from Red Sunset Hotels and use this PivotTable to determine the yearly income and expenditures for each hotel department:

1. Open the `RedSunsetHotelChain.xlsx` file.

2. Select cell A1. Choose Insert ➡ Tables ➡ PivotTable.

The Create PivotTable dialog box appears, as shown in Figure 6-3.

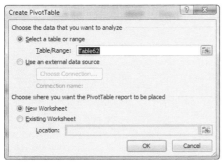

Figure 6-3: The Create PivotTable dialog box.

Because the cell you selected (cell A1) is in a table, the Table/Range field is filled in with the table name. In addition, Excel has selected the New Worksheet radio button, which means that the PivotTable will appear in a new worksheet.

If the cell you selected had not been in a table, you could have used the grid button (which is to the right of the Table/Range field) to select the range of cells for the PivotTable.

Information Kiosk

If you're working with data from a SQL database, you define the data source by selecting the second radio button in the Create PivotTable dialog box: Use an External Data Source. This option enables you to select records from an external database and import the data as an OLAP (Online Analytical Processing) cube. In this case, Excel looks at the external data but works with it as though it were in your actual spreadsheet. (For more information on working with OLAP cubes, look for the Help topic and the OLAP tools in the Tools group on the PivotTable Tools tab.)

3. **Click OK to create the new sheet containing your PivotTable.**

The new sheet opens, and the PivotTable Field List task pane appears on the right side of your screen, as shown in Figure 6-4.

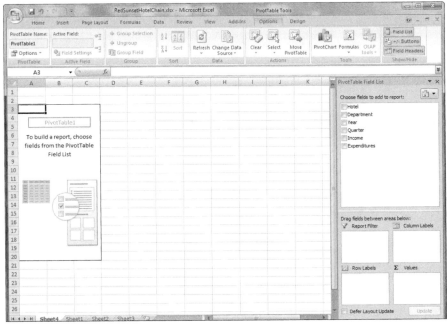

Figure 6-4: A PivotTable field list.

Excel displays, as an information message, a quick explanation of how to build the PivotTable. This message continues to be shown until you select your first field to add to the table. In addition, two new tabs appear on the Ribbon. You can use them to change the PivotTable manually and to work with the design of your table.

4. **Select the Hotel check box in the task pane.**

Notice that column A is filled with row labels based on the names of the properties in the hotel chain and that the Hotel field is added to the Row Labels area of the task pane. Excel has defined the rows for your PivotTable based on its best guess of where you want these values placed. You learn how to move the fields from rows to columns to values in Step 7.

5. **Select the Department check box.**

Notice that the data was again placed in the row. You have now set up the subcategory for your PivotTable. Subcategories can either be shown or hidden. If you want to hide the subcategorization, click the minus sign to the left of each hotel name.

6. **Select the Year check box.**

This time, Excel guessed wrong. Because the data in the year column cells are all numerical, Excel guessed that you wanted that information summed as the values for the PivotTable cells. You don't want to sum the years, however; instead, you want to break down the data by year. You need to move the year values from the Values list in the task pane to the Column Labels list.

7. **Select the Sum of Year box in the Values list, and then drag it to the Column Labels area.**

The years are now shown across the top of the PivotTable. The last column in the table shows the grand total. Next, you tell Excel on which data you want to base the values.

8. **Select the Income check box.**

Notice that the cells in your PivotTable are now filled in with the sum of the income for each year, as shown in Figure 6-5.

	A	B	C	D	E	F	G	H
3	Sum of Income	Column Labels						
4	Row Labels	2002	2003	2004	2005	2006	Grand Total	
5	⊟Jackson Hotel	1040523	704694	1058226	904136	960668	4668247	
6	Catering	190672	96690	240473	184243	215052	927130	
7	Conference Facilities	240334	166611	168047	200075	180081	955148	
8	Restaurant	206476	165955	183095	162891	177774	896191	
9	Rooms	403041	275438	466611	356927	387761	1889778	
10	⊟Miguel Ranch	547900	708976	491017	497686	631171	2876750	
11	Catering	69757	173907	91591	69979	130783	536017	
12	Conference Facilities	137681	152482	114575	144003	141406	690147	
13	Restaurant	211669	270894	202282	205251	245995	1136091	
14	Rooms	128793	111693	82569	78453	112987	514495	
15	⊟Pengueno Place	527524	718803	541046	698309	495816	2981498	
16	Catering	201698	302208	212078	259604	227233	1202821	
17	Conference Facilities	84555	140904	137380	133983	86631	583453	
18	Restaurant	125556	109903	100091	133783	96738	566071	
19	Rooms	115715	165788	91497	170939	85214	629153	
20	Grand Total	2115947	2132473	2090289	2100131	2087655	10526495	

Figure 6-5: A basic PivotTable containing data from Red Sunset Hotels.

You have now created your first PivotTable. It doesn't quite answer your question (to find out the overall yearly income and expenditures for each department) because you have only the income, not the expenditures, for each department.

9. Select the Expenditures check box.

Notice that each year column now has two subcolumns — one for income and one for expenditures. If you scroll to the right side of the PivotTable, you see the comparison of income to expenditures across this time period for each hotel and department. As you can see, none of the hotels is breaking even.

You can learn much more from this data. The first step you might want to take is to remove the categorization by year so that all you see is flat income versus expenditures.

10. Either deselect the Year check box in the PivotTable task pane or drag the Year box from the Column Labels area to the Field List area.

The summarization table and the field layout for it are shown in Figure 6-6.

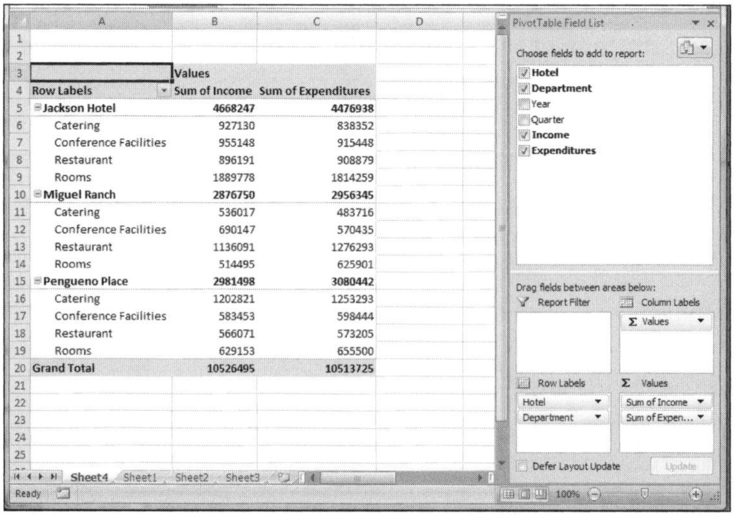

Row Labels	Sum of Income	Sum of Expenditures
Jackson Hotel	4668247	4476938
Catering	927130	838352
Conference Facilities	955148	915448
Restaurant	896191	908879
Rooms	1889778	1814259
Miguel Ranch	2876750	2956345
Catering	536017	483716
Conference Facilities	690147	570435
Restaurant	1136091	1276293
Rooms	514495	625901
Pengueno Place	2981498	3080442
Catering	1202821	1253293
Conference Facilities	583453	598444
Restaurant	566071	573205
Rooms	629153	655500
Grand Total	10526495	10513725

Figure 6-6: A summarization table of income and expenditures for the three hotels.

Another change you might want to make is to see the hotel income and expenditures by department rather than by year.

11. At the bottom of the task pane, drag the Department box from the Row Labels area to the Column Labels area.

This change produces a much shorter but wider table. In fact, the information in that table is not easy to interpret at first glance.

12. Swap the Hotel values to the columns and the Department values to the rows by dragging each label from one area to the other at the bottom of the task pane.

The table narrows somewhat, as shown in Figure 6-7, because the names of the fields for the hotels are shorter than the names for the departments. You can now see the expenditures and income for each department by hotel.

	A	B	C	D	E	F	G	H
1								
2								
3		Column Labels						
4		Sum of Income			Sum of Expenditures			Total Sum of Income Total Sur
5	Row Labels	Jackson Hotel	Miguel Ranch	Pengueno Place	Jackson Hotel	Miguel Ranch	Pengueno Place	
6	Catering	927130	536017	1202821	838352	483716	1253293	2665968
7	Conference Facilities	955148	690147	583453	915448	570435	598444	2228748
8	Restaurant	896191	1136091	566071	908879	1276293	573205	2598353
9	Rooms	1889778	514495	629153	1814259	625901	655500	3033426
10	Grand Total	4668247	2876750	2981498	4476938	2956345	3080442	10526495
11								
12								
13								
14								
15								
16								
17								
18								
19								
20								
21								
22								
23								
24								
25								
26								
27								

Sheet4 Sheet1 Sheet2 Sheet3

Figure 6-7: This PivotTable compares income and expenditures for each department by hotel.

Expanding Your PivotTables

In addition to merely summing the data in your table, PivotTable values can be based on almost any formula or function you can imagine. In the exercise in this section, you change the calculations for the PivotTable in a number of different ways to learn from this data. In this exercise, you adjust the PivotTable to find the average expenditures and income amounts rather than the totals:

1. Return to the chart you created in the preceding section, or open the `RedSunsetHotelChain1.xlsx` file.

2. On the PivotTable sheet, select cell B4. Right-click the cell and choose Summarize Data By → Average from the context menu.

The column title, as shown in cell B4, changes from Sum of Income to Average of Income. In addition, the values for the cells in the Income columns change to the average for that department for each hotel. In addition, the values in column H are changed to show Total Average of Income. If you look in the task pane at the items in the Values area, it also displays Average Of rather than Sum Of.

3. Select cell E4. Right-click the cell and choose Summarize Data By → Average from the context menu.

The remaining value cells in the table change to contain averages rather than sums, as shown in Figure 6-8.

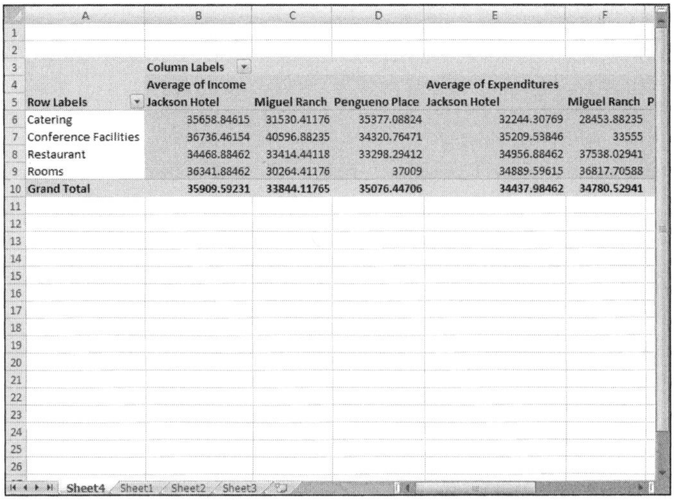

Figure 6-8: The income and expenditure cells contain averages.

After this change is made, it becomes obvious that the default formatting for the PivotTable leaves something to be desired. You fix that problem in the next step.

4. Select cell B4. Choose PivotTable Tools Options ➜ Active Field ➜ Field Settings.

The Value Field Settings dialog box appears, as shown in Figure 6-9.

Figure 6-9: The Value Field Settings dialog box.

This dialog box is another way to change the values in your PivotTable. On the Summarize By tab, you change the calculation to be performed for the cells that are generated in this part of the table, which is the Average of Income section (cells B6 through D9). Below the tab, you see the Number Format button.

5. Click the Number Format button.

The Format Cells dialog box appears. There, you can select any format for the numbers generated by your PivotTable.

Step Into the Real World

The data in your PivotTable can also show you the relationship between the information in each column. You can get this information by using the relationships set up on the second tab of the Value Field Settings dialog box.

To see these relationships, look at the Show Values As tab in the Value Field Settings dialog box. You can see the differences between the values in the current column and in the other columns. As an example, find out how the income for the departments at each hotel compares to the income for Pengueno Place:

1. **In the task pane, click the Average of Income drop-down arrow button. From the list, select Value Field Settings.**

   The Value Field Settings dialog box opens.

2. **On the Show Values As tab, select Difference From in the Show Values As drop-down list.**

3. **From the Base Field list box, select the basic comparison; in this example, it is by hotel.**

4. **From the Base Item list box on the right, specify which hotel you want to compare the data with; in this case, select Pengueno Place.**

5. **Click OK.**

   The resulting change to the income data (cells B6 through D9) is shown in the figure.

Row Labels	Column Labels ▾ Average of Income Jackson Hotel	Miguel Ranch	Pengueno Place
Catering	$281.76	-$3,846.68	
Conference Facilities	$2,415.70	$6,276.12	
Restaurant	$1,170.59	$116.15	
Rooms	-$667.12	-$6,744.59	
Grand Total	$833.15	-$1,232.33	

As you can see, the Jackson Hotel and Miguel Ranch columns now contain the numerical differences between that department at that property and the same department at Pengueno Place. The Pengueno Place column is empty because there is no difference between the same data.

6. **Select Currency and click OK. When you return to the Value Field Settings dialog box, click OK again.**

Cells B6 through D9 of the PivotTable are formatted as currency, as are those for the Total Average of Income section, as shown in Figure 6-10.

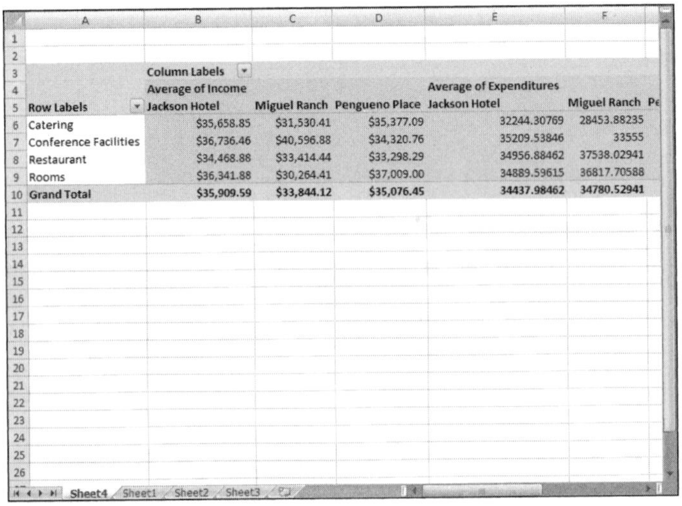

	A	B	C	D	E	F	
1							
2							
3		Column Labels ▾					
4		Average of Income			Average of Expenditures		
5	Row Labels ▾	Jackson Hotel	Miguel Ranch	Pengueno Place	Jackson Hotel	Miguel Ranch	Pe
6	Catering	$35,658.85	$31,530.41	$35,377.09	32244.30769	28453.88235	
7	Conference Facilities	$36,736.46	$40,596.88	$34,320.76	35209.53846	33555	
8	Restaurant	$34,468.88	$33,414.44	$33,298.29	34956.88462	37538.02941	
9	Rooms	$36,341.88	$30,264.41	$37,009.00	34889.59615	36817.70588	
10	Grand Total	$35,909.59	$33,844.12	$35,076.45	34437.98462	34780.52941	
11							
12							
13							
14							
15							
16							
17							
18							
19							
20							
21							
22							
23							
24							
25							
26							

Sheet4 Sheet1 Sheet2 Sheet3

Figure 6-10: The first set of values are formatted as currency.

Notice that cells E6 through G9 and cells I6 through I9 remain as regular numbers.

7. **In the task pane, click the Average of Expenditures drop-down arrow button. From the list, select Value Field Settings.**

The Value Fields Settings dialog box appears again, allowing you to access the calculation and formatting information for these cells.

8. **Click the Number Format button.**

The regular Format Cells dialog box appears. There, you can select any format for the numbers generated by your PivotTable.

9. **Select Currency and click OK. When you return to the Value Field Settings dialog box, click OK again.**

Cells E6 through G9 and I6 through I9 of the PivotTable are formatted as currency, as shown in Figure 6-11. Now that all the numbers in the PivotTable are shown as dollar amounts, the information is easier to understand.

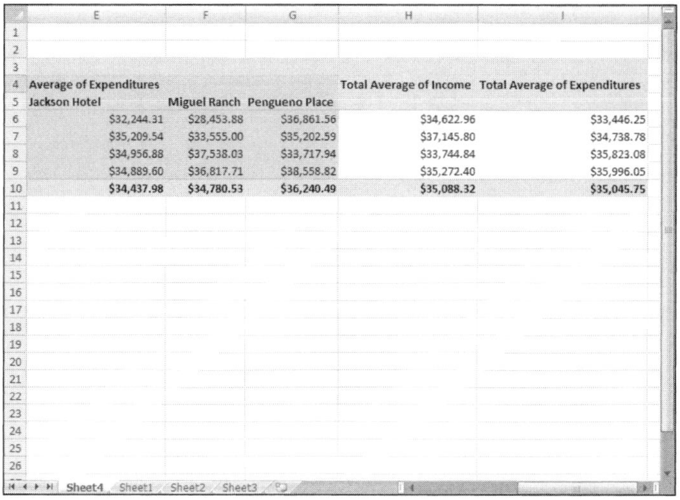

Figure 6-11: All the income and expenditure values are formatted as currency.

Using PivotCharts to Display Your Data in a Way That People Can Understand

PivotTables are a useful way to organize your data, but they are not a highly graphical means of displaying that data. Just as a chart shows off the data in a table clearly, a PivotChart shows off the data in a PivotTable clearly.

Creating a PivotChart

In this exercise, you use the same basic data as in the previous exercises. In this case, you are using only the annual data, not the total income and expenditure data. By using only the annual data, you create clearer, more understandable charts. Follow these steps to create a PivotChart based on the PivotTable:

1. Open the **RedSunsetHotelChainCharts.xlsx** file. Select cell **PivotTable!A6.**

You will use this table to create a series of basic PivotCharts.

2. Choose **PivotTable Tools Options ➜ Tools ➜ PivotChart.**

The Insert Chart dialog box appears, as shown in Figure 6-12.

The dialog box for creating a PivotChart is the same as for creating regular charts. The difference lies in the arrangement and display of the data that goes into the PivotChart.

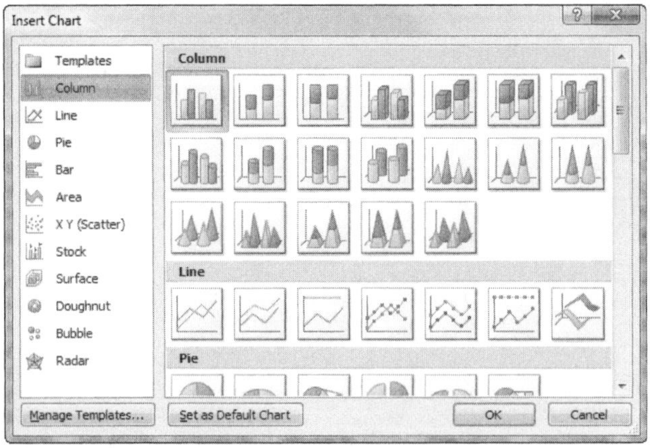

Figure 6-12: The Insert Chart dialog box.

3. **Click OK.**

The PivotChart Filter Pane task pane appears, as shown in Figure 6-13.

This task pane has three parts:

- **Axis Fields:** In the top section, you choose fields to be the categories, or x axis fields. They are usually the groupings of the data from your chart. By default, all values of each subcategory are shown for each category. You can filter visible items by clicking the drop-down arrow button next to the field and either sorting or filtering the data, as you learned earlier.

- **Legend Fields:** In this section of the task pane, you can choose the values to be used for the bars in the chart. In this case, the values are the sums of the department income and expenditures. For each department, values are broken down by year.

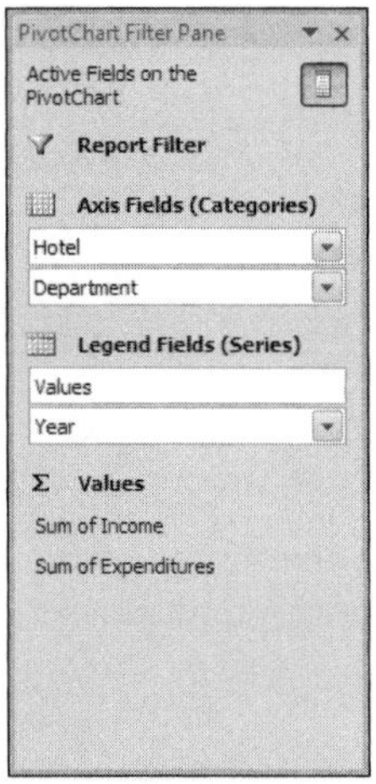

Figure 6-13: The PivotChart Filter Pane.

- **Values:** This section contains the information from the cells in your PivotTable. In this case, the values are the sums of the income and expenditures for the quarters.

4. **If the pane is not already docked to the right of the chart, drag the pane to the right side of your screen until it docks.**

The chart is shown behind the pane but in front of the data. Because the size of the chart makes reading difficult, you will move the chart to a separate page so that you can see it better. Before you do that, notice that several contextual tabs now appear on the Ribbon, as shown in Figure 6-14.

Figure 6-14: A Ribbon with many contextual tabs.

5. **Choose PivotChart Tools Design → Location → Move Chart.**

The Move Chart dialog box appears.

6. **Select the New Sheet radio button and give the new sheet the name** Pivot Chart 1. **Click OK.**

The chart appears on a new sheet, as shown in Figure 6-15.

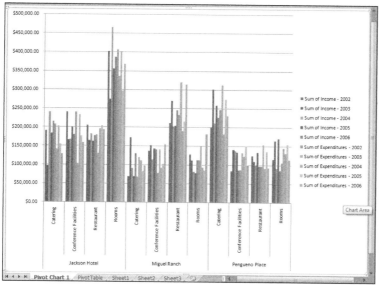

Figure 6-15: A default PivotChart.

This chart has too much data in it to be readable. Each property has a total of 40 bars, which makes it difficult to see the data. Next, you will summarize the data one step further to produce a more readable chart.

7. In the PivotTable Field List task pane, deselect the Year check box.

The number of bars in the chart is reduced to eight per hotel, as shown in Figure 6-16.

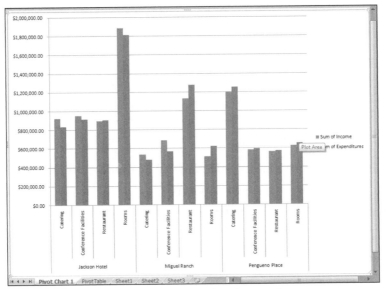

Figure 6-16: This PivotChart is more readable than the preceding one.

This chart is simpler, but still communicates information. The chart shows the overall income and expenditures for each department at each property. When you look at the chart, one characteristic jumps out: Each property specializes in one department and does much less business in the others. The Jackson Hotel area of specialization is the Rooms department; the Miguel Ranch area of specialization is the Restaurant department; and the Pengueno Place area of specialization is the Catering department.

In the real world, you would use this information to start finding out how the other departments can learn from the ones that specialize in each area.

What else can you do with a PivotChart? Because the PivotChart is based on the data in your PivotTable, you can specify which values are displayed by moving them into, out of, and around the field areas. You have already seen a basic example, when you turned off the year display in the chart.

You can also change the computations performed for each value by changing the information in the PivotTable Values section of the PivotTable Field List. To see how this affects the chart, deselect the Expenditures check box and notice that the bars that show the expenditures are no longer shown in the chart.

Information Kiosk

When you're working with a PivotChart, you can specify which task panes are visible by clicking the buttons in the Show/Hide group on the PivotChart Tools Analyze tab. If your screen is so "busy" that you cannot easily understand the chart, use these two buttons to expand the visible space for the chart.

Working with other chart types

In some circumstances, you want to see the PivotTable in other ways. In the next few steps, you change the type of chart used to show the data. When you complete these steps, you can determine which chart types to use, or not use, with your PivotTables:

1. Open the **RedSunsetHotelChainCharts1.xlsx** file. Then select the sheet named Lines.

This sheet contains a line chart of the pivoted data, as shown in Figure 6-17.

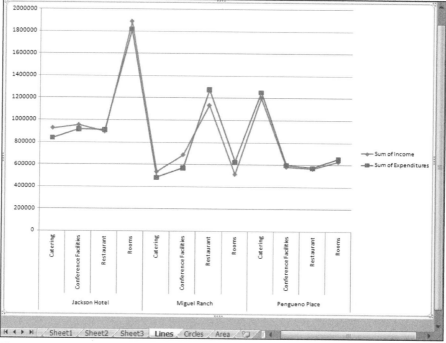

Figure 6-17: This line chart has markers from a PivotTable.

With the data shown this way, you can see the general trend of the data across the departments and the properties. The trend is a little more obvious from the line chart than it was from the bar chart in the preceding section (refer to Figure 6-16).

When you look at the data as a line chart, you might want to look at just the expenditures or just the income. If you no longer see the task panes, click the chart. The task panes become visible again.

To see just the expenditures, deselect the Income check box. To see just the income, select the Income check box, and then deselect the Expenditures check box.

Watch Your Step

If you deselect both the Expenditures and Income boxes at the same time, you don't do any harm. However, you end up with a chart with no data on it.

2. **Select the sheet named Circles.**

This sheet contains a pie chart of the pivoted data, as shown in Figure 6-18. In this case, the chart content has been changed to show a comparison of the expenditures by each department across the entire time frame.

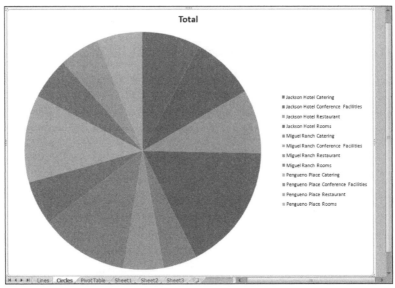

Figure 6-18: A pie chart from a PivotTable.

This chart would lead you to believe that a pie chart generated from a PivotTable isn't useful. However, with a slight change, it becomes a highly useful chart.

3. **Deselect all selections except for Hotel and Expenditures.**

Your pie chart should now show only the overall expenditures for the hotels, split by property, as shown in Figure 6-19.

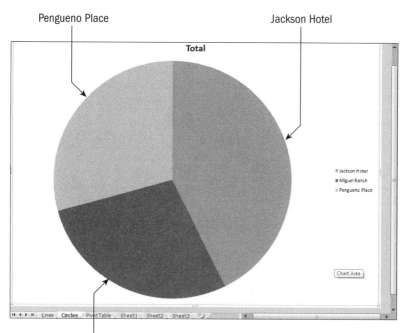

Pengueno Place   Jackson Hotel

Miguel Ranch

Figure 6-19: A pie chart with markers from a PivotTable.

You can now see that Jackson Hotel has a very large percentage of the expenditures for the three properties.

4. **Deselect the Expenditures check box and select the Income check box.**

The chart changes slightly. Jackson Hotel has the highest percentage of income of the three properties, but the percentage of the total income is not as high as the percentage of the total expenditure.

5. **Change the pie chart so that you can see the income breakdown for the departments rather than the hotels. To do this, deselect the Hotel check box and select the Department check box.**

6. **Change the pie chart so that you can see the expenditures breakdown for the departments rather than the hotels. To do this, deselect the Income check box and select the Expenditures check box.**

As you can see, there isn't much of a change between the two charts because the income and the expenditures for the four departments are fairly evenly split.

7. Select the sheet named Area. Set the field selections back to show the income and expenditure values by hotel, department, and year. In this case, the order in which you select the check boxes makes a difference in how the data is sorted. First, deselect all the check boxes except for Income and Expenditures. Then select the Year check box, the Hotel check box, and the Department check box. In addition, remember that you need to move the Year from the Values box to the Legend box.

When you create a PivotChart or PivotTable, the order in which you select the check boxes tells Excel how you want the data sorted. After you have the data sorted correctly, you see that this sheet contains an area chart of the pivoted data, as shown in Figure 6-20.

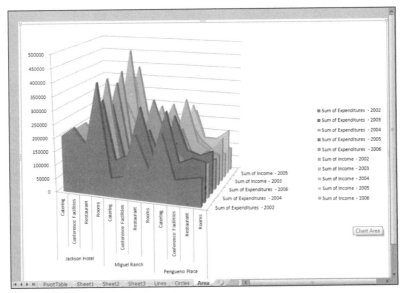

Figure 6-20: A 3-D area chart from a PivotTable.

If your Excel file has more than one PivotChart built from the same PivotTable, changing the field selections for one of the charts changes the selections for all the charts. In addition, changing the selection of visible fields for the charts changes the visibility of the fields for the table itself.

When you look at the pivoted data as a 3-D area chart (see Figure 6-20), you can see more of the relationships between all the data points. In this case, the multitude of data points shown in the full chart actually make some sense. Because of the additional dimension and color selections, you can tell more about the relationships between the income and expenditures for each of the departments across each of the hotels.

Watch Your Step

Only some chart types can be created from PivotTables. If you attempt to create an XY (scatter) chart, a bubble chart, or a stock chart from a PivotTable, Excel displays an error message asking you to select a different type of chart.

cube: A set of three-dimensional data pulled into Excel from a database.

fields: The rows, columns, and values used to build a PivotTable. Unlike regular cells, fields are either classifications of data (months, departments, or years, for example) or results of formulas generated from the cells summarized with the data.

field layout: The location and organization of the fields in the PivotTable.

flat file: A two-dimensional spreadsheet; used to create the three-dimensional sheet known as a PivotTable.

OLAP (Online Analytical Processing): Databases that are three-dimensional cubes, arranged so that the data can be easily pulled from the database into an Excel spreadsheet for analysis with a PivotTable or PivotChart.

PivotChart (also Pivot Chart): The charts built from PivotTables.

PivotTable (also Pivot Table): A summarization table of large lists of data that are related to each other by common names, data, and information.

summarize: To evaluate and analyze selected items from a particular column.

Last Stop

Practice Exam

1. True or False: Everything you can do with a PivotTable, you can also do by hand.

2. Which of the following is not an advantage of using PivotTables?

   a. Speed.

   b. Additional understanding of the data.

   c. Colors in tables that are not available anywhere else in Excel.

   d. Flexibility.

3. True or False: PivotTables can help you analyze inventory data.

4. Which of the following is required for the creation of a PivotTable?

   a. Blank lines within the data.

   b. A header row for the data.

   c. A connection to an SQL server.

   d. A minimum of 100 rows of data.

5. True or False: In the field definitions for a PivotTable, Q1 and Quarter 1 are the same.

6. Which of the following cannot be automatically determined with a PivotTable?

   a. The number of times a name appears in a table.

   b. The sum of the years in a table.

   c. The minimum number of items sold in a month.

   d. The longest customer name in the data.

7. You can change the visibility of the data in a PivotTable in which of these ways:

    a. Click the minus sign for a cell in the first column of the table.

    b. Click the minus sign for the first row of the table.

    c. Change the formula for the value cells.

    d. Right-click a value cell.

8. True or False: Data in a PivotTable cannot be formatted.

9. Describe one case where you would change the settings of the Show Values As tab in the Value Field Settings dialog box.

_____

_____

10. Changing the visible data for a PivotChart affects

    a. only the visible data on that PivotChart.

    b. the visible data on all PivotCharts.

    c. the visible data for the current PivotChart and the PivotTable it is based on.

    d. the visible data for the current PivotTable and all PivotCharts based on that table.

11. Give one reason why you would limit the detail level on a PivotChart.

_____

12. Which of the following charts cannot be based on a PivotTable?

    a. Line chart.

    b. Pie chart.

    c. Bubble chart.

    d. None. Any chart type can be created from a PivotTable.

7

Adding Data from Other Sources

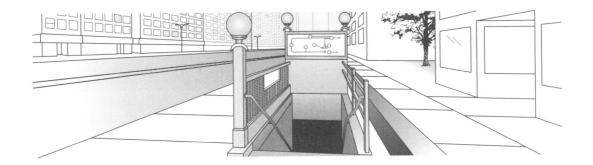

Enter the Station

Questions

1. Why pull data from somewhere else rather than retype it?

2. What is an advantage of pulling data from Word rather than from a text file?

3. What is a CSV file?

4. What is a fixed-width file?

5. What is a Web query?

6. Why would you want to pull data from an Access database?

7. Beyond an Access database, what other types of connections to data can Excel 2007 make?

Express Line

If you are already familiar with importing data from other sources into Excel 2007, skip ahead to the next chapter. Be aware that even if you know how to pull data into Excel in its earlier versions, you might not know how to do it here.

Chapter 7: Adding Data from Other Sources

So far in this book, you have added data to your Excel 2007 worksheets by either typing it or using a formula to get more information from existing data. In the real world, the sets of data you work with aren't usually data that you type by hand. Instead, you are likely to work with data that already exists somewhere else. Your job in these cases is to get the data into Excel from the other sources in such a manner that you can work with it.

In this chapter, you work with data from three main sources:

- Data that has been saved in files other than Excel files. You then import that data into Excel.

- Data that exists in other Excel files.

- Data pulled from an Access database.

After you learn how to get this data into Excel and work with it, you close out this chapter by learning how to refresh your data from other sources. Refreshing the data updates it in its original location so that you can see the changes reflected in your Excel files.

Importing Existing Data into Excel

Much of the external data you work with exists already in the world. The data can exist in a Word table or on a Web page, or you might even have scanned it from a stack of papers. No matter how the data got on your computer, you need to have it in Excel 2007 to work with it and draw your conclusions.

Moving data from a Word table to Excel

In this exercise, you open a Word document that contains a table of data and move the data to a new Excel worksheet:

 Information Kiosk

If you don't have Word installed, you can download the 2003 Word Viewer from Microsoft and add the Compatibility Pack to it (also available from Microsoft). The combination of these two downloads allows you to open the Word document. If you search Google.com for the term **Word viewer**, you should find the viewer easily.

1. Start Word and open the file **SampleWordData.docx**.

In this exercise, you create an Excel worksheet from data that already exists in Word. In this case, you are working with the satisfaction data for HighLowe

Corporation's new-employee orientation sessions. Historically, these sessions have not been well received by new employees, and you have been working to improve the sessions. You want to generate a report showing the progress.

To this point, you have been tracking the data in a Word table. Because you now want to build charts and evaluate the data, you want to copy the data to Excel.

2. **Select the entire Word table and press Ctrl+C to copy it to the Clipboard.**
3. **Open Excel. In the blank sheet that appears, select cell A1 and press Ctrl+V to paste the Word table.**

   Notice that when you paste the data, Excel retains most of the formatting you had applied in Word, as shown in Figure 7-1.

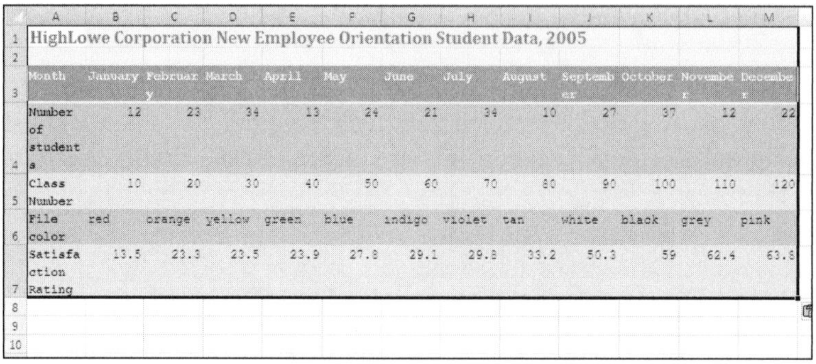

	A	B	C	D	E	F	G	H	I	J	K	L	M
1	HighLowe Corporation New Employee Orientation Student Data, 2005												
2													
3	Month	January	February	March	April	May	June	July	August	September	October	November	December
4	Number of students	12	23	34	13	24	21	34	10	27	37	12	22
5	Class Number	10	20	30	40	50	60	70	80	90	100	110	120
6	File color	red	orange	yellow	green	blue	indigo	violet	tan	white	black	grey	pink
7	Satisfaction Rating	13.5	23.3	23.5	23.9	27.8	29.1	29.8	33.2	50.3	59	62.4	63.8
8													
9													
10													

Figure 7-1: This Excel table looks similar to the way it looks in Word.

   The data you have pasted is normal Excel data. Anything you can do with Excel data, you can do with this data.

4. **Close Excel. When Excel prompts you to save your work, name the file** Ch7WordData.xlsx**.**

   Although you will import this data several more times from other sources, you want to compare the data as you go along.

Moving data from a text file to Excel

Another common way to get data into Excel is by using a text file. A *text* file contains just the information, not the formatting that goes with the information. A text file with data usually comes in one of two formats:

- **Delimited:** A file containing delimited data separates each column of data by using a specific character. The most common type of delimited data is the Comma Separated Values (CSV) file. In CSV files, the data in each column is separated from the next by a comma. Rows of data are separated by hard returns. CSV data is used when the width of the data within a column isn't the same from one row of data to the next.

 Fixed: A file containing fixed-width data always has the same amount of space reserved for each column, no matter how wide the data in the column is for the current row. Fixed-width data is also used when there is no single character that is never used within the data, so there is no possible delimiter.

Generally, you see fixed-width data whenever the data was formatted for people, rather than the computer, to look at. Another common use is for data that is formatted for printing, but saved in a text file. Sometimes, what seems to be fixed-width data is in reality tab-delimited data.

If you work in an environment where data comes from an older computer system, that data is usually in fixed-width format. Older computers format data for printing, not expecting it to be imported into Excel. Older printers were not as sophisticated as the ones we all use now. People have found that by importing fixed-width data into Excel, they can save hundreds of hours of conversion time. They just let Excel do the work rather than do it by hand.

Each file format has good points and bad points. Fixed-width files take up a lot more room because each row has the maximum amount of space reserved for each response. Delimited files don't have that wasted space, but they limit which characters can be used in the data itself.

In the following exercises, you import some data into Excel from text files. Each Excel file has the same data as was in the text file. As you work with each file, notice the differences in how the data is processed by Excel.

Step Into the Real World

One common example of CSV data is the data you download from a Web site, such as your bank's site or a Web affiliate program. The people creating the files know that the information will fall into the same categories of data for each record being downloaded. What they don't know is the size of the numbers or descriptions for each downloaded row. To make the data easier to work with, it is separated by commas.

Fixed files are commonly used when the data is likely to contain multiple text fields. If you have ever filled in the data for a survey where you were asked for your comments about the questions but told that your response must be limited to only 256 characters, you are likely to have created a fixed-width file. Because a comma or other common delimiter is commonly used in responses, the people designing the data limit the field width rather than risk having your data split at the wrong point.

Importing a delimited .txt file

Follow these steps to import a delimited `.txt` file into Excel:

1. **Open Excel, click the Office Button, and choose Open. Using the drop-down arrow on the Files of Type list, change the file type to Text Files.**

If it isn't on your list, scroll down to find it.

Notice that Excel defines a text file as one of three types: `.prn` (print), `.txt` (text), or `.csv` (comma-separated values).

2. **Navigate to the file `SampleCommaData.txt` and click Open.**

The first screen of the Text Import Wizard appears, as shown in Figure 7-2.

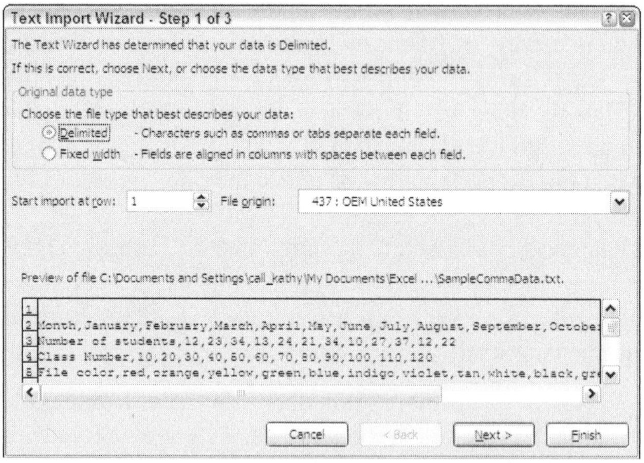

Figure 7-2: Step 1 of the Text Import Wizard for a CSV text file.

Watch Your Step

Two elements make a CSV file a CSV file: The data in the file is separated by commas, and the file extension is `.csv`. In most cases, both conditions are true. On rare occasions, however, you may find files that have been saved in CSV format that don't use commas as delimiters. In this exercise, you work with a file that uses commas as delimiters but is not named with the `.csv` file extension. In the exercise after that, you work with a CSV file that is CSV in format and in filename.

Notice that Excel has already determined that this file is delimited. It is asking you whether you want to start the import at row 1 and whether the file is from the United States Although the data is from the United States, if you look closely, you see that the first line of data is blank. If your computer is set up to handle information from another region of the world, this screen indicates that the file origin is something other than US-437.

 Information Kiosk

When would you not want to start your import at row 1? If the beginning of the file contains information that isn't CSV-delimited data, you would not want to import it. Sometimes, a paragraph at the top of the file contains information about the file layout or the data collection circumstances. Or, maybe the data file has been updated since you last did your import. In that case, you don't want to import data again that you already have, so you skip down to the new data.

3. **Enter** 2 **in the Start Import at Row box to change the starting row, and click the Next button.**

The second screen of the Text Import Wizard appears, as shown in Figure 7-3.

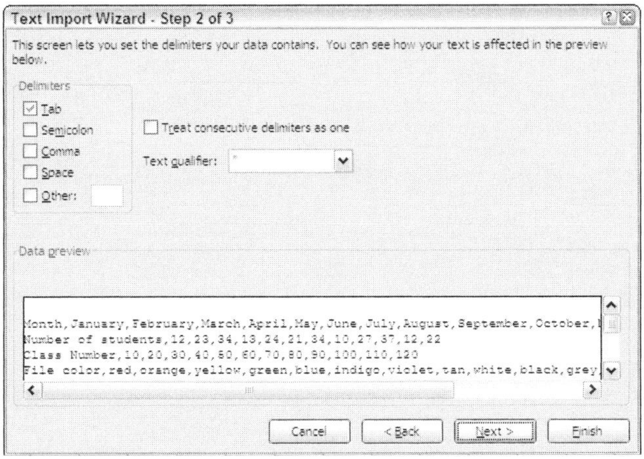

Text Import Wizard - Step 2 of 3

This screen lets you set the delimiters your data contains. You can see how your text is affected in the preview below.

Delimiters
- ☑ Tab
- ☐ Semicolon
- ☐ Comma
- ☐ Space
- ☐ Other:
- ☐ Treat consecutive delimiters as one
- Text qualifier: "

Data preview

```
Month,January,February,March,April,May,June,July,August,September,October,N
Number of students,12,23,34,13,24,21,34,10,27,37,12,22
Class Number,10,20,30,40,50,60,70,80,90,100,110,120
File color,red,orange,yellow,green,blue,indigo,violet,tan,white,black,grey
```

[Cancel]   [< Back]   [Next >]   [Finish]

Figure 7-3: Step 2 of the Text Import Wizard for a CSV text file.

On the second page of the wizard, you define how the data is delimited. You can see that Excel expects the file to be delimited by tabs, but that it offers you several other options to choose from.

 Information Kiosk

Tab-delimited files are referred to as TSV files, but are saved as text files. This format is a common one for data coming from another spreadsheet, a database, a Word table, or an online location.

4. **In the Delimiters area, deselect the Tab option and select the Comma option.**

When you deselect the Tab check box, nothing happens. However, when you select the Comma check box, vertical lines replace the commas in the data, as shown in Figure 7-4.

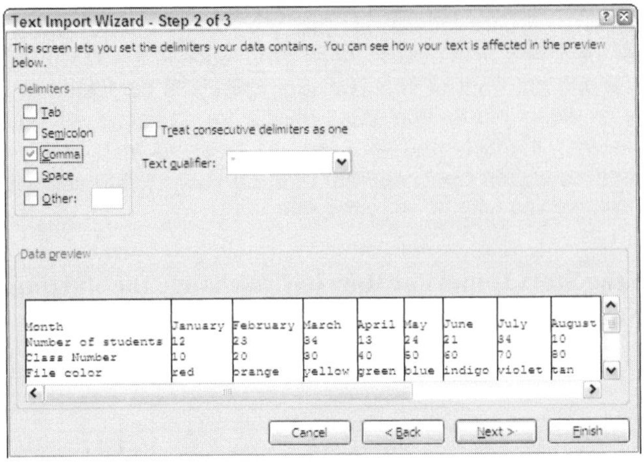

Figure 7-4: Step 2 of the Text Import Wizard for a CSV text file with the comma delimiter selected.

5. **Click the Next button to continue.**

The third screen of the Text Import Wizard appears, as shown in Figure 7-5.

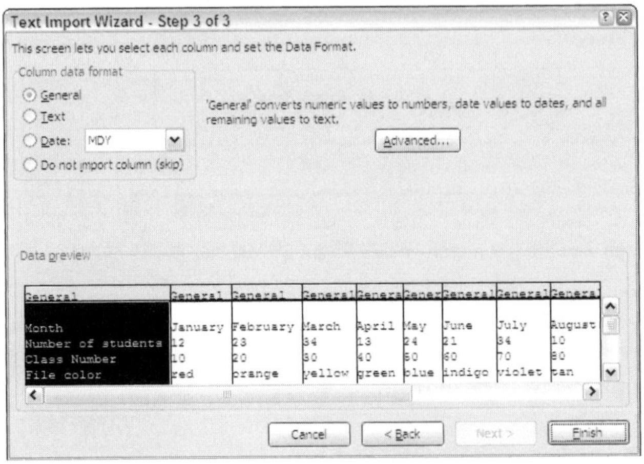

Figure 7-5: Step 3 of the Text Import Wizard for a CSV text file.

On the third page of the wizard, you define the format for the data as it is imported. You can also choose not to import a specific column. Each column can be formatted as general data, text data, or a date.

To the right of the Column Data Format list is an Advanced button. You use the advanced options to further define how numbers in your data are imported.

6. Leave all the columns with General formatting.

In your data, no columns contain only dates or numbers, so you can reasonably leave the formatting alone.

7. Click the Finish button.

The wizard closes, and the data appears in columns in an Excel sheet, as shown in Figure 7-6.

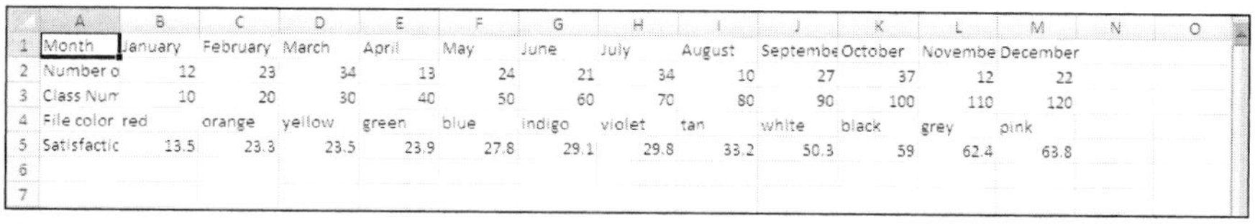

	A	B	C	D	E	F	G	H	I	J	K	L	M	N	O
1	Month	January	February	March	April	May	June	July	August	Septembe	October	Novembe	December		
2	Number o	12	23	34	13	24	21	34	10	27	37	12	22		
3	Class Num	10	20	30	40	50	60	70	80	90	100	110	120		
4	File color	red	orange	yellow	green	blue	indigo	violet	tan	white	black	grey	pink		
5	Satisfactic	13.5	23.3	23.5	23.9	27.8	29.1	29.8	33.2	50.3	59	62.4	63.8		
6															
7															

Figure 7-6: An imported CSV file.

You can now format this data as a table or work with it as it exists.

8. Use the Save As command to save your work as a new Excel file named Ch7CSVDataFromTextFile.xlsx**.**

You can, before you close the file, compare the data formatting to that of the data copied from Word in the preceding exercise.

Importing a CSV file

In the following steps, you import a CSV file into Excel:

1. In Windows Explorer, copy the file `SampleCommaData.csv` to your workspace.

Because Excel knows what a CSV file is, you can open a CSV file by double-clicking it. You do this now to see whether there are any differences in the process.

2. Double-click the copy of `SampleCommaData.csv` that you just created.

This step should be much easier than importing a `.txt` file. Because Excel recognized the extension as containing a CSV file, it knew that your file was a delimited file with commas as delimiters. It didn't need to ask you anything; it just processed the file and opened it.

Watch Your Step

Because Excel knows how to handle CSV files, you don't get the chance to tell it not to open the first records. If your file is saved as a CSV file, it needs to start with the right data and contain only valid data.

If the data isn't right (if there are commas in a CSV file other than as column delimiters, for example), Excel assumes that you intend for the commas to be delimiters. The cell is split at the extra comma, and all further columns are one column "off." You can fix this problem by editing your data in Excel, but it is something that you should know can happen. In these cases, it is usually easier to edit the CSV file before, rather than after, you bring it into Excel.

3. Use the Save As command to save your work as a new Excel file named **Ch7CSVDataFromCSVFile.xlsx,** and then close Excel.

If you want, you can compare the data formatting to that of the other Word and text files you created in the previous exercises before you close the file.

Importing a fixed data file

Your next step is to open a file that isn't delimited. Again, the data is the same as in the two previous exercises, but you notice differences in the process:

1. Open Excel, click the Office Button, and choose Open. Using the drop-down arrow, change the file type to Text Files.

If it isn't in the list, scroll down to find it.

2. Select the file **SampleFixedData.txt.**

The first screen of the Text Import Wizard appears, just as it did earlier in this chapter, in the section "Importing a delimited .txt file."

3. Change the starting row to 2 and click the Next button.

The second screen of the Text Import Wizard appears, as shown in Figure 7-7. Notice that it is significantly different now.

Excel doesn't know where your column breaks are. It has made its best guess that you want a column break every ten spaces. That number isn't what you want, though, so you have to change the column width for the first column. The other columns are correct.

4. Click the first vertical line. Drag it to the left so that it appears to go off the preview. Let go of the mouse button. This will delete the extra column break.

When you finish, the column markers align with your data. If you decide to remove one of the column separators, you can do so by double-clicking the line. If you need a new separator, you can add it by clicking where you need it.

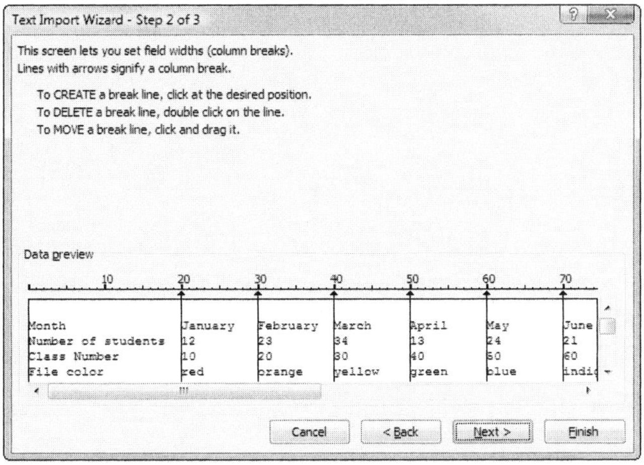

Figure 7-7: Step 2 of the Text Import Wizard for a fixed-width text file.

5. When you have all the separators positioned, click the Next button.

The third screen of the Text Import Wizard appears just as it did in the earlier exercise.

6. Just as before, you don't do any special formatting on this data, so click the Finish button.

The wizard closes, and the data appears in columns in an Excel sheet, just as it did earlier.

7. Click in cell F1, and click again on the Formula Bar at the end of the word.

Notice that Excel removed the extra spaces from your data as it imported it. Each column now contains only the data and not the extra spaces that were dividing the columns.

8. Use the Save As command to save your work as a new Excel file with the name Ch7FixedDataFromTextFile.xlsx, **and then close Excel.**

You can, before you close the file, compare the data formatting to that of the other files you created in this chapter.

The process you just completed is one that can save you much time and effort as you work with data in the future. Knowing how to import data from other sources can save you hours of typing time and ensure that the data you are importing looks just as it did in the source file.

Information Kiosk

Sometimes, it seems that no matter what you do, getting data from a text file into Excel is difficult. In these cases, using Find and Replace in Word can be a great time-saver. For example, if a document has data that was laid out by using the Tab key for spacing, you find that replacing two tabs with a single tab throughout the entire document gives you a cleaner import. In addition, if you are importing numerous blank rows, you can search for double returns and replace them with single ones.

Grabbing data from the Web

One of the cooler features of Excel is its ability to grab data from a Web page and then store the data in Excel and keep it updated (as long as you are connected to the Web). This feature is one that you will either use all the time or never touch again after you finish this chapter. I use it, so I show it to you. Follow these steps:

1. **Open a blank sheet in Excel. Choose Data → Get External Data → From Web.**

The New Web Query window opens to your selected home page.

2. **Change the URL to** http://www.erh.noaa.gov **and click Go. Enter** 12345 **for the zip code in the Local Forecast box in the top-left corner of the Web page and click Go.**

The Web page changes to show the weather data for Schenectady, New York. The page looks normal, except that a number of yellow arrows are scattered over the page, as shown in Figure 7-8.

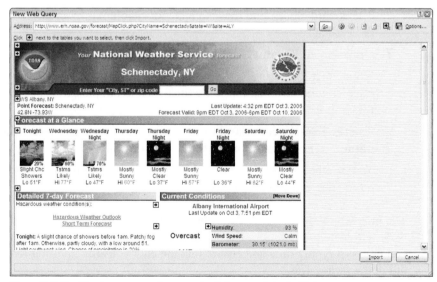

Figure 7-8: The Weather.com weather page for Schenectady in the Web query page.

3. Click the yellow arrow next to the word Humidity. You might need to expand the page to see this section of the page.

The arrow changes from yellow to green and becomes a check mark. You have told Excel that the data in this table is the data you want to link to live.

4. Click the Import button in the lower-right corner of the window. The Import Data window appears. Click OK to accept the default location.

The first cell is temporarily filled in with a statement that your query is being created and updated. When the update is done, cells A1 through B7 contain the data from the Web site, as shown in Figure 7-9.

	A	B	C	D	E	F	G	H
1	Humidity:	32%						
2	Wind Speed:	W 8 MPH						
3	Barometer:	29.92" (1013.7 mb)						
4	Dewpoint:	-9°F (-23°C)						
5	Wind Chill:	5°F (-15°C)						
6	Visibility:	10.00 mi.						
7	More Local Wx:	2 Day History:						
8								
9								
10								
11								
12								
13								
14								
15								
16								
17								
18								

Sheet1   Sheet2   Sheet3

Figure 7-9: Results of the weather Web query.

The power of the Web query is that the data is updated live as long as you are connected to the Web. To see it happen, leave the page alone for about 15 minutes, and then come back and continue.

5. If the data on your screen has not changed, choose Data → Connections → Refresh All.

If the Refresh All button doesn't appear, click the drop-down arrow to find the Refresh selections on the list.

Watch Your Step

When you click the Refresh All button, you might see a security notice warning you that the data you are connecting to comes from an outside source and can potentially be harmful. In this case, because you created the Web query and know that it is from a safe source, you can click OK and update the data. If you open a file that isn't from a known safe sender, you should think twice before casually clicking the OK button.

As with other imported data, you can work with this data in any way you work with data from any other source. Although this simple example doesn't make it obvious, there is much power behind this feature.

If you track stocks, you can log in to your stock account and set up a Web query to gather the past few months' worth of data for the stocks you follow. Setting up charts to see how the stocks are doing, as explained in Chapter 6, gives you current stock information at a glance at any time.

If you are responsible for tracking your company's inventory from a Web site, you can set up a Web query to gather the current inventory numbers and save the sheet with the query. Create conditional formatting rules for the data gathered by the query, and you can see at a glance when inventory is low or out.

Information Kiosk

You can (and often will) import files from other sources to existing Excel sheets. To do this, use the selections in the Get External Data group on the Data tab. Use these options to select data from a text file as you have just done, or from the other sources you are about to explore.

Linking to Data in Other Excel Worksheets

Another powerful way to get data into your Excel 2007 files is to link to the data in other Excel files. You have two options:

- Paste the data and keep it linked.
- Reference the data directly by using formulas.

How do you choose?

You really don't have to follow any hard-and-fast rules about when to reference the data directly and when to paste the data and link it. If you want to see the data, you should paste and link it. The data is always there, and you can set it to update automatically so that it is current. If you have a large amount of data, you probably should reference it to keep your worksheet content manageable.

Pasting and linking to the data

In this exercise, you again work with the satisfaction data for the HighLowe Corporation new-employee orientation sessions. This time, you replace the satisfaction rating for each of the sessions in the text data with a link to the cell that computes the values. By linking to the actual data rather than just having it pasted in as a number, you ensure that the data is current when you need it. Follow these steps:

1. Click the Office Button and choose Open, select both **ExcelToExcelBaseFile.xlsx** and **LinkedDatasheet.xlsx**, and click Open.

Two different Excel files are now open.

2. **Switch between the files by using the taskbar or pressing the Alt+Tab key combination. Switch back the same way.**

Make sure that you end in the `LinkedDatasheet.xlsx` file.

3. **Select cells B5 through M5 (the course averages). Press Ctrl+C to copy the cells.**

4. **Switch back to the `ExcelToExcelBaseFile` file. Select cells B5 through M5, and then press Ctrl+V to paste the copied cells.**

Each cell displays an error message. That is because Excel is trying to use the formulas on the data in this sheet rather than in the other sheet.

5. **To fix the error, find the Paste Options flag. From its drop-down list, select the Link Cells option.**

If you notice the value on the Formula Bar, it should now say `=[LinkedDatasheet.xlsx]Sheet1!B5` — that is the reference link to the cell in the other file for cell B5, as shown in Figure 7-10. If you scroll through the cells, you see that each of the other cells contains a similar formula with a different (but correct) cell reference for each cell.

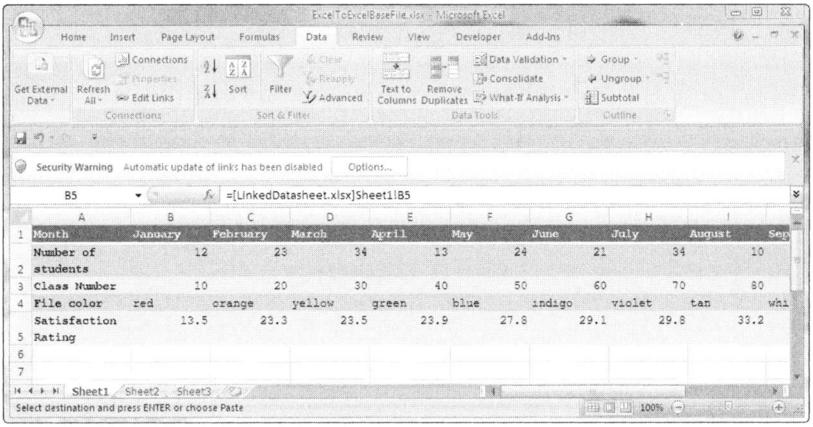

Figure 7-10: The Formula Bar for a cell with a linked equation.

6. **Close and save the `ExcelToExcelBaseFile` file.**

You see the linked data again from `LinkedDatasheet.xlsx`. You will now change some data in the linked file so that you can see it change when you open the other file.

7. **Change the value for cell B10 to** 16.1**. Change the value for cell C21 to** 21.8**. Change the value for cell D23 to** 69**.**

As you have changed each cell, the average for that course also has changed. Now you will open the other file to see the data update there.

8. Choose Office → Open to open `ExcelToExcelBaseFile.xlsx` from the location where you saved it.

If you prefer, you can open the file by selecting it from the Recent Documents list on the right side of the Office Button menu.

When you opened the file, the data should have been automatically updated to show the values as they are in the other sheet, as shown in Figure 7-11.

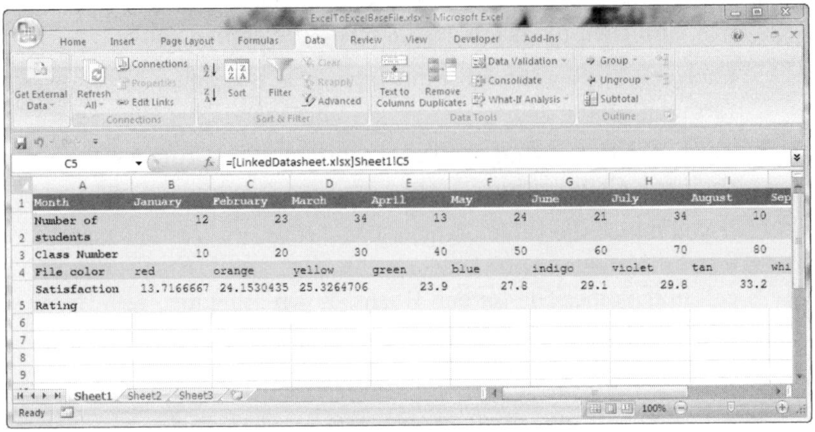

Figure 7-11: Updated data from the linked file.

9. Close and save the `ExcelToExcelBaseFile` file.

Even though you have made no changes to the file, you are prompted to save changes because Excel automatically updated the linked data and knows that the data has changed.

Referencing the data directly

You probably figured it out already, but the process for referencing the data directly is just about the same as pasting with a link. The difference is that you put the cell references into your formula rather than copy the cell. To reference the data directly, follow these steps:

1. Open `ExcelToExcelBaseFile.xlsx` from the location where you saved it in the preceding section.

Now that both files are open, you will re-create the formula from the data file in the base file. When you keep the formulas separate from the data, you can update data without having to worry about wiping out your formulas.

2. In cell B7 of `ExcelToExcelBaseFile.xlsx`, type =Sum(.

3. Move to the file `LinkedDatasheet.xlsx`, and select cells B7 through B56.

4. Type the close parenthesis.

The close parenthesis is shown in the formula box for cell B7, as is the formula you have entered so far:

```
=Sum([LinkedDatasheet.xlsx]Sheet1!$B$7:$B$56)
```

5. Type /Count(.

6. Select the same range of cells a second time.

7. Type the close parenthesis.

The entire formula should now appear in this box, like this:

```
=Sum([LinkedDatasheet.xlsx]Sheet1!$B$7:$B$56)/Count
([LinkedDatasheet.xlsx]Sheet1!$B$7:$B$56)
```

If you accidentally press Enter before typing either of the parentheses, Excel tells you that your formula is wrong and asks whether you want it corrected. Click OK to accept the correction.

8. Press Enter to apply the formula.

If you got the formula right, the result is the same as it is in cell B5.

Why use the reference rather than copy the cell with the formula? Mostly, it is a matter of circumstance. If your data will be refreshed from text files regularly, you likely want to keep the formula separated from the data. If not, you might want to keep the formulas with the data and paste-link the cell containing the formulas.

Pulling Data from Access

Access is the Office product that handles databases. Databases contain linked data that crosses multiple dimensions. Whereas an Excel file can handle data and calculations well, an Access database is used to maintain connections between the data. Many databases are out there that you might use regularly. For example, when you run a search on Google, you access its database of Web pages and get back the data that meets the criteria you request.

You might or might not have Access installed on your machine. If you do, you can work along with this exercise; if you don't, read the exercise and skip to the next section:

1. Copy the file **Northwind2007.accdb** to either your desktop or your My Documents folder. If necessary, download the file from the Microsoft site. To find it, search for Northwind 2007.

2. Open Access. Click the Office Button and choose Open to open the copy of the file.

3. Follow the directions on the opening screen to enable the disabled content.

In this exercise, you pull data from the Northwind Traders database into Excel. Northwind Traders, the sample database that is available from Microsoft to all

Access users, is preset with tables of data so that you can pull data into your Excel file without your having to know how to use Access.

4. **After you have enabled the content, you are prompted to log in as a member of the Northwind team. Click the Login button to log in as the user Andrew Cencin, one of the default names associated with the database.**

When you reach this point, you have a database that is available for you to link to from Excel.

5. **Close Access and open a blank file in Excel. Choose Data → Get External Data → From Access. Browse to and open the Northwind Access file you just created.**

The Select Table dialog box appears, as shown in Figure 7-12.

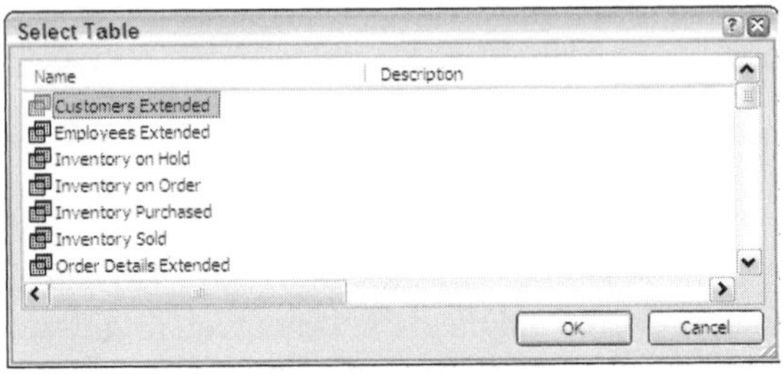

Figure 7-12: The Select Table dialog box.

This dialog box lists the tables and queries in the database and allows you to choose the one you want to pull your data from. You want to work with orders that have been processed, so you use the Product Orders query.

6. **Click the Product Orders entry from the list and click the OK button.**

The Import Data dialog box appears, as shown in Figure 7-13.

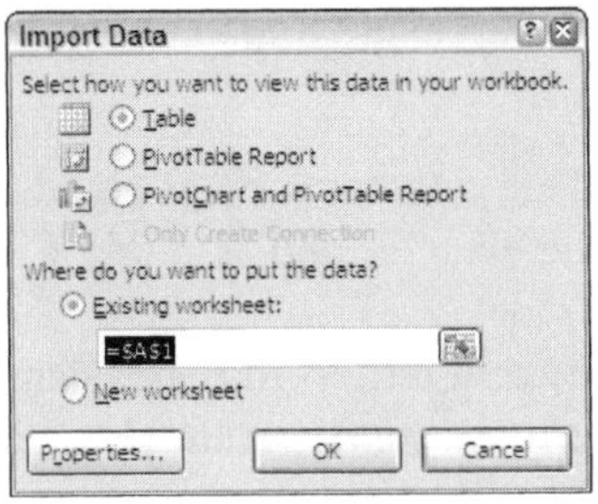

Figure 7-13: The Import Data dialog box.

In this dialog box, you pick which data you want to import into your worksheet and where you want it to go. In a real world situation, your next step with this data would be to place it in a PivotTable to learn what you can from the data. Because this scenario is likely for data pulled from Access, you can use the

Import Data dialog box to pull the data directly into a PivotTable or both a PivotTable and a PivotChart.

 Transfer

PivotTables and PivotCharts are described in detail in Chapter 6.

7. **Click the PivotChart and PivotTable Report radio button, and then click the New Worksheet radio button to place the data on a new worksheet. Click OK.**

Your screen changes to show a PivotTable waiting to be created. As you select fields for the PivotTable, you see corresponding changes in the chart.

Now you can create a chart to answer your questions about the data. In this case, you create a simple PivotChart to see how much product was sold during the reported period.

8. **Select the Order Date field and drag it to the Axis Fields list at the bottom of the task pane. Select the Product ID field and drag it to the Values list. Summarize the data by the Count of Product ID. (If you don't remember how to set up the PivotTable, refer to Chapter 6.)**

Your chart should now show the number of different products sold on any given day, as shown in Figure 7-14.

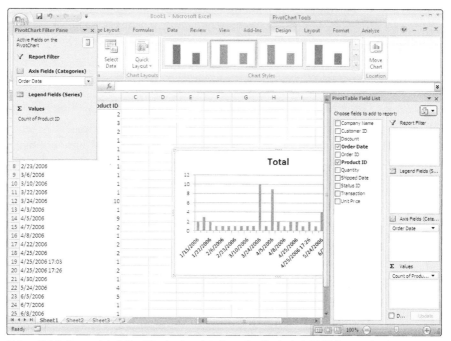

Figure 7-14: A completed PivotChart using data from the Northwind 2007 Access database.

Information Kiosk

You can pull data from other databases in the same way that you pull it from Access. You are prompted to set up a connection to the database and log in, but from there the process is the same as doing it from Access. If you expect to pull data from databases other than Access, work with your database administrator to get your account information and determine the setup of the data you want to evaluate.

Pulling Data from an Existing Database Connection

In addition to pulling data from places you set up, several database connections are preset for you within Excel 2007. After you have added a connection to a database, as you did in the preceding section, you can pull data by using that connection in any other Excel file that is on the same machine and has the same login information.

To pull data from an existing connection, you create a worksheet by using the data you can pull from the MSN currency rate database:

Watch Your Step

Two of the advantages to using data stored in a database are that the data can be updated automatically and your Excel sheet doesn't grab the new data until you establish the connection. In this exercise, therefore, what you see on-screen will look similar but contain different data. You see the currency rates for your dates rather than the data shown here.

1. **If the file from the preceding Access exercise is still open, close it, and then open a blank file in Excel.**

2. **Choose Data → Get External Data → Existing Connections.**

The Existing Connections dialog box appears, as shown in Figure 7-15.

You see the connections available from your machine, listed in order of access to the connection. After you establish a connection, it is shown on this list. As you can see, the Northwind 2007 Product Orders table is at the bottom of the list because it was the most recently established connection.

Next, you connect to the currency rate database.

3. **Click the MSN MoneyCentral Investor Currency Rates entry, and then click Open.**

The short version of the Import Data dialog box appears so that you can tell Excel where you want the data placed when it is imported.

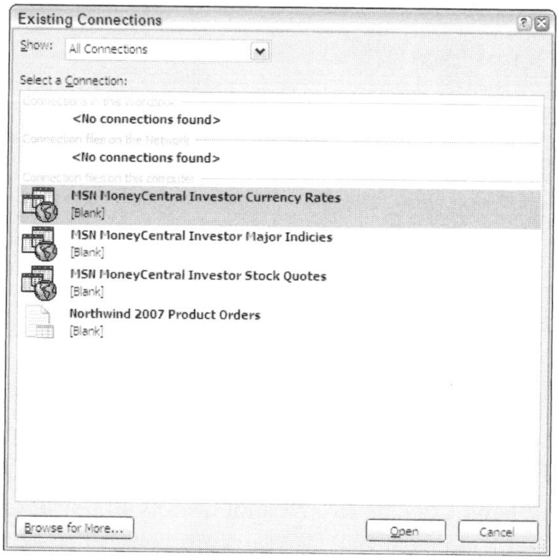

Figure 7-15: The Existing Connections dialog box.

4. Click the OK button to import the data into the current worksheet.

Just as with the Web connections, a slight delay might occur while the site is contacted and the data gathered. After the data is gathered, it is added to your worksheet, starting in cell A1. The top of the sheet is shown in Figure 7-16.

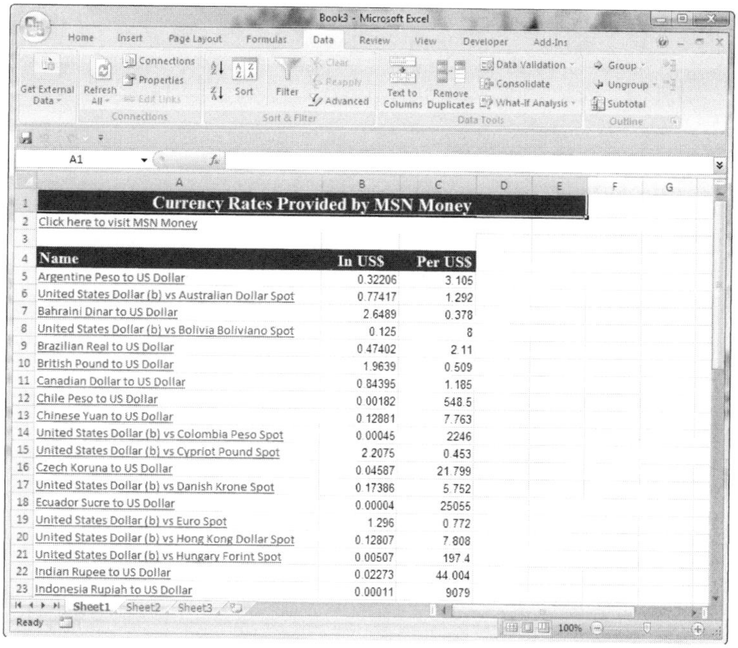

Figure 7-16: Currency rates for February 2007.

You now know how to pull and use data from a wide variety of non-Excel files. Being able to pull data from other sources means less work for you, better data, and more consistent results. By using either linked cells or connections to databases to link to data, you ensure that the data you are using needs to be updated in only one place, saving time and money. That's always a good thing!

CSV (comma-separated values): A special kind of text file where the data in the file is made up of values separated by commas.

database: A multidimensional storage facility for data. Data in a database is related to another in any of a number of ways, including by hierarchy and by relation.

database connection: The mechanism for pulling external data from a database.

delimiter: The character used to separate columns or fields of data in a file.

external data: Data that is stored in Excel but originates in another program or on another computer.

import: To add data to an Excel file from a file that exists elsewhere. The importing of data saves time and effort by reducing the time spent having to rework data. In addition, data imported into a file is less likely to have errors in it than data that is retyped.

linked data: Data that resides in another file but is connected to the current file by reference.

pulling data: Using one program to get data from another; the reverse of pushing data.

pushing data:. Sending data from one program to another; the reverse of pulling data.

text file: A file on your computer that contains only printable characters, not formatting or control characters. Data that is imported into Excel is separated into columns by way of a delimiter or a specific number of characters.

Last Stop

Practice Exam

1. Which of the following is not an advantage of importing data into Excel?

    a. Importing data removes errors placed there originally.

    b. Importing data is faster than retyping it.

    c. Importing data eliminates the addition of new typing errors.

    d. b and c.

2. Name one advantage to working with data in Excel rather than in Word.

_____

3. True or False: A comma is the only delimiter that Excel knows how to handle.

4. Survey questions with a limit of 256 characters per answer are an example of _____ data.

5. When you import data from a CSV file, extra commas

    a. are ignored.

    b. create new columns.

    c. divide large numbers.

    d. tell Excel that the data is a paragraph.

6. True or False: You can change the length of the fields in a nondelimited file.

7. Data grabbed from the Web

    a. cannot be refreshed.

    b. cannot be stored locally.

    c. must be grabbed from the entire Web page or not at all.

    d. can be of any type.

8. Name one situation where you would link to data rather than import it.

_____

_____

9. True or False: Access is the only database program that Excel can talk to.

10. One reason that Excel can now handle larger amounts of data is the prevalence of data being imported from _____.

8

Designing Your Data for Viewing and Printing

- Using Page Layout view to design a worksheet that will look good when printed
- Setting print areas to control what you print
- Adding graphical elements
- Applying a theme to improve the look of your worksheet

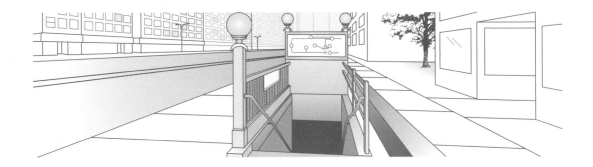

 # Enter the Station

Questions

1. How do you change to Page Layout view?

2. How do you show gridlines when you view a worksheet but not when you print it?

3. Can a print area cross worksheet boundaries?

4. Can a print area cross page boundaries?

5. Which two Excel elements can use theme information?

Express Line

If you are already familiar with creating worksheets for printing and then printing them in Excel 2007, skip ahead to the next chapter.

When most people think of Excel, they visualize row after row of numbers and formulas that are shown on a screen. If they picture printed information at all, it is either in the form of charts, which we covered in Chapter 4, or data sheets added to Word or PowerPoint and formatted there.

With Excel 2007, Microsoft emphasizes allowing you to create and format your data at the same time. The idea is to help you to work smarter. For example, rather than let you ignore what the formatting looks like until later, Excel 2007 is designed to encourage you to think about how the data looks and is shared as well as what the data is.

In this chapter, you will learn how to set up your data to look good from the moment you enter it into Excel. You have already learned about one of the first steps in creating good-looking data: using tables. The more you get used to using tables, the easier it will be to format your data from the beginning.

Information Kiosk

In this chapter, you need to have a printer attached to your machine from which you can print test documents. Then you can see what the printed pages look like and compare them to what you see on the screen.

Determining What and When to Print

The Ferguson Farms employee time sheet you use in this chapter is a good example of an Excel worksheet that can be used either interactively or off the printed page. How do you know when to print and when not to? Here are a couple of scenarios:

- If every employee has access to a common computer or to a file on a shared drive, the individual time sheet forms can be completed online and may never need to be printed. The summary form can be printed for recordkeeping and time evaluation.

- If not all employees have access to the computer, the form as it has been designed can be printed. Then employees can fill in their time sheets weekly, and someone else can enter the data into the Excel file.

Another scenario where documents need to be printed is when you use signature documents. Although it is helpful to have a computer record indicating the hours that were worked and reported, most companies need to have printed time sheets signed and then filed for audit purposes.

I believe in printing the least possible amount of paper. If a worksheet can be made to look good in a small area, print it. If the worksheet needs to be larger to be understood, consider printing only those parts that are applicable and needed. After all, in today's world of constant access, you can just as easily open a spreadsheet and look at it on a computer or by using a projector as you can look at it on paper.

Even so, sometimes a printed sheet is needed. In that case, always verify that you are printing only the data you need. Also, always verify that the sheet you are printing looks professional and that it is readable and available to those who need it.

Designing a Worksheet in Page Layout View

Picturing your data as a table is a great place to start. However, Excel 2007 has a built-in way — Page Layout view — for you to think about formatted data, not just rows and columns of information.

In previous versions of Excel, to see how your data would look when printed, you had to use Print Preview and hope that you could see your data on-screen. It was hard to work with the data in individual cells while looking at it in Print Preview mode, so people left the task of formatting their work until after the data was entered and they were ready to create final printouts of it.

Now you can view your data directly in Page Layout view and set it up the way you want it to print. In this chapter, you start with a worksheet that is in progress and adjust it for data entry, data computations, and printing all at one time.

In the following exercise, you create a time sheet for employees of Ferguson Farms. This single time sheet can be used in two different ways: Employees can enter their data directly into the worksheet or print it and fill in their information on paper.

Adding a header and footer

Follow these steps to add a header and footer to the time sheet in Page Layout view:

1. Open the file named **FergusonFarms.xlsx**.

2. Choose View → Workbook Views → Page Layout View.

Notice that the look of your worksheet changes drastically. Excel has added horizontal and vertical rulers to the column letter and row number headings, as shown in Figure 8-1.

Additionally, rather than start immediately with row 1, your page now has these characteristics:

- The page starts with the words *Click to add header*.

- The page margins are shown.

- Fewer cells are shown at a time. In fact, only those cells that fit on a page are shown.

- The first part of the page to the right is shown.

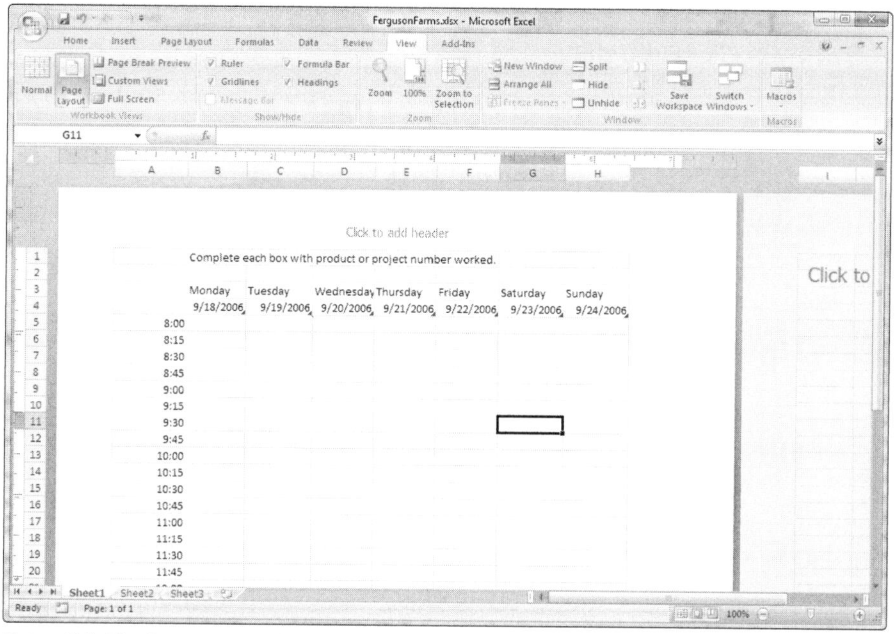

Figure 8-1: Viewing your spreadsheet in Page Layout view.

If you scroll down the page, you notice that the page ends with the words *Click to add footer.* If you scroll further down the page, you move to the top of another page. The same thing happens if you scroll to the right — you end up on a new page.

Excel has started you down the path toward thinking about pages rather than just about raw data. To be able to continue down this path, you need to change to the Page Layout tab and start working with the worksheet formatting.

You start with some of the setup options that Excel provides. As you work through the rest of this chapter, you learn when to use the options that Excel 2007 offers for formatting and when to create what you need from scratch.

Information Kiosk

Working in Page Layout view, you can instantly tell when the data you are working with no longer fits on a single printable page. You can then fix column widths and page margins as you go rather than try to fix problems later, such as when you have to meet a deadline.

3. Click in the area labeled Click to Add Header. Type Ferguson Farms. Press Enter and type Employee Time Tracker.

4. Scroll down the page and click in the area labeled Click to Add Footer.

5. Choose **Header & Footer Tools Design → Header & Footer Elements → Current Date.**

Notice that the footer is filled in with the date code for today's date.

6. Click in the box on the right. Choose **Header & Footer Tools Design → Header & Footer Elements → Sheet Name.**

The footer now shows the sheet name on the right (Sheet 1) and today's date in the middle, as shown in Figure 8-2.

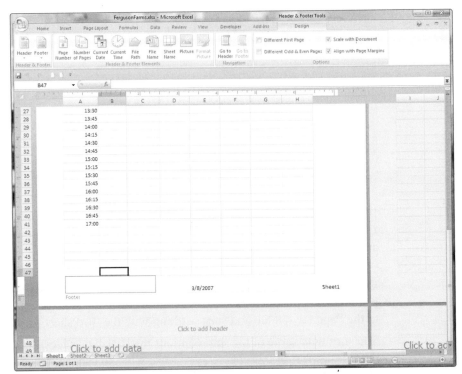

Figure 8-2: The bottom of the time sheet with footer information added.

7. Double-click this worksheet's sheet name (which is now Sheet 1) and change it to your name. Click in any cell on the first page to see the change in the footer.

Notice that the right-hand box is filled in with your name.

8. Select cells B3 through H3. From the font list on the Home tab, change the font for the days of the week to Franklin Gothic Medium, 14 point. Adjust the column width so that the days fit in the columns.

9. Select cells B4 through H4. Right-click, choose Format Cells, and change the date format to 18-Sep-06.

When you complete these steps, the top of your time sheet should look somewhat like Figure 8-3. To be sure that you are getting what you need, print the document.

		A	B	C	D	E	F	G	H	I

B4 ▾ ⨍ₓ 9/18/2006

Ferguson Farms
Employee Time Tracker
Complete each box with product or project number worked.

	Monday	Tuesday	Wednesday	Thursday	Friday	Saturday	Sunday
4	18-Sep-06	19-Sep-06	20-Sep-06	21-Sep-06	22-Sep-06	23-Sep-06	24-Sep-06
5	8:00						
6	8:15						
7	8:30						
8	8:45						
9	9:00						
10	9:15						
11	9:30						
12	9:45						
13	10:00						
14	10:15						
15	10:30						
16	10:45						
17	11:00						
18	11:15						
19	11:30						
20	11:45						

Click to

Kathy Jacobs / Sheet2 / Sheet3

Ready   Page: 1 of 1   Average: 21-Sep-06   Count: 7   Sum: 30-Jan-47   100%

Figure 8-3: Your time sheet should look like this one after you format the days and dates.

10. **Print your worksheet and verify that it looks similar to what you expect.**

Notice that I said "similar to," not "exactly like." Excel 2007 calculates the page size based on the printer you are using and the drivers installed on your computer. That page size tells Excel how much data can fit on a single page. Your computer stores the page size information in the default print settings.

If you print your worksheet with different kinds of printers, you may see different numbers of cells on each page. To prepare the sheet for this potential problem, I have designed a sheet with very large margins. If your pages don't fit the way you expect, choose Page Layout ➜ Page Setup ➜ Margins and select from the list of potential margins to change your specific settings.

Your printout may differ from the one shown in Figure 8-4 and the one you see on-screen. Although gridlines are turned on for viewing, they are not turned on for printing.

11. **Verify that the Gridlines Print and View check boxes in the Sheet Options group of the Page Layout tab are deselected.**

Watch Your Step

In previous versions of Excel, gridlines were always on when you viewed a sheet, but could be turned on or off for printing. In Excel 2007, gridline visibility is determined separately for printing and viewing. You control the display of gridlines by selecting or deselecting two check boxes in the Sheet Options group on the Page Layout tab. When you select both check boxes, all gridlines are shown. When you deselect both boxes, gridlines aren't shown on-screen or on your printouts. In addition, you can have one set of gridlines turned on and the other turned off.

Now none of the gridlines for this sheet appears on-screen or on any printouts, as shown in Figure 8-4. After the data is entered into Excel, the lack of gridlines gives a cleaner appearance both on-screen and in print.

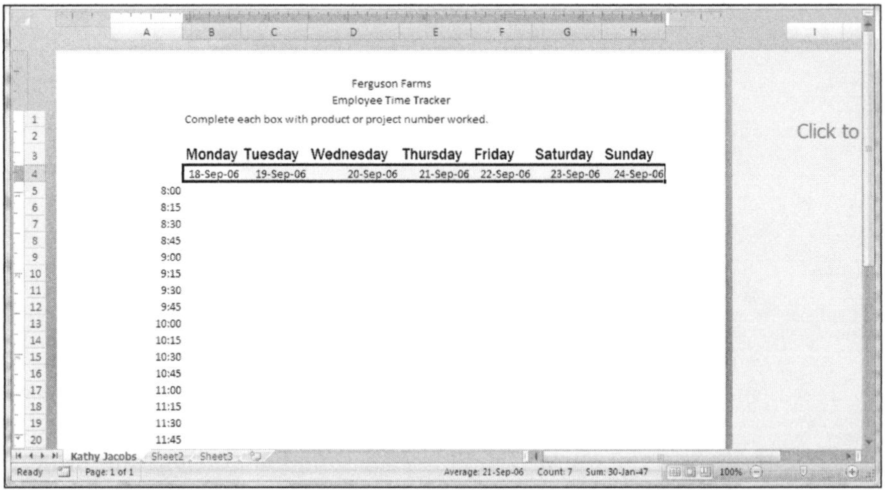

Figure 8-4: The time tracker sheet has gridlines turned off.

Adding cell borders

Even though you don't want to see the gridlines for this sheet, you want its cells to have a border in a particular section of the sheet. By adding cell borders to the main cells of the Ferguson Farms time sheet, employees can more easily fill in the time sheet either on paper or on the computer.

Continuing with the Ferguson Farms time tracker worksheet that you created in the preceding section, follow these steps to add cell borders to the main cells and to a Totals row at the bottom of the worksheet:

1. **Select cells B5 through H41. Right-click in the selected area and choose Format Cells.**

   The Format Cells dialog box appears. You can set the border for any cell or group of cells by using this dialog box.

2. **Click the Border tab, as shown in Figure 8-5.**

3. **In the Style box, click the lower-right border style from the list and then, in the Presets area, click the Inside button.**

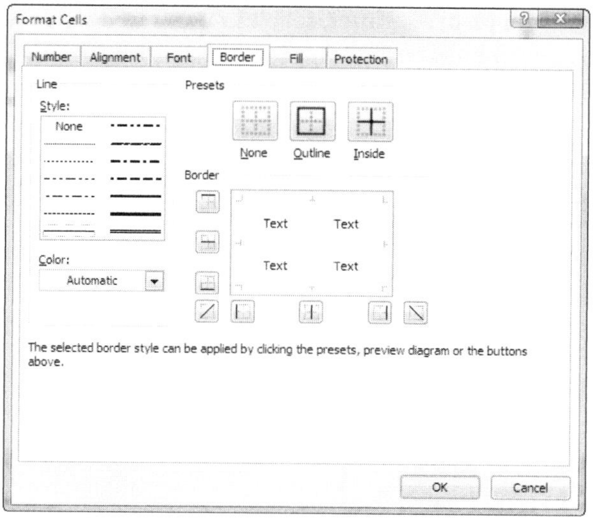

Figure 8-5: The Border tab in the Format Cells dialog box.

4. **In the Style box, click the heavy solid line (the one just above the double line that you clicked in Step 3), and then click the Outline button.**

The dialog box should look like the one shown in Figure 8-6.

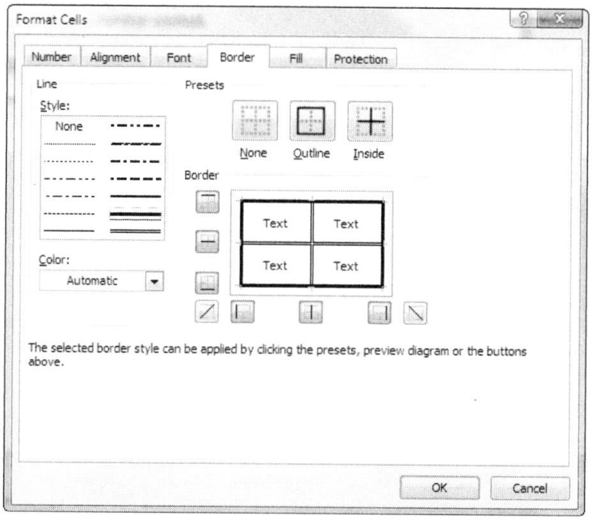

Figure 8-6: The cell border settings for the time grid area.

5. Click the OK button or press Enter. Click in a cell to deselect the entire range and see the cell borders.

Steps 1 through 5 apply a double-line border to the individual cells and apply a heavy black line to the outside of the time block area, as shown in Figure 8-7. This process sets off the data area distinctively from the rest of the worksheet.

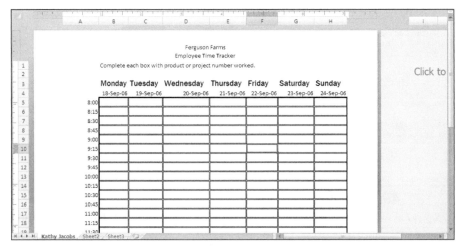

Figure 8-7: This time sheet has a grid added for time sections.

6. Scroll down to row 42. Select cells B42 through H42.

7. Choose Home → Styles → Cell Styles. Select the Total option for the cell style.

8. Print your worksheet, and verify that it looks similar to what you expect.

The bottom of your time sheet should look like the one shown in Figure 8-8, in both the printed and on-screen versions.

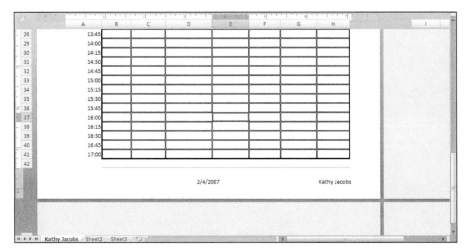

Figure 8-8: A time sheet with cell borders applied.

Step Into the Real World

Because all employees of Ferguson Farms will use the same worksheet setup for their time sheets, it becomes a simple matter to create an overall time summary sheet.

To add this functionality, you start by adding a summary sheet in the same format as the individual sheets and placing it in front of the current sheet. After that, you add one sheet for each employee.

On the summary sheet, set up a formula to summarize the hours worked for each project in an hour and pull the data from each individual time sheet. When the formulas are completed, the summarization sheet shows the total hours for each type of produce or product.

Performing these simple steps takes this single page of data to a whole new level. You can now evaluate how time is being spent, determine whether project estimates are correct, and find out who is working too much overtime. You can even go a step further and evaluate which produce takes the most interaction to grow so that you can factor the extra time into the cost of the produce.

Adding another page of data

As you scroll to the right in your worksheet, notice that the next page to the right is shown. However, rather than show cells, the page shows the words *Click to add data.* This is the Excel 2007 way of telling you that if you need more columns of data, you can add them — although, until you do, the unused columns are not printed or shown on-screen.

On the other hand, if you scroll down your worksheet to see the rows on the next page, you notice that the page is blue. Excel 2007 does not tell you to click to add data, however, because it knows that you have defined the appearance of columns A through H. The data on pages below the first one take on the same width as, and look the same as, the data that is already in the upper parts of the columns. To add data below the current page, merely click in the cell you want to use and add your data.

Defining a Print Area for Your Worksheet

The amount of data that fits on a single worksheet in Excel is much more than the amount that fits on a printed page. Moreover, the amount is more than you usually would want to print in a given session. Usually, you do not print every cell that you use to store data in an Excel file. Instead, you most often want to print the data that you need to share with someone else.

To tell Excel which part of your worksheet you want to print, you define a print area. In some worksheets, such as the Ferguson Farms time sheet you just created, identifying the *print area* is easy: It is the area you have defined as one time sheet. In other worksheets, the area you need to print spreads across multiple pages. However, you cannot set a print area that crosses a worksheet boundary. Each worksheet has its own print area whether you have explicitly defined one or not.

Follow these steps to set the print area for your worksheet:

1. Continue with the Ferguson Farms Employee Time Tracker worksheet or open the `FergusonFarms2.xlsx` file.

2. Choose Page Layout ➜ Page Setup ➜ Print Area.

Two options appear: Set Print Area and Clear Print Area. Even though you have not yet set a print area, one is already defined. By default, the print area for a worksheet is the area containing all the cells with data.

 ## Watch Your Step

Before you print an Excel worksheet, choose Office ➜ Print ➜ Print Preview to ensure that you are printing only the data you need. Many times, I have seen someone print what was supposed to be a small worksheet, only to have 20 or 30 blank pages be printed before stopping the printer. All those blank pages were the result of the user not checking the print preview to catch any cells with data in them somewhere outside the intended print area. You may recall from Chapter 4 that you stored one of the values down in cell B99. If you were to print that document, you would get all the data in the top part of your summary sheet, a couple of blank sheets, and then a single sheet with the label and the value for the number of expected survey responses.

3. From the list of Print Area functions, select Set Print Area.

An error box appears, as shown in Figure 8-9.

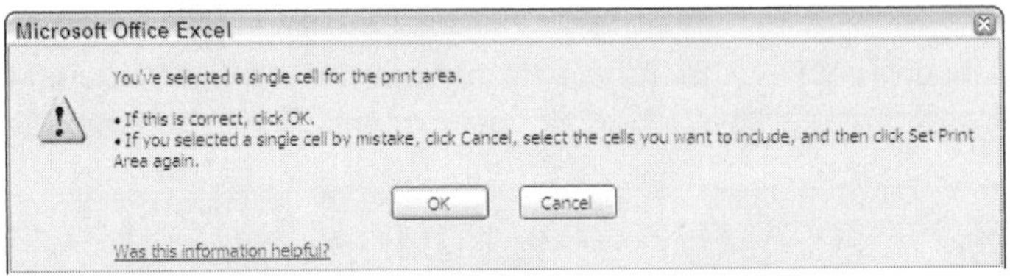

Microsoft Office Excel
You've selected a single cell for the print area.
• If this is correct, click OK.
• If you selected a single cell by mistake, click Cancel, select the cells you want to include, and then click Set Print Area again.
[OK]   [Cancel]
Was this information helpful?

Figure 8-9: You receive this error message if you try to set the print area with only one selected cell.

4. Click OK to close the error message, and then select cells A1 through H42 — the area that contains a single copy of the Time Tracker. Then repeat Steps 2 and 3 to set the print area.

Notice that the selected area is now bordered by a dotted box. Although this box is not printed, it helps you remember the area you have selected as your print area.

Watch Your Step

After you set your print area, it stays set until you either clear it or reset it. If you add data on another page of the current worksheet, that data is not printed unless you add that page to the print area.

Adding Graphical Elements: Photo Backgrounds and Logos

So far in this chapter, you have created basic-looking sheets. However, the printout that this file creates is rather plain and boring. In today's world of graphics, branding, and sophisticated users of documents, you are expected to create documents that look great — whether they are printed from Excel or Word or some other application. Luckily for you, Excel 2007 is built to help you do just what you need.

Your first step is to add some color to the sheet, to give it a little zip: You can either print the page on colored paper or set the background of each sheet to a color or graphical image.

Using a picture as a background

If you want to add a picture to the background of your worksheet, you can choose Page Layout ➔ Page Setup ➔ Background. However, before you add the picture, make sure that your new background will not make it harder to see the data in your worksheet. You also want to make sure that the background you add to the Ferguson Farms time sheet doesn't prevent employees from reading their time sheets on paper or on-screen.

Follow these steps to add a pictorial background to the Ferguson Farms time sheet:

1. Open the file **FergusonFarms2.xlsx**.

2. Choose **Page Layout ➔ Page Setup ➔ Background**.

   The Sheet Background dialog box appears, showing the My Pictures default folder.

3. Select the sample picture for your sheet background. Use **Blue hills.jpg** if you're using Windows XP, or use **Creek.jpg** if you're using Windows Vista. Click Insert.

   Notice that the background of the data area for each page is now the selected graphic, as shown in Figure 8-10. Notice also that the Background button has changed to the Delete Background button.

Figure 8-10: This time sheet uses `Creek.jpg` as its background.

If this picture were more washed out, it would work better as the background for the worksheet. You can create the washout effect in a separate graphics program or simply choose another picture.

4. Choose Page Layout → Page Setup → Delete Background.

The white background of the sheet is restored.

Information Kiosk

Another way to add a background to your worksheet is to select the cells in the sheet and choose Home → Font → Fill Color. You can use the Fill Color button to add a solid tint to the entire background of your worksheet, just as you can use the Background button to add a pictorial background.

Adding a logo to your worksheet

Another common way to create a professional-looking worksheet is to add a picture or logo to it. Using the same worksheet from the preceding section, follow these steps to add a logo:

1. Choose Insert → Illustrations → Picture.

Notice that the Insert Picture dialog box shows the same folder as before.

2. Select the file same file as you did in Step 1 in the preceding exercise, and then click Insert.

Notice that the picture is full size and appears on each page of the sheet. That isn't what you want, so you need to adjust the picture's properties.

3. **Right-click the picture and choose Size and Properties from the pop-up menu.**

The Size and Properties modal dialog box is shown. It is different from other dialog boxes you have seen in Excel. Any changes you make in the options are immediately applied to the selected object.

4. **On the Size tab, change the scale in both the Height and Width boxes to 8% of the current size, and then click Close.**

After the logo has been added in the upper-left corner, the sheet should look like the one shown in Figure 8-11.

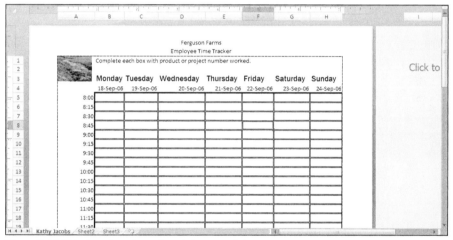

Figure 8-11: This time sheet has a logo in its upper-left corner.

Applying a Theme to Quickly Change the Look of Your Worksheet

One of the additions that Microsoft made to the Office suite is its themes. *Themes* allow you to define font sets, colors, and effects for your company documents and apply these sets in just a few clicks.

Although theming is extensively implemented in Word and PowerPoint, Excel 2007 has only a certain amount of theme interpretation built in. In this section, you look at some of the theme elements incorporated into Excel and how they can affect your work.

You can best see the effect of theming in documents that are set up from the beginning to handle theme elements. Because this book is about Excel 2007 and not about design, you will work with a document that is based on one of the Microsoft templates to explore how the theme elements can affect the look of your work. Follow these steps:

1. **Open the file named `FergusonFarmsMarketingBudget.xlsx`.**
2. **Explore the look of both the data and chart sheets. Then return to the data sheet.**
3. **Choose Page Layout ➜ Themes ➜ Themes. Hover the mouse over several themes to see how they affect the look of your worksheet.**
4. **After you explore the effect of the themes, select the Concourse Theme.**

   Notice that the fonts and colors used in the table have changed. Notice also that the width of the columns has changed to allow for the increased font size. The look for the new table is shown is Figure 8-12.

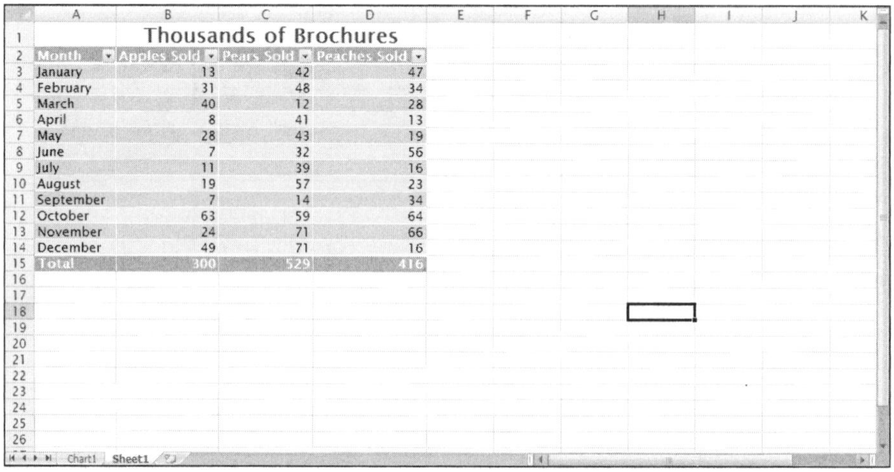

Thousands of Brochures

Month	Apples Sold	Pears Sold	Peaches Sold
January	13	42	47
February	31	48	34
March	40	12	28
April	8	41	13
May	28	43	19
June	7	32	56
July	11	39	16
August	19	57	23
September	7	14	34
October	63	59	64
November	24	71	66
December	49	71	16
Total	300	529	416

Figure 8-12: The rethemed table.

5. **Click the tab for the chart, and notice that it has been updated to use the colors for the theme.**

   Notice that as you move to the chart, the colors and fonts for the chart change in the same manner as the table. The new chart look is shown in Figure 8-13.

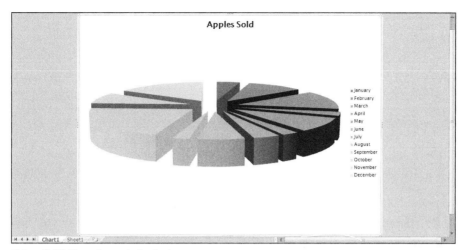

Figure 8-13: The rethemed pie chart.

footer: The text that is designated to appear at the bottom of every printed page. This text also appears when the worksheet is viewed in Page Layout view.

gridline: A border that Excel automatically places around each cell to allow you to see where one cell ends and the next one begins.

header: The text that is designated to appear at the top of every printed page. This text also appears when the worksheet is viewed in Page Layout view.

page size: The size of the paper to be used for a printed worksheet. The page size can be any size that the selected printer can handle. Common page sizes are Letter (8½ x 11 inches) and A-4 (210 x 297 millimeters).

print area: The group of cells to be printed when the selected worksheet is sent to the printer. If the print area for a sheet is not explicitly set, the print area consists of all the cells containing data.

Last Stop

Practice Exam

1. True or False: Interactive worksheets can only be designed for use on the computer.

2. Name two advantages to working in Page Layout view when you first begin creating a worksheet.

_____

_____

3. Why would you turn gridlines on when viewing a worksheet but turn them off when printing it?

_____

4. What is one possible consequence of not setting a print area for a large worksheet?

_____

5. Describe two ways to add a background to your worksheet.

_____

_____

6. True or False: Adding a background to your worksheet covers the entire printed page.

7. Name three elements of an Excel file that are affected by changing the theme for the file.

_____

_____

8. Name one print scenario where you are usually likely to print your worksheet and one where you are not likely to print your worksheet.

_____

_____

EXIT

CHAPTER

9

Exporting Data to Other Applications

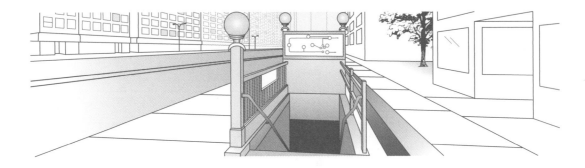

Enter the Station

Questions

1. Why should Excel data be saved in CSV format?

2. What is the difference between pasting Excel data and pasting a link to the Excel data?

3. What is the advantage of using worksheet contents to create a Word mail merge?

4. What is the most common use of Excel data in PowerPoint?

5. What is SharePoint?

6. What is a document library?

7. What is the difference between opening a document from a library and checking out a document?

Express Line

If you are already familiar with using Excel 2007 data in other programs, such as Word and PowerPoint, skip ahead to the next chapter.

Be aware that even if you know how to use Excel data in other programs in earlier versions, changes have taken place in how the process works.

ow that you understand how to get data into Excel from other places and how to print the data, it is time to go in the other direction: using your Excel data in other programs.

Just as you needed to bring some data into Excel from other programs in Chapter 7, in this chapter you learn how to save your Excel data so that you can use it in other programs and on other platforms.

In addition to saving Excel data in other file formats, you can use the data stored in Excel in Word and PowerPoint. In fact, if you want to build charts in either of those programs, you work in Excel. You can also store your Excel data in a document library on a SharePoint site *and* import it into SharePoint to use for the basis of custom lists.

In this chapter, you start by looking at how to save your Excel data in other formats and why you might want to do that. After that, you learn how to access your Excel data from Word to create a mail merge. From there, you move on to using Excel charts in PowerPoint. The closing sections talk about storing and working with your Excel data in SharePoint.

Storing Excel Data in Other Formats

You store Excel data in other formats when you need to use that data in other programs or on other platforms. If you are sharing data with an application that doesn't run on a PC, it may or may not understand the XML-based file format that Excel creates. Mac applications, including Mac Office, may not be able to read the new 2007 file format until Mac Office 2008 is available.

If you are using Excel on the Mac, you can save your work as an Excel 97–2003 file. But, if you are saving data for other software on the Mac, you need to save your data as special versions of either text files or CSV files.

To use the Excel data in some older computer programs, you need to save the data in a format that the system can understand. The most common format needed here is also text or CSV.

No matter which file format you use, you follow the same process, and you have to watch for the same potential problems with your content.

Saving Excel data as CSV files

In this exercise, you save an existing Excel file as a CSV file and then as a CSV Macintosh file:

1. Open the file **KellieKonsultingClients.xlsx**.

In this chapter, you save customer information for Kellie Konsulting for use in programs on other applications. The first sheet of customer information lists the contact information. The second sheet of information shows the date and total amount owed for the customer's last consulting project.

2. **Click the Office Button and choose Save As to save the document.**

3. **Click the Save As Type drop-down arrow, and then scroll to select CSV (Comma Delimited).** Add CSV1 **to the beginning of the filename.**

4. **Click Save to save the file.**

You see the warning message shown in Figure 9-1.

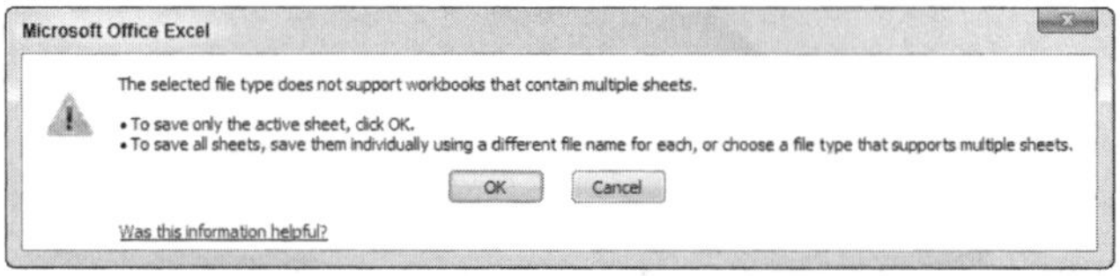

Microsoft Office Excel

The selected file type does not support workbooks that contain multiple sheets.

• To save only the active sheet, click OK.
• To save all sheets, save them individually using a different file name for each, or choose a file type that supports multiple sheets.

[OK] [Cancel]

Was this information helpful?

Figure 9-1: This warning message appears whenever you try to save multiple sheets as a CSV file.

Only Excel-based formats understand what to do with data on multiple sheets. Clicking OK saves the first sheet as a CSV file. To save the second sheet, you navigate to that sheet and choose Save As again, described in Step 7.

5. **Click OK to save just this sheet.**

When you click OK, you see another warning message.

Only Excel-based formats understand how to handle the formatting that has been applied to this data. In this case, the only formatting that was applied adjusted the column width. No formatting is understood by text-based file formats, including CSV formats. If you want, click Help to learn what else besides the column width isn't carried over to the CSV file format.

6. **Click Yes to save this sheet without the formatting.**

Notice that the title of the sheet changed to CSV1KellieKonsultingClients. This title helps you to remember which unformatted files are associated with which sheets in your file.

7. **Repeat Steps 2 through 6 to save the second sheet. Change the name to start with** CSV2.

You have now created two generic CSV files from the Excel data. Before you leave Excel, you will create two more files for comparison.

8. **Repeat Steps 1 through 7. This time, choose CSV (Macintosh) from the list both times and change the names to start with** MCSV1 **and** MCSV2.

You now have two CSV files that can be read on the Mac.

9. **Close Excel and do not save your work.**

Step Into the Real World

You can save files in Excel in 25 different text-based formats. To see the entire list, open the Save As dialog box and click the drop-down arrow at the bottom. Use your favorite search engine to find out when you might use each of the different types. The only reason you would need one of the other text-based formats is when you use Excel data in a specific program that requires a different format.

10. Open Windows Explorer and navigate to where you saved the files. Be sure that you are in Details view (choose View → Details).

Notice that although the file extensions are the same for all four files, their sizes are all slightly different. The Mac files are just slightly smaller than the PC files.

You might need to look at the properties of the files (right-click and choose Properties from the context menu) to see the differences in them.

Saving Excel data to use in previous Excel versions

You can also save a workbook in the format Excel 97-2003 workbook (*.xls). This format allows your document to be used directly by users of some older versions of Excel. You may see the Compatibility Checker warning message about functionality that may be lost when you save the file in the older format.

If you need to give workbooks to users of older versions of Office and cannot downgrade the functionality, you may want to look into the Microsoft Office Compatibility Pack. This free download from Microsoft (when installed on computers with Excel 2000 or newer) allows Excel to open the newer formats and use much of the newer functionality. Your ability to make changes is limited. See the Microsoft Web site (www.microsoft.com) for more details.

Using Excel Data in Word

There are a number of ways you might use your Excel data in Word, ranging from simple reporting of data and charts to creating mail merged letters based on the data in your Excel files. In this section, you learn how to do both these tasks.

Using Excel data to create a report in Word

To place your Excel data into a Word document, you copy a table of data and then paste that data into an existing Word document. This task involves more than a simple copy-and-paste operation, however, because when the paste is done, the data remains *linked* to the Excel file so that any updates to the Excel file are shown in the Word document.

Follow these steps to paste an Excel table into a Word memo about a 10 percent discount for Kellie Konsulting customers:

1. **Open the file named `KellieKonsultingClientsTables.xlsx`.**

2. **Select cells Sheet2!A1 through Sheet2!C12.**

3. **Press Ctrl+C to copy the cells.**

You are now ready to paste and link the Excel data into the Word document.

4. **Open Word. Click the Office Button and choose Open to open `KellieKonsultingMemo.docx`.**

5. **Select the words (Place table here).**

6. **In Word, choose Home → Clipboard, and select Paste Special from the Paste list.**

Word opens the Paste Special dialog box, in which you indicate how to paste the content.

7. **Click the Paste Link radio button and the Excel Worksheet option for the format, as shown in Figure 9-2.**

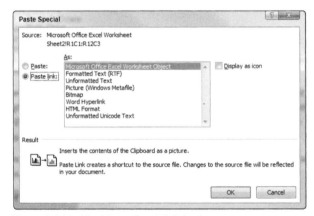

Figure 9-2: The Word Paste Special dialog box.

By selecting these two options, you tell Word that you want the data to remain connected to Excel and to be displayed as a worksheet object. This process is called *linking the data.* By linking the data, you ensure that the data in the Word document matches the data in the Excel document at all times.

8. **Click OK.**

Your table is pasted into the Word document as live Excel data. Now you will change the data in Excel and look at the change in the Word document.

9. **Close Word and save your new document to your hard drive.**

10. Return to Excel and change cell C3 to 7/13/2005. Save the change.

11. Reopen the Word document.

Word warns you that the linked data has changed and asks whether you want to update your document, as shown in Figure 9-3.

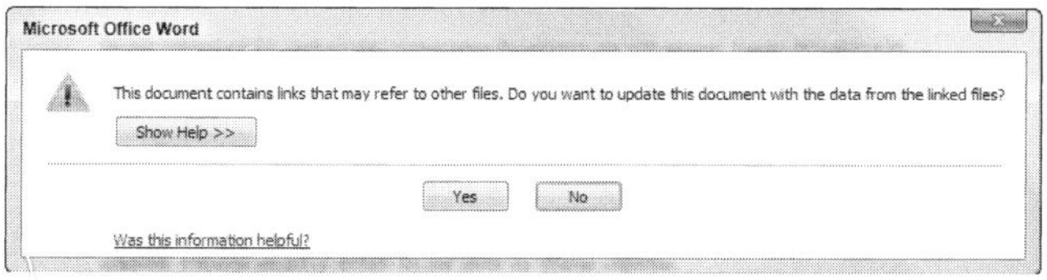

Figure 9-3: Word asks whether you want to update the data in the document.

12. Click Yes to update the data.

Your memo opens, and the data changes are shown.

Using Excel data in a mail merge

After the memo you created in the preceding exercise is distributed, your next step is to send a letter to these clients telling them about the 10 percent discount offer. You could just create a letter for each client, by copying and pasting the contact information from the Excel file in each letter. However, you can much more efficiently create the letter by using a mail merge and pulling the customer data from the Excel file. To do this, you add the mail merged data to an approved letter:

1. Open Word and then open `KellieKonsultingMergeLetter.docx`.

2. Click in the blank line immediately below the date.

3. Choose Mailings → Start Mail Merge → Start Mail Merge, and select Step by Step Mail Merge Wizard.

The Mail Merge task pane appears on the right side of your screen, as shown in Figure 9-4.

4. On the Document Type list, click the Letters radio button. Click the Next link at the bottom to continue.

5. Leave the Starting Document selection set to Use the Current Document, and click Next.

6. Leave the Use an Existing List option selected. Click the Browse button to find the file for the list.

The Select Data Source dialog box opens.

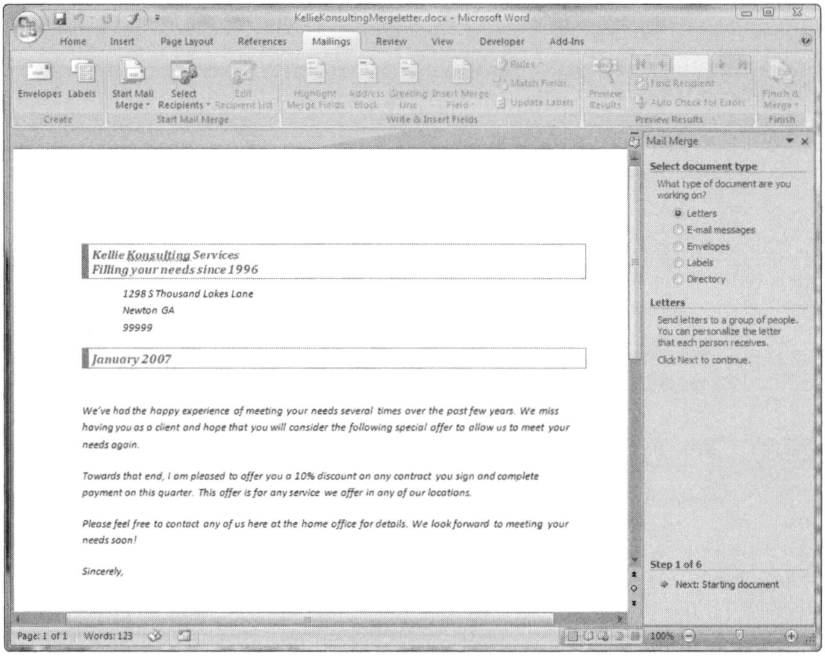

Figure 9-4: The Word 2007 Mail Merge task pane is ready to start a merge.

7. **Navigate and select the Excel file KellieKonsultingClients.xlsx. Then click OK.**

The Select Table dialog box opens, as shown in Figure 9-5, and you're prompted to choose which sheet contains your data.

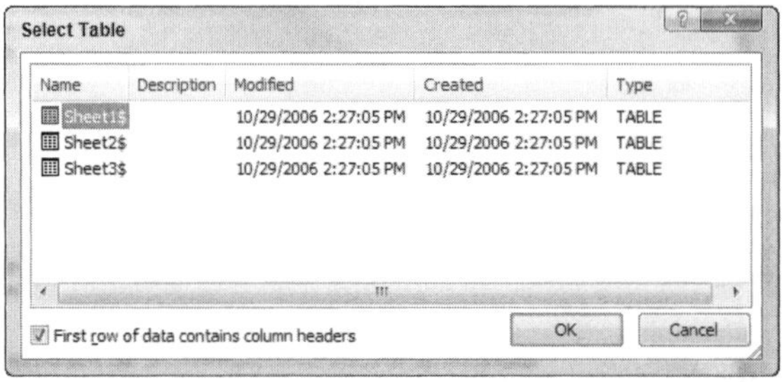

Figure 9-5: Select the sheet that contains the data to use for the mail merge.

8. **Sheet1$ should be selected. If it isn't, select it. Click OK.**

You're prompted to choose the recipients of the letter.

9. **Because all the recipients in your Excel sheet will receive the letter, leave everything selected, as shown in Figure 9-6. Then click OK.**

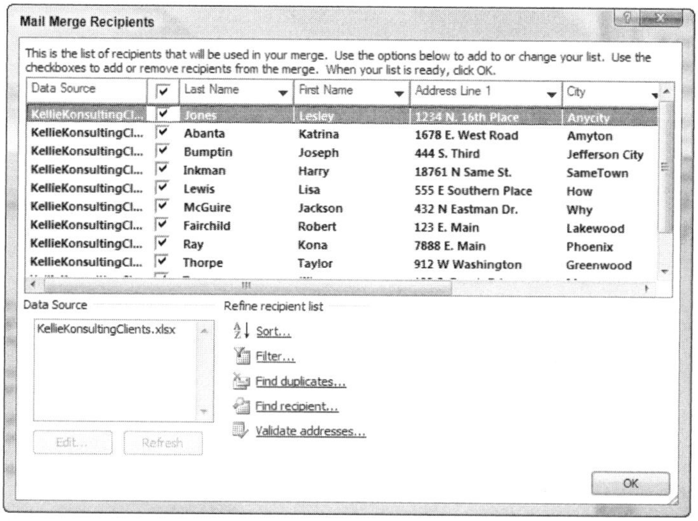

Figure 9-6: The Word Mail Merge Recipients dialog box.

10. When you return to the task pane, click Next to connect the letter to the list.

11. Click Address Block to add the addresses underneath the letter date.

The Insert Address Block dialog box opens and prompts you to format the names and addresses, as shown in Figure 9-7.

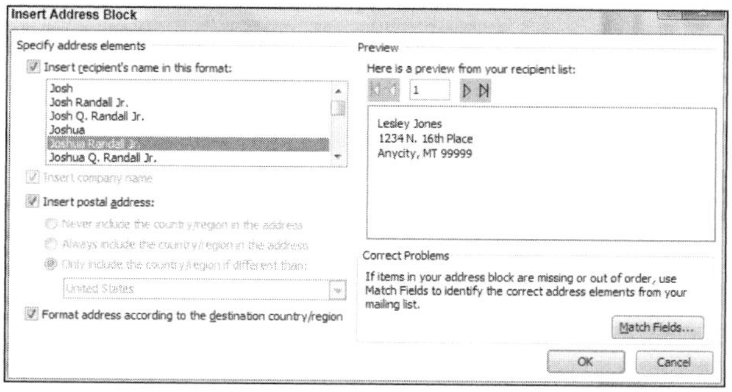

Figure 9-7: Format recipients' names and addresses in the Word Insert Address Block dialog box.

Although the first address looks fine, if you scroll through the list, you notice a problem. The second line of the address isn't being picked up. You need to match that line of the Excel file to a spot on the merged letter.

12. Click the Match Fields button to show the fields in the Excel sheet and the merge fields they have been merged with.

The list of fields in the address block and their matching Excel column headers are shown in Figure 9-8.

Figure 9-8: Select the address block fields to include in the Match Fields dialog box.

13. **Click the Address 2 drop-down arrow and change the (Not Matched) value to Address Line 2. Click OK.**

After matching the new column with a mail merge field, you return to the Insert Address Block dialog box.

14. **Click the arrow buttons to move through the addresses to ensure that they are now shown correctly. Then click OK.**

You see the Mail Merge task pane again, and your addresses are now set. Next, you set up the greeting line.

15. **In the document, press Enter to move the cursor to where you want to set up the greeting line. In the task pane, click the Greeting Line link.**

The Insert Greeting Line dialog box appears with the options you want already selected.

16. **Click OK to return to the task pane.**

The top of your document should now look as shown in Figure 9-9.

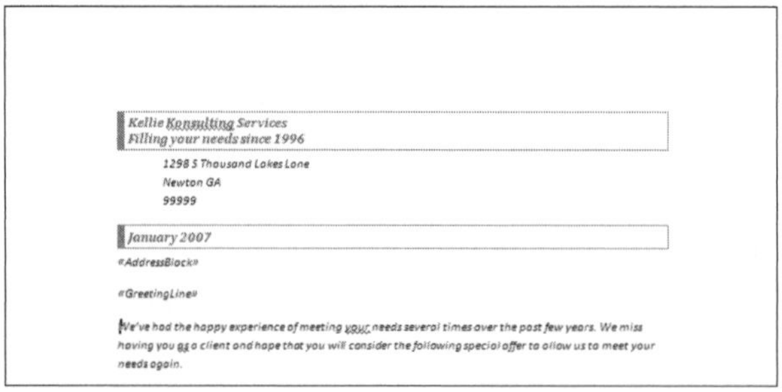

Figure 9-9: Your Word document should look like this one after adding the mail merge fields.

You are ready to preview and create your letters.

17. **Click the Next link to preview your letters.**

The letter for the recipient you last looked at should appear. Click the arrow buttons on the task pane to ensure that all the letters look right.

18. **Click the Next link to complete the merge of your letters.**

The final step is to either edit your individual letters or send the whole set of letters to the printer.

19. **Choose whether you want to edit the letters or send the letters to the printer, and then close and save the document.**

Your mail merge is complete.

Using Excel Data in PowerPoint

Although the most common use of Excel data in Word is to create mail merges and reports (as described in the preceding section), in PowerPoint, Excel data is most often used to create charts. You learned how to create and work with charts in Excel in Chapter 5, so in this section you just create a simple linked chart so that you can see how to link the Excel data to a PowerPoint file.

To create a chart in PowerPoint that uses existing Excel data, you work with both PowerPoint and Excel. You open an Excel file that has a chart created, copy the chart, and then paste the chart onto a slide in PowerPoint. The resulting chart is linked to your data. You test this link at the end of this exercise.

In this exercise, you copy a bar graph showing billing information to Kellie Konsulting clients and then paste the graph into a PowerPoint slide for a management presentation:

1. **Open the file KellieKonsultingClientsGraph.xlsx.**

2. **Select the chart sheet. Select the chart and press Ctrl+C to copy it.**

Now that you have the chart copied to the Clipboard, you are ready to open a PowerPoint presentation and paste the chart on a slide.

3. **Open PowerPoint and press Ctrl+V to paste your chart on the blank slide, as shown in Figure 9-10.**

By default, your chart is pasted as a chart linked to your original Excel data. Clicking the Paste Options tag (located in the lower-right corner of Figure 9-10) gives you a few more options. You can change the element you have pasted from the linked chart to a linked chart with the entire workbook included in the PowerPoint presentation or to a picture of the chart that isn't linked.

In addition, the Paste Options tag lets you decide whether the pasted chart takes on the formatting from the Excel file's theme or from the presentation file's theme (the default).

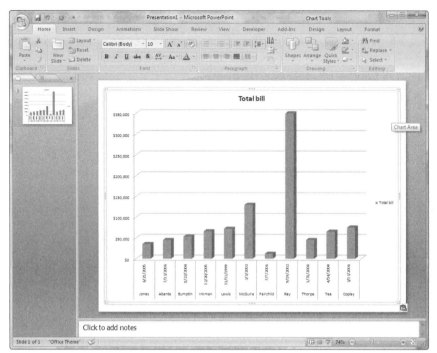

Figure 9-10: An Excel chart pasted into PowerPoint.

4. **Save the presentation to your hard drive and close PowerPoint.**

Now that you have linked the chart to your presentation, it is time to see the linked data change.

5. **Return to Excel. Change the value for cell Sheet2!D9 to** 120,000.

6. **Reopen the saved PowerPoint presentation.**

When you open the presentation, PowerPoint automatically uses the new data from the Excel spreadsheet to update the chart in the presentation file.

Unlike in previous versions of Office, where adding charts to PowerPoint required you to decide whether the data should reside in the presentation or in Excel, all charting with Office 2007 is done by using Excel. Although the data can either be in a presentation-based file or in a separate Excel file, all the functionality of Excel is available in either case.

In addition, you can add the Excel data to your presentation as a table in exactly the same manner as you added it to Word (as described in the earlier section "Using Excel data to create a report in Word"). Copy the data in Excel, move to PowerPoint, use Paste Special to paste the data, and then link it.

Using Excel Data with SharePoint

SharePoint is a Microsoft Office product that lets you create storage areas, discussion areas, and Web sites for your team. It is designed to improve how your team communicates and collaborates. SharePoint, which is usually implemented in enterprise-size companies, requires a separate server for storing and controlling your information. Usually, a SharePoint server is implemented and controlled by an IT department.

In exchange for the additional resources and complexity that are needed to implement and maintain SharePoint, you get a place to store any document that needs to be accessed or seen by multiple people. SharePoint controls access to the documents and maintains the history of changes made to them.

In this section, you learn how to create a document library on a SharePoint system, store your Excel documents in that library, and retrieve Excel documents from the library.

Accessing your SharePoint site

When you were given access to your SharePoint site, you should have also been given instructions on how to log in and access the areas you need. This information should have included these items:

- The URL for the site
- Your personal ID or user name for the site
- Your password for the site

To access your site, enter the URL into your browser. You should be prompted for your login information (the ID and password). Complete the information and press Enter. Your browser should navigate to the default page of your site. An example is shown in Figure 9-11.

Step Into the Real World

If you do not have a big business, it's not a problem. With Office 2007, Microsoft has added Office Live, a Web-based alternative to SharePoint. With Office Live, you can create sites and store documents without the internal overhead of SharePoint. Office Live sites are aimed at small businesses that need to track documents and customer interactions and maintain a Web presence.

Office Live works much like SharePoint. If you prefer to do the document-storage and -retrieval exercises on Office Live, you can.

Links to site content   Click to add or edit pages

Figure 9-11: The default SharePoint home page.

Watch Your Step

One of the strengths of SharePoint is its customization options. For the purposes of these exercises, no customization was applied to the sites. That means that your screen may look very different from these figures. The functionality and the buttons used should be the same, but the locations of the buttons may be different.

In the upper-right corner of your browser window, you see a Site Actions button. Use this button to add and edit pages to your site and maintain the site settings.

In the left column, you see a series of links to the site content that already exists. Use these links to navigate your site. As you add document libraries and other items to your site, they are added to this list.

Creating a document library on your SharePoint site

A *document library* is the place where SharePoint stores your documents so that others can access them. Document libraries can contain many different kinds of documents. By storing a document in a library, you ensure that everyone looking at that document is looking at the same version. Because the document is stored in only one place (in the library) rather than in multiple places (on everyone's hard drives), you know that everyone is looking at the same information. When one person changes the document, everyone else can be notified about the changes.

Before you can store your documents in a library, the library must be created. You might have to create it yourself, or it might already have been created. Follow these steps to create a library yourself:

1. **From your SharePoint site, click the Site Actions button and select Create.**

You see the Create screen.

> # ⓘ Information Kiosk
>
> If you do not have a Create option, you have not been given permission to create new site elements. In this case, jump past this exercise to the section "Uploading an Excel file by using SharePoint."
>
> In addition, if your company is using MOSS 2007 or SPS 2003, you may have been given access to MySite, which is an area on the SharePoint site that you control and that only you can access. If you have access to a MySite location, use it for the exercises in the rest of this chapter. If you aren't sure whether you have access to MySite, ask your IT support person.

2. **From the first column, click the first link, Document Library.**

You see the New window for document libraries, as shown in Figure 9-12.

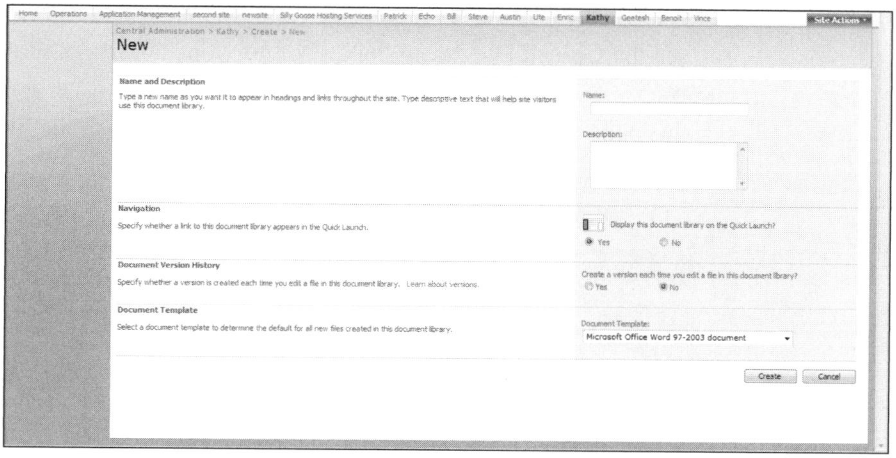

Figure 9-12: The New Document Library SharePoint page.

Use this dialog box to define the document library you will use to store your Excel files.

3. **Fill in the following information:**

- *Name:* Type **KellieKonsultingExcelDocuments**.

- *Description:* Type **Document library for Kellie Konsulting's sales and tracking Excel files**.

- *Create a Version Each Time You Edit a File in This Document Library:* Select Yes.

- *Document Template:* From the drop-down list, change the template type to Microsoft Office Excel Spreadsheet.

4. **Click Create.**

Now that you have defined the setup for the library, SharePoint creates the library and changes your view to the library. Because the library doesn't yet have any documents, the page that is shown is mostly empty.

You are ready to add documents to the library. You can add documents from either SharePoint or Excel. Because you are already in SharePoint, you start there.

Uploading an Excel file by using SharePoint

To upload an Excel document to the library from SharePoint, you use the Upload feature from the library. You have two options: Upload a single document at a time, or upload multiple documents at a time. In the following exercise, you upload a single document:

1. **From your document library, click the Upload drop-down arrow and select Upload Document.**

You see the Upload Document dialog box for your library, as shown in Figure 9-13.

Use this page to find and upload your Excel spreadsheet to the library.

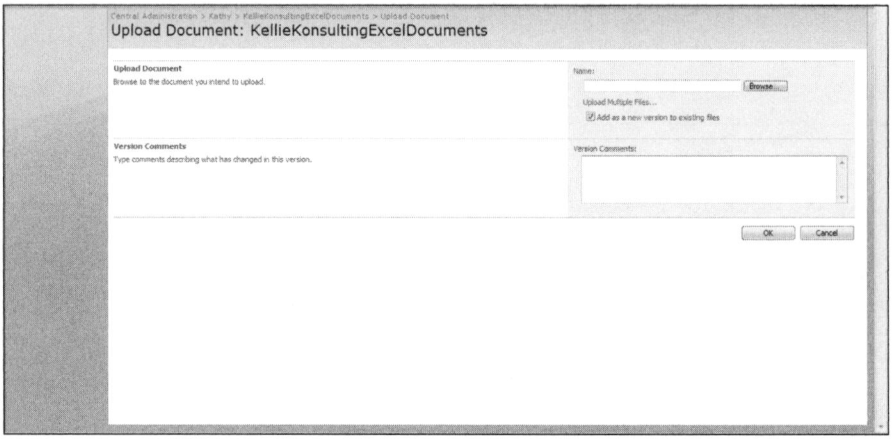

Figure 9-13: Uploading an Excel document from SharePoint to the library.

2. Click the Browse button and navigate to the file `KellieKonsulting ClientsTables.xlsx` on your hard drive. After you have selected the file, click Open.

3. In the Version Comments box, type Initial Upload. Click OK. (If your installation of SharePoint doesn't have versioning enabled, you don't see the Version Comments box. In this case, just click OK.)

You return to your document library list, which now lists your document, as shown in Figure 9-14.

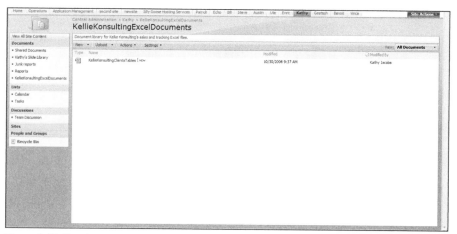

Figure 9-14: The document you uploaded appears on the SharePoint document library page.

Now that you have a document in your library, you can work with it from SharePoint in any of the following ways:

- Download it to your computer to have a local copy for viewing and research.
- Check it out of the library to make changes, and then check it back in so that others can access the updated file.
- Change the name and other properties of the document.
- Add other properties to the document to make searching on the document easier.
- Delete the document from the library.

You can learn more about working with your documents in the library from the Help system within SharePoint. If you work regularly with SharePoint, you might want to check into a SharePoint-specific class.

Uploading an Excel file by using Excel

To upload an Excel document to the library from Excel, you open the document from Excel and use the publishing options built into Excel 2007. Follow these steps:

1. **Open Excel. Choose Office → Open to open the file named `KellieKonsultingClientsGraph.xlsx`.**

2. **Choose Office → Publish → Document Management Server to publish the file to your document library.**

   You see what looks like an ordinary Save As window. However, in this case, the path looks different. Excel is trying to save your document to a network shortcut. Because you have not yet told Excel where the SharePoint server is, it is trying to guess.

3. **Return to the SharePoint document library in a browser window, and select the current URL, up to the slash in front of the word Forms. Copy that part of the URL.**

   From now on, I refer to this URL as the *path* for your library.

4. **Flip back to the Excel Save As dialog box. Paste the URL in front of your document name in the Save As dialog box. Press Enter.**

5. **If you are prompted for your SharePoint user name and password, provide it.**

6. **Return to the SharePoint document library in a browser window. Refresh the window.**

   Your document should have been added to the library, giving you two documents in the library, as shown in Figure 9-15.

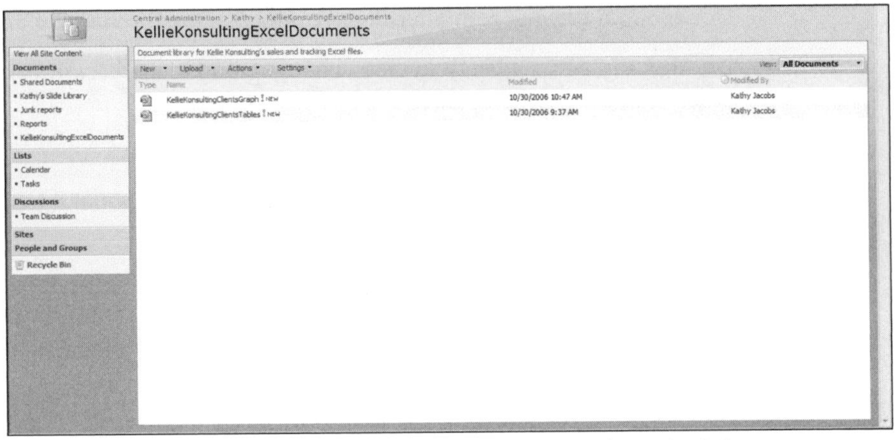

Figure 9-15: Your document library contains the two documents you just uploaded.

Retrieving documents from the library

If someone else has stored in the library a document that you need to look at, you can retrieve the document. You are not retrieving an editable copy of the document at this point; you are merely retrieving a copy that you can look at and use for research.

You can retrieve documents from either Excel or SharePoint. However, you are likely to find that the process is so much easier from SharePoint that you do not use the Excel process.

Using SharePoint

You can retrieve documents from the library by using either Excel or SharePoint. Because the process is easier and cleaner from SharePoint, you do that first:

1. **From your SharePoint site, navigate to your document library.**

2. **Click the name of the document you want to retrieve. If you are prompted for your user name and password, provide them. If the Document Management Task Pane did not open, choose Server → Document Management Information to open the task pane.**

   A local copy of the document is created on your hard drive and opened in Excel. In addition, the Document Management task pane opens, as shown in Figure 9-16.

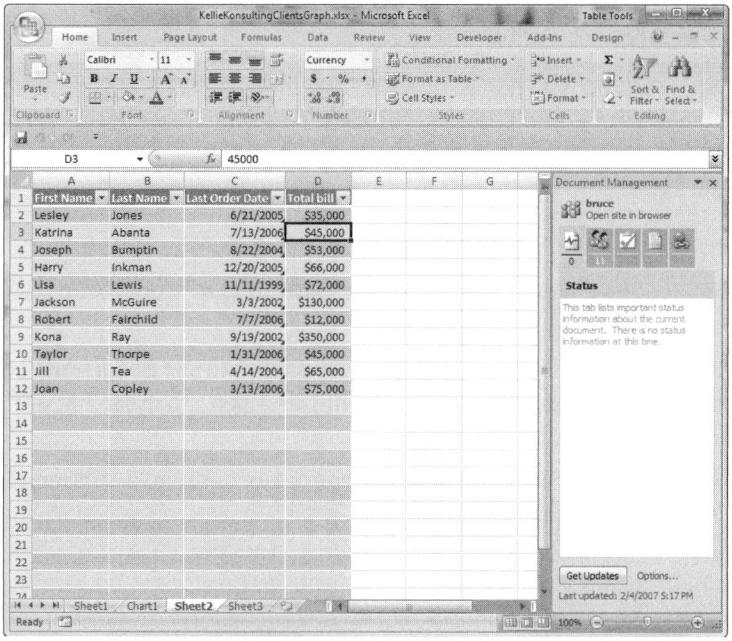

Figure 9-16: The Document Management task pane.

The Document Management task pane shows you a variety of information about the status of your document and the users of your SharePoint site. This task pane has five tabs, each of which tells you different information about your site:

Status: Indicates whether you have the most up-to-date copy of the document. If someone else makes changes to the document while you are looking at it, a notification is shown here.

Members: Specifies which members of the site are online and which are not. If you use one of the Microsoft instant messaging products, this tab also shows you each user's status (online or away, for example). You can determine the status of a user by the color of the dot in front of his or her name.

Tasks: Indicates the active tasks associated with the SharePoint site. Some of these tasks are global to the project, some are specific to your username, and some are even specific to the document you are working with.

Documents: Lists the documents in this library. You can use this tab to open documents from the site, whether they are Excel documents or not.

Links: Shows you the links to other sites that have been stored in your site. These can be anything from links to the corporate site to links to customer and client sites, and to useful sites that someone on the team thinks should be tracked.

Using Excel

If you are already connected to the SharePoint site, you can use the links on the Documents tab in the Document Management task pane to open your documents. If you are not already connected to the site, navigate to the site and then open the document:

1. From Excel, choose Office ➜ Open.

2. Replace the current path with the path to your document library. Press Enter.

The Open window changes slightly. Rather than see documents in the view you are used to, you see the name of your library and then the list of documents, as shown in Figure 9-17.

3. Click the name of the document you want to open, and then click Enter.

A local copy of the document is created on your hard drive and opened in Excel. In addition, the Document Management task pane opens. You can now use this document for research and information.

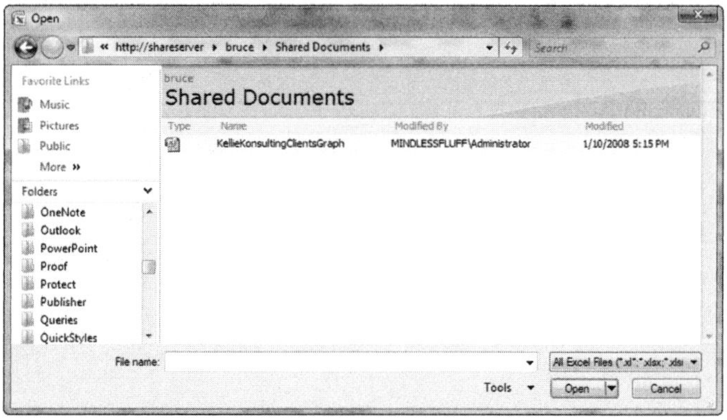

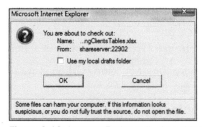

Figure 9-17: The document library's Open window.

Making changes to an Excel file from a library

After you add a document to the library, you should check out the document in order to make changes. Checking out the document from the library to make changes ensures that only one person is changing the document at any given time and that the changes are made to the most recent copy of the document.

You can check out your documents from either your browser session or Excel.

Checking out a document by using SharePoint

You check out a document from SharePoint from the Document Library view:

1. **From your SharePoint site, navigate to your document library.**

2. **From the drop-down list for one of the document names, select Check Out.**

A message warns you to be careful when you open documents from other locations, as shown in Figure 9-18.

Nothing appears to change. The reason is that checking out a document in this manner does not download your document to your hard drive — it merely changes the status of the document. You must now download the document to make changes to it.

Figure 9-18: Internet Explorer displays this warning whenever you check out a document.

3. **From the drop-down list for your checked-out document, choose Edit from the Excel menu.**

4. **When prompted, complete your username and password and click OK.**

The document opens in Excel with the Document Management task pane displayed. This time, the Status tab shows that you have the document checked out, as shown in Figure 9-19.

Your document is now available for you to edit.

Figure 9-19: The Document Management task pane indicates a checked-out document.

Checking out a document by using Excel

In contrast to the preceding process, checking out a document in Excel is done from an open document and is straightforward:

1. **Follow the steps in the section "Using Excel," earlier in this chapter, to open your document in Excel.**

When you have a document from a server open, you see a new set of commands that you can access by choosing Office ➜ Server.

2. **After the document is opened, choose Office ➜ Server ➜ Check Out.**

You see a message telling you where the document will be stored locally so that you can work on it, as shown in Figure 9-20.

3. **Click OK to change to the editable copy of the document.**

Figure 9-20: This message indicates where the checked-out document will be stored.

The document opens in Excel with the Document Management task pane displayed. This time, the Status tab indicates that you have the document checked out (refer to Figure 9-19).

Checking in a document using Excel

After you have made changes to the document, you must check in the document again so that others can see it. To do this, do one of the following:

ONE PANE From Excel, use either of these methods:

- Click the Check In link on the Status tab in the Document Management task pane.

- Choose Office ➜ Server ➜ Check In.

ONE PANE From SharePoint, select Check In from the drop-down list available from the document name.

No matter which way you choose to check in your document again, you are prompted to provide version history information. This information tells other users which changes you made to the file and why you made them.

In addition, if you plan to make more changes to the document, each method of checking in the document allows you to keep the document checked out. By uploading only the document, you continue to block others from making changes to the document while still allowing them to see the changes you have checked in.

Discarding a checkout

If you find that you have checked out the wrong document or if you don't need to make changes after all, you can discard the checkout for your document:

ONE PANE From Excel, choose Office ➜ Server ➜ Discard Check Out.

ONE PANE From SharePoint, choose Discard Check Out from the drop-down list available from the document name.

check out: The process of retrieving a file from a library and allowing only the person who checked it out to make changes. When the person is finished making changes, he checks in the document to make it available to other users.

document library: A controlled area for storing documents that multiple people will need to access; usually stored on a remote computer or server rather than a local computer.

download: To save a copy of a document from a server or site on a local hard drive.

mail merge: To create a number of letters, labels, or documents, all of which are basically the same but whose content is customized based on the contents of a separate file. In the exercise in this chapter, the mail merge created a series of Word documents customized for each client based on information pulled from an Excel document.

Office Live: A Microsoft product that is similar to SharePoint but hosted by Microsoft for smaller businesses. Although Office Live does not have all the capabilities of SharePoint, it is based on the same principles.

platform: The computer and operating system combination that you use to run your presentation. Examples of computer platforms are Linux boxes, Macs, and PCs.

SharePoint: A Microsoft product consisting of software that runs on a server and facilitates communication between team members, both internal and external. SharePoint as a whole allows the creation of document libraries, discussions, link information, calendars, task tracking, signature processes, work flows, and Web sites.

upload: To save a copy of a document from your local hard drive to a remote drive on a server or site; the opposite of *download*.

URL: Uniform Resource Locator, in geek speak; to the rest of us, the address of a Web site.

version: A copy of a document created and stored at a specific time. A version helps track the state of the document at a particular time.

version history: The set of annotations and dates that indicate when a document was updated, how it was updated, why it was updated, and who updated it.

Last
Stop

Practice Exam

1. What is the difference between the three different CSV file formats Excel can create?

_____

_____

2. True or False: You can save two sheets of data in the same CSV file.

3. Name two advantages to linking Excel data when pasting into another application.

_____

_____

4. In which of the following cases can you not create a single mail merge from your Excel document?

a. Data from the Excel spreadsheet is in multiple sheets.

b. Column names for the data in the spreadsheet don't match the predefined names in the mail merge.

c. The Excel sheet contains more columns of data than you want to use in the mail merge.

d. The Excel sheet contains more rows of data than you want to use in the mail merge.

5. Name one reason that you should check more than one record when preparing for a mail merge.

_____

_____

6. True or False: By default, a chart pasted into a PowerPoint presentation is linked and editable.

7. Give a reason why you might choose SharePoint over Office Live or vice versa.

_____

_____

8. Which of the following is needed to create a document library?

   a. A username.

   b. A password.

   c. A URL for the site.

   d. All of the above.

9. True or False: You must have permission to create libraries in order to store documents in them.

10. Which of the following is not possible from Excel?

   a. Upload a document.

   b. Check in a document.

   c. Create a library on SharePoint.

   d. Discard the check-in of a document.

11. Name the main difference between retrieving a document and checking it out.

_____

_____

12. Explain why version history is important.

_____

_____

CHAPTER

10

Sorting and Filtering Data

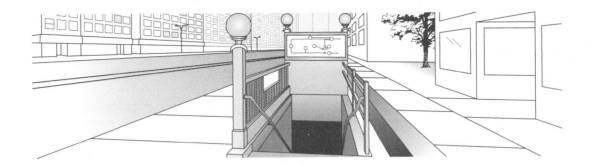

 # Enter the Station

Questions

1. What is the difference between sorting data and filtering data?

2. What is the biggest advantage to sorting data?

3. Can you sort on elements other than numbers?

4. Can you sort on more than one field at a time?

5. What is the biggest advantage to filtering data?

6. When you add a filter to your data, does it remove the previous filter?

Express Line

If you are already familiar with sorting and filtering your data in Excel 2007, skip ahead to the next chapter.

So far in this book, you have worked with datasets that are small enough that you could see and understand the data in a reasonable manner. However, in the real world, you often work with sets of raw data that you need to make understandable to the people with whom you need to communicate.

You already looked at how to make sense of data by publishing it in graphs and charts. In this chapter, you learn about two more common ways to make data understandable: sorting and filtering.

You also work with some public data from the Arizona Department of Education. This data concerns the standardized test results for various high schools in the state of Arizona. Although this data is available on the Web, it is also included on this book's Web site to make it easy for you to find. In each exercise in this chapter, you sort or filter your data to discover the answers to specific questions.

Because Excel 2007 tables enhance your ability to work with data, the raw data from the Arizona Department of Education has been formatted as a table. In addition, the data downloaded from the site has been formatted so that each column shows the full width of the data.

Deciding Whether to Sort or Filter Your Data

When you sort and filter your data, you can narrow the data you are looking at from the full dataset to just those records that help you answer a specific question. Usually, that question has to do with some correlation between the records in your worksheet.

For example, the data you look at in this chapter consists of 4,202 records. Each of those records has 28 columns of unique data. That is a lot of information to look at — let alone use to find answers to questions. To make the data more manageable, you have two excellent choices:

Sort the data so that the answers float to the top of the worksheet.

Filter the data so that the only records you see are those that answer your questions.

When should you sort your data, and when should you filter it? In general, you want to sort data when you want to see the whole set of data, grouped together into logical, related units. You filter your data when you want to see only the data that helps you answer the question at hand.

Sorting Your Data

Sorting your data allows you to determine the order of the data records you are looking at. Sorting is helpful for seeing top and bottom results, looking at geographical distributions, and doing much more. Sorting data keeps it all visible but changes the order of the rows within the worksheet.

Doing a quick sort

As delivered, the standardized test results for Arizona high schools are sorted by school and district. In the following exercise, you change this sort so that you can find out the number of schools that reported data for Indian students, and then you change the sort criteria to find the lowest average score in the M-MSS test for the Indian students:

1. **Open the file `AIMSSpring2005RawData.xlsx`.**

2. **Move through your worksheet so that column J, labeled Ethnicity, is the first visible column on the left side of your screen.**

For now, the data to the left of Column J is not data you need. You want answers about *the number of* schools that meet the criteria, not which schools meet them (yet).

In the case of this data, each cell in Column J has one of five values:

All	All students reported as one population
A	Asian
B	Black
H	Hispanic
I	Indian
W	White

The view of your worksheet is the same as the one shown in Figure 10-1.

3. **Click the Ethnicity drop-down arrow. From the list, select the Sort A to Z option.**

Notice that the order of the rows changes so that the first rows are those with an ethnicity of 0, followed by those with no ethnicity reported. The first 219 rows show no ethnicity. In fact, in this sort order, the first record providing Indian test scores is in row 2,798.

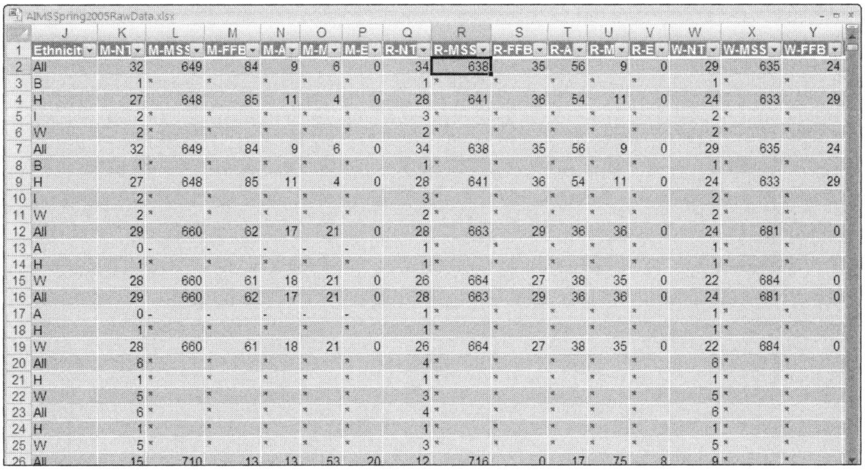

AIMSSpring2005RawData.xlsx

	J	K	L	M	N	O	P	Q	R	S	T	U	V	W	X	Y
1	Ethnicit	M-NT	M-MSS	M-FFB	M-A	M-M	M-E	R-NT	R-MSS	R-FFB	R-A	R-M	R-E	W-NT	W-MSS	W-FFB
2	All	32	649	84	9	6	0	34	638	35	56	9	0	29	635	24
3	B	1	*	*	*	*	*	1	*	*	*	*	*	1	*	*
4	H	27	648	85	11	4	0	28	641	36	54	11	0	24	633	29
5	I	2	*	*	*	*	*	3	*	*	*	*	*	2	*	*
6	W	2	*	*	*	*	*	2	*	*	*	*	*	2	*	*
7	All	32	649	84	9	6	0	34	638	35	56	9	0	29	635	24
8	B	1	*	*	*	*	*	1	*	*	*	*	*	1	*	*
9	H	27	648	85	11	4	0	28	641	36	54	11	0	24	633	29
10	I	2	*	*	*	*	*	3	*	*	*	*	*	2	*	*
11	W	2	*	*	*	*	*	2	*	*	*	*	*	2	*	*
12	All	29	660	62	17	21	0	28	663	29	36	36	0	24	681	0
13	A	0	-	-	-	-	-	1	*	*	*	*	*	1	*	*
14	H	1	*	*	*	*	*	1	*	*	*	*	*	1	*	*
15	W	28	660	61	18	21	0	26	664	27	38	35	0	22	684	0
16	All	29	660	62	17	21	0	28	663	29	36	36	0	24	681	0
17	A	0	-	-	-	-	-	1	*	*	*	*	*	1	*	*
18	H	1	*	*	*	*	*	1	*	*	*	*	*	1	*	*
19	W	28	660	61	18	21	0	26	664	27	38	35	0	22	684	0
20	All	6	*	*	*	*	*	4	*	*	*	*	*	6	*	*
21	H	1	*	*	*	*	*	1	*	*	*	*	*	1	*	*
22	W	5	*	*	*	*	*	3	*	*	*	*	*	5	*	*
23	All	6	*	*	*	*	*	4	*	*	*	*	*	6	*	*
24	H	1	*	*	*	*	*	1	*	*	*	*	*	1	*	*
25	W	5	*	*	*	*	*	3	*	*	*	*	*	5	*	*
26	All	15	710	13	13	53	20	12	716	0	17	75	8	9	*	*

Figure 10-1: Unsorted standardized test results for various high schools in Arizona.

You can get to this row in two ways: Either scroll down, or use the Find command. Either way, you have a lot of data to scroll through to find your answer. An easier way is to sort the data in reverse alphabetical order. This action "floats" the data you need closer to the top of the worksheet and makes it easier to find your answers.

4. **Scroll back to the top of the sheet, if you are not already there. Click the Ethnicity drop-down arrow. From the list, select the Sort Z to A option.**

5. **Scroll down to find the first instance of the letter I. Click in cell J773.**

   The first school reporting data on Indian students is now in row 773, which is closer to the top and easier to find and work with. Your next step is to find how many schools reported data on Indian students.

6. **Press Shift+↓ to move down to the last row with an I (row 1399).**

   You have now selected each school that is reporting data for Indian students. Your next step is to find out how many schools are selected. You could count the entries or subtract the row numbers, but you can use an easier way instead.

7. **Right-click at the bottom of the Excel 2007 window and choose Count from the menu that pops up.**

   Notice that the lower-right corner of the Excel 2007 window now indicates the count of selected cells with data, as shown in Figure 10-2. This count shows the number of schools that reported data on Indian students.

Watch Your Step

If you don't click and select the cells, you won't get the count.
If you only have one cell selected, you won't get the count either.

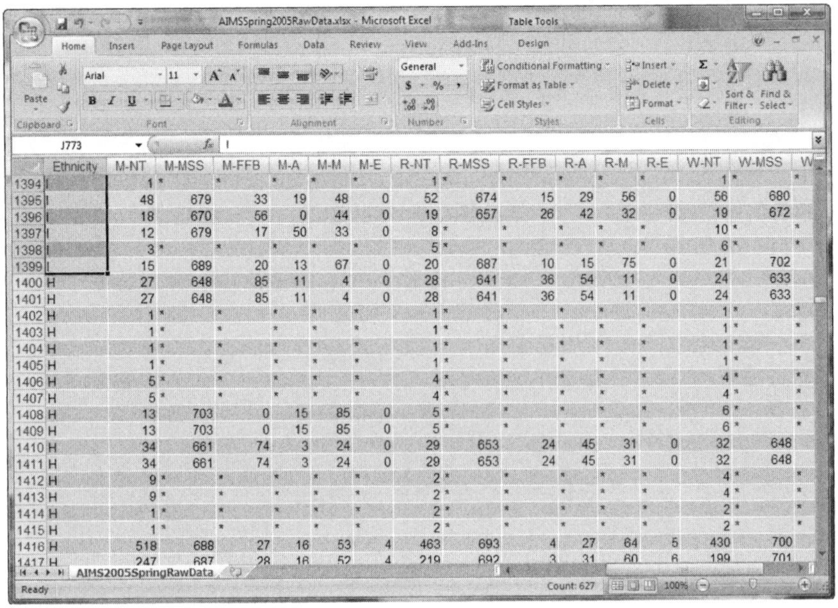

Figure 10-2: The count of selected cells of data.

Now that you know how many schools reported data on Indian students, it is time to move to the next question, posed in the following section. When you are working with data, finding the answer to one question usually helps you either figure out the next question to ask or see the answer to the overall question.

Entering sort criteria in the Sort dialog box

The next question to be answered is which of the schools reported the lowest average score in the M-MSS test for the Indian students. You can calculate this number by using a second sort on the data with the quick sort options. However, after you get past two or three levels of sorts, you can use a better way to set up the sorts. Continue with the same file you used in the previous section and follow these steps to specify sort criteria:

1. Choose Data → Sort & Filter → Sort.

This step opens the Sort dialog box, as shown in Figure 10-3. Notice that it already lists one sort criteria: Sort by ethnicity in Z to A order. (This is the sort criteria you applied in the last exercise.) You use this dialog box to add your next sort criteria.

2. Click the Add Level button.

A new row (it starts with the words *Then by*) appears in the sort list. In the Sort dialog box, the order of the rows tells Excel 2007 that you want it to sort by the rows listed first and then work its way down the list of criteria. You want to sort first by Ethnicity and then by the new criteria you are about to define.

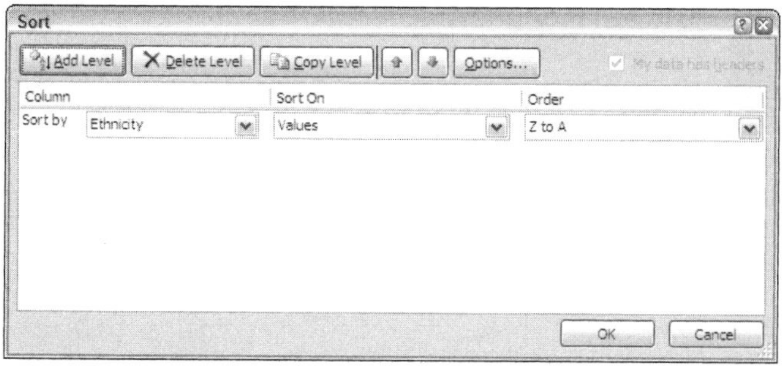

Figure 10-3: Enter your sort criteria in the Sort dialog box.

3. **From the Then By box, select M-MSS. Leave the Sort On option as-is. Leave the Order option alone also. (You want the lowest average score, so you want the smallest value on top.)**

This sort criteria sorts the data so that the M-MSS column displays the lowest average score at the top of the list of schools reporting data for Indian students.

4. **Click the OK button or press Enter.**

The sort is executed. You now need to find the cell in the data that tells you which school answers your question. Because you already know that the first school reporting data is in row 773, and because you just sorted to bring into this row the school with the lowest score on this test, you can find the answer to your question in the School Name column for that row. To see this answer, either scroll down or find the first instance of the letter *I* in the Ethnicity column and then scroll back to the left to find the school and district names. Four different high schools reported the lowest average score (645) in the M-MSS test for the Indian students, as shown in Figure 10-4.

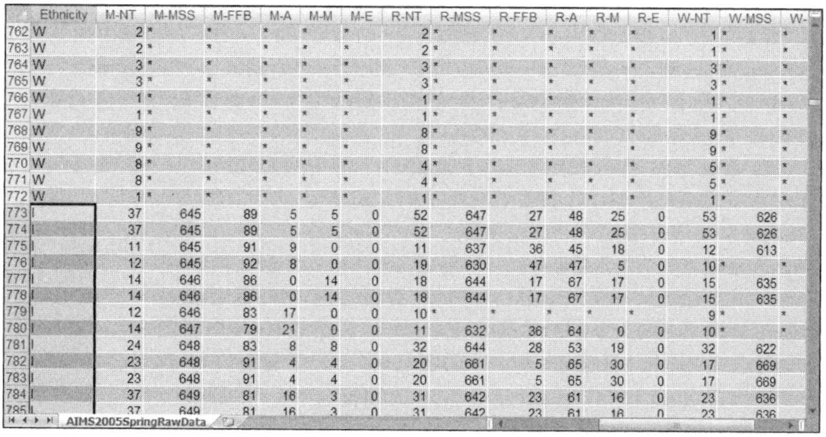

	Ethnicity	M-NT	M-MSS	M-FFB	M-A	M-M	M-E	R-NT	R-MSS	R-FFB	R-A	R-M	R-E	W-NT	W-MSS	W-
762	W	2 *	*	*	*	*	*	2 *	*	*	*	*	*	1 *	*	
763	W	2 *	*	*	*	*	*	2 *	*	*	*	*	*	1 *	*	
764	W	3 *	*	*	*	*	*	3 *	*	*	*	*	*	3 *	*	
765	W	3 *	*	*	*	*	*	3 *	*	*	*	*	*	3 *	*	
766	W	1 *	*	*	*	*	*	1 *	*	*	*	*	*	1 *	*	
767	W	1 *	*	*	*	*	*	1 *	*	*	*	*	*	1 *	*	
768	W	9 *	*	*	*	*	*	8 *	*	*	*	*	*	9 *	*	
769	W	9 *	*	*	*	*	*	8 *	*	*	*	*	*	9 *	*	
770	W	8 *	*	*	*	*	*	4 *	*	*	*	*	*	5 *	*	
771	W	8 *	*	*	*	*	*	4 *	*	*	*	*	*	5 *	*	
772	W	1 *	*	*	*	*	*	1 *	*	*	*	*	*	1 *	*	
773	I	37	645	89	5	5	0	52	647	27	48	25	0	53	626	
774	I	37	645	89	5	5	0	52	647	27	48	25	0	53	626	
775	I	11	645	91	9	0	0	11	637	36	45	18	0	12	613	
776	I	12	645	92	8	0	0	19	630	47	47	5	0	10 *	*	
777	I	14	646	86	0	14	0	18	644	17	67	17	0	15	635	
778	I	14	646	86	0	14	0	18	644	17	67	17	0	15	635	
779	I	12	646	83	17	0	0	10 *	*	*	*	*	*	9 *	*	
780	I	14	647	79	21	0	0	11	632	36	64	0	0	10 *	*	
781	I	24	648	83	8	8	0	32	644	28	53	19	0	32	622	
782	I	23	648	91	4	4	0	20	661	5	65	30	0	17	669	
783	I	23	648	91	4	4	0	20	661	5	65	30	0	17	669	
784	I	37	649	81	16	3	0	31	642	23	61	16	0	23	636	
785	I	37	649	81	16	3	0	31	642	23	61	16	0	23	636	

AIMS2005SpringRawData

Figure 10-4: Result of the sort by average score for the M-MSS.

Watch Your Step

What if you want to find out the highest average score? In this case, it is not simple to find. Excel sorts characters higher than numbers, which can change the results from what you expect to something that appears out of order. If you sort the data for the M-MSS column from highest to lowest, you see that the first rows that appear in the sort order contain asterisks. The asterisk in this worksheet means that the school did not report scores for that test. Unfortunately, asterisks are sorted higher than any number, so the schools reporting no data are listed higher than the schools reporting data. The data here cannot be easily cleaned. (In Chapter 11, you learn how to clean most data.) If you try to replace the asterisk with anything else, Excel reads the asterisk as a wildcard and replaces every character in the worksheet with the character you chose.

Sorting data by color

In addition to sorting your data by the contents of the cells, you can sort by the color of the cell. I have found this sort type to be most useful when I use conditional formatting to apply a color to cells. I can then use the Sort dialog box to pull the data I want to the top of the list.

In this exercise, your goal is to find out whether any correlation exists between ethnicity and high results in two particular columns: M-NT (column K) and R-NT (column Q).

You do this by first sorting any rows that contain invalid data to the bottom. You push rows that are not itemized by race to the bottom. Then within the remaining rows, you push the rows that have invalid data (not between 1 and 10000) for the two test scores you are concerned about to the bottom. Finally you sort the remaining records so that the highest M-NT scores are on top.

In this exercise, data elements with a value of * (asterisk) or 0 are not valid data items. Your first step is to change the color of the valid data elements so that they show up. After that, you sort on the color of the data as well as on the data itself, to see whether a correlation exists. Follow these steps:

1. **Use the file from the previous section or open the file named AIMSSpring2005RawData1.xlsx.**

2. **Select columns K through AB (the test-result columns).**

    By selecting the test score columns and applying the conditional formatting to all of them at one time, you save yourself some work and make it easy to see at a glance which data does not meet your criteria.

3. **Use conditional formatting to give all cells whose values are between 0 and 10,000 a green fill with dark green text.**

To do this, choose Home → Styles → Conditional Formatting → Highlight Cells Rules → Between. In the Between dialog box, enter **1** in the first box, enter **10000** in the second box, and select Green Fill with Dark Green Text from the drop-down list. Click OK.

By adding the color to the data that is valid, you make it easy to see and ignore any invalid data. In addition, because you can sort on the color of the cells, you can then sort for exactly what you want rather than search for the answer after you complete the sort.

4. **Click to deselect the data.**

You want to be sure to sort all the data in the table, so start the sort with no data selected. If you have more than one cell from your table selected, you will get different sort results than you expect.

5. **Select the Z to A option from the sort drop-down list for column J to ensure that your data is sorted in reverse alphabetical order by Ethnicity. Doing this will also add the sort criteria to the Sort dialog box.**

6. **Choose Data → Sort & Filter → Sort.**

The Sort dialog box appears.

7. **In the Ethnicity sort row: From the Order drop-down list, select Custom List.**

You already know that some schools report their scores by ethnicity and some schools lump all scores together. Because you are looking for a correlation between scores and ethnicity reporting, you want to sort the specific ethnicities to the top of the list. To do this, you create a custom list for the sort order: Use the Custom Lists dialog box, shown in Figure 10-5.

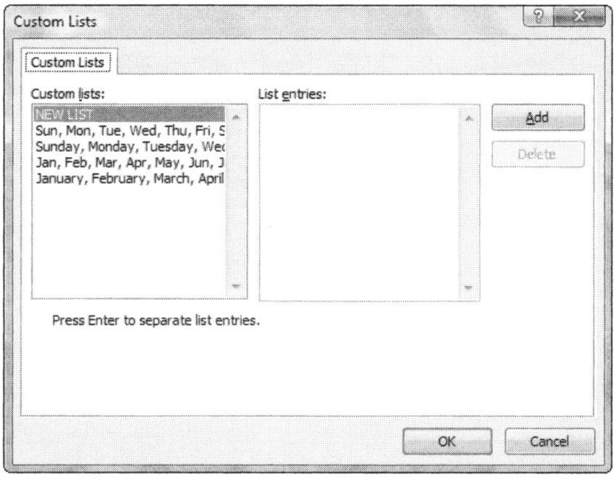

Figure 10-5: The Custom Lists dialog box.

8. Click in the List Entries box, and type W, I, H, B, A.

9. Click the Add button to add your new list to the options. If the list isn't automatically selected, select it.

Your new list appears and is selected in the Custom Lists column so that you can use it, as shown in Figure 10-6.

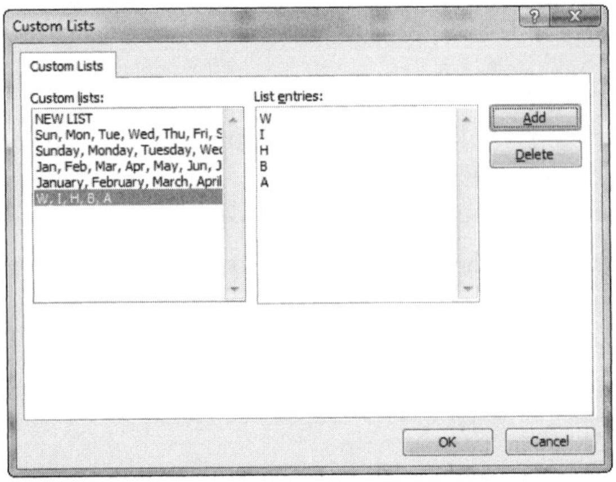

Figure 10-6: The Modified Custom Lists dialog box.

10. Click the OK button.

You have defined the custom list. If you return to the Sort dialog box, you can see that your list is selected in the Order box, as shown in Figure 10-7. All of the rows where the results are broken down into one of the races will be sorted together by race.

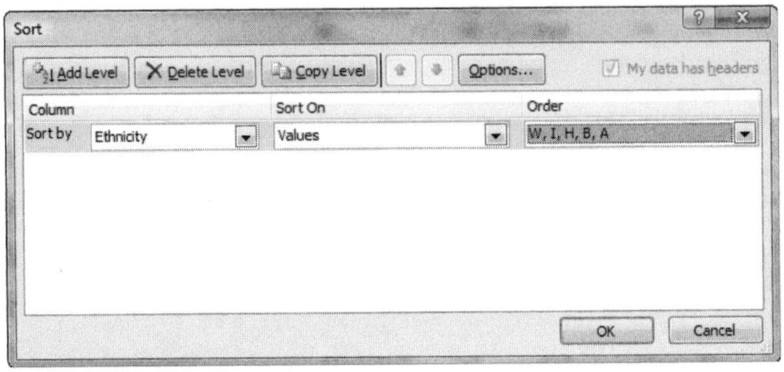

Figure 10-7: The results will be sorted by race.

11. If a second sort criteria isn't listed, click the Add Level button to add it again. If the criteria is there, set it to sort the M-NT values on cell color, where the no cell color cells are on the bottom, as shown in Figure 10-8.

Because of the conditional formatting, this sort moves all records with invalid M-NT data to the bottom of the list.

12. Add three more conditions to your Sort dialog box. They should match the set shown in Figure 10-9.

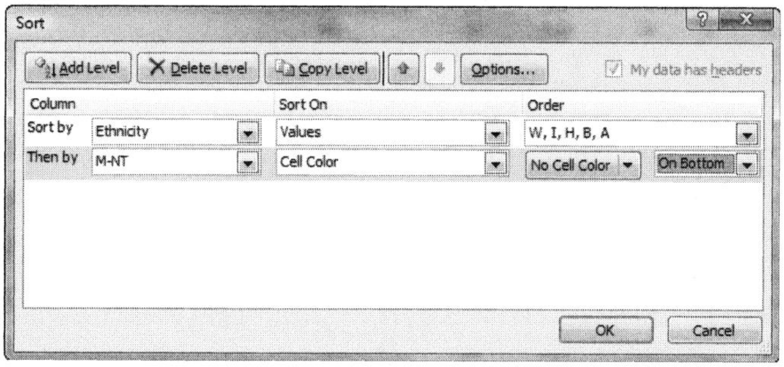

Figure 10-8: This modified Sort dialog box shows a two-level sort.

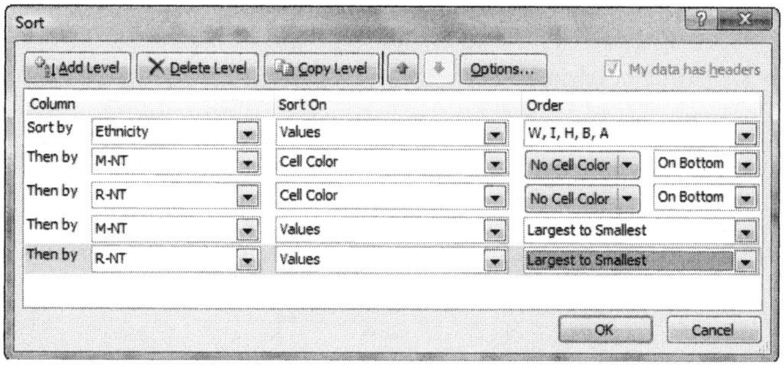

Figure 10-9: After you enter all your sort criteria for the exercise, the Sort dialog box should look like this.

Information Kiosk

You can sort on as many as 255 different criteria. That number represents a lot more criteria than you want to set up during class time. However, I recommend that you play around with adding more criteria to your sorts. Repeated sorting takes practice to make sure that your sort is really giving you the answers you want.

13. Click OK to apply the sort.

After a few moments, your data should sort in the order you requested. How long this process takes depends on the power of your computer and on which other programs are running at the time. The resulting sheet looks like the one shown in Figure 10-10.

Ethnicity	M-NT	M-MSS	M-FFB	M-A	M-M	M-E	R-NT	R-MSS	R-FFB	R-A	R-M	R-E	W-NT	W-MSS	W-FFB
W	3798	730	6	6	57	32	3706	721	2	11	73	14	3619	716	
W	2539	722	7	8	63	24	2331	723	2	10	72	16	2440	706	
W	2528	724	10	7	54	28	2333	721	3	12	69	15	2306	717	
W	2352	713	16	10	53	21	2234	716	5	13	67	14	2321	704	
W	2352	717	8	8	65	19	2140	722	2	10	75	13	2191	706	
W	2349	729	5	6	58	30	2245	731	2	8	71	20	2297	719	
W	2347	732	5	6	56	33	2353	723	2	10	73	15	2420	716	
W	2264	726	5	6	62	27	2110	724	1	9	76	14	2115	715	
W	2068	729	5	7	57	31	1970	730	1	8	74	17	1964	722	
W	1483	724	7	7	61	24	1371	729	2	8	72	18	1349	726	
W	1075	713	15	8	54	23	973	724	5	10	68	18	984	713	
W	912	702	19	9	61	11	789	708	5	16	70	9	811	708	
W	858	738	4	3	54	39	883	731	1	7	72	20	852	726	
W	854	697	23	13	53	11	969	696	12	19	62	8	999	696	
W	806	737	2	3	59	36	767	727	1	8	76	14	760	722	
W	754	694	23	15	55	8	568	694	8	22	65	5	546	688	
W	715	703	17	12	58	12	630	713	4	12	74	10	627	709	
W	673	738	5	3	56	36	634	731	1	7	73	19	660	710	
W	673	725	7	5	60	28	573	731	1	5	77	17	597	713	
W	661	710	12	12	59	17	627	713	3	15	70	11	623	706	
W	646	724	6	8	61	26	633	722	1	11	74	14	661	712	
W	645	746	2	4	49	44	717	743	1	5	66	28	738	729	
W	643	738	4	5	51	40	629	736	0	5	73	21	641	727	
W	636	698	20	15	55	10	612	692	9	24	62	5	661	682	

Figure 10-10: After Excel sorts the data according to your criteria, your results should look like this.

The first lines of the results show the schools that reported high test results for both these columns (M-NT and R-NT) for the White population. If you scroll down the Ethnicity column to the first row with an ethnicity of Indian (a letter I in the Ethnicity column), as shown in Figure 10-11, you find the schools in the Indian population that reported high results for both these columns. Continue scrolling and you can find out which schools reported high test results for both these columns for each of the other ethnicities.

Ethnicity	M-NT	M-MSS	M-FFB	M-A	M-M	M-E	R-NT	R-MSS	R-FFB	R-A	R-M	R-E	W-NT	W-MSS	W-FFB	W-A	W-M
W	0	-	-	-	-	-	0	-	-	-	-	-	0	-	-	-	-
W	0	-	-	-	-	-	0	-	-	-	-	-	0	-	-	-	-
W	0	-	-	-	-	-	0	-	-	-	-	-	0	-	-	-	-
I	542	678	36	24	39	1	450	670	11	42	47	1	382	666	7	49	43
I	533	679	35	24	40	1	435	670	10	42	47	1	367	667	7	47	45
I	348	685	23	25	49	3	330	668	9	45	45	1	288	676	2	46	50
I	348	685	23	25	49	3	330	668	9	45	45	1	288	676	2	46	50
I	345	683	33	18	47	2	310	677	6	40	52	1	257	673	5	46	47
I	345	683	33	18	47	2	310	677	6	40	52	1	257	673	5	46	47
I	335	698	20	13	62	5	304	685	4	31	63	2	263	696	2	23	71
I	316	673	43	23	34	0	280	663	11	55	33	0	227	665	5	57	37
I	316	673	43	23	34	0	280	663	11	55	33	0	227	665	5	57	37
I	293	684	32	18	45	5	378	667	14	42	41	3	323	671	7	41	49
I	278	681	34	18	47	1	223	676	7	37	55	1	182	679	1	41	58
I	278	681	34	18	47	1	223	676	7	37	55	1	182	679	1	41	58
I	262	686	29	19	47	6	353	668	14	42	42	3	296	673	6	40	51
I	242	691	26	15	56	3	229	682	7	30	60	3	223	683	7	31	57
I	233	700	19	18	50	12	234	687	3	32	64	2	204	690	4	26	65
I	218	670	49	22	29	1	216	659	24	41	34	1	197	647	16	55	28
I	218	670	49	22	29	1	216	659	24	41	34	1	197	647	16	55	28
I	218	676	44	18	37	1	216	652	20	52	27	0	180	652	12	57	32
I	218	676	44	18	37	1	216	652	20	52	27	0	180	652	12	57	32
I	219	677	43	18	36	3	211	671	12	40	47	1	187	671	11	37	49
I	210	697	15	16	62	7	242	684	7	30	62	1	244	684	2	34	61
I	210	697	15	16	62	7	242	684	7	30	62	1	244	684	2	34	61
I	173	665	60	17	23	1	153	853	24	44	31	0	127	649	22	47	30
I	173	665	60	17	23	1	153	853	24	44	31	0	127	649	22	47	30
I	173	658	66	17	17	0	102	659	18	49	33	0	119	631	30	55	14
I	173	658	66	17	17	0	102	659	18	49	33	0	119	631	30	55	14
I	172	695	16	16	64	5	142	679	4	39	56	1	136	681	3	44	49
I	172	695	16	16	64	5	142	679	4	39	56	1	136	681	3	44	49
I	164	704	10	14	68	9	161	684	4	31	64	1	143	686	3	36	59
I	164	704	10	14	68	9	161	684	4	31	64	1	143	686	3	36	59
I	162	697	26	20	50	4	142	682	11	32	54	3	134	678	7	37	56

Figure 10-11: Results of the multilevel sort, starting at cell J770.

Filtering Your Data

When you filter your data, you see only the data that matches the criteria you want. Unlike sorting, where all the data remains visible, when you filter data, only rows that contain data that matches your criteria remain visible. The other data is still in your worksheet, but is hidden from view.

At the end of the previous sort exercises, you had a way to find out which schools reported data for all tests, but you had to scroll through each set to find out whether any single school reported data for each ethnicity for each test. By filtering the data and showing only data that meets your specific requirements, you could have made that chore easier.

Filtering data with a single criterion

To ensure that you are starting with data that is sorted in an appropriate way for this exercise, start over with a new file that already has the sorts from the preceding section applied. The first type of filtering you perform on the data is a quick filter to show only those schools that reported their data in the All category (which indicates that all students were reported as one population):

1. **Open the file AIMSSpring2005ReadyToFilter.xlsx.**

2. **Move through your worksheet so that column J, the Ethnicity column, is the first visible column on the left side of your screen.**

3. **Choose Data → Sort & Filter → Filter.**

   Each cell in the title row is displayed with a drop-down arrow. You can use the lists to either quick-filter the data or set up custom filters for the data.

4. **Click the drop-down arrow to filter column J.**

   The bottom half of the list, shown in Figure 10-12, shows you the values in this column. You want to see only the rows for schools that reported useful data.

5. **Deselect the (Select All) check box.**

   Because all the other boxes are deselected, you can quickly apply the filter so that only the schools reporting all their population data together are shown.

6. **Select the All check box. Click OK.**

   You have now filtered the data so that only the rows containing an Ethnicity value of All are shown. Notice that the number of rows has greatly decreased. The first row that is shown is row 3382. If you scroll down, you see that the last row you see is row 4195. You now have a set of data that meets a single criterion and is small enough to work with.

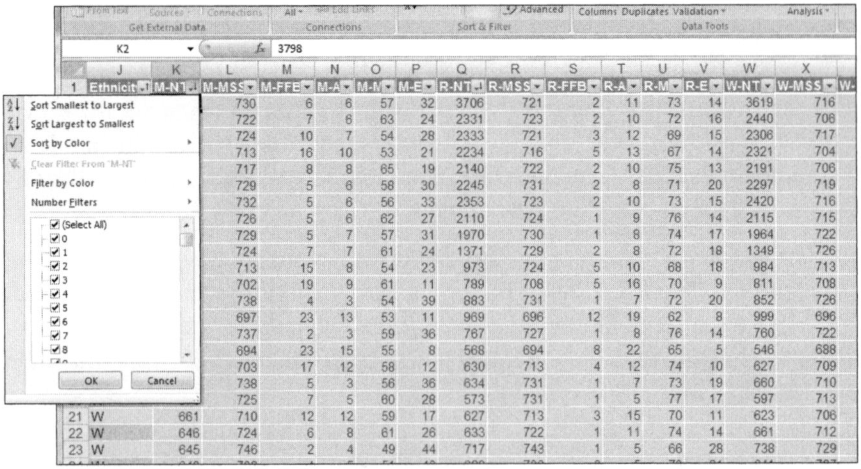

Figure 10-12: List of options for filtering on column J — the Ethnicity column.

Filter dropdown menu options (for column M-NT):

- Sort Smallest to Largest
- Sort Largest to Smallest
- Sort by Color ▸
- Clear Filter From "M-NT"
- Filter by Color ▸
- Number Filters ▸
- ☑ (Select All)
- ☑ 0
- ☑ 1
- ☑ 2
- ☑ 3
- ☑ 4
- ☑ 5
- ☑ 6
- ☑ 7
- ☑ 8

[OK] [Cancel]

Cell K2 = 3798

M-MSS	M-FFE	M-A	M-M	M-E	R-NT	R-MSS	R-FFB	R-A	R-M	R-E	W-NT	W-MSS	W-
730	6	6	57	32	3706	721	2	11	73	14	3619	716
722	7	8	63	24	2331	723	2	10	72	16	2440	708
724	10	7	54	28	2333	721	3	12	69	15	2306	717
713	16	10	53	21	2234	716	5	13	67	14	2321	704
717	8	8	65	19	2140	722	2	10	75	13	2191	708
729	5	6	58	30	2245	731	2	8	71	20	2297	719
732	5	6	56	33	2353	723	2	10	73	15	2420	716
726	5	6	62	27	2110	724	1	9	76	14	2115	715
729	5	7	57	31	1970	730	1	8	74	17	1964	722
724	7	7	61	24	1371	729	2	8	72	18	1349	726
713	15	8	54	23	973	724	5	10	68	18	984	713
702	19	9	61	11	789	708	5	16	70	9	811	708
738	4	3	54	39	883	731	1	7	72	20	852	726
697	23	13	53	11	969	696	12	19	62	8	999	696
737	2	3	59	36	787	727	1	8	76	14	760	722
694	23	15	55	8	568	694	8	22	65	5	546	688
703	17	12	58	12	630	713	4	12	74	10	627	709
738	5	3	56	36	634	731	1	7	73	19	660	710
725	7	5	80	28	573	731	1	5	77	17	597	713
(21 W) 710	12	12	59	17	627	713	3	15	70	11	623	706
(22 W) 724	6	8	61	26	633	722	1	11	74	14	661	712
(23 W) 746	2	4	49	44	717	743	1	5	66	28	738	729

The view of your worksheet is the same as the one shown in Figure 10-13.

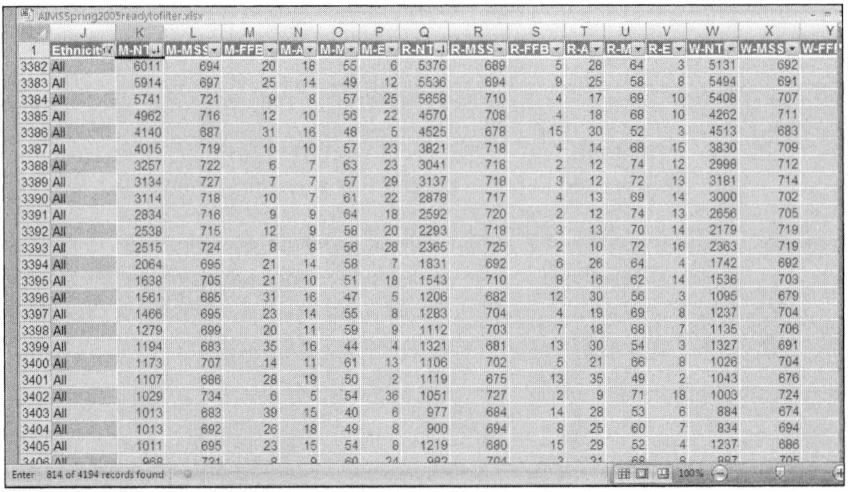

	Ethnicit	M-NT	M-MSS	M-FFE	M-A	M-M	M-E	R-NT	R-MSS	R-FFB	R-A	R-M	R-E	W-NT	W-MSS	W-FFI
3382	All	6011	694	20	18	55	6	5376	689	5	28	64	3	5131	692	
3383	All	5914	697	25	14	49	12	5536	694	9	25	58	8	5494	691	
3384	All	5741	721	9	8	57	25	5658	710	4	17	69	10	5408	707	
3385	All	4962	716	12	10	56	22	4570	708	4	18	68	10	4262	711	
3386	All	4140	687	31	16	48	5	4525	678	15	30	52	3	4513	683	
3387	All	4015	719	10	10	57	23	3821	718	4	14	68	15	3830	709	
3388	All	3257	722	6	7	63	23	3041	718	2	12	74	12	2998	712	
3389	All	3134	727	7	7	57	29	3137	718	3	12	72	13	3181	714	
3390	All	3114	718	10	7	61	22	2878	717	4	13	69	14	3000	702	
3391	All	2834	718	9	9	64	18	2592	720	2	12	74	13	2656	705	
3392	All	2538	715	12	9	58	20	2293	718	3	13	70	14	2179	719	
3393	All	2515	724	8	8	56	28	2365	725	2	10	72	16	2363	719	
3394	All	2064	695	21	14	58	7	1831	692	6	26	64	4	1742	692	
3395	All	1638	705	21	10	51	18	1543	710	8	16	62	14	1536	703	
3396	All	1561	685	31	16	47	5	1206	682	12	30	56	3	1095	679	
3397	All	1466	695	23	14	55	8	1283	704	4	19	69	8	1237	704	
3398	All	1279	699	20	11	59	9	1112	703	7	18	66	7	1135	706	
3399	All	1194	683	35	16	44	4	1321	681	13	30	54	3	1327	691	
3400	All	1173	707	14	11	61	13	1106	702	5	21	66	8	1026	704	
3401	All	1107	686	28	19	50	2	1119	675	13	35	49	2	1043	876	
3402	All	1029	734	6	5	54	36	1051	727	2	9	71	18	1003	724	
3403	All	1013	683	39	15	40	6	977	684	14	28	53	6	884	674	
3404	All	1013	692	26	18	49	8	900	694	8	25	60	7	834	694	
3405	All	1011	895	23	15	54	8	1219	680	15	29	52	4	1237	886	

Enter   814 of 4194 records found   100%

Figure 10-13: The results of filtering column J (Ethnicity) to show only the value All.

Notice that filtering the data does not affect the order of the data. All it did was limit which rows of data are visible. Now that you have less data to work with, you can easily see which school or district reported the highest numbers for both M-NT and R-NT and reported all their data under one ethnic category. In this case, it is a district, and the district's name is in cell I3382.

You might want to know how many schools report this way. In the lower-left corner of the screen, next to the word *Ready,* notice the indication of how many rows are shown out of the number of rows in the worksheet: 814 of 4194.

Or, maybe you want to work with the whole set of data so that you can sort it a different way. In this case, you clear the sort so that all rows are shown again.

7. Choose Data → Sort & Filter → Clear.

All the data rows appear again.

Just as with sorts, you can apply repeated filters by applying a series of quick filters to each column. To see this process, you do one more filtering exercise.

Applying quick filters

For this exercise, you apply quick filters to find out which schools that reported data for the White population reported test scores higher than 700 (a passing score) for all three of the R-MSS, M-MSS, and W-MSS tests:

1. Return to the same file you used in the previous exercise.

2. Click the Ethnicity column's drop-down arrow, and set it to filter for just the rows that have a value of W. Click OK.

The set of visible rows narrows to only the schools reporting data in the W category of ethnicity, a total of 771 rows.

3. Using the drop-down arrow for the R-MSS column (column R), choose Sort by Color → Sort by Font Color → Green, as shown in Figure 10-14.

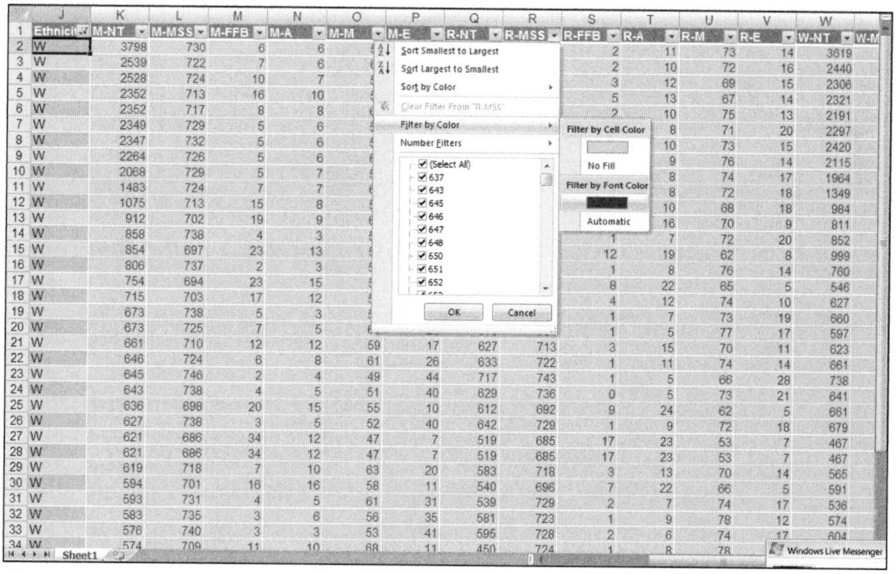

Figure 10-14: Filter list for the R-MSS column.

If at any time from now on you notice a delay before the drop-down list appears, do not be surprised. Excel 2007 has to work through the entire column to determine each unique value in the column, because any value can be used in the quick filter.

The set of visible rows narrows to only the schools reporting valid data in column R, the column containing test results for the R-MSS test. This is a total of 554 rows.

4. Repeat Step 3 for columns M-MSS (column L) and W-MSS (column X).

So far, you have shrunk the data set so that the invalid data for the R-T, M-MSS, and W-MSS test scores are the only ones shown. Notice that the final number of visible rows is 526.

You are shrinking the dataset to a useable number of rows. However, as is the case in the real world, now you add one more criteria to the filter: Delete all M-MSS and R-MSS scores below the value of 700. To do this step, you will add a numeric filter to this column.

5. Bring up the drop-down filter for column M-MSS (column L). From the list of possible filters, choose Number Filters → Greater Than.

This step opens the Custom AutoFilter dialog box, as shown in Figure 10-15.

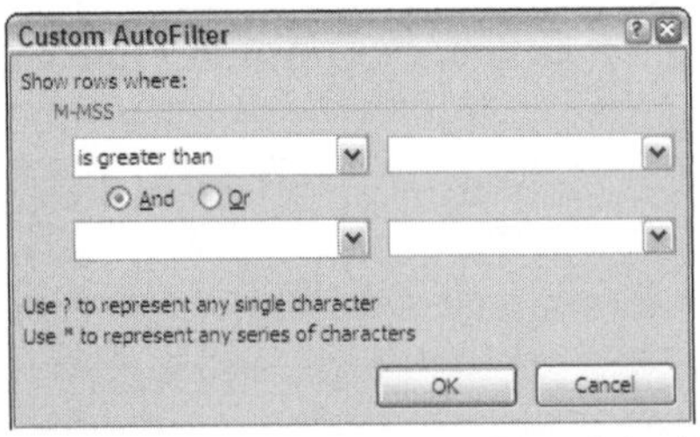

Figure 10-15: The Custom AutoFilter dialog box.

6. The cursor should appear in the second box in the first row. Fill in this box with a value of 700. Click OK.

You have filtered out any M-MSS scores below the value of 700, so next you do the same for the R-MSS scores.

7. Repeat Steps 5 and 6 for the R-MSS column (column R).

This step filters out any R-MSS scores below 700.

Notice that the number of rows you see decreased dramatically. You now have only 195 of the original 4,194 records showing. This set of data is manageable. The top of your worksheet should look like the one shown in Figure 10-16.

8. Choose Data → Sort & Filter → Clear.

All data is shown again.

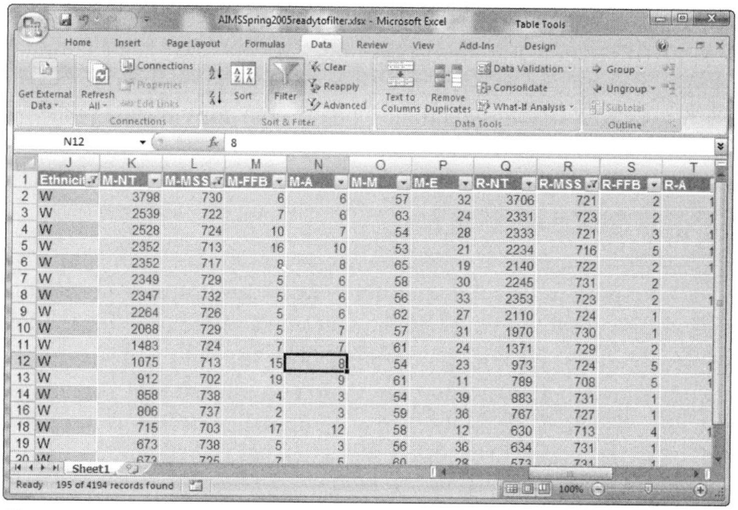

Figure 10-16: After applying the quick filters, your worksheet should look like this.

Using advanced filters

Quick filters are the way to go as you learn to filter your data. Eventually, you might be tempted to play with the advanced filtering button in the Sort & Filter group on the Data tab. *Note:* Be very careful when using this option.

In the Advanced Filter dialog box, shown in Figure 10-17, you click and drag in your data to set up the range and criteria for your sort.

Figure 10-17: The Advanced Filter dialog box.

If you know your data extremely well, this method works. Otherwise, this dialog box can be an invitation to disaster. Because you are depending on your memory to select the filter criteria, you can easily miss a value that you want to include. (I prefer to work with the quick-filter options that are built into your table definitions and then filter based on the actual values of my data.)

The one feature in the Advanced Filter dialog box that might seem to be helpful is the option to copy your filtered data to another location within your file (to another worksheet, for example). The risk of accidentally filtering out data you might need greatly outweighs the advantage of having this dialog box do the copying for you.

Organizing Assorted Data

You can organize your data in Excel in another way: by grouping it. *Grouping,* or *outlining,* allows you to combine your data so that you can see more of the logical connections within the rows. Grouping combines both filtering and sorting. In addition, grouping allows you to add subtotal rows and columns so that you can easily summarize your data. These subtotal rows may be actual subtotals, or they may be any other formula you wish to use. Think about it as a way to sort and pivot your data in a single group of steps.

There is one catch: You can't group or outline data that is in a table. You must perform these functions on data that has not yet been changed to a table. So, why do it? Because this is how the summary rows within the table you have been working with throughout this chapter were actually created.

To group or outline your data, you must have labels in each row of the first column. In addition, no blank lines can appear within the set of data you are using. In fact, it is a good idea to start with a file that has a value of some kind in each cell.

For this exercise, you are going to work with the data for four school districts. You will use the outlining and grouping features to discover the high test score for the M-FFB test for each school and each district:

1. Open the file **AIMSSpring2005OutliningData.xlsx.**

2. Choose **Data → Outline → Subtotal.**

The Subtotal dialog box appears, as shown in Figure 10-18.

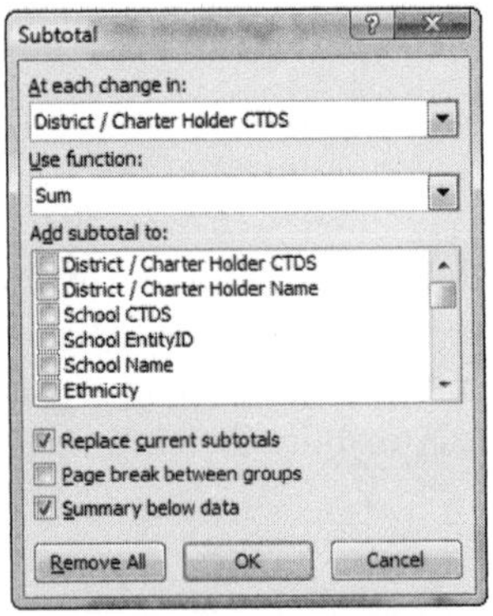

Figure 10-18: The Subtotal dialog box.

You use this dialog box to set up where you want the subtotal lines added. By adding the subtotal lines, you also turn on the outlining and grouping functions for the rows of data.

This dialog box needs three pieces of information to set up the subtotal lines:

- The column for which you need to track the changes

- The function to be computed

- The value to be used in the computation

In addition, you can use the check boxes at the bottom of the dialog box to tell Excel exactly where you want the subtotals created.

3. From the At Each Change In drop-down list, choose School Name.

This tells Excel that you are setting up the subtotal line for the schools first. You will add the subtotal lines for the districts after you set up the school lines.

4. From the Use Function drop-down list, choose Max.

The default function is the Sum function. Because you want to find the high score instead of the total of all the scores, you need to set the function to Max instead of Sum.

5. Uncheck the check box for W-E. Check the check box for M-FFB.

You could select multiple tests to find the high score on the same subtotal line. To keep things concise, you'll show only the high score for the M-FFB test.

6. Leave the check boxes at the bottom of the dialog box at their default settings.

If you had added any subtotals prior to this point, you would want to remove them in order to create this set of subtotals. In this case, you do not need page breaks between each group of data, so leave that box unchecked. Finally, you want the summary line to appear below the group of data, so leave the bottom box checked. If you want the summary line above the group of data, uncheck this box. When you're done, the dialog box should look like Figure 10-19.

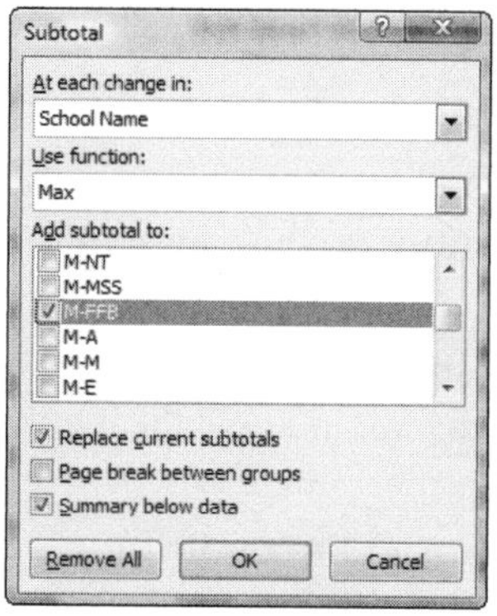

Figure 10-19: The Subtotal dialog box set to create the outline that will find the max value for the M-FFB test for each school.

7. **Click OK.**

Excel takes a moment or two to add the subtotal lines and group the data. When Excel is done, your sheet should look like Figure 10-20.

Outline levels

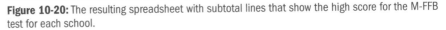

	District / Charter CTDS	District / Charter Holder Name	School CTDS	School EntityID	School Name	Ethnicity	M-NT	M-MSS	M-FFB	M-A	M-M	M-E
2	70297000	Deer Valley Unified District	70297224	5162	Barry Goldwater High Sch	W	404	715	10	9	63	
3	70297000	Deer Valley Unified District	70297224	5162	Barry Goldwater High Sch	I	3	*	*	*	*	*
4	70297000	Deer Valley Unified District	70297224	5162	Barry Goldwater High Sch	H	78	700	18	14	60	
5	70297000	Deer Valley Unified District	70297224	5162	Barry Goldwater High Sch	B	15	692	27	20	40	
6	70297000	Deer Valley Unified District	70297224	5162	Barry Goldwater High Sch	All	516	713	12	10	61	
7	70297000	Deer Valley Unified District	70297224	5162	Barry Goldwater High Sch	A	15	754	7	13	40	
8	70297000	Deer Valley Unified District	70297224	5162	Barry Goldwater High Sch	-	1	*	*	*	*	*
9					**Barry Goldwater High School Max**				27			
10	70297000	Deer Valley Unified District	70297245	85850	Boulder Creek High Schoc	W	254	711	10	14	62	
11	70297000	Deer Valley Unified District	70297245	85850	Boulder Creek High Schoc	I	1	*	*	*	*	*
12	70297000	Deer Valley Unified District	70297245	85850	Boulder Creek High Schoc	H	18	706	17	11	56	
13	70297000	Deer Valley Unified District	70297245	85850	Boulder Creek High Schoc	B	3	*	*	*	*	*
14	70297000	Deer Valley Unified District	70297245	85850	Boulder Creek High Schoc	All	284	711	10	13	62	
15	70297000	Deer Valley Unified District	70297245	85850	Boulder Creek High Schoc	A	8	*	*	*	*	*
16	70297000	Deer Valley Unified District	70297245	85850	Boulder Creek High Schoc	-	0	-	-	-	-	-
17					**Boulder Creek High School Max**				17			
18	70297000	Deer Valley Unified District	70297219	5161	Deer Valley High School	W	447	720	5	6	71	
19	70297000	Deer Valley Unified District	70297219	5161	Deer Valley High School	I	3	*	*	*	*	*
20	70297000	Deer Valley Unified District	70297219	5161	Deer Valley High School	H	69	707	6	13	70	
21	70297000	Deer Valley Unified District	70297219	5161	Deer Valley High School	B	26	705	4	8	85	
22	70297000	Deer Valley Unified District	70297219	5161	Deer Valley High School	All	564	718	5	7	71	
23	70297000	Deer Valley Unified District	70297219	5161	Deer Valley High School	A	19	730	0	0	74	
24	70297000	Deer Valley Unified District	70297219	5161	Deer Valley High School	-	0	-	-	-	-	-
25					**Deer Valley High School Max**				6			
26	70297000	Deer Valley Unified District	70297233	5163	Mountain Ridge High Schc	W	673	725	7	5	60	
27	70297000	Deer Valley Unified District	70297233	5163	Mountain Ridge High Schc	I	8	*	*	*	*	*
28	70297000	Deer Valley Unified District	70297233	5163	Mountain Ridge High Schc	H	55	711	15	11	60	
29	70297000	Deer Valley Unified District	70297233	5163	Mountain Ridge High Schc	B	33	707	15	12	61	
30	70297000	Deer Valley Unified District	70297233	5163	Mountain Ridge High Schc	All	816	724	8	6	60	
31	70297000	Deer Valley Unified District	70297233	5163	Mountain Ridge High Schc	A	47	731	6	2	55	
32					**Mountain Ridge High School Max**				15			

Sheet1 | Sheet2 | Sheet3

Figure 10-20: The resulting spreadsheet with subtotal lines that show the high score for the M-FFB test for each school.

The left side of your sheet now has a series of outline levels showing. You can expand or collapse these levels by using the Show Detail and Hide Detail buttons at the far right of the Outline group on the Data tab.

In addition, a new line has been added for each change in school. This line shows the high score for the M-FFB test for that school. For example, the highest score for the M-FFB test from Arcadia High School is 34.

Your next step is to add the subtotal lines for the school districts.

8. **Choose Data → Outline → Subtotal.**

9. **From the At Each Change In drop-down list, choose District/Charter Holder Name.**

10. **Leave the function and the subtotal options as they were in the first part of the exercise.**

While you are adding a second level of subtotal, you still want the data reported on the same column. In addition, you still want to know the maximum value for that column within this district.

11. **Uncheck the check box for Replace Current Subtotals.**

This time, you want to add a new set of subtotal lines to the ones that are already there. Notice that when you tell Excel not to replace the existing subtotal lines, you are no longer able to change the location of the summary line. When you are done, the dialog box should look like Figure 10-21.

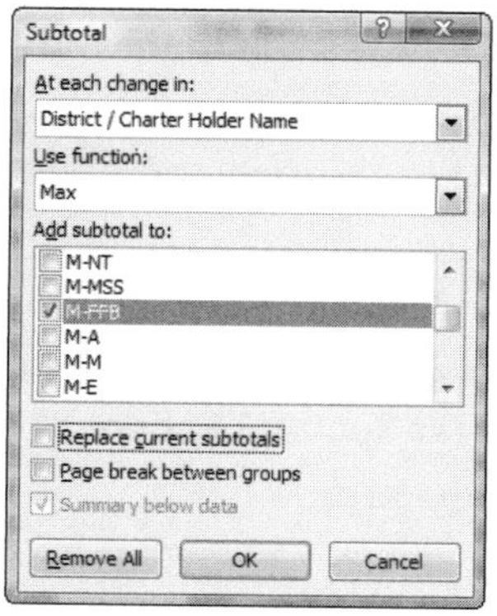

Figure 10-21: The Subtotal dialog box set to create the outline that will find the max value for the M-FFB test for each district.

12. **Click OK.**

Excel takes a moment or two to add the subtotal lines and group the data. When Excel is done, your sheet should look like Figure 10-22.

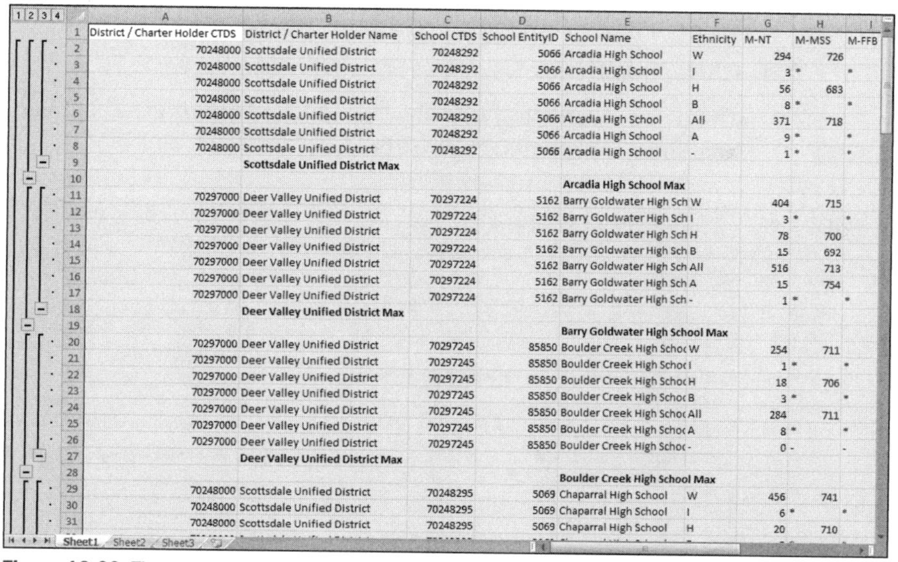

Figure 10-22: The resulting spreadsheet with subtotal lines that show the high score for the M-FFB test for each district.

Where previously you had two sets of grouping options, you now have three sets. Notice also that you now have two lines of subtotals for each school, which isn't quite what you want.

Unlike a PivotTable, the order in which you add the subtotals makes a difference. You are now going to clear the subtotals and create them in the opposite order so that you see what you expected to see.

13. Choose Data → Outline → Subtotal. At the bottom of the Subtotal dialog box, click Remove All.

The dialog box closes, and your subtotal lines are removed. You are now ready to re-create them.

14. Choose Data → Outline → Subtotal.

15. From the At Each Change In drop-down list, choose District/Charter Holder Name. Leave the function and the subtotal options as they were in the first part of the exercise. Click OK.

Excel takes a moment or two to add the subtotal lines and group the data. When Excel is done, you see subtotal lines for each district.

16. Choose Data → Outline → Subtotal.

17. From the At Each Change In drop-down list, choose School Name. Leave the function and the subtotal options as they were in the first part of the exercise. Click OK.

Excel takes a moment or two to add the subtotal lines and group the data. When Excel is done, you see subtotal lines for each school, and the district lines only appear at the end of the set of schools for the district.

18. Click Hide Detail.

The detail records for your sheet are filtered out of view, and you see just the total lines as shown in Figure 10-23.

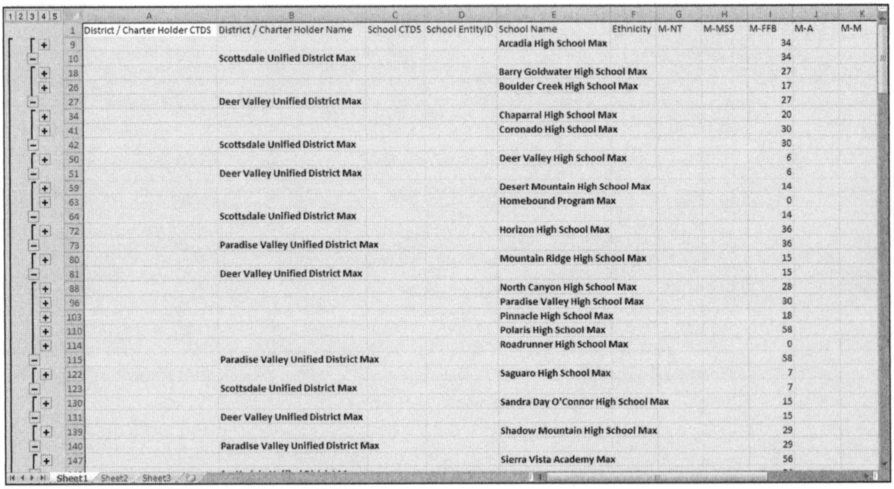

Figure 10-23: The final worksheet shows only the total lines.

Subtotal lines are good for generating reports when you don't have a table of data. They allow you to fairly quickly see the summarization information when you don't need to create a PivotTable.

correlation: The relationship between two pieces or sets of data.

criteria: The information used to determine the answer to the question being investigated. In sorting, criteria are used to determine the order of the rows of data. In filtering, the criteria determine which rows are visible and which are not.

group (or outline): When different data in a worksheet is related, grouping (or outlining) is used as another way to show relationships between the data. One advantage to groups or outlines is that levels within the groups can have subtotals applied for data evaluation. Another advantage is that levels of data can be collapsed so that only summary data is visible.

hidden cell: A cell that is not visible, but is still in the worksheet.

level: When creating sorts and filters, each of the multiple criteria that can be applied to a data set.

raw data: Data that has not been filtered or sorted to find answers. Raw data can also be referred to as the full set of data in a workbook.

record: A row of data; a term used especially where a relationship exists between cells within a given row.

visible cell: A cell that can be seen in the current view of the data.

Last Stop

Practice Exam

1. Name one situation where you would sort your data and one where you would filter your data.

_____

_____

2. Name one way to define the sort criteria for your data.

_____

3. Name two ways that you can find the count of rows in a range of data.

_____

_____

4. Describe a situation where using conditional formatting with sorting improves your productivity as well as the understandability of your data.

_____

_____

5. You can't complete which of the following tasks from the Custom Lists dialog box?

a. View any existing custom lists.

b. Delete a custom list.

c. Name a custom list.

d. Edit a custom list.

6. Name the biggest advantage to filtering your data.

_____

_____

7. To clear the filters in use in your document, use the _____ button in the _____ group on the _____ tab.

8. True or False: You can filter only on numeric data.

9. Which addressing method is used when you create an advanced filter: relative addressing or absolute addressing?

10. Which of the following does not prevent Excel from grouping and outlining your data? (More than one answer is possible.)

a. No labels are defined for the data set.

b. Empty cells are in the data set.

c. You have empty rows of data.

d. Text data is within the data set.

Ensuring Your Data Is Right

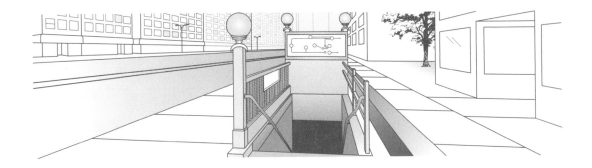

Enter the Station

Questions

1. What are two common causes of invalid data?

2. Should duplicate data always be removed?

3. How do you remove duplicate data from one column while leaving the other columns alone?

4. What is the difference between a duplicate cell and a duplicate record?

5. What is a validation rule?

6. Which types of data can be validated?

7. Which sheets in a file are affected if you turn on the Circle Invalid Data feature?

8. What is the difference between an input message and an error message?

9. What is a validation list?

10. What do you learn when you consolidate data?

Express Line

If you already fully understand how to ensure that the data in your Excel 2007 files is correct, skip ahead to the next chapter.

In a perfect world, all the data you receive is perfect. You don't get any duplicate data, formulas work correctly every time, data is totally valid, and data is in only one place at a time. Unfortunately, you don't live in that world; you live in the real world.

In this world, you have to *clean* the data you're given so that you can get good use from it. You need to be able to examine your data and find the problems. You can do this task by hand, but that can be an error prone process. Instead, this chapter leads you through the processes involved in validating your data with Excel:

- Find and remove duplicate cells from rows or columns.
- Validate that the data in the spreadsheet is correct.
- Ensure that data that's added, both its range of value and its type, is correct.
- Consolidate groupings of data into workable chunks.

Removing Duplicate Data

Duplicate data can get into your spreadsheets in a variety of ways. Usually, duplicates are caused by human error of some kind, such as data being entered more than once. Another common cause of duplicate data is that data from two sources is merged into a single sheet.

On the other hand, sometimes duplicate data is legitimate. If someone does something every day, it will be logged in a receipt list once per day. However, if the same transaction is entered more than once, it is not valid. For example, if you buy coffee at the same time every day, the store you buy it at will show duplicate times for the coffee purchases, but the dates for the purchases will be different.

In all these cases, finding unique values by hand can be a tedious, error prone process. You would need to sort the data and then select the duplicates and delete them. Although this process sounds simple, it can be time consuming and problematic. By contrast, the process built into Excel 2007 is easier to do than to describe and is less prone to human error and frustration.

In the following exercises and throughout this chapter, you work with the data from an archeological dig. The dig constitutes a one-semester class. Each time a student discovers an item, he fills out a form for that item. Then, at the end of the week, the student turns in all the filled-out forms for that week. The forms show where the item was found, what type of object it is, who found it, and its weight in grams.

Removing duplicate cells from a single column

In this exercise, you will be using Excel functions to automatically remove duplicate entries from a single column of data. Later in this chapter, you will do an exercise that shows how to remove rows that contain duplicate information that crosses multiple columns.

1. Open the file `DigResults.xlsx`.

2. Select column B (Object Type).

Your have to find which unique object types were found this week. To do this task, you will make a copy of this column and use the Remove Duplicates button to create a list of the types.

3. Copy column B to column G so that you have a copy to work with.

Unlike filtering or sorting your data, removing duplicates changes the data. In the computer world, this process is *destructive*. Whenever you perform a destructive process, work on a copy of data until you are sure that what you are doing will generate the result you want.

4. With column G selected, choose Data ➔ Data Tools ➔ Remove Duplicates.

The Remove Duplicates dialog box opens, as shown in Figure 11-1. In preparation for finding the duplicates, you're prompted to select which columns to evaluate for duplicates, as shown in Figure 11-1.

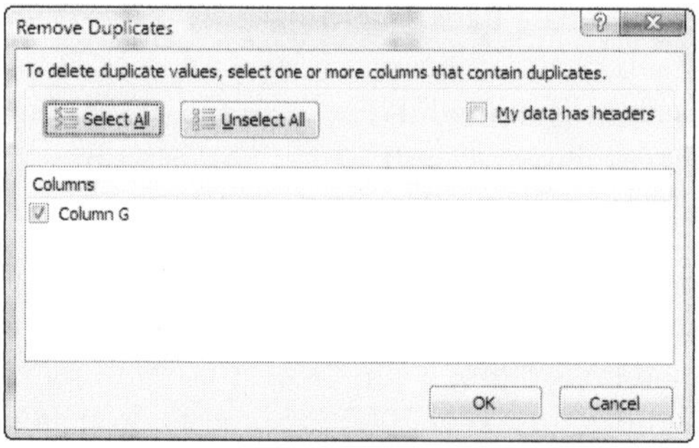

Figure 11-1: The Remove Duplicates dialog box.

Because you have selected only one column, only one column is shown in the list. Because the data was not in a table and was textual in nature, Excel doesn't automatically know that the data has a header. If you don't tell it that the first row is a header row, Excel considers the first row to be just another row of data to be handled.

5. Select the My Data Has Headers check box and then click OK to remove the duplicates.

When you click OK, Excel quickly skims the data and finds the number of unique items and the number of duplicate items. After Excel completes this process, it removes the duplicates and reports the results to you, as shown in Figure 11-2.

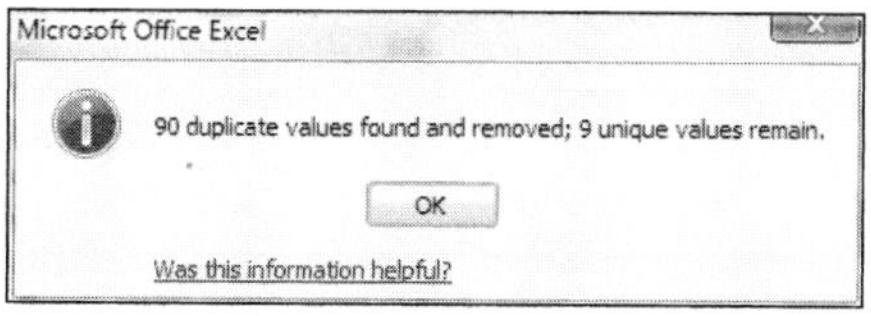

Figure 11-2: Excel reports that it found and removed 90 duplicates.

In this case, Excel found and removed 90 duplicates and left 9 unique types of items found in the dig during the week.

6. **Click OK.**

You see the list of unique object types found and reported this week, as shown in Figure 11-3.

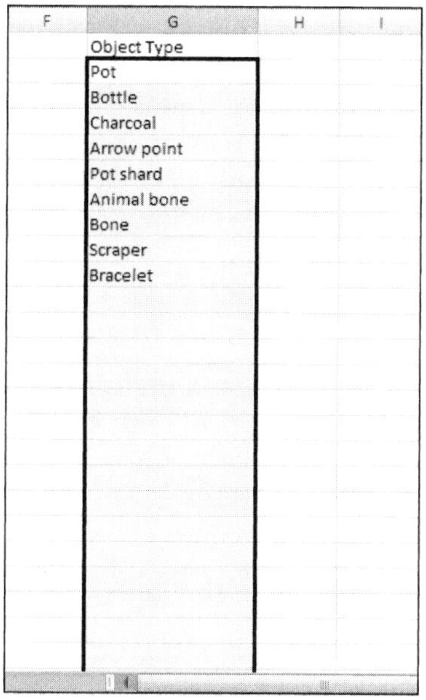

Figure 11-3: A list of unique object types found by removing duplicates in a single column.

Removing duplicates from the columns in a table

Duplicate cells are simplistic examples of duplicate data. A more complex use of the remove-duplicates process is to find and remove duplicates where the data to be verified runs across several columns.

Step Into the Real World

A very real use of removing duplicates from data in a single column is the mainte-nance of e-mail address lists. If you are merging data from multiple lists into a single list, finding and removing duplicates can be a hassle. Rather than do it by hand, drop the e-mail addresses into an Excel spreadsheet, and use the Remove Duplicates button to do the cleanup for you.

A client of mine had a series of e-mail lists that contained addresses from a number of sources. In all, more than a thousand unique addresses were spread across five lists. The client spent hours each month removing the duplicates by hand.

I had the client drop all the addresses into a single column and then use the remove-duplicates process to clean them up. What had taken hours to do then took about three minutes to do automatically.

In this exercise, you begin to clean up the data from the week's archeological digs. Each day, the results of the dig are written on a two part tracking form. At the end of the week, one part of each form is turned in, and the data from that copy is entered into the computer. The students are supposed to keep the other copy.

Unfortunately, at the end of the first week, many of the students turned in both copies, and both were entered into the computer. Your task is to remove the duplicate entries so that only the real entries remain. To do this task, you select the entire data-entry table and use the Remove Duplicates feature to whittle it down:

1. **Return to the table that starts at cell A1 and select the entire table by press-ing Ctrl+A. Choose Data → Data Tools → Remove Duplicates.**

This time, when Excel displays the column list for you to choose from, it recog-nizes that your data has headers and lists all four columns in the table, as shown in Figure 11-4.

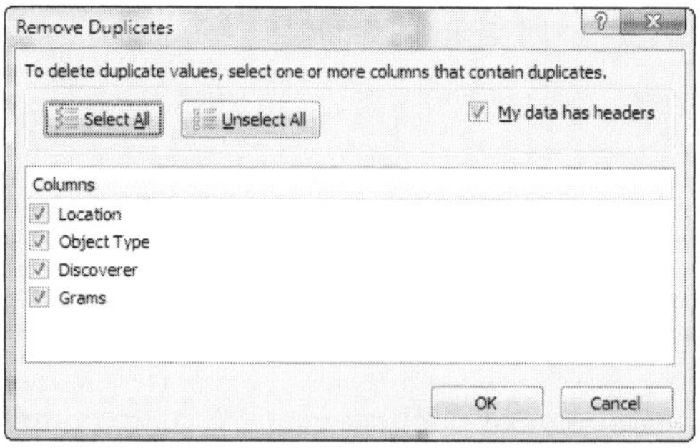

Figure 11-4: The Remove Duplicates dialog box lists the four columns in your table.

2. **Click OK to remove the duplicates.**

When you click OK, Excel skims through the data and finds the number of unique values and the number of duplicate values. This time, rather than just check the values of a single cell, it checks for duplicates across all the cells in the columns you selected.

For example, whereas earlier any copy of an object type was considered a duplicate, now it is a duplicate only if the location, discoverer, and weight are the same.

After the duplicates are removed, Excel reports the results to you, as shown in Figure 11-5.

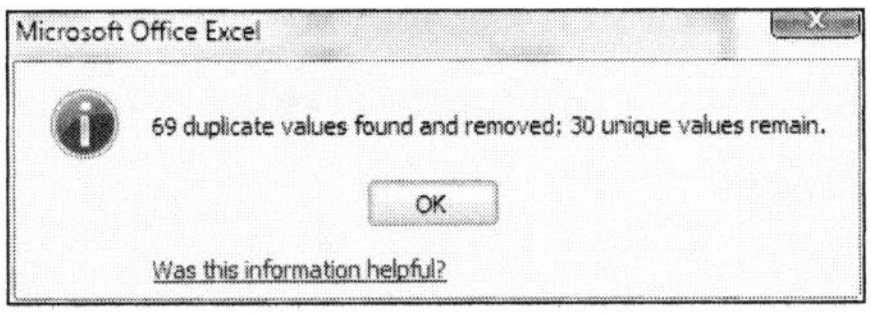

Figure 11-5: Excel reports that it found and removed 69 duplicates.

In this case, Excel found and removed 69 duplicates, leaving 30 unique items found in the dig during the reporting week.

3. **Click OK.**

You see the list of unique item records for this week, as shown in Figure 11-6.

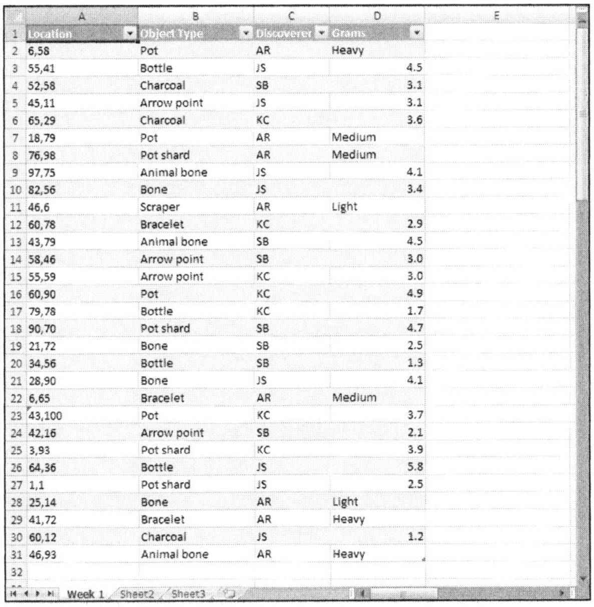

	A	B	C	D	E
1	Location	Object Type	Discoverer	Grams	
2	6,58	Pot	AR	Heavy	
3	55,41	Bottle	JS	4.5	
4	52,58	Charcoal	SB	3.1	
5	45,11	Arrow point	JS	3.1	
6	65,29	Charcoal	KC	3.6	
7	18,79	Pot	AR	Medium	
8	76,98	Pot shard	AR	Medium	
9	97,75	Animal bone	JS	4.1	
10	82,56	Bone	JS	3.4	
11	46,6	Scraper	AR	Light	
12	60,78	Bracelet	KC	2.9	
13	43,79	Animal bone	SB	4.5	
14	58,46	Arrow point	SB	3.0	
15	55,59	Arrow point	KC	3.0	
16	60,90	Pot	KC	4.9	
17	79,78	Bottle	KC	1.7	
18	90,70	Pot shard	SB	4.7	
19	21,72	Bone	SB	2.5	
20	34,56	Bottle	SB	1.3	
21	28,90	Bone	JS	4.1	
22	6,65	Bracelet	AR	Medium	
23	43,100	Pot	KC	3.7	
24	42,16	Arrow point	SB	2.1	
25	3,93	Pot shard	KC	3.9	
26	64,36	Bottle	JS	5.8	
27	1,1	Pot shard	JS	2.5	
28	25,14	Bone	AR	Light	
29	41,72	Bracelet	AR	Heavy	
30	60,12	Charcoal	JS	1.2	
31	46,93	Animal bone	AR	Heavy	
32					

Week 1 / Sheet2 / Sheet3

Figure 11-6: A list of objects found after the Remove Duplicates feature was used on a set of columns.

Removing duplicates from select columns in a table

Because Excel lets you select exactly which columns to use for the comparison, you can use the same process you used in the preceding section to find out many other things about your data. As an example, you first revert to the original data and remove the duplicates again. This time, you don't care where the item was found or how much it weighs; you just want to know what types of objects each student found. To do this task, you repeat the remove-duplicates process with only the Object Type and Discoverer columns selected:

1. **Continuing with the same file you used in the preceding section, select the entire table and then click the Remove Duplicates button.**

2. **Deselect the check boxes for the Location and Grams columns.**

3. **Click OK to remove the duplicates.**

   This time, Excel reports back to you that it found and removed six duplicates, as shown in Figure 11-7.

   Figure 11-7: Excel found and removed six duplicates.

4. **Click OK.**

   You see the list of unique object types that each person found and reported during the week, as shown in Figure 11-8.

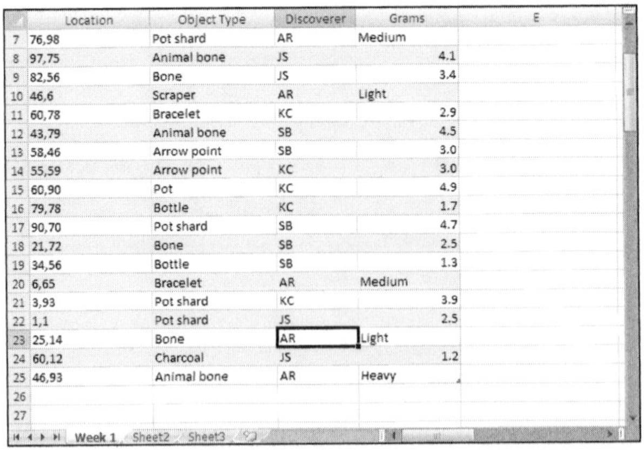

	Location	Object Type	Discoverer	Grams	E
7	76,98	Pot shard	AR	Medium	
8	97,75	Animal bone	JS	4.1	
9	82,56	Bone	JS	3.4	
10	46,6	Scraper	AR	Light	
11	60,78	Bracelet	KC	2.9	
12	43,79	Animal bone	SB	4.5	
13	58,46	Arrow point	SB	3.0	
14	55,59	Arrow point	KC	3.0	
15	60,90	Pot	KC	4.9	
16	79,78	Bottle	KC	1.7	
17	90,70	Pot shard	SB	4.7	
18	21,72	Bone	SB	2.5	
19	34,56	Bottle	SB	1.3	
20	6,65	Bracelet	AR	Medium	
21	3,93	Pot shard	KC	3.9	
22	1,1	Pot shard	JS	2.5	
23	25,14	Bone	AR	Light	
24	60,12	Charcoal	JS	1.2	
25	46,93	Animal bone	AR	Heavy	
26					
27					

Figure 11-8: List of unique items found by each person after removing duplicates.

Validating Data

Duplicate data is only one kind of problem data. You can find other problem data by using the data validation tools to build your own validation rules for correct data. *Validation rules* let you determine how data should look and what type of data is allowed for any given column of data.

For example, take a look at the Grams column in the archeological dig results in the previous section. Although most of the team members weighed their items and provided a weight in grams, the team member with the initials AR misunderstood the directions and gave a *description* of the weight instead.

With an error like this one, you can fix the data in two ways:

- If the data is already in the spreadsheet, you can have Excel find and mark the incorrect values.

- If the data is being added to the spreadsheet, you can restrict the entry of the data in many different ways.

In this section, you learn how to do both kinds of validation.

Creating a basic validation rule

When working with large amounts of data, you generally know what kind of data to expect for each column. In some cases, you even know the range of values or which specific values can be used for each column. You can use that knowledge to create data validation rules that help clean your data.

In the following exercise, you create a validation rule to restrict the weights in the Grams column to actual numbers:

1. Open the file `DigResultsWk1UniqueRecords.xlsx`.

2. Select column D (Grams). Choose Data → Data Tools → Data Validation.

The Data Validation dialog box opens, as shown in Figure 11-9.

Using the three tabs in this dialog box, you will create a validation rule to restrict the weights in this sheet to actual numbers.

3. From the Allow drop-down list, select Decimal.

When you change the allowed data from Any Value to a specific item, you activate the remainder of the interface. For simplicity's sake, the first rule you make requires only that the values are numbers. When you create a number-based rule, you must also define something about the number for Excel to validate against. Because you are working with weights, the number must be greater than 0.

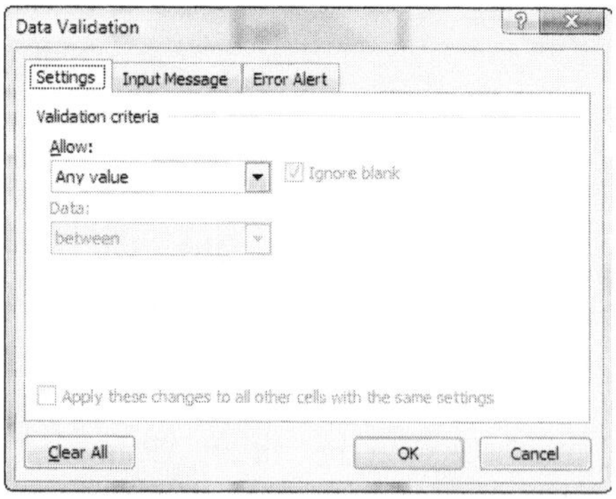

![Data Validation dialog box]

Figure 11-9: The Data Validation dialog box.

4. **From the Data drop-down list, select Greater Than. In the Minimum box, type 0 (zero). Click OK to create the rule.**

You have now created and applied a data validation rule for the Grams column. Notice that each of the entries that contains a word has an error triangle in the upper-left corner of the cell.

When you have only a few rows of data, as in this case, visually checking for the error indicator is a good way to find all the errors. However, when you have more data, you are likely to miss items. Instead, you can have Excel mark the errors much more obviously.

5. **Choose Data → Data Tools → Data Validation → Circle Invalid Data.**

As shown in Figure 11-10, Excel circles all the cells in your sheet that contain invalid data.

In the real world, at this point you would go find the correct information and enter it into the cells. As you correct each cell, Excel would remove the circle and the error flag would clear.

If you want to remove all the flags at one time, you can select the Clear Validation Circles option from the Data Validation drop-down list.

 ## Watch Your Step

Turning on and off the error circles applies to all errors on the active spreadsheet. To see the error circles for other sheets, you select each sheet and turn on the circles.

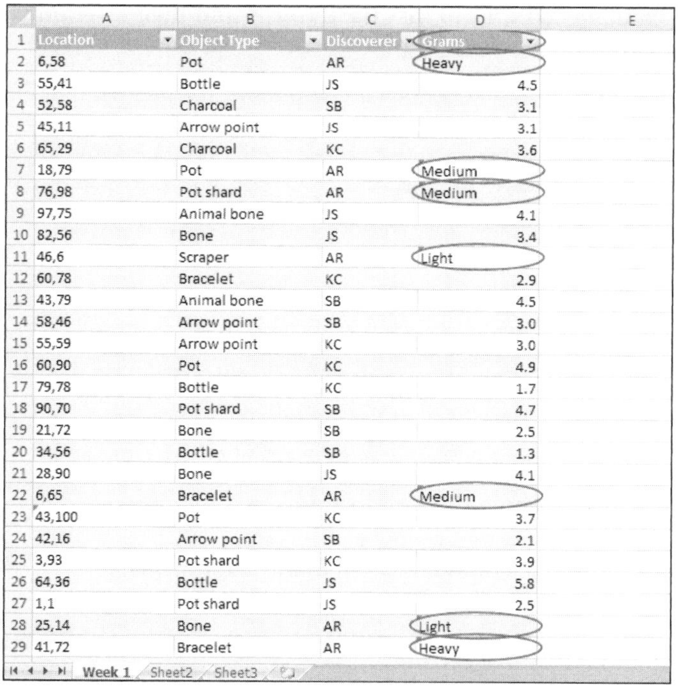

	A	B	C	D	E
1	Location	Object Type	Discoverer	Grams	
2	6,58	Pot	AR	Heavy	
3	55,41	Bottle	JS	4.5	
4	52,58	Charcoal	SB	3.1	
5	45,11	Arrow point	JS	3.1	
6	65,29	Charcoal	KC	3.6	
7	18,79	Pot	AR	Medium	
8	76,98	Pot shard	AR	Medium	
9	97,75	Animal bone	JS	4.1	
10	82,56	Bone	JS	3.4	
11	46,6	Scraper	AR	Light	
12	60,78	Bracelet	KC	2.9	
13	43,79	Animal bone	SB	4.5	
14	58,46	Arrow point	SB	3.0	
15	55,59	Arrow point	KC	3.0	
16	60,90	Pot	KC	4.9	
17	79,78	Bottle	KC	1.7	
18	90,70	Pot shard	SB	4.7	
19	21,72	Bone	SB	2.5	
20	34,56	Bottle	SB	1.3	
21	28,90	Bone	JS	4.1	
22	6,65	Bracelet	AR	Medium	
23	43,100	Pot	KC	3.7	
24	42,16	Arrow point	SB	2.1	
25	3,93	Pot shard	KC	3.9	
26	64,36	Bottle	JS	5.8	
27	1,1	Pot shard	JS	2.5	
28	25,14	Bone	AR	Light	
29	41,72	Bracelet	AR	Heavy	

⊮ ◀ ▶ ▶⊮ **Week 1** / Sheet2 / Sheet3 / 🔲

Figure 11-10: Excel has circled the cells that contain invalid data.

Extending the validation rules

Now that you have a basic validation rule, it's time to see what else you can do with validation rules. Most numerical rules are self explanatory, but what if you need to set up a rule for a column with text data in it? To find out, in this exercise you create a validation rule to ensure that all the values in the Discoverer column have exactly two letters:

1. Select column C (Discoverer). Choose Data ➔ Data Tools ➔ Data Validation.

The Data Validation dialog box opens.

2. From the Allow drop-down list, select Text Length. Set up the rule so that the data length is equal to 2. Click OK to create the rule.

You have created and applied a data validation rule for the Discoverer column. Because no errors are in the current data, no error flags are shown.

3. **Change the value in cell C11 to just the letter B and then attempt to leave the cell by pressing Enter or Tab.**

As shown in Figure 11-11, Excel does not allow you to enter a value that is outside the bounds of the rule you created.

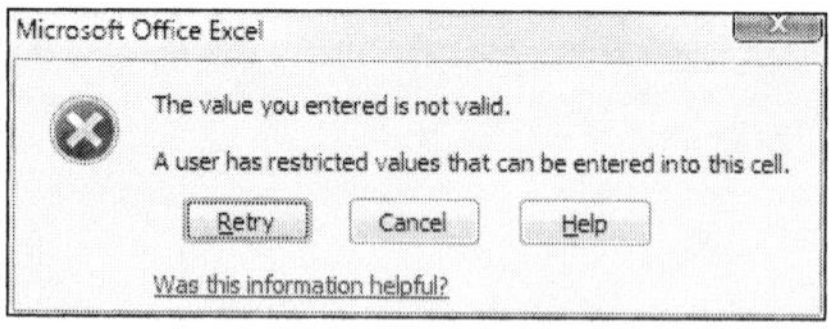

Figure 11-11: The value you tried to enter is not valid.

The problem with this error message is that it isn't very useful or complete. All it tells you is that something is wrong with the data you tried to enter.

4. **Cancel the attempt to change the cell value.**

Your next step is to improve the communication of the error message.

Creating custom input messages for data validation

The validation rule you just created tells you that something went wrong. What if you could give users more information about what to enter and help them to avoid the problems in the first place? Follow these steps:

1. **Select column C (Discoverer). Choose Data → Data Tools → Data Validation.**

Your two-character rule is shown on the Settings tab in the Data Validation dialog box.

The first decision you make is whether to show the message. By default, when you create a message, it is set to be shown any time a cell with that rule is selected. Whenever you hover the mouse over that cell, the message pops up to the right of the cell. If the Show Input Message When Cell Is Selected check box is not selected, the message is never shown — whether you edit the cell or hover the mouse over the cell.

After you decide whether to show the message, you need to give the message a title and a message describing what the content of the cell should be.

2. **Click the Input Message tab so that you can create a new message. In the Title box, enter** Discoverer. **For the input message, type** Enter the first and last initials of the person who found the artifact, **as shown in Figure 11-12.**

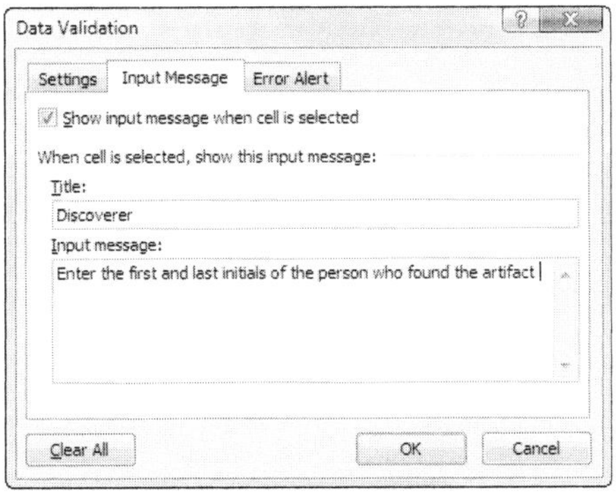

Figure 11-12: Enter the custom input message to display to users.

3. **Click OK to save the changes to the rule, and then select one of the cells in column C.**

As shown in Figure 11-13, the message is shown near the active cell. The exact placement of the message will change depending on how much space there is between the active cell and the edge of the Excel window. The title is in bold, and the text is underneath the title.

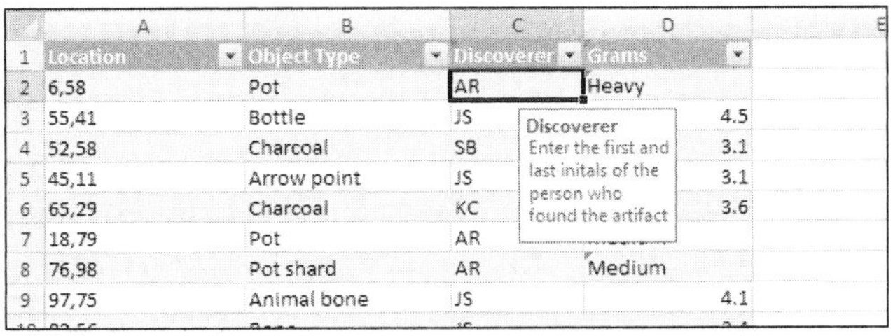

Figure 11-13: This message appears any time a cell in column C is selected.

You have now told anyone using this worksheet what to enter in the cells in this column. Your next step is to create an error message so that a user who puts the wrong value in a cell knows what to do to correct the value.

Creating custom error messages for invalid data

Fixing a problem with data you have entered in a cell is easier when the error message is clear and specific. By default, as you saw in Figure 11-11, all Excel tells you is that you have broken a data validation rule. When you create rules, make sure that your error messages are as clear and succinct as possible so that users can fix problems quickly.

In the following exercise, you create a custom error message that is displayed whenever users try to enter more than two characters in the Discoverer column:

1. **Select column C (Discoverer). Choose Data → Data Tools → Data Validation.**

   Your two-character rule is shown on the Settings tab.

2. **Click the Error Alert tab so that you can create your new message.**

   As shown in Figure 11-14, the error alert lets you set up the style, title, and error message for your alert. The error is set to be shown whenever invalid data is entered.

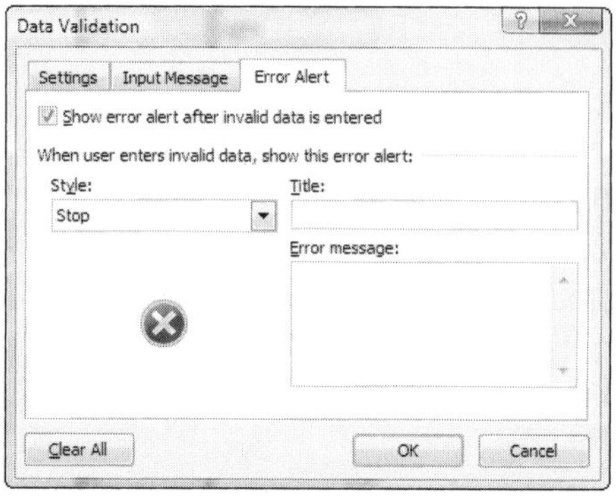

Figure 11-14: User the Error Alert tab to create a custom error message.

You can create three levels of alerts:

- *Stop error:* The most restrictive level of error message. The error must be corrected before the cursor can leave the cell. Your only options are to retry, cancel, or get help. Because you (not Excel) create the rule, you won't find any more information from Excel's Help system.

- *Warning error:* The middle level of error message. The user must choose whether to continue with the change, knowing that it's wrong, or to wipe it out by clicking either the No or Cancel button. Clicking the No button leaves the value in the cell but leaves the cell contents selected for change. Clicking the Cancel button wipes out any change that has been made and reverts to the previous value in the cell.

- *Informational error:* The least restrictive level of error message. The user can ignore the error and leave the new value by clicking OK or cancel the change and revert to the previous value in the cell.

3. **Create a stop message for the cells in column C, as shown in Figure 11-15:**

   - In the Style box, select the Stop option.

   - In the Title box, enter **Two Characters!**

   - In the Error Message box, enter the text **All artifacts must be tagged with the first and last initial for the discoverer as an identifier.**

Figure 11-15: Select a message type, and then enter a title and the message text.

4. **Click OK and then attempt to change the value in cell C12 to** Q.

Excel displays the error alert you just created, as shown in Figure 11-16.

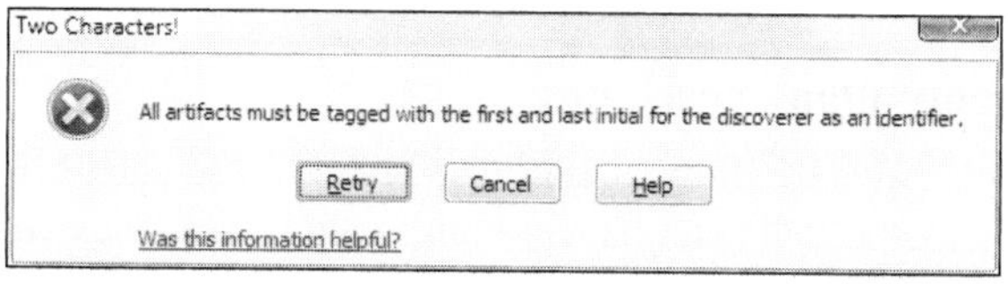

Figure 11-16: The error alert you just created.

5. **Click Cancel to wipe out the change and revert to the previous cell value.**

Using a list of items for data validation

Sometimes, more restrictive data validation rules are required to ensure that data is correct. A good example is the Object Type column in the table you've been working with. When data is typed in this column, the value has no predefined length, nor is it a numeric value that can be restricted in other ways. However, only certain types of objects can be found in the current dig site. It would be useful to be able to pull the values from a list for this column.

In this exercise, you create a list and a validation rule based on this list. Follow these steps:

1. **Look at cells AA1 through AA10.**

The cells in column AA of this sheet contain the distinct types of objects that can be found on this site.

2. **Select column B (Object Type). Choose Data → Data Tools → Data Validation.**

Next, you set up a data validation rule to pull the legal Object Type values from the items on this list.

3. **From the Allow drop-down list on the Settings tab, select List.**

The settings for a list-based rule are different from those used until now, as shown in Figure 11-17.

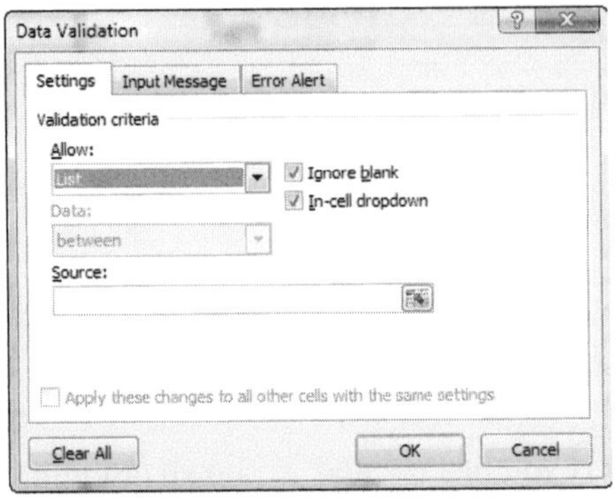

Figure 11-17: The options that are available for a list rule.

4. **Deselect the Ignore Blank check box.**

You can set up list rules to allow or ignore blanks. If you select the Ignore Blank check box, the selected cells can have a blank value. Because every artifact found must have a type, deselect this option.

5. **Leave the In-Cell Dropdown check box selected so that users can select the options from a list.**

When this option is not selected, any value can be typed and is then verified. Because this goes against the reason for using the validation rule, be sure to select the In-Cell Dropdown check box. When this option is selected, the list of possible elements is shown to the side of the cell so that users can easily choose a type.

6. **To set up the source for the list, click the grid button to the right of the Source box. Select cells AA1 through AA10. Click the grid button to return to the Data Validation dialog box.**

To create the list, you must tell Excel where to find the items for the list. You can either type the list directly into the Source box or get the values from a list located somewhere on your active sheet. For this exercise, you select cells AA1 to AA10.

Watch Your Step

If you type in the Source box, you must be careful about capitalization and punctuation. An element you type qualifies as a match only if it matches the value from the source exactly.

7. (Optional) Provide appropriate input and error messages.

8. Click OK to close the dialog box and create the rule.

Your rule is created and ready for use.

9. Select cell B5. Click the drop-down arrow to the right of the cell to bring up the choices for the cell values. Click Charcoal to change the value to Charcoal.

Notice that the entries in your list are in exactly the order you entered them. If you want them in a different order, you can change the order of the list in cells AA1 to AA10. If you change the order of the values, you don't need to change the rule. If you make the list longer or shorter, then you will need to adjust the rule definition.

10. Select cell B5. Press the Delete key to remove the contents of the cell. Attempt to move away from the cell.

Notice that although you can delete the cell contents, a warning marker appears in the upper-left corner of the cell. If you had left the Ignore Blanks check box selected, the warning marker would not even appear.

11. Select cell B5. Press the spacebar and then attempt to move away from the cell.

This time, an error message says that the value you chose is not in the list. Cancel the change to revert to the blank cell.

For practice, set up full validation rules for each of the columns in this table. Experiment with the various combinations of options so that you can best understand when to use each one.

Consolidating Data

In Chapter 6, you learned one way to consolidate your data: by using PivotTables. However, when Excel power users talk about consolidating data, they're referring to using the Consolidate button to validate and combine your data at the same time.

Sometimes, you want to create a single spreadsheet that will be used repeatedly to record data. Some examples are time sheets, sales information, and delivery statistics. In each case, after the individual sheet data is entered into Excel, you need a simple way to consolidate the data from all the different sheets into a single master sheet.

When you consolidate data, you combine all the data from the various sheets to find the sum, average, or maximum, or some other type of calculation, across the fields.

You use consolidation, rather than merely create the formulas manually, for two reasons:

- **It's quicker.** You just define the range of data to be consolidated, and then you can view the various calculations by changing the consolidation formula rather than each individual formula.

- **It's easier to add and remove data sets from the formulas.** Because all the consolidation formulas draw their data sources from one dialog box at one time, you change the data sources only one time. If you do the consolidation by hand, you have to change each formula individually.

For the remainder of this chapter, you use sales data from a pet shop. Each day, using the total sales for each type of animal, an employee enters the daily gross sales and the tax amount into a spreadsheet page. Each month, the sheets for each type of animal are consolidated, and a summary of daily sales is created.

Consolidating data in a single workbook

In the following exercise, you create the consolidation page that lists the pet shop's total daily sales for January:

1. Open the **DataConsolidation.xlsx** file.

2. Create a new sheet in the file and name it Consolidation. Select cell A1 of this sheet.

   The cell you select is the starting point where the consolidation results will be placed on the sheet.

3. Choose Data → Data Tools → Consolidate.

   The Consolidate dialog box opens, as shown in Figure 11-18.

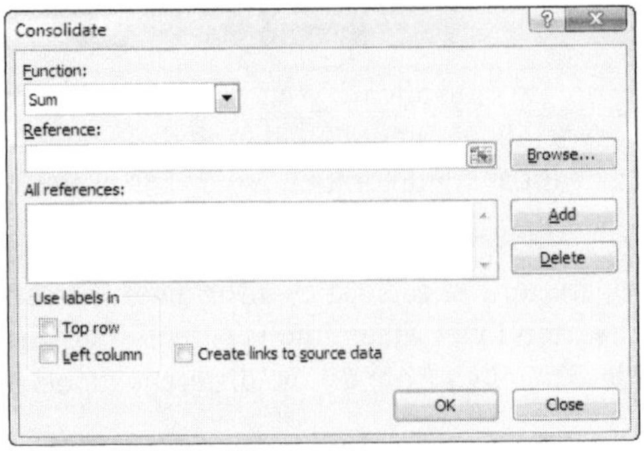

Figure 11-18: The Consolidate dialog box.

The Consolidate dialog box is divided into these main areas:

- *Function:* From this drop-down list, choose the function to perform during the consolidation. The default function is Sum. Other choices include the usual range of statistical functions for data.

- *Reference:* Define the areas to be consolidated. (Excel calls them *consolidation references.*) You add references one at a time.

- *All References:* Select the full list of references you have added.

- *Use Labels In:* Select the check boxes in this area to define which labels and links you want associated with your consolidation data.

 ## Watch Your Step

When you use Excel to consolidate data, the data labels must match exactly, or else the consolidation doesn't give you the results you expect. For example, *Jan* is not the same as *January*. More importantly, because the labels must match exactly, you cannot use dates if you want to consolidate data across months. The data you are about to work with is all from one month, so the actual date can be used to label the rows. However, when you work with data from different months, you need to label the days with the day number rather than with the date. Although you know that the January 1 data should get consolidated with February 1 data, Excel does not see 1/1 as the same label as 2/1 and therefore does not consolidate the numbers.

4. Click in the Reference text box, and then click the grid button to collapse the dialog box. Click the Dogs tab to show the Dogs sheet, select cells A1 through C32, and then click the grid button again to expand the dialog box. Click the Add button to add this reference to the All References list box.

Your first set of referenced cells is shown in the All References list. You're ready to add the references for the other sheets.

5. Click the Cats tab to show the Cats sheet.

Notice that Excel automatically completes the range based on the range you previously selected.

6. Click the Add button to add the Cats references to the list.

7. Repeat Steps 5 and 6 for the Fish, Snakes, Birds, and Gerbils sheets.

You have defined the data to be consolidated. The Consolidate dialog box looks like the one shown in Figure 11-19.

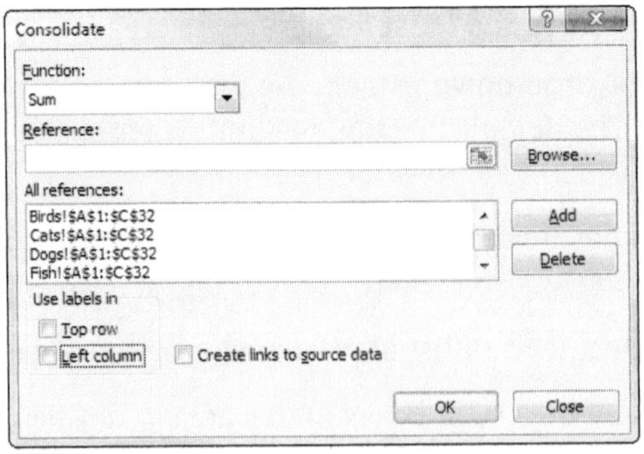

Figure 11-19: After you select all the data from each sheet, the completed dialog box looks like this one.

In the next step, you tell Excel which labels to use.

8. Select both the Top Row and Left Column check boxes in the dialog box. Click OK to start the consolidation.

The consolidation report appears in cells Consolidation!A1 through Consolidation!C32, as shown in Figure 11-20.

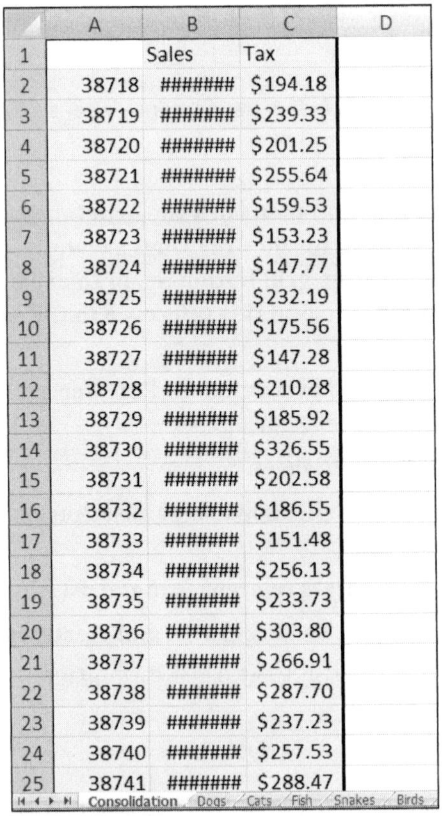

	A	B	C	D
1		Sales	Tax	
2	38718	######	$194.18	
3	38719	######	$239.33	
4	38720	######	$201.25	
5	38721	######	$255.64	
6	38722	######	$159.53	
7	38723	######	$153.23	
8	38724	######	$147.77	
9	38725	######	$232.19	
10	38726	######	$175.56	
11	38727	######	$147.28	
12	38728	######	$210.28	
13	38729	######	$185.92	
14	38730	######	$326.55	
15	38731	######	$202.58	
16	38732	######	$186.55	
17	38733	######	$151.48	
18	38734	######	$256.13	
19	38735	######	$233.73	
20	38736	######	$303.80	
21	38737	######	$266.91	
22	38738	######	$287.70	
23	38739	######	$237.23	
24	38740	######	$257.53	
25	38741	######	$288.47	

Consolidation | Dogs | Cats | Fish | Snakes | Birds

Figure 11-20: The result of the consolidation.

When the consolidation is complete, the data that is generated is placed on the sheet, starting with the cell you selected.

Notice that the data is not formatted the way you would expect. Column B may not be wide enough to show the data, but may show pound signs instead. Or, Column A may show a series of 5 digit numbers instead of the dates. You need to fix these formatting problems before continuing.

9. Select columns A and B on the consolidation sheet. Double-click between the two columns to autoexpand the columns to the needed width. Select Column A and change it to be formatted as dates by selecting Short Date from the drop-down list in the Number group of the Home tab.

You can see the amount of total sales and taxes paid each day for the pet store, as shown in Figure 11-21.

	A	B	C	D
1		Sales	Tax	
2	1/1/2006	$2,774.00	$194.18	
3	1/2/2006	$3,419.00	$239.33	
4	1/3/2006	$2,875.00	$201.25	
5	1/4/2006	$3,652.00	$255.64	
6	1/5/2006	$2,279.00	$159.53	
7	1/6/2006	$2,189.00	$153.23	
8	1/7/2006	$2,111.00	$147.77	
9	1/8/2006	$3,317.00	$232.19	
10	1/9/2006	$2,508.00	$175.56	
11	1/10/2006	$2,104.00	$147.28	
12	1/11/2006	$3,004.00	$210.28	
13	1/12/2006	$2,656.00	$185.92	
14	1/13/2006	$4,665.00	$326.55	
15	1/14/2006	$2,894.00	$202.58	
16	1/15/2006	$2,665.00	$186.55	
17	1/16/2006	$2,164.00	$151.48	
18	1/17/2006	$3,659.00	$256.13	
19	1/18/2006	$3,339.00	$233.73	
20	1/19/2006	$4,340.00	$303.80	
21	1/20/2006	$3,813.00	$266.91	
22	1/21/2006	$4,110.00	$287.70	
23	1/22/2006	$3,389.00	$237.23	
24	1/23/2006	$3,679.00	$257.53	
25	1/24/2006	$4,121.00	$288.47	

Consolidation / Dogs / Cats / Fish / Snakes / Birds / Ger

Figure 11-21: Total sales and takes for each day after consolidation.

If you want to see average sales rather than total sales, a simple change to the function used in the consolidation provides this information.

10. Click in cell Consolidation!A1. Choose Data → Data Tools → Consolidate.

11. In the Consolidate dialog box, change the function from Sum to Average and then click OK.

The consolidation information in the sheet changes to show the average sales and taxes for each day rather than the total sales.

Because you started the consolidation from the same cell as you used previously, the new result falls into the same cells, and you don't need to do any reformatting.

Although the consolidation information is complete, a problem has occurred: Any updates made to the data on individual sheets do not also update the consolidation. You can run the consolidation again, but you would need to do it by hand every time the data changes. You can use a better method: Link the results of the consolidation to the cells, and keep the results up-to-date at all times.

12. Click in cell Consolidation!A1. Choose Data → Data Tools → Consolidate. Select the Create Links to Source Data check box and then click OK.

The consolidation is performed again. This time, the result looks like the one shown in Figure 11-22.

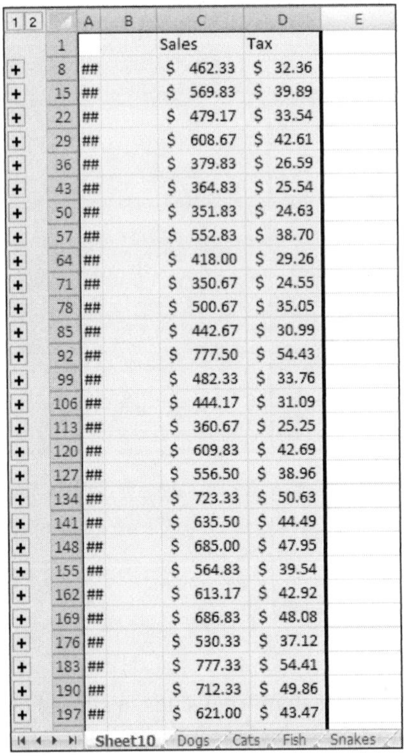

	A	B	C	D	E
1			Sales	Tax	
8	##		$ 462.33	$ 32.36	
15	##		$ 569.83	$ 39.89	
22	##		$ 479.17	$ 33.54	
29	##		$ 608.67	$ 42.61	
36	##		$ 379.83	$ 26.59	
43	##		$ 364.83	$ 25.54	
50	##		$ 351.83	$ 24.63	
57	##		$ 552.83	$ 38.70	
64	##		$ 418.00	$ 29.26	
71	##		$ 350.67	$ 24.55	
78	##		$ 500.67	$ 35.05	
85	##		$ 442.67	$ 30.99	
92	##		$ 777.50	$ 54.43	
99	##		$ 482.33	$ 33.76	
106	##		$ 444.17	$ 31.09	
113	##		$ 360.67	$ 25.25	
120	##		$ 609.83	$ 42.69	
127	##		$ 556.50	$ 38.96	
134	##		$ 723.33	$ 50.63	
141	##		$ 635.50	$ 44.49	
148	##		$ 685.00	$ 47.95	
155	##		$ 564.83	$ 39.54	
162	##		$ 613.17	$ 42.92	
169	##		$ 686.83	$ 48.08	
176	##		$ 530.33	$ 37.12	
183	##		$ 777.33	$ 54.41	
190	##		$ 712.33	$ 49.86	
197	##		$ 621.00	$ 43.47	

Sheet10 Dogs Cats Fish Snakes

Figure 11-22: Consolidation results with linked source data.

Notice that now the data is arranged in an outline. The full set of data is available, but only the summaries are shown. You need to expand column A to see the dates.

13. Click in cell Consolidation!C8.

Check the Formula Bar. Rather than see just a number, you now see the formula that created the number. Just *that* quick, you created the formulas to average the entire consolidation. Just as in any outline, you can expand the outline to see the details or leave it collapsed to show just the summary. In the case of outlines created by using the consolidation process, the detail lines are the links to the data points, and the summary lines are the formulas.

Consolidating data from multiple workbooks

Consolidation across a single file is useful, but when you take the consolidation out another layer, the feature is even more useful. In addition to being able to consolidate data across the sheets in a single file, you can consolidate data from multiple files. In fact, you can even stack the consolidations across multiple files to consolidate consolidated data even further. This is called *nesting your consolidations.*

To see the result of nesting consolidations, you are going to consolidate the data for each month of the first quarter of the year into a sheet in a new file.

For this exercise, use these Excel files:

    DataConsolidationJanuary.xlsx

    DataConsolidationFebruary.xlsx

    DataConsolidationMarch.xlsx

You will create a series of consolidations that tell you the amount of total income and sales for the first quarter. You complete this task by creating the consolidations using information from these monthly files. Each of the files has the sheets detailing how many animals were sold of each type that month as well as a consolidation sheet. You use the individual consolidation sheets to create your full consolidation sheet.

Watch Your Step

When you consolidate data across files, you must use named ranges to access the data in the other files. If your file doesn't have a named range in it, you don't get any results from the consolidation. To avoid this problem, the files for this part of the exercise have named ranges already created. The January data is in a range named JanuaryConsolidation, the February data is in a range named FebruaryConsolidation, and the March data is in a range named MarchConsolidation.

Follow these steps to consolidate data for the pet shop's first quarter:

1. **Open Excel to a new, blank file. Save this file to your hard drive in the same folder where you saved the other data files for this chapter. With cell A1 selected, choose Data → Data Tools → Consolidate.**

2. **Click the Browse button and browse until you find the files you copied to your hard drive. Select the name of the January file, and press Ctrl+C to copy the name for future use. Click the file again and click Open.**

   (This process allows you to get the name of the file and open it in one step, instead of going to Windows Explorer to get the name and then coming back to Excel to open the file.)

   The name of your file appears in the Reference box. However, you need to add the name of the range to the end of the filename. Although you may think that you can press the Home and End keys to move to either end of the filename and add your sheet name, you may not be able to do that. Moving the cursor within the Reference box probably changes the location of the selected cell in your spreadsheet and adds the reference for that cell to the name of the other file.

3. **Select the full path that shows as the reference and press Ctrl+V to paste the name of the file you just copied in its place. After the name of the file, type an exclamation point and the name of the range** JanuaryConsolidation. **Click Add to add the range to the list.**

   Because the name of the reference stays in the box after you add it to the list, you can edit it to make it what you want.

4. **Change the name of the reference in the box so that it references February for both the filename and the cell range. Click the Add button.**

5. **Repeat Step 4 to add the March data to the consolidation.**

   When you have finished adding the consolidation ranges, your dialog box should look like Figure 11-23.

6. **Select the Top Row and Left Column check boxes. Click OK to perform the consolidation.**

   The results of your consolidation appear starting in cell A1, as shown in Figure 11-24.

Just as you can change the function for the consolidation on local consolidations, you can easily change the function for the consolidation across files. You can also link the data from the other sheets by selecting the Create Links to Source Data check box in the Consolidate dialog box. If you link data that has already been linked, updating any piece of information within one of the subsheets gives you updated information on your final consolidation.

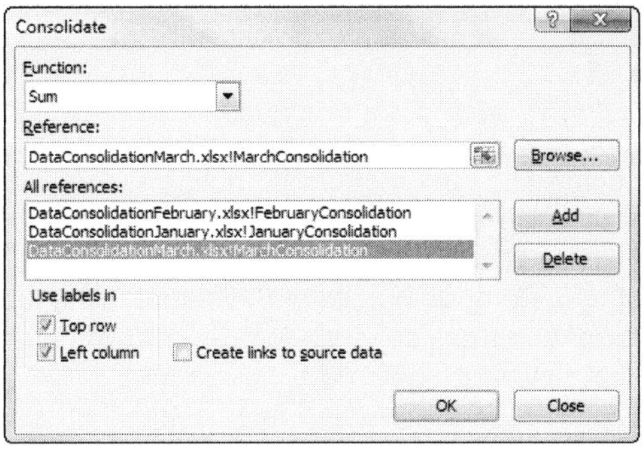

Figure 11-23: The Consolidation dialog box for data from other files.

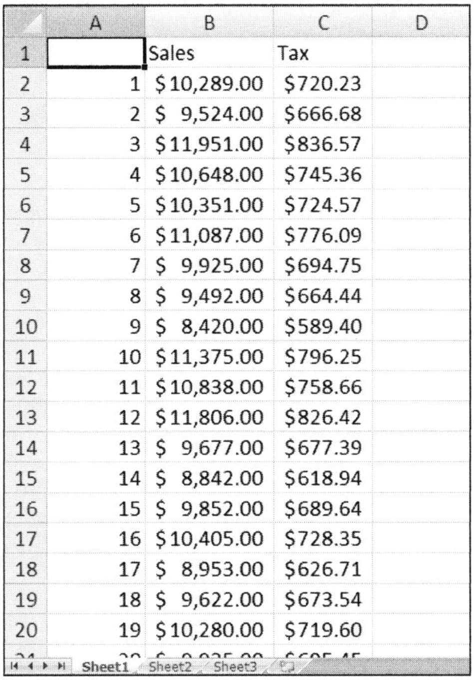

	A	B	C	D
1		Sales	Tax	
2	1	$10,289.00	$720.23	
3	2	$ 9,524.00	$666.68	
4	3	$11,951.00	$836.57	
5	4	$10,648.00	$745.36	
6	5	$10,351.00	$724.57	
7	6	$11,087.00	$776.09	
8	7	$ 9,925.00	$694.75	
9	8	$ 9,492.00	$664.44	
10	9	$ 8,420.00	$589.40	
11	10	$11,375.00	$796.25	
12	11	$10,838.00	$758.66	
13	12	$11,806.00	$826.42	
14	13	$ 9,677.00	$677.39	
15	14	$ 8,842.00	$618.94	
16	15	$ 9,852.00	$689.64	
17	16	$10,405.00	$728.35	
18	17	$ 8,953.00	$626.71	
19	18	$ 9,622.00	$673.54	
20	19	$10,280.00	$719.60	

Figure 11-24: Consolidation results with data from other files.

Transfer

In Chapter 12, you learn about analyzing your data. You can use the consolidation features on validated data to help you do some of the same types of analysis in a clearer, more user-friendly way.

Step Into the Real World

Changing the consolidation function and graphing the results provides an accurate picture of how your business is doing and how it could be doing. When you chart information, such as day-by-day averages, from the top-level consolidation, you can see on which days of the month you do the most business. Using consolidation data can give you a good idea of how things are going across a wide span of time. Take advantage of the sample data provided for this chapter, and play around with the information that consolidation can give you about the health of a business. You might be surprised at how much your data can tell you.

consolidate data: To merge data from multiple sheets into a new sheet by using an automated process.

consolidation reference: The cells to be consolidated or merged.

criteria: Rules defining types of content, values, and range boundaries for a cell value.

destructive process: Making a permanent change to something. In this case, to change the data in a way that cannot easily be undone without reverting the file to its previously saved state.

error circle: A red circle drawn around a cell by Excel to show that a problem exists in the content — an error in the formula or a validation error, for example.

validate data: To ensure that the data that is entered falls within the criteria defined for the cell.

validation rule: The grouping of rule message, input message, and error message that defines a valid value for a cell.

Last Stop

Practice Exam

1. Which one of these examples has duplicate cell content?

   a. Jenny and jenny

   b. 99.00 and 99

   c. 1/1/2006 and 1-Jan-06

   d. sixty and 60

2. Describe a situation where you would use the Remove Duplicates feature on cells in a single column.

_____

_____

3. Describe a situation where you would use the Remove Duplicates feature on cells in multiple columns at once.

_____

_____

4. True or False: All columns in a sheet must be checked for duplicates at the same time.

5. True or False: Duplicate data can be valid data.

6. Name the three parts of a validation rule.

_____

_____

_____

7. Error circles

   a. can be applied to more than one sheet at a time.

   b. stay active when a file is closed.

   c. disappear when the error is fixed.

   d. can be different colors at different times.

8. Input messages can be set to be shown

   a. to the left of the cell.

   b. only when a cell is selected.

   c. whenever a cell is blank.

   d. always, no matter whether the cell is selected.

9. Name the two buttons that appear on an informational error message.

_____

_____

10. True or False: Data lists for a validation rule can be on a different sheet from the data.

11. True or False: Text data can be consolidated.

12. When are consolidation results refreshed?

   a. When the consolidation is linked to the data and the data changes

   b. Whenever the file is opened

   c. Whenever the data used for the consolidation is changed

   d. When the consolidation sheet is copied

13. True or False: Consolidation results can be nested.

12 Analyzing Data with Excel

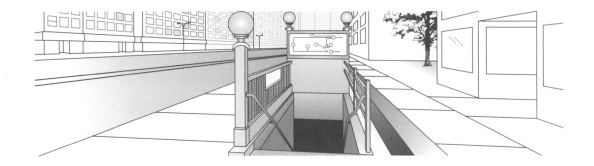

Enter the Station

Questions

1. What is the difference between analyzing data and filtering or sorting it?

2. What is the difference between the scenario process and the goal-seeking process?

3. Can you have nonconsecutive cells in a scenario definition?

4. Can you have cells from different worksheets in a scenario definition?

5. What is a target cell?

6. Can you use nonconsecutive cells when you're using Goal Seek?

7. Can you use cells from different worksheets when you're using Goal Seek?

8. What type of trendline is the most accurate?

Express Line

If you're already skilled at analyzing your data by using Excel 2007, skip ahead to the next chapter.

When you analyze data with Excel, you're using known data to find out what would happen if circumstances changed. Analyzing your data with Excel lets you change pieces of your data and find out what would happen to the overall picture.

Just as you can use filters and sorting to learn from your data in its current state, analyzing your data can help you answer questions about the data available to you. The difference is that with the tools used in this chapter, you can learn what might happen. Filtering and sorting can tell you only what the data already says.

The Excel what-if analysis tools are built to help you find out how changes to certain cells are reflected across the whole set of data. By setting up a series of what-if scenarios and using Goal Seek, you can find out exactly what would happen across the spreadsheet if you changed a single value.

In this chapter, you look at the data from the James Restaurant. Current data shows that you will make a profit, but as with most businesses, the margin is smaller than desired.

By using the Scenario Manager and the Goal Seek feature, you learn where to focus your effort so that the changes have the greatest effect. After that, you learn how to use the charting capabilities to extend your predictions into the future.

Exploring the Excel What-If Analysis Tools

Data in Excel can tell you how things look now and how they looked in the past. Sometimes, you need to go beyond that stage and project what would happen in the future if you changed certain variables. This process of projecting future outcomes is *what-if analysis.*

You can use the various tools in the what-if process to look at the current state of your data, make changes, and see how those changes would affect the rest of your data. You use each tool to analyze the changes you want to make. Which tool you use depends on what you know and what you want to find out.

Looking at different scenarios

The Scenario Manager enables you to change values in a number of cells and then save that condition, or *scenario,* under a unique name. When you select the scenario name in the Scenario Manager, Excel applies the changes you've designated to the appropriate cells in the sheet. You can then see the effect of those changes throughout the workbook.

Scenarios are useful for what-if analysis if all the data you need to change is on the same sheet. They're also helpful if the values you want to change are numbers, not formulas. Examples of good questions to answer with the Scenario Manager are shown in this list:

- What happens to my annual profit if I at least break even every month in my first year?
- What happens to my monthly expenses if I hire fewer people?
- What happens to my annual profit if I do more business of one type than another?

Goal seeking

Goal seeking looks at what-if analysis from a perspective that is the opposite of scenarios. When you seek a goal, you already know the outcome you want, and you need Excel to determine which values need to change to achieve that outcome. Goal seeking works across multiple sheets, but it requires that the cells be related by a trail of equations in order for the seek process to find a valid answer. Examples of goals you might seek are shown here:

- How many employees do I need to lay off to increase profits to X?
- How much do I need to increase business in June to increase profits to X?

Extending charts into the future

You can also project future outcomes by extending your charts into the future. In Chapter 5, you learned how to create a trendline for your scatter charts. You can also apply some types of trendlines to line charts. Then you can see the future outcome if your data continues along the same historical paths.

Transfer

In Chapter 14, you learn about some of the add-ins that have been developed to help you analyze your data. One add-in allows you to create a Moving Average chart, which is another analysis tool that Excel offers. You also learn in that chapter about installing the Solver tools.

Information Kiosk

How do you find answers when you're away from the office? If you use SharePoint, you have another option for analyzing your data: You can place your Excel spreadsheet on an Excel Server. You can then use your Excel files as the basis for parameter-driven analysis from any browser. If you want to learn more about this topic, check out *Microsoft SharePoint Bible* by Wynne Leon, et al. (Wiley).

Setting Up Scenarios with the Scenario Manager

Scenarios within Excel allow you to change the values for cells on a single sheet and determine how those changes will affect the other sheets in the file. In this section, you create several scenarios to determine the effect on your bottom line if you could expand the to-go orders for James Restaurant.

To expand the to-go orders, you will have to increase your expenses by hiring more kitchen staff and increasing your advertising budget. However, you also know that the to-go orders will generate more income for the restaurant. You want to find out whether the increased to-go income will be greater than the increased expenses.

Examining the effect of increased expenses

In the following exercise, you create a scenario to see how an increase in advertising and kitchen staff expenses would affect your annual profits:

1. **Open the `JamesRestaurant.xlsx` file. Make sure you have the Average Expenses per Month sheet selected.**

   In this chapter, you analyze how the restaurant will do financially throughout its first year based on changes to expected situations. The file you use has two worksheets, which detail the following information:

   - *Average Expenses per Month:* Known monthly expenses for the restaurant.

   - *Expected Income:* Expected income from both eat-in orders and to-go orders for each month. This worksheet also computes the expected profit and loss for the restaurant for each month.

2. **Choose File → Save As to save a copy of the document as a regular Excel 2007 file.**

   Work on a copy of your data whenever possible while analyzing your data with the Excel tools. When you run your scenarios in the Scenario Manager, you add sheets with the scenario summaries. In addition, you change your data as you run the scenarios. Because you do not want to save these changes on top of your real data, always make a copy first and work there.

3. **Choose Data → Data Tools → What-If Analysis → Scenario Manager.**

   An empty Scenario Manager dialog box appears, as shown in Figure 12-1.

   The Scenario Manager lets you create and work with the scenarios for the active sheet.

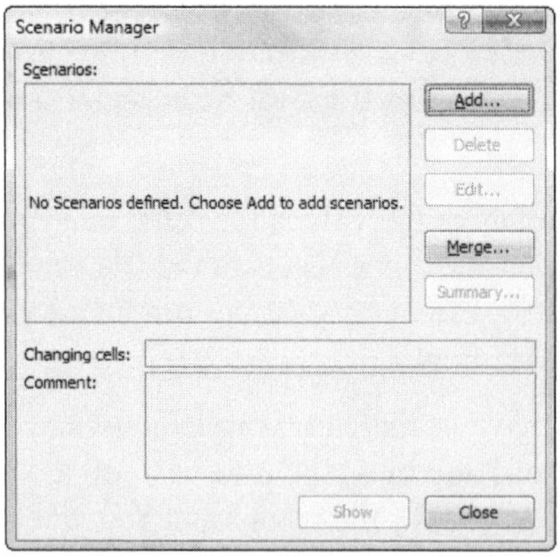

Figure 12-1: The Scenario Manager dialog box.

4. Click Add to create a new scenario.

The Add Scenario dialog box appears, as shown in Figure 12-2.

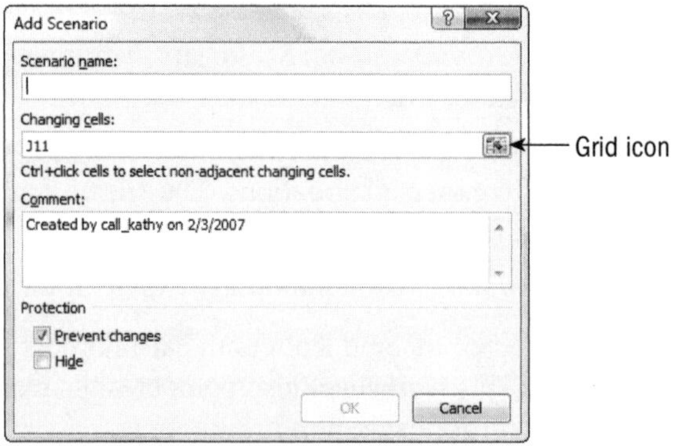

Grid icon

Figure 12-2: The Add Scenario dialog box.

Notice that a cell value is already in the Changing Cells box. This cell is the active cell at the time you open the Scenario Manager.

You're ready to create your first scenario by naming it and defining the cells you want to change.

5. In the Scenario Name box, type Additional Expenses for Expanded To-Go Orders.

6. Click the grid icon to the right of the Changing Cells box.

You are ready to define which cell or cells you want to change for your scenario. For this exercise, the variables you want to change are the advertising budget and the number of employees on your kitchen staff.

7. Click in cell H8 to add your advertising costs to the list of cells to change. Ctrl+click in cell C20 to add the number of kitchen employees to the cells to change. Click the grid icon to expand the Add Scenario dialog box back to its full view.

When you Ctrl+click, you see the two cell references added as absolute addresses, with a comma separating them:

```
$H$8,$C$20
```

Each scenario refers to a specific cell, so absolute addressing is used. Because you are choosing two cells that are not adjacent to each other, they are separated by commas.

If you want to choose a consecutive range of cells, select the first cell and drag to the last cell. When you do this, you get an absolute range of cells.

8. Click OK to close the dialog box and continue defining your scenario.

The Scenario Values dialog box appears, as shown in Figure 12-3. In this dialog box, you define the values you want to use for these two cells when you run the scenario.

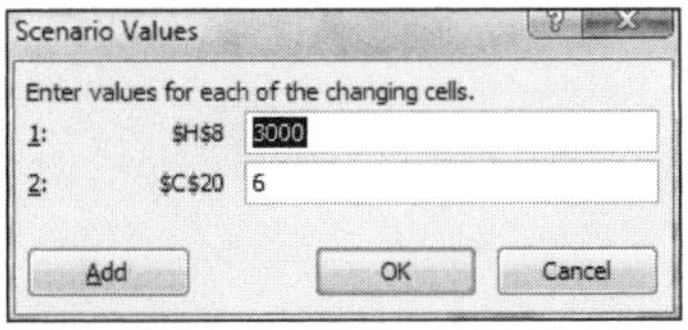

Figure 12-3: Enter the values for the changing cells in this dialog box.

The current values for the two cells — H8 and C20 — are already filled in, as shown in the figure. You change these two values to the values for your scenario.

Information Kiosk

If more than five cells are in your scenario definition, the first five are shown, with a scroll bar to the right to give you access to the other cell values.

You can type the values in the dialog box or use a simple formula to do the calculation. If you use a formula, Excel changes it to the value. Be sure to preface your formula with an equal sign. If you don't, you won't get the results you expect, because the Scenario Manager will interpret your new value as a string rather than as a number.

You can use any formula that you can type in. You can't choose cells for your formulas, but if you can type or paste in the reference to the cell, you can use it.

9. Type 3500 **for the value in H8, and then press Tab to move to the value for C20. Type** 8 **and click OK to complete the process.**

You have defined the values for the scenario ($3,500 for advertising and 8 for the number of kitchen staff employees) and returned to the Scenario Manager list. Your definition appears as the first (and only) one on the list.

You have a number of choices of what to do next, depending on which button you click in the Scenario Manager dialog box:

- *Show:* Your changes are applied to the active worksheet, and the results are shown.

- *Close:* Your scenario is defined, but not applied to, the spreadsheet now.

- *Summary:* Your changes are made to the sheet, and a new sheet that shows the difference between the original cell values and the new sheet values is added to the workbook. The summary button also allows you to define what you want as the result in the summary sheet. You do this step next.

10. **Click Summary.**

The Scenario Summary dialog box appears, as shown in Figure 12-4.

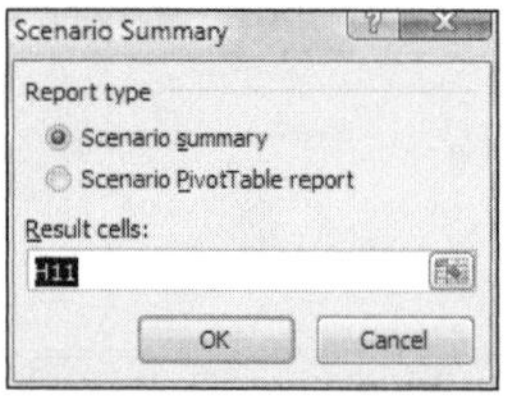

Figure 12-4: The Scenario Summary dialog box.

This dialog box lets you choose what kind of summary sheet you want to see — either a summary report or a PivotTable — and the specific cell you expect to contain the result of your changes.

You are creating a summary, not a PivotTable, in this exercise, so leave the default radio buttons selected.

If a value is in the Result Cells box, Excel was able to guess where the changes would cascade on the active sheet. If Excel has guessed, the value is a relative cell address, as shown in Figure 12-4. Therefore, click in the cell; the reference changes to an absolute address.

11. **Click OK to generate the summary.**

A new sheet is added to your file, as you can see in Figure 12-5.

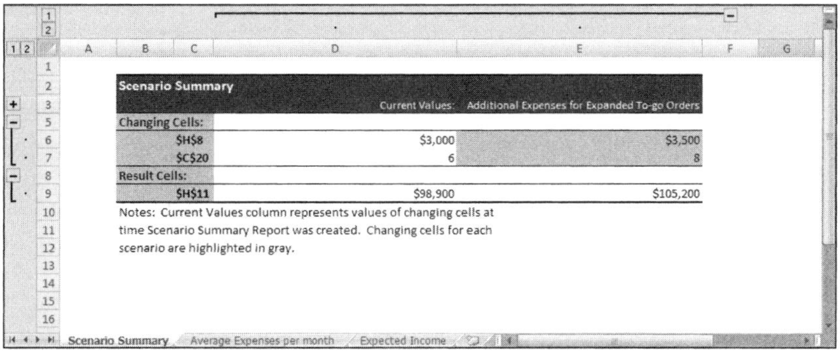

Figure 12-5: The Scenario Summary Sheet lists the scenario you just defined.

This sheet shows you the cells you changed, their original values, their new values, and the resulting change. These changes have not been made to the original cells themselves; rather, they're made only to this sheet. Although the summary is useful for seeing how your scenario would affect monthly expenses, you probably want to see how it would affect the overall profit or loss for the restaurant.

12. **Change your view back to the Average Expenses per Month sheet.**

13. **Choose Data → Data Tools → What-If Analysis → Scenario Manager.**

Notice that the scenario you just created is still shown as an available scenario. You will show these new values in the sheet next so that you can see the cascaded result through the entire file.

14. **Click the Show button.**

Nothing changes in the Scenario Manager dialog box. If you look at the data in your sheet, the values there have been updated. You're ready to see how the changes affected the profit of your business.

You can't change worksheets with the Scenario Manager open, but after you close it, you can.

15. **Click the Close button.**

You return to the worksheet. You can change to the Expected Income sheet, as shown in Figure 12-6, to see the effect of these additional expenses. The annual profit with this change is $23,600. The original annual profit was $99,200. But this example shows only half the story; you also need to consider increased sales, as outlined in the next exercise.

Considering increased income

In the real world, you would hope that increasing expenses to get more to-go business would pay off so that you would receive additional income for these orders. To see how the increased income would affect your bottom line, create a scenario for this sheet that changes the income for the to-go orders for each month.

Changed values

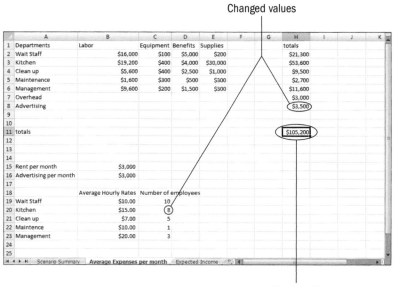

Final result

Figure 12-6: The preliminary result of the what-if analysis.

From the Expected Income sheet, follow these steps:

1. **Choose Data → Data Tools → What-If Analysis → Scenario Manager.**

Notice that the Scenario Manager is blank. That is because you have no scenarios set up for this sheet.

2. **Click the Add button to open the Add Scenario dialog box (refer to Figure 12-2).**

3. **In the Scenario Name box, enter** Increased To-Go Income.

4. **Click the grid icon to the right of the Changing Cells box. Select cells C2 through C13. Click the grid icon to expand the Add Scenario dialog box back to its full view. Then click OK.**

5. **In the Scenario Values dialog box, replace the value with the value for that month's eat-in orders divided by 4. For example, the formula for cell C2 would be =B2/4, the formula for cell C3 would be =B3/4, and so on. Be sure to use the scroll bar on the right to see all of the values that need to be changed. When they are all changed, click OK.**

6. **Click the Show button to run the scenario and see whether you think that the additional income would be substantial enough to justify the expense.**

Working from the assumption that the to-go orders will be at least one quarter of the eat-in results, you see that the change will increase profits almost immediately. The results of the analysis are shown in Figure 12-7.

Changed cells

	A	B	C	D	E	F	G	H
1		Eat in Orders	To Go Orders	Total Income		Expenses	Profit	
2	Jan	$ 79,000.00	$ 19,750.00	$ 98,750.00		$ 105,200.00	$ (6,450.00)	
3	Feb	$ 86,000.00	$ 21,500.00	$ 107,500.00		$ 105,200.00	$ 2,300.00	
4	Mar	$ 85,000.00	$ 21,250.00	$ 106,250.00		$ 105,200.00	$ 1,050.00	
5	Apr	$ 82,000.00	$ 20,500.00	$ 102,500.00		$ 105,200.00	$ (2,700.00)	
6	May	$ 100,000.00	$ 25,000.00	$ 125,000.00		$ 105,200.00	$ 19,800.00	
7	Jun	$ 100,000.00	$ 25,000.00	$ 125,000.00		$ 105,200.00	$ 19,800.00	
8	Jul	$ 95,000.00	$ 23,750.00	$ 118,750.00		$ 105,200.00	$ 13,550.00	
9	Aug	$ 110,000.00	$ 27,500.00	$ 137,500.00		$ 105,200.00	$ 32,300.00	
10	Sep	$ 110,000.00	$ 27,500.00	$ 137,500.00		$ 105,200.00	$ 32,300.00	
11	Oct	$ 102,000.00	$ 25,500.00	$ 127,500.00		$ 105,200.00	$ 22,300.00	
12	Nov	$ 124,000.00	$ 31,000.00	$ 155,000.00		$ 105,200.00	$ 49,800.00	
13	Dec	$ 119,000.00	$ 29,750.00	$ 148,750.00		$ 105,200.00	$ 43,550.00	
14								
15		$ 1,192,000.00	($298,000.00)	$ 1,490,000.00		$ 1,262,400.00	($227,600.00)	
16								
17								
18								
19								
20								
21								

Scenario Summary / Average Expenses per month / Exp

New results

Figure 12-7: The what-if analysis result after completing the second stage.

Goal Seeking with Excel

Goal seeking goes in the other direction from scenarios. When you are seeking a goal, you already know the result you want, and you need for Excel to determine what needs to change in order to achieve it.

Goal seeking allows you to base the change of one cell on a change in another cell. These two cells should be connected by one or more formulas that have been created before running the Goal Seeker. For example, cell A1 may contain the number of glasses of lemonade sold, and A2 may contain the cost of each glass. Cell A3 contains the formula =A1*A2. When you initiate Goal Seek, Excel iterates through a series of changes to values to find the closest possible change to create the new value. In the lemonade example, you would be seeking the goal value for cell A3.

When you seek a goal, you set up three values in the Goal Seek dialog box:

- **Set Cell:** The cell you want to set (the *target cell*)
- **To Value:** The value for the target (the *target value*)
- **By Changing Cell:** The cell that changes to achieve the goal

In the following exercise, you use Goal Seek to find out how many wait staff you would need to lay off to increase your James Restaurant profits to $110,000 per year:

1. Open the file **JamesRestaurant.xlsx**. Save a new copy of the file for use in this exercise.

You work with the restaurant data again. If you have made changes to the data, close the current file and create a new copy of the original file. As when you show the changes caused by creating a scenario, goal seeking changes the values of your current spreadsheet. To avoid problems, work on a copy of the data, not the original data.

2. **Display the Expected Income sheet and then choose Data → Data Tools → What-If Analysis → Goal Seek.**

The Goal Seek dialog box appears, as shown in Figure 12-8.

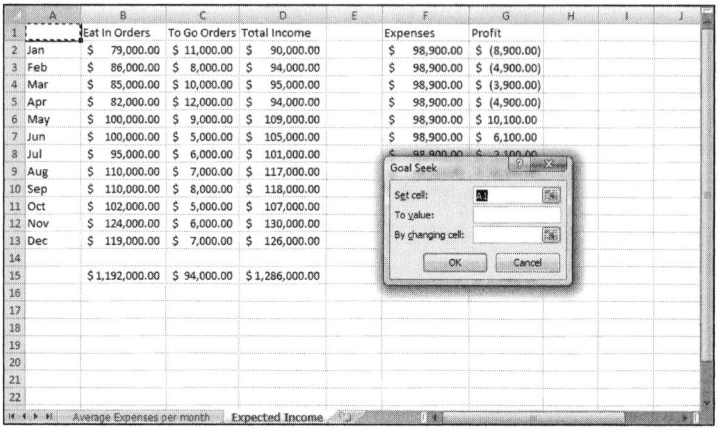

Figure 12-8: The Goal Seek dialog box.

To seek a new goal, you need to define the cell to be changed, its new value, and the cell you want to change to get to that value. When you open Goal Seek, the default cell to set is the selected cell.

3. **Click the grid icon for the Set Cell field. Select cell 'Expected Income'!$G$15. Click the grid icon again to return to the Goal Seek dialog box.**

Cell G15 shows the total yearly profit for James Restaurant. This cell is the target cell.

4. **In the To Value box, type 110000 for the target value.**

You want to increase the James Restaurant yearly profits to $110,000 per year.

5. **Click the grid icon to the right of the By Changing Cell field. Select cell 'Average Expenses per month'!$C$19. Click the grid icon again.**

Cell C10 is the number of employees on the wait staff.

6. **Click OK to seek your goal.**

The Goal Seek feature runs and lets you know whether it obtained your result. In this case, the result is shown in Figure 12-9.

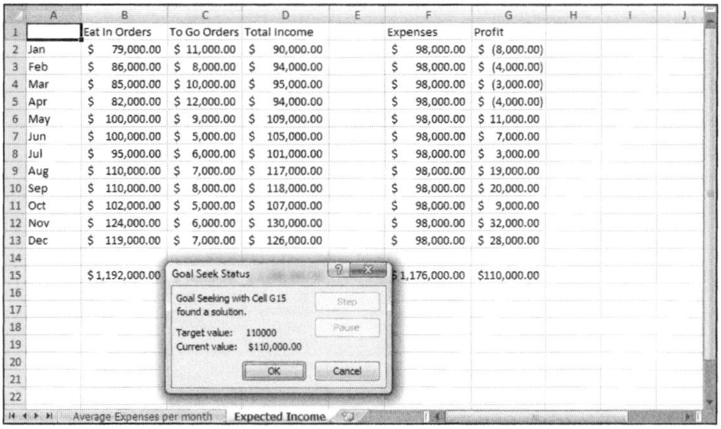

Figure 12-9: The Goal Seek Status dialog box.

To see the number of wait staff that are needed to make this change in profits, check the value in cell 'Average Expenses per month'!$C$19. The value has changed from 10 to about 9.57, so to meet your profit goal, you only need to cut one of the wait staff to half time.

7. Click Cancel.

Goal Seek has changed your data already. If you click OK, the changes remain in the spreadsheet. By clicking Cancel, you revert the sheets to their original states.

Although these steps all seem straightforward, they can be a big problem. If the cells you want to change are not directly related to the target cell, Goal Seek may run through a number of iterations and then tell you that it can't find a solution, as shown in Figure 12-10.

Another potential problem with goal seeking occurs when you want to make a change to the target cell, but Excel cannot make enough of a change to find a solution using the cell you selected. To see what happens, try to cut expenses to $50,000 per month by cutting cleanup staff. The solution is roughly –25.18, as shown in cell C21 in Figure 12-11. Although Excel found a viable numeric solution, in the real world, you can't have a negative number of employees.

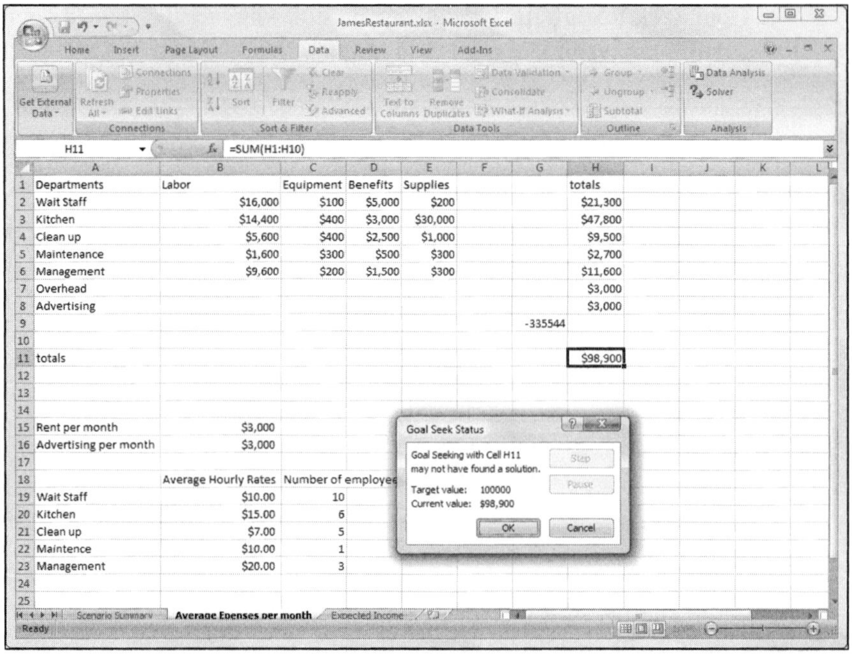

Figure 12-10: The Goal Seek Status dialog box indicates that Goal Seek couldn't find a solution.

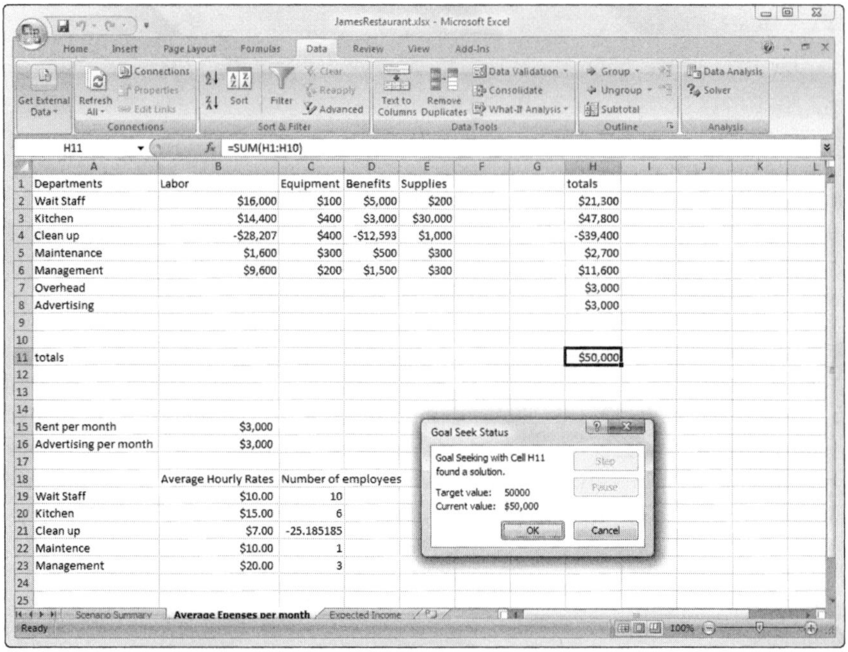

Figure 12-11: The Goal Seek solution is invalid for this example.

Using Excel Charts to Forecast Future Outcomes

You already know how to use a line chart to create a visual representation of your data. By adding trendlines to your line charts, Excel can make different kinds of best guesses about what the future will bring if conditions stay the same. Using the data you provide, *trendlines* use one of three different computations to project future results. After you add a trendline to a line in a chart, you can then extend that line into the future.

In the following exercise, you will chart the trends for the eat-in orders, the to-go orders, and the profit. By looking at the relationships among these lines, you can tell if the changes you are considering will actually achieve the result you want.

1. **Open the file `JamesRestaurantChart.xlsx`. Save a new copy of the file for use in this exercise. Change the view to show the chart, if it isn't already shown.**

You work with the James Restaurant data again, but this time you start with a file that has a line chart built for you. The chart shows the eat-in orders, to-go orders, expenses, and profit.

2. **Click in the chart area to activate the Chart tabs.**

3. **Choose Chart Tools Layout → Analysis → Trendline → Linear Trendline.**

The Add Trendline dialog box appears so that you can select the series that will be the basis of the trendline. You can create only one trendline at a time, but you can have multiple trendlines on a single chart. You add trendlines to each of the data series except for the Expenses line. Because expenses are forecasted to remain the same for the year, you have no need to create a trendline for its series. Another way to look at it is that if there are not enough different points of data, Excel won't create a useable trendline.

4. **Select Profit, and then click OK.**

A linear trendline is added to the Profit series, as shown in Figure 12-12.

Linear trendlines project your data into the future by using the current data as a basis for a straight-line projection. This projection is not always the one that fits best, but it gives you a good idea of whether you are seeing an upward trend or a downward trend.

5. **Choose Chart Tools Layout → Analysis → Trendline → Exponential Trendline.**

The Add Trendline dialog box appears so that you can select the series that will be the basis of the trendline.

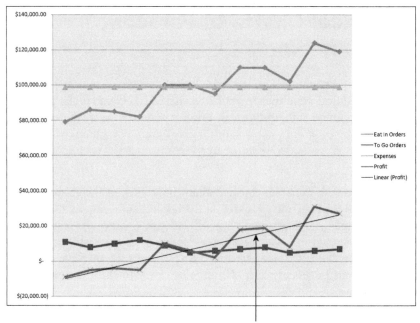

Linear trendline for Profit

Figure 12-12: A linear trendline for the Profit series.

6. **Select Eat In Orders, and then click OK.**

An exponential trendline is added to the Eat In Orders series, as shown in Figure 12-13.

The exponential trendline uses a more accurate estimation method for determining the future than the linear method does. Rather than assume that everything will continue in a straight line, the exponential trend uses the data to project the data along a curve.

Both these trendlines show the trend of the current data. Next, you move into the future to see what the data says might happen. You can use the trendlines to predict the future in two ways:

- Add a 2-period linear trendline directly from the Ribbon.

- Extend an existing trendline into the future by using the line properties.

7. **Choose Chart Tools Layout ➜ Analysis ➜ Trendline ➜ Linear Forecast Trendline.**

The Add Trendline dialog box appears so that you can select the series that will be the basis of the trendline.

8. **Select To Go Orders, and then click OK.**

A linear forecast trendline is added to the To Go Orders series, as shown in Figure 12-14.

Exponential trendline for Eat In Orders

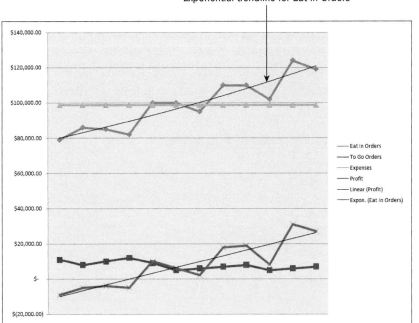

Figure 12-13: An exponential trendline for the Eat In Orders series.

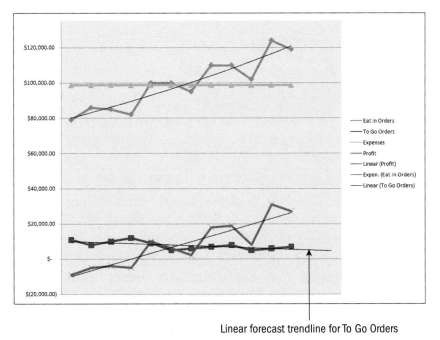

Linear forecast trendline for To Go Orders

Figure 12-14: A linear forecast trendline for the To Go Orders series.

Notice that the new trendline has extended the chart two periods into the future. Your next step is to extend that line, and others, further into the future.

9. Choose Chart Tools Layout → Current Selection and then select the Eat In Orders trendline from the drop-down list. Click the Format Selection button in that group.

The Format Trendline dialog box appears with the Trendline Options shown, as shown in Figure 12-15.

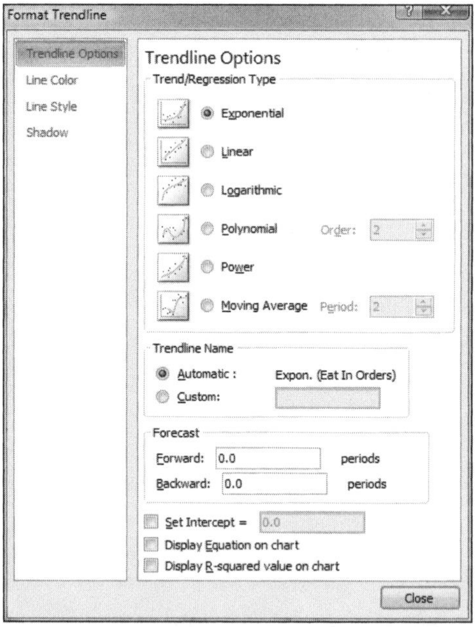

Figure 12-15: The Format Trendline dialog box.

Notice the Forecast section of this dialog box. You can set how far forward or backward you want to predict from the current data. Next, you change the line so that it forecasts 12 months into the future.

10. Change the 0.0 in the Forward box to 12.0 and press Tab.

The chart behind the dialog box changes to show the new forecasting period. If you can't see the chart, drag the dialog box to the left side of your screen.

In exponential forecasting, the line approximates a curve rather than a straight line, which provides a slightly better guesstimate of future performance.

11. Without closing the dialog box, select To Go Orders Trendlines from the drop-down list in the Current Selection group on the Chart Tools Layout tab.

12. **Change the 2.0 in the Forward box to** 12.0 **and press Tab.**

Now that the two sets of orders trendlines are shown, you can see the trend prediction. Unless something changes, the eat-in profits continue on an upward trend over the next year, and the to-go orders start to fall off. The updated chart is shown in Figure 12-16.

Because the exponential trendlines make a more realistic forecast on the data, the final step in the forecasting process is to show a 12-month exponential forecast for each of the three lines. You already created this trendline for the eat-in orders, so now you need to adapt the one for the to-go orders.

13. **If you closed the Format Trendline dialog box, reopen it.**

14. **Select the To Go Orders trendline. In the Format Trendline dialog box, select the Exponential option button and enter** 12 **in the Forward text box.**

You want to change to-go orders to a 12-month exponential trendline.

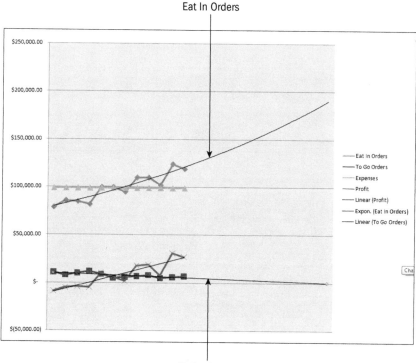

Figure 12-16: The Eat in Orders and To Go Orders trendlines are forecasted 12 months into the future.

Watch Your Step

You cannot directly change the profit trendline to an exponential trendline because it has negative values. A series with negative values can't be given an exponential trendline. These lines can be given only a linear trendline. However, you can extend linear trendlines with negative numbers into the future as far as you need to by using the Format Trendline dialog box.

15. **Select the Profit trendline. In the Format Trendline dialog box, select the Linear option button and enter** 12 **in the Forward text box. Close the dialog box.**

When you're done, the final chart appears, as shown in Figure 12-17.

As you can see, even though the profit trendline is a linear trendline, it still approximates the angle of the eat-in orders. Because to-go orders are such a small part of the restaurant's business now, they do not affect the projected growth of the profits.

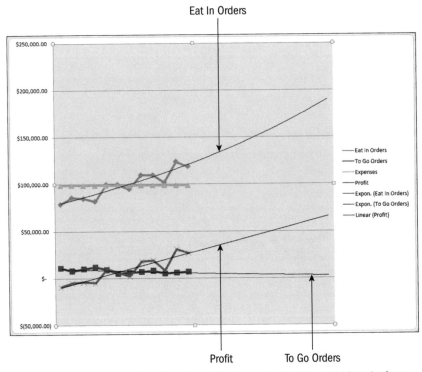

Figure 12-17: The final line chart with all possible lines extended 12 months into the future.

exponential: A nonlinear relationship between pieces of data. Exponential trend-lines are created by approximating the changes between known data using an exponential function.

forecast: A projection of the future based on known data and trends.

goal seeking: The process of determining which changes need to be made to reach a desired result.

linear: The type of relationship that exists between pieces of data when the rate of change occurs in a straight line. Linear trendlines are estimates that assume the rate of change for the line is constant.

scenario: A circumstance in which the expected result is based on changes to known data.

summary sheet: A type of sheet added to an Excel file that shows the state of the data before the changes are defined in the scenario and the state of the data after the changes are defined in the scenario.

target cell: The cell that contains the value to be changed when seeking a goal.

target value: The value desired for the target cell when seeking a goal.

trendline: An extension of a line in a line chart that shows how the existing points on the line will best fit if changes to the data are made over time.

what-if analysis: The process of using pieces of current data to make a guess about future states of the data.

Practice Exam

1. **Which of the following statements is true?**

    a. When you're using Goal Seek, the results can be stored in a range of cells.

    b. Cells in multiple sheets can be changed during the creation of a single scenario.

    c. Formulas can be used to define the change to a cell when creating a scenario.

    d. Cells containing formulas can be used as the *by changing cell* of a goal.

2. **What does the Show button in the Scenario Manager do when a scenario is selected?**

_____

_____

3. **True or False: Only five cells can be used to create a single scenario.**

4. **Name one difference between the target cell and the *by changing cell* when goal seeking.**

_____

5. **True or False: Goal Seek always finds an answer.**

6. **True or False: All answers found by Goal Seek are valid.**

7. **Suppose that cell R5 contains the number of employees and cell B17 contains the profit. Using Goal Seek, which of the two cells would you change and which one would Excel change?**

_____

_____

8. Which of the following situations prevents you from being able to create an exponential trendline?

a. Too many data points are in the series.

b. Negative data points are in the series.

c. Too few data points are in the series.

d. Too much of a difference exists between data points in the series.

9. By default, how far in the future does a Linear Forecast Trendline reach?

_____

CHAPTER

13

Customizing Excel

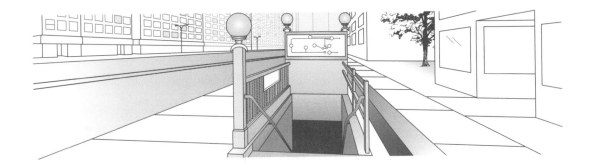

Enter the Station

Questions

1. What is the Quick Access Toolbar (QAT)?

2. Can you move buttons and groups around on the Ribbon?

3. What are the default buttons on the QAT?

4. Can you add tabs to the Ribbon?

5. Can an application add tabs to the Ribbon?

6. How do you add buttons to the QAT?

7. Where are the two places you can put the QAT?

8. How can you use the Customize QAT options to find the location of specific commands on the Ribbon?

Express Line

If you already fully understand the QAT and what you can and cannot customize in Excel 2007, skip ahead to the next chapter.

In Chapter 1, you explored the Excel 2007 interface. Since then, you have been working with that interface as it comes out of the box in your use of Excel. Although the Ribbon adjusts itself by displaying and hiding various contextual tabs, you haven't done much to change the interface yourself. If you're used to previous versions of Excel or other Office products, you might be wondering why I haven't shown you how to customize the interface yet.

The simple answer is that you can customize very few elements in the Excel 2007 interface without creating a program or XML set to do the customization for you. You cannot move items between tabs on the Ribbon, change which items show, or add items to any tab other than the Add-Ins tab.

Watch Your Step

The QAT (Quick Access Toolbar) is the only part of the Ribbon you can change. You might be used to adding menus, moving buttons, and adding other elements to your Excel interface. To make these types of changes, you need an external tool, a separate program, or a piece of code or custom XML that you have written.

This situation isn't as dire as it sounds. Other users are writing Ribbon customization tools that you can use. The one I have found most stable is from Patrick Schmid, a Microsoft MVP. You can find his Ribbon customizer on his site (http://pschmid.net/office2007/ribboncustomizer/index.php) or by doing a Google search for his blog (www.google.com).

One main idea behind the Ribbon concept is that it should be so easy to use that you shouldn't need to customize it. The Ribbon is supposed to be so logical to use that you can find and use everything you need in just a few clicks. That statement might be true, but you're likely to find some small adjustments you want to make.

In this chapter, you learn how to customize your Excel 2007 interface. Most of the customization revolves around the QAT. The other customizations you learn about are made by using the Excel Options button, found at the bottom of the Office Button menu.

Examining the Quick Access Toolbar (QAT)

When you open Excel 2007 for the first time, you see the default QAT, a set of three buttons that sit just to the right of the Office Button, as shown in Figure 13-1.

By default, the QAT contains three buttons: Save, Undo, and Redo. You perform these three actions regularly in Excel, no matter which tasks you are performing.

This toolbar, which is always available, contains the buttons you need to access in one click, no matter which ribbons are available or which tasks you are performing.

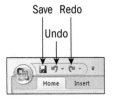

Figure 13-1: The Quick Access Toolbar.

In the following exercise, you will add items to the QAT by choosing from the drop-down list of additional buttons:

1. **Open Excel, if you haven't already.**

2. **Locate the QAT.**

3. **Click the drop-down arrow to the right of the QAT.**

The Customize Quick Access Toolbar menu appears, as shown in Figure 13-2.

> Customize Quick Access Toolbar
>
> New
> Open
> ✓ Save
> E-mail
> Quick Print
> Print Preview
> Spelling
> ✓ Undo
> ✓ Redo
> Sort Ascending
> Sort Descending
> More Commands...
> Show Below the Ribbon
> Minimize the Ribbon

Figure 13-2: Making quick additions to the QAT.

Down the left side of the menu are check boxes for the three buttons that are already on the QAT.

4. **From the menu, choose Print Preview.**

Notice that the list closes and the button is added (by default) to the right of the QAT. You learn later in this chapter how to rearrange these toolbar buttons.

5. **Repeat Steps 3 and 4.**

When you remove the check mark from the customized list item, the item is removed from your QAT. This method is the most basic way to update the QAT.

If the 11 listed items were the only elements you could add to the QAT, most Excel users wouldn't be happy. But you can add almost any item from the Ribbon. In addition, as you can see later in this chapter, you can get to some parts of the Excel 2007 interface only by adding them to the QAT.

Before you customize this toolbar further, you need to understand how to use one other option that you can access from this menu: Minimize the Ribbon.

6. Click the drop-down arrow to the right of the QAT.

7. From the list, select Minimize the Ribbon.

The Ribbon shrinks to show just the tab names. When you click a tab name, the tab expands to cover the top of the current worksheet. You can then access the elements on the tab. When you click somewhere off the tab (and on your sheet), the Ribbon collapses again to show just the tabs.

You can achieve the same effect at any time by double-clicking any tab on the Ribbon.

Changing the Location of the QAT

In many programs, including all versions of Excel before 2007, you could move pieces of the interface around. You could undock toolbars and move them, for example, and you could place the menu bar somewhere other than at the top of the screen. However, with the implementation of the Ribbon, your options have been limited.

The Ribbon can be located only at the top of your screen. As you discovered in the previous exercise, you can shrink the amount of space the Ribbon occupies, but you cannot move it. On the other hand, you can move the QAT — but only slightly.

By default, the QAT is located above the Ribbon on the left side of your screen. For two reasons, this location might not be the optimal one for you:

You have to move the mouse a long distance from the cells in your worksheet to the top of the window where the QAT sits.

Having too many buttons on your QAT shortens the length of the document name shown on the title bar and moves some QAT buttons to a separate drop-down list. This effect is shown in Figure 13-3.

Figure 13-3: A QAT with too many buttons on it.

The solution to this problem is to move the QAT to the one other place where it can reside — below the Ribbon:

1. Click the drop-down arrow to the right of the QAT.

2. From the list, select Show Below the Ribbon.

The QAT moves to a spot between the Ribbon and the cell reference box, as shown in Figure 13-4. The QAT can now extend from one side of your window to the other.

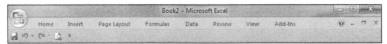

Figure 13-4: The QAT with four buttons below a minimized Ribbon.

3. **Click the drop-down arrow to the right of the QAT. From the list, unselect Minimize the Ribbon.**

Information Kiosk

If you fill the QAT with buttons, you still see the drop-down list. However, if your screen resolution is high enough that you can see the fully expanded Ribbon, you can have more than 50 buttons on your QAT before the buttons wrap to the drop-down list.

Customizing the Quick Access Toolbar

You have already learned one way to add buttons to the QAT. If the button you want isn't on the customize list for the QAT, however, you need to customize it by using the full customization interface.

Adding buttons

You can access the full customization interface in two ways:

- From the QAT drop-down list, select More Commands.
- From the Office Button, click the Excel Options button and go to the Customize section.

Because you already know how to use the QAT drop-down list, you learn the other way now:

1. **Click the Office Button, and then in the lower-right area of the menu that appears, click the Excel Options button.**

The Excel Options window opens. You learn about more of these options at the end of this chapter. For now, go directly to the Customize section.

2. **From the list of option categories on the left side of the window, select Customize.**

Notice that the full Customize the Quick Access Toolbar section of the Excel Options window appears, as shown in Figure 13-5.

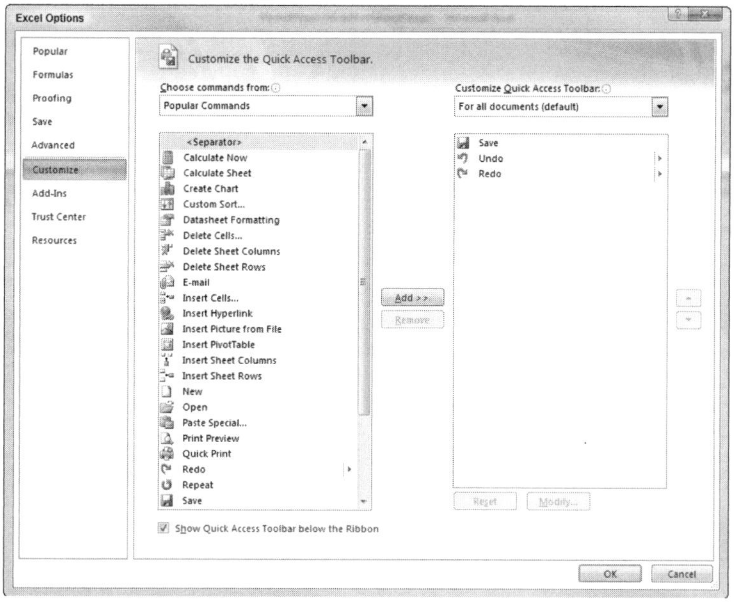

Figure 13-5: Customize the Quick Access Toolbar.

The left column of the window contains the various buttons, galleries, groups, macros, and commands that are available to you. The right side contains the list of items that are now on your QAT.

Using the Choose Commands From drop-down list at the top of the left column, you can choose from a number of command groupings, including all commands, most popular commands, commands on a specific tab, or items you can't access from the Ribbon. Using the drop-down list at the top of the right column, you can choose whether the commands are always shown on the QAT or only for the current document.

Next, you add to the QAT two commands to all documents.

3. **From the Choose Commands From drop-down list, select Office Menu. Scroll down the list until you find the New... option.**

4. **Click New... in the left column to select it. Click the Add button, which appears between the two columns.**

The New... button appears in the right column, showing that you have added it to your global QAT.

5. **From the Choose Commands From drop-down list, select Popular Commands. Select New from this list.**

6. Click the Add button.

The word New appears in the right column, showing that you have added it to your global QAT.

You have now added two different buttons to the QAT, as shown in Figure 13-6. Although they appear to do the same thing (open a new document), in reality, they do two different things. Next, you save the changes to your QAT and see what these buttons do.

7. Click OK to close the Excel Options window.

Figure 13-6: Your QAT with both the New... and New buttons added.

8. Click the lefthand New button on your QAT.

The New Workbook dialog box appears, allowing you to open a new document of any type.

9. Click Cancel, and then click the New button on the right on your QAT.

Excel now automatically opens a new, blank file whenever you click this button. This functionality is not available from the main Excel interface. The only way to open a new blank document in one click is to add the New button to the QAT. This is one important use of buttons on the QAT: to access functionality that has been hidden from you.

Because you already know how to access the New Workbook dialog box, your next step is to remove that button from the QAT.

10. Repeat Steps 1 and 2 to return to the Customize the Quick Access Toolbar section of the Excel Options window. Select the New... entry from the right-hand column by clicking it.

11. Click the Remove button.

The New... button no longer appears on the list for the QAT.

12. Click OK to close the Customize interface and save your changes to the QAT.

Your QAT now has only four buttons on it: Save, Undo, Redo, and New.

Rearranging buttons and adding separators

Adding buttons to, and removing them from, the QAT is only part of what you can do by using the Customize the Quick Access Toolbar section of Excel Options. You can also use it to rearrange the buttons on the QAT and to add separators to it. *Separators* are dividing lines that help you logically organize your buttons into groups. Organizing the buttons helps you remember what type of functionality you can access from your QAT.

To best see how to work with your QAT as it gets more complex, you start this exercise by adding several buttons to the QAT. After you add them, you reorder them and group them:

1. **Repeat Steps 1 and 2 in the previous exercise to open the Customize the Quick Access Toolbar section of Excel Options window.**

2. **Use the customization interface to add these buttons to your QAT:**

- *From the Popular Commands list:* Create Chart, Quick Print, Repeat.

  (Repeat is different from Redo. Repeat performs the command again on whatever is now selected; Redo redoes only what you undid.)

- *From the Office Menu list:* Print, Properties, Save As Other Format.

- *From the Formulas Tab list:* Function Library, Date and Time.

When you complete this step, your QAT has 12 buttons, as shown in Figure 13-7.

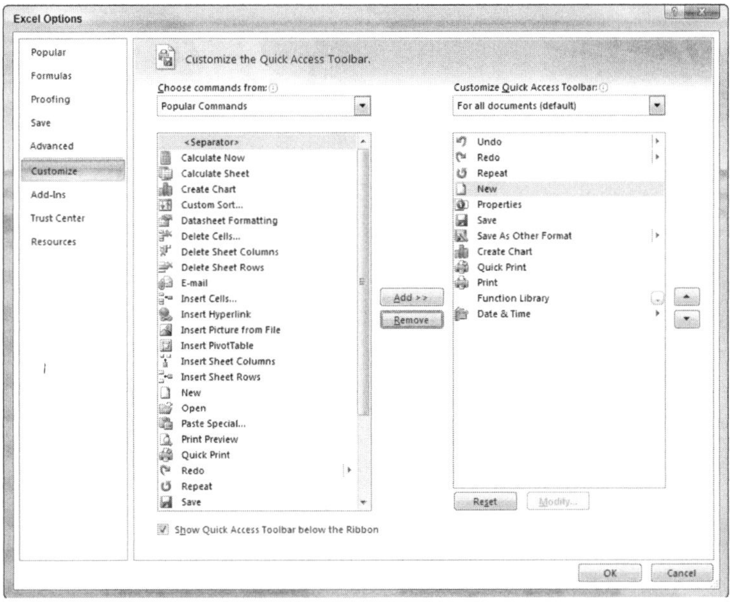

Figure 13-7: An unordered QAT list.

You are ready to add separators to the list so that you can group the buttons logically.

3. Click <Separator> in the lefthand list. The separator is always the top item on the list, no matter which category is shown.

4. Click the Add button four times.

You have added four separators to the bottom of your list. You can add any button or group to the QAT once, at most. However, you can add as many separators to the QAT as you want.

Your next step is to move the separators up on the list to divide your buttons into groups.

5. Click the up and down arrows to arrange the buttons and separators so that the list appears as shown in Figure 13-8.

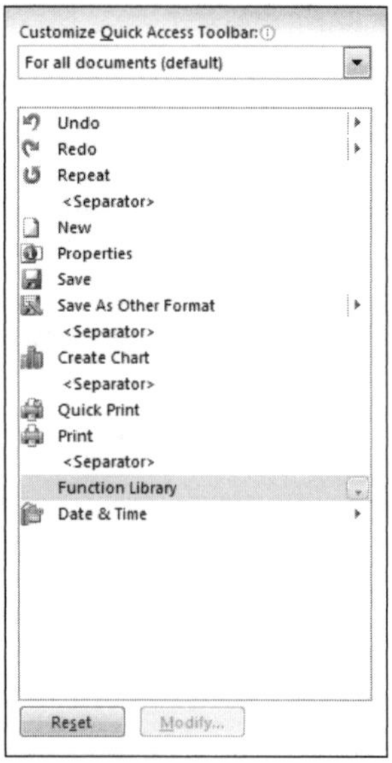

Figure 13-8: An organized QAT list.

6. Click the OK button to save your changes to the QAT.

Your expanded and organized QAT now looks similar to Figure 13-9.

The QAT you just created should make doing basic tasks within Excel easier. As you discover other items that you want to have on the QAT, add them.

Step Into the Real World

As you become more experienced in using the Ribbon, you find that you want items on your QAT for some documents but not for others. When you are working in a document made up of tables, for example, you're likely to want to change the look and feel of the table without using the contextual Design tab. When I am working with the design of tables, I find it useful to add the Table Styles group to the QAT. One advantage is that the gallery that makes up this group is a live preview gallery. By adding it to the QAT, I have one-click access to live previews.

If you work with conditional formatting, you're likely to want the conditional formats on your QAT. Even though they're on the Home tab, which is shown most of the time, having them handy on the QAT saves you from having to remember where they are. One additional advantage of having the Conditional Formatting items on the QAT is that you can skim over them to see (or show) the state of your data without needing to add the formatting to the data.

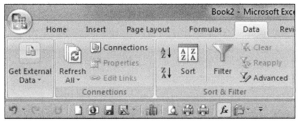

Figure 13-9: An organized QAT.

The Function Library item on your expanded QAT is an example of adding a group to the QAT. If you click it, you see that the Function group appears below the QAT. You get easier access to all the functions without needing to use the Formulas tab to find them.

Finding the location of buttons with the customization list

You can also use the Customize section of the Excel Options window for the QAT as a way to remember where commands you don't use frequently are located on the Ribbon. Each entry in the list of items you can add to the QAT tells you where it is located in the interface. All you need to do is hover the mouse cursor over it. Follow these steps:

1. Repeat Steps 1 and 2 in the earlier section "Adding buttons" to open the Customize the Quick Access Toolbar section of the Excel Options window.

2. From the Choose Commands From drop-down list, select All Commands.

3. Click in the list and then type the letter L.

   Notice that the list scrolls down to the Label entry (the first entry that starts with the letter *L*).

4. Scroll down until Last Column is shown on the list.

5. Hover your mouse cursor over the words Last Column.

   Notice that the ToolTip that pops up shows you exactly where the command can be found, as shown in Figure 13-10.

Step Into the Real World

Now that you know how to add elements to the QAT that you're used to seeing on the Ribbon, it's time to learn about the other reason for the QAT: Some functionality that you need isn't available directly from the Ribbon. These items are on the customization list in a group named Commands Not in the Ribbon. If you add the elements from this list to your QAT, you can access them, even though they are not on the Ribbon.

You have already seen two examples of elements that are not available from the Ribbon, but which are very handy to have available: the New button and the Repeat button. In fact, so many people add the Repeat button to the QAT that Microsoft added it to the Popular Commands list.

Commands that aren't on the Ribbon fall into a few basic categories:

- **Commands that are accessible from other areas of the interface:** An example is the Undo button. It needs to be listed as something you can add to the QAT. However, because its default location is the QAT, it isn't in any other command category. Another example are the buttons near the View adjustment. These buttons also are not on the Ribbon, but are popular commands. A third example are items like the Save and New buttons, which are included in the Office Button list.

- **Commands that are accessible from a gallery or group and usually hidden or that exist on a contextual tab:** Examples include shapes, 3-D operations, and effects.

- **Commands from previous versions of Excel:** Items that you're used to using with a previous Excel version, but whose functionality wasn't added to the Ribbon because Microsoft didn't think that most users would need it. Examples in this category are the Back button, the Close All button, and the various VB controls you can add to your worksheets.

You add these commands to the QAT in the same way as you add any other command. The only difference is that these commands are all grouped alphabetically in the category Commands Not in the Ribbon.

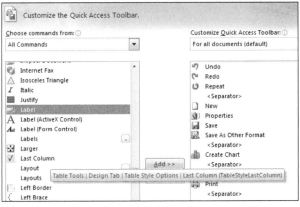

Figure 13-10: A button location ToolTip.

Changing Excel Settings

You can make customizations to Excel other than those you make to its interface, such as the changes you made to the timing of spreadsheet re-calculation in Chapter 4. You access these customizations by using the Excel Options button on the Office Button menu. In this exercise, you explore a few of the other customizations you might want to make to your Excel installation:

1. Click the Office Button. In the lower-right area of the menu that appears, click the Excel Options button.

The default category of customizations or options you can control is labeled Popular, as shown in Figure 13-11. These options are the ones that Microsoft knows that almost everyone will eventually want to change.

The changes you can make using the Popular options fall into three categories:

- *Options that you're likely to want to change:* The first group contains options that Microsoft developed but knew that users might want to turn off. If you find that the Mini Toolbar gets in your way when you're entering data into cells, deselect the first check box to turn off the option. If Live Preview slows down your computer too much, deselect that check box. If you work with very large amounts of data, you will definitely want to turn off Live Preview. If you don't need full-screen ScreenTips and prefer to see less information when you hover the mouse cursor over a button, or if you don't want to see ScreenTips, change the ScreenTip style by using the drop-down list.

Transfer

If you're a developer, turn on the Developer tab so that you can access related VBA information. You learn about this tab in Chapter 15.

- *Options for creating new workbooks:* In the second group of options, you specify settings for new Excel workbooks. If you know that you will use more than three sheets in most of your workbooks, increase this number. If you're doing a lot of development for print, change the default view for new sheets to Page Layout view rather than Normal view.

- *Options for personalizing Office:* Use these two settings to change your name and change which language you use. These two default settings are picked up from your Windows account.

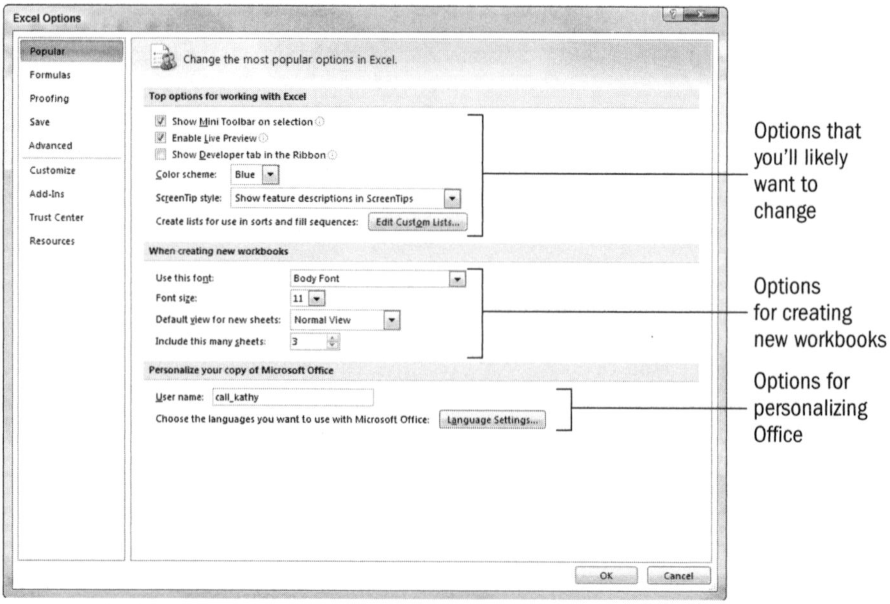

Figure 13-11: Popular Excel options.

2. **Select the Save category to change how your workbooks are saved.**

You have already seen the information in both the Formulas and Proofing categories, so the next type of customization you work with is the Save category. The changes you can make by using the Save options fall into four categories, as shown in Figure 13-12. Two of the customization categories are described in the following list (you aren't likely to need the other two categories in normal Excel use):

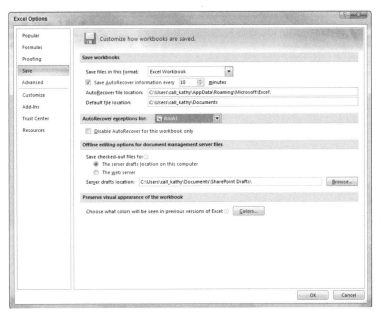

Figure 13-12: The Save options.

- *Where and when you want to save your work:* In the first group of options, you customize how your workbooks are saved. If you are working on important material, you might want to change the AutoRecover time to 5 minutes rather than 10 because losing 10 minutes of data entry in Excel can result in your having to reenter a lot of numbers. If you want to put your workbook and AutoRecover files in a location that you choose rather than in the Microsoft default locations, change that information here.

- *Turn off AutoRecover:* The only option in the second section is to turn off AutoRecover for the current workbook.

3. **Click the Advanced category to change how you work with Excel.**

The changes on the Advanced tab are the changes that Microsoft spread across the Tools → Options tabs in previous versions. You use these options to make advanced customizations to your work environment. You aren't likely to need to change many of the settings in this category. You should browse through the options in this category to find out whether you need to make specific changes.

4. **Select the Resources category to contact Microsoft, get updates, and find more information about your Excel installation.**

The Resources category is the Excel Options area that you will want to access regularly. The changes you can make are shown in Figure 13-13.

Figure 13-13: The Resources options.

- *Check for Updates:* Click this button to check for updates to your Office 2007 installation. If you aren't running Microsoft Update, you should check for updates every couple of weeks. To get the updates, you need to be connected to the Web. When you click this button, you go to the Office Online site. From there, you can check for and install any patches, service packs, or security updates as they are released.

- *Diagnose:* If your copy of Excel is running slowly, crashing or hanging frequently, or just not behaving the way you expect, click the Diagnose button. This action initiates the diagnosis-and-repair process, which determines whether you have problems with Office and then fixes any problems that it can.

- *Contact Us:* This button connects you to the Office Online page that summarizes where you can get help with your copy of Excel. You can use the links on this page to send feedback to Microsoft about your Excel experience.

- *Activate:* If you haven't yet activated your Excel installation, this button initiates the process. If you have already activated your copy of Excel, it tells you that as well.

- *Go Online:* When you're connected to the Web, clicking this button takes you to the front page of the Office Online site. Use this page to get information on Office and its associated products, download additional templates and clip art, and find many other online resources.

- *About:* Clicking this button brings up information about Excel and your system.

  If you aren't sure whether you have any updates or service packs installed, check the end of the first line in this window. If a service pack is installed, it's shown after the version number.

  Clicking the System Info button displays a wealth of information about your computer. This information can tell you how much memory you have installed, how big your hard drive is, which operating system you are running, and many other useful technical details about your system.

  Finally, if you are having problems with your Excel installation, you can click the Tech Support button and get the contact information for Microsoft Product Support. Calls about installation issues are free, as are certain others. However, most calls aren't free.

5. **After you finish customizing Excel, click OK to save your changes.**

AutoRecover: An Excel feature that periodically saves your document in the background to a special file. If Excel closes unexpectedly, use this file to recover changes you have made since the last time you saved your work.

customize: To change your program environment so that you can better accomplish daily tasks.

global change: A change made across all documents that are open in Excel.

local change: A change made to only the current document in Excel.

Office Online: The Microsoft online resource for all Office-related information for Excel users; contains articles, tutorials, training information, templates, clip art, and much more.

Quick Access Toolbar (QAT): A special toolbar used to store buttons that users need frequently. The QAT is the only toolbar in Excel 2007.

separator: A vertical bar added to the Quick Access Toolbar that logically groups toolbar items.

Last Stop

Practice Exam

1. True or False: Excel 2007 makes it easy for any user to add buttons to any tab.

2. What is the QAT?

    a. Quick Access Toolbar

    b. Quick Action Toolbar

    c. Quietly Accessible Tools

    d. Quality Assurance Tools

3. Name the three buttons that are on the QAT by default.

4. Which of the following actions does not hide the Ribbon?

    a. Right-clicking a tab on the Ribbon.

    b. Double-clicking a tab on the Ribbon.

    c. Pressing Alt+H on the keyboard.

    d. Selecting the More Commands option on the Customize Quick Access Toolbar menu.

5. True or False: You can put the QAT anywhere you want.

6. True or False: You can have only 50 buttons on the QAT.

7. QAT changes

    a. can be applied to all Excel documents on the computer.

    b. go away when the current Excel session is closed.

    c. can be applied to only the current document.

    d. A and C.

8. Buttons are added to the QAT

    a. from right to left and cannot be moved around.

    b. from left to right and cannot be moved around.

    c. from right to left and can be moved around.

    d. from left to right and can be moved around.

9. True or False: Buttons on the QAT can be moved by dragging.

10. True or False: All buttons that can be added to the QAT are found elsewhere on the Ribbon.

11. To change the default location of your AutoRecover files, which category of options do you need to access from the Excel Options window?

    a. Popular

    b. Advanced

    c. Resources

    d. Save

12. To find out whether you need to add any updates to your copy of Excel, which category of options do you need to access from the Excel Options window?

    a. Popular

    b. Advanced

    c. Resources

    d. Save

Extending Excel: Using Existing Add-Ins

STATIONS ALONG THE WAY

- Taking a look at add-ins
- Examining the add-ins that come with Excel 2007
- Installing and uninstalling add-ins
- Exploring additional add-ins available from Microsoft
- Looking for add-ins from other sources

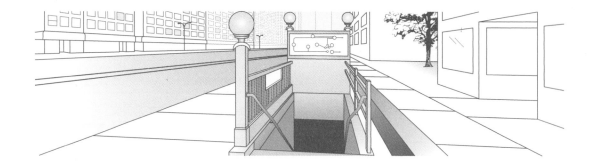

Enter the Station

Questions

1. What is the benefit to using an add-in?

2. How do you find out whether any add-ins are available to you?

3. Where can you find a comprehensive list of the add-ins that are delivered with Excel?

4. How do you install an add-in?

5. How do you remove an add-in?

6. Where can you find more Excel add-ins from Microsoft?

7. What other common add-ins are available?

8. How do you find a comprehensive list of Excel add-ins available from the Web?

Express Line

If you already know how to install and remove the add-ins available for use in Excel 2007 and you know why you would want to install them, skip ahead to the next chapter.

It is time to think outside the box or, rather, "outside the cell." In earlier chapters, you learned how to use Excel to work with your data. In this chapter, you find out how to make Excel work for you by automating it to perform steps repeatedly without your having to do each step manually.

As you work with your data, you will find that you have to do some tasks over and over again. These repeated processes can be turned into macros and add-ins. *Macros* are pieces of software (or programs) that you create to tell Excel what you want it to do. These programs are usually written in VBA (Visual Basic for Applications). Macros are attached to a single Excel file. *Add-ins* are groups of macros that you make available for use no matter which file is open.

Macros evolve into add-ins over time. When you need to automate a series of steps, you create a macro that is available for use when you have that file open. As you use the macro, you may find that you could use that macro in other files. At this point, you would turn the macro into an add-in. Eventually, you may even want to share your add-in with other users.

Transfer

Although you don't learn how to program in this book, you do learn how to record steps that you perform repeatedly and then turn those recordings into programs you can use. If you want to jump directly to those lessons, skip to Chapter 15.

Another reason to create an add-in is when you want to add functionality to Excel beyond that which is available from the Ribbon. In fact, many users have, over time, created add-ins that extend what Excel can do. This type of add-in program is created especially to enhance or extend the existing functionality of Excel.

Add-ins are installed after you install Excel. Some add-ins come with Excel, but are not installed when you do a typical install. Other add-ins must be acquired from the developers, either for free or for a fee. Microsoft delivers a set of add-ins with Excel that allow you to extend its functionality. It also makes more add-ins available from the Office Online site. A third common place to find add-ins is from various Excel support Web sites on the Internet.

By creating add-ins, developers allow you to add functionality to Excel that will be available no matter which Excel files you have open. You gain flexibility in using the new functionality without having to enable macros for each file that needs the extra functionality.

In this chapter, you learn what add-ins are and how to install, use, and uninstall them. While learning how to install and uninstall add-ins, you will add one of the Microsoft add-ins to your system. After you understand the basics of using add-ins, you will learn how to find other add-ins that are available to you from Microsoft and other developers.

Introducing Add-Ins

At their basic level, add-ins enhance the functionality of your Excel installation. Each add-in is a separate program that has been designed and written to allow you to complete a task that is not currently available or easy to do from within Excel. Two common add-ins that you might have come across already are the following:

- The **SnagIt** screen capture program, from TechSmith, installs an Excel add-in that allows you take a screen shot and add it directly to your Excel spreadsheet.

- **Adobe Acrobat** installs an add-in to allow you to create PDFs in one click if you have the full Adobe Acrobat product installed.

In both these cases, the company that created the add-in has integrated the installation of the add-in into the installation of the main product. This is not the only way to install an add-in, however. You can also install an Excel add-in by clicking the Office Button and clicking the Excel Options button at the bottom of the menu that appears. After the Excel Options window appears, click the word Add-Ins in the left column to bring up the list of active and inactive add-ins for your computer. A typical set of available add-ins is shown in Figure 14-1.

Add-ins		
Name	Location	Type
Active Application Add-ins		
SnagIt Add-in	C:\...s\TechSmith\SnagIt 8\SnagItOfficeAddin.dll	COM Add-in
Inactive Application Add-ins		
Analysis ToolPak	analys32.xll	Excel Add-in
Analysis ToolPak - VBA	atpvbaen.xlam	Excel Add-in
Conditional Sum Wizard	sumif.xlam	Excel Add-in
Custom XML Data	C:\...iles\Microsoft Office\Office12\OFFRHD.DLL	Document Inspector
Date (Smart tag lists)	C:\...Files\microsoft shared\Smart Tag\MOFL.DLL	Smart Tag
Euro Currency Tools	eurotool.xlam	Excel Add-in
Financial Symbol (Smart tag lists)	C:\...Files\microsoft shared\Smart Tag\MOFL.DLL	Smart Tag
Headers and Footers	C:\...iles\Microsoft Office\Office12\OFFRHD.DLL	Document Inspector
Hidden Rows and Columns	C:\...iles\Microsoft Office\Office12\OFFRHD.DLL	Document Inspector
Hidden Worksheets	C:\...iles\Microsoft Office\Office12\OFFRHD.DLL	Document Inspector
Internet Assistant VBA	C:\...icrosoft Office\Office12\Library\HTML.XLAM	Excel Add-in
Invisible Content	C:\...iles\Microsoft Office\Office12\OFFRHD.DLL	Document Inspector
Lookup Wizard	lookup.xlam	Excel Add-in
Person Name (Outlook e-mail recipients)	C:\...les\microsoft shared\Smart Tag\FNAME.DLL	Smart Tag
Solver Add-in	solver.xlam	Excel Add-in
Document Related Add-ins		
No Document Related Add-ins		
Disabled Application Add-ins		
No Disabled Application Add-ins		

Figure 14-1: A typical add-ins list.

Examining different add-in categories

The list of add-ins is split into four categories:

- **Active application add-ins:** These add-ins, which are installed and working properly, are ordinary add-ins that you can access from any Excel file.

- **Inactive application add-ins:** These add-ins are not installed, but are available for installation. This list consists primarily of add-ins that you have installed and removed or that were delivered with Excel 2007 and are not installed. After these add-ins are installed, they are available for use in any open Excel file.

- **Document-related add-ins:** In rare cases, complicated macros are turned into add-ins associated with a single document or template. If any of these add-ins is available with the active document or from the template on which the document is based, it is listed here. In general, you do not see any document-related add-ins.

- **Disabled application add-ins:** Add-ins in this category were installed, but have been disabled because they were causing some kind of problem. Either Excel disabled them because of repeated errors, or you disabled them but did not uninstall them. Other disabled add-ins have been disabled for security reasons.

 Watch Your Step

If you are sure that you have installed an add-in, but it continues to be shown as disabled, you likely have turned off add-ins in your trust settings. To find out, click the Office Button and then click the Excel Options button. In the Excel Options window, select the Trust Center section and click the Trust Center Settings button. Click the Add-ins link and make sure that you have not disabled all application add-ins.

In addition, if you selected the Require Application Add-Ins to Be Signed by Trusted Publishers check box, you may have problems with some of the add-ins available from the Web. In that case, you need to decide whether you want to risk running an add-in that does not have a signed security certificate.

You may find that your IT department has disabled add-ins for you and that you cannot reenable them. If so, contact your IT department to find out whether this policy decision can be overridden.

Examining types of add-ins you can use with Excel

Before you begin adding add-ins to your computer, you need to understand the four basic types of add-ins you can use with Excel:

- **Excel add-ins:** Excel files with VBA code that have been stored with the XLAM extension. These add-ins usually start life as a macro or series of macros that someone created for a single workbook. As the idea behind the macro grew, the developer decided to make the functionality available to files other than the original one. At this point, the programs changed from macros attached to a single file to add-ins available for installation on any Excel system.

- **.COM add-ins:** Programs written in a language other than VBA. These programs are stored outside of Excel, even after they are installed. .COM add-ins, which are generally saved as DLL files, are more advanced versions of simple VBA macros, written in C++ or other Visual Studio–based languages.

- **Smart tags:** Ways of attaching functionality to specific content within an Excel file. One smart tag you may be familiar with is the tag that pops up when you add contact information to a spreadsheet and that contact information already exists in your Outlook Contacts list. Excel automatically understands that the content is linked and provides specific functionality for that content.

- **XML expansion packs:** Packs created to allow you to work with the XML created by other, non-Office programs. When you use an expansion pack, you can understand the XML schemas created elsewhere and read data files based on these schemas directly in Excel.

Exploring Add-Ins That Come with Excel 2007

Depending on which edition of Office 2007 you use and the decisions you make during installation, your list of add-ins may be shorter than the one shown in Figure 14-1. However, for the purposes of this chapter, you will work only with add-ins from this list.

Before you practice installing and uninstalling Excel add-ins, you need to understand the add-ins that you are most likely to use from this list. You can think of these add-ins as chunks of functionality:

- **Analysis tools:** Five add-ins on the list help you extend the Excel 2007 analysis and solving capabilities. These add-ins help you to analyze, sum, find, and solve complicated formulas. Each of the add-ins in this category is a true add-in.

- **Document inspectors:** Five of the add-ins are additions to the document inspection functions available in Excel 2007. These add-ins are not run from the Add-ins tab; they run automatically when a document is inspected for changes or when it is saved. As a group, these add-ins help you hide data, find hidden data, work with the XML in your files, and work with Internet data.

- **Other types of add-ins:** The remaining four add-ins help you improve the lookup functions within Excel for data that exists outside of Excel. The Euro Currency Tools add-in is accessed from the Add-ins tab; the others are new smart tags that appear when the add-in is installed and data of that type is added to a file.

These add-ins are not installed by default because you need them only if you do very specific tasks. In general, you don't ever need most of these add-ins. When you need them, however, you must know how to add and remove them from your system, as described in the next section.

Installing and Uninstalling Add-Ins

Now that you have a basic understanding of which kinds of add-ins are available, you can add a couple of add-ins to your system and then remove them.

Installing Excel add-ins

Follow these steps to install an Excel add-in:

1. **Open Excel if you haven't already.**

2. **Click the Office Button. At the bottom of the menu that appears, click the Excel Options button. Click the Add-Ins link.**

The full add-in interface appears, as shown in Figure 14-2. Your system may not have any active add-ins yet, but the remainder of your list should look similar.

Next, you install the Solver Add-in, which expands the available equation and analysis tools.

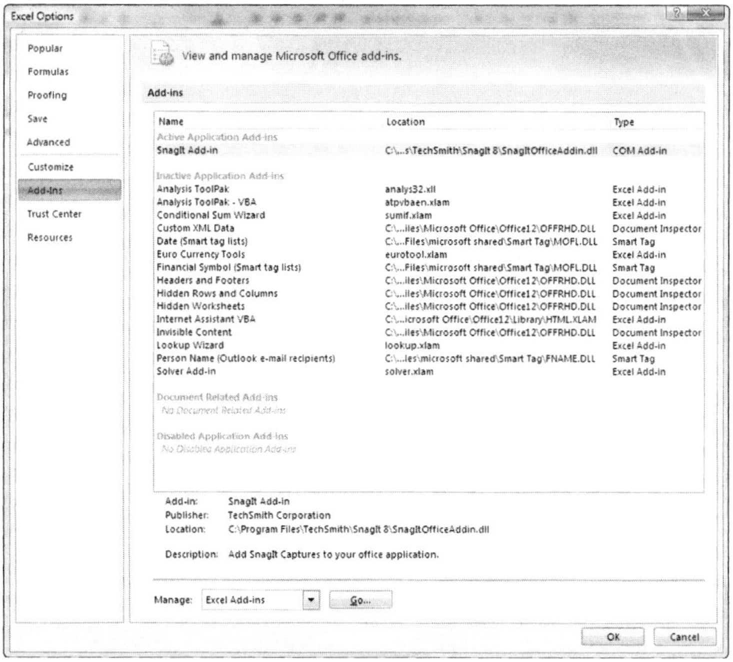

Figure 14-2: The full add-in interface from the Excel Options window.

3. **Make sure that Excel Add-Ins is selected in the Manage drop-down list, and then click the Go button immediately to its right.**

The list of available add-ins of this type appears, as shown in Figure 14-3.

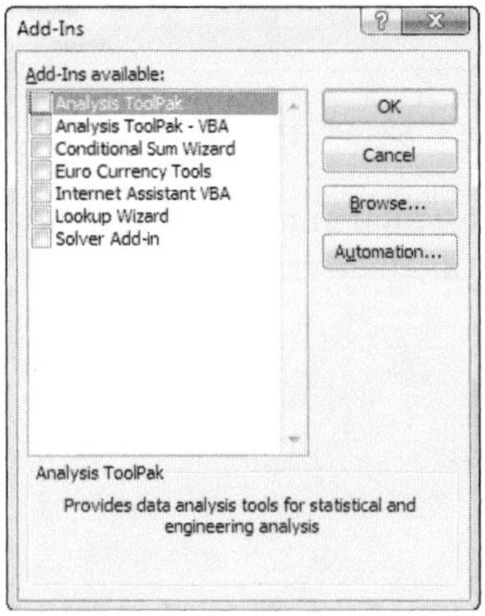

Figure 14-3: The Add-Ins Available list.

Your list may look slightly different, depending on your Office edition. The only thing that matters at this point is that the Solver Add-In appears on the list.

Each available add-in is preceded by an empty check box. If the check box were selected, it would indicate that the add-in is already installed. In this dialog box, you can install an add-in, cancel the installation, or browse your hard drive for more add-ins.

Watch Your Step

The other button in the Add-Ins dialog box is the Automation button. Unless you are developing an add-in for wide distribution, do not click this button. Its purpose is to help developers install and uninstall add-ins while they create, test, and perfect their programs before making them available to the general public.

4. **Select the Solver Add-In check box and click OK.**

Excel responds with the message shown in Figure 14-4.

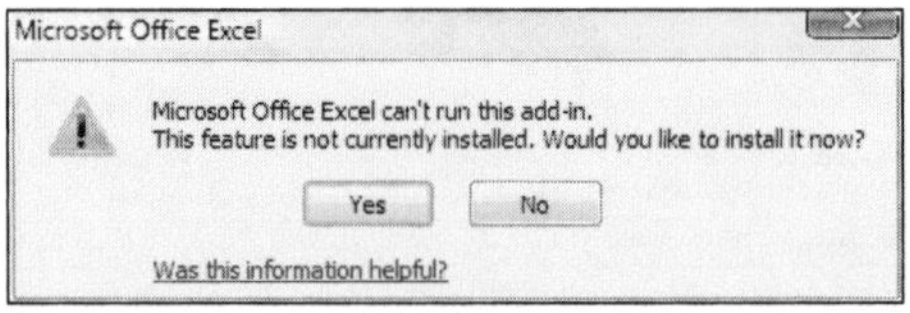

Figure 14-4: A feature is not installed.

All this message is saying is that you must install the add-in before running it. If someone else installed the Solver package on your computer, you may not see this message. Instead, you see the window shown in the figure in the next step.

5. Click Yes in the message box that appears.

Excel displays the configuration screen and a green progress bar as it installs the add-in, as shown in Figure 14-5.

Figure 14-5: The configuration progress.

When the installation is completed, you return to the main Excel interface. Although nothing appears to have changed, changes have been made.

6. Click to select the Data tab.

Excel has installed the add-in and added a new group (Analysis) and button (Solver) on the far right side of the Data tab, as shown in Figure 14-6.

The solver has been installed. Click the Solver button to activate the Solver interface. For now, leave the Solver alone. You install one of the other types of add-ins in the next section.

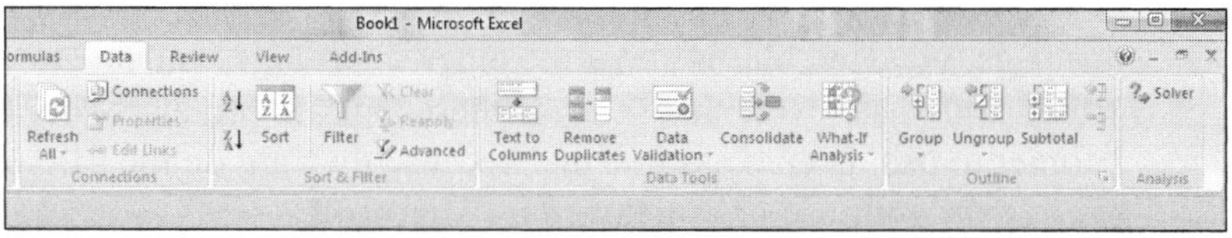

Figure 14-6: The new Analysis group on the Data tab.

Installing smart tags

In the following steps, you install a smart tag:

1. **Click the Office Button. At the bottom of the menu that appears, click the Excel Options button. Click the Add-Ins link.**

2. **Select Smart Tags from the Manage drop-down list and then click the Go button.**

The AutoCorrect dialog box appears, with the Smart Tags tab active, as shown in Figure 14-7.

Figure 14-7: The smart tags list.

Again, your list may look slightly different, depending on your Office edition. Before you can activate one of the smart tags, you have to activate the smart tag functionality.

3. **Select the Label Data with Smart Tags check box.**

The list of available smart tags is now available for use. By default, both the Financial Symbol tag and the Person Name tag are selected. Before you add the Date tag, check for other available smart tags on your system.

4. **Click the More Smart Tags button.**

If you are connected to the Web, a new window (or tab, if you are running a tabbed browser) opens to the Available Smart Tags page in Office Online. On this page, you find blurbs about the other smart tags available to you as an Office 2007 user. Note that some of these tags are products you must purchase in order to use. Do not assume that because they are on the Microsoft site, they are free for your use or sanctioned by Microsoft.

5. **Minimize the browser window and return to Excel. Select the Date Smart Tag check box to install the smart tag. Click OK.**

Although it does not look as though anything has changed in your Excel installation, you have activated all three default smart tags. Next, you test one of them to ensure that they are installed correctly.

6. **In cell A3, type** 11/12/08 **and press Enter.**

To the right of the cell, a smart tag indicator appears, as shown in Figure 14-8.

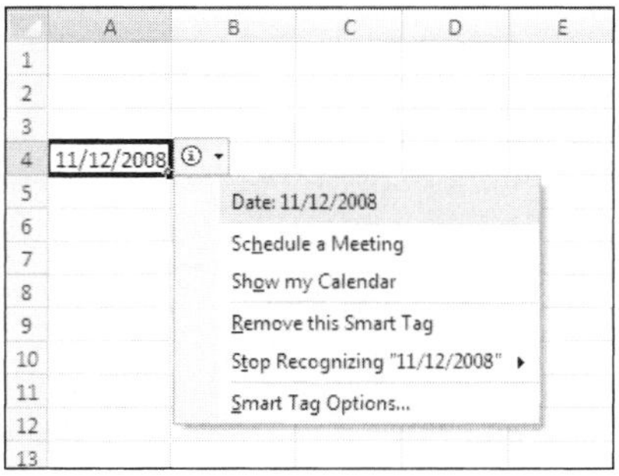

Figure 14-8: The Date smart tag options.

By adding the Date smart tag when you type a date in Excel, you can more easily work with the calendar for that date. Selecting the last item on the options list returns you to the AutoCorrect dialog box.

Installing .COM add-ins

Unless you have added functionality by using another program, you don't have any .COM add-ins to enable on your list. If you do, you install them in much the same manner as you install regular add-ins:

1. **Click the Office Button. At the bottom of the menu that appears, click the Excel Options button. Click the Add-Ins link.**

2. **Select COM Add-Ins from the Manage drop-down list at the bottom of the window, and then click the Go button.**

The COM Add-Ins dialog box appears, as shown in Figure 14-9.

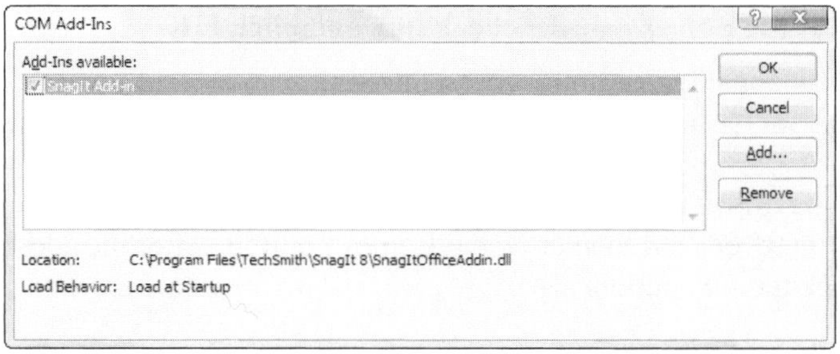

Figure 14-9: The COM Add-Ins dialog box.

As you can see, one .COM add-in is installed — the one for SnagIt. Other than the difference in the list, the buttons for adding and removing .COM add-ins are the same as for regular add-ins.

3. Because you probably don't have any .COM add-ins to install yet, click Cancel to close the COM Add-Ins dialog box.

Information Kiosk

What about those document inspector options? They come into play when you want to send confidential documents to other users. In Excel 2007, you can inspect your file for any hidden information and then remove it from the file. You access this information by choosing Office → Prepare → Inspect Document.

When you run the inspector, Excel tells you to save the document before you continue. After you decide whether to save it, you are prompted with the list of inspection options. Miraculously, when you initiate the inspection, the inspection classifications that were inactive are activated and selected. After the document is inspected, you are asked which changes you want Excel to make automatically.

After you run your first document inspection, all the inactive inspectors move to the active add-ins list at the top of the Add-Ins list in the Excel Options window — like magic.

Removing add-ins

You may install an add-in and then decide later that you don't want it. The uninstall process for both .COM and XLAM add-ins is much like the install process. Follow these steps to remove the Solver Add-In you just added:

1. Click the Office Button. At the bottom of the menu that appears, click the Excel Options button. Click the Add-Ins link.

2. Select Excel Add-Ins from the Manage drop-down list, and then click the Go button.

Next, you remove the Solver Add-In from the list.

3. Deselect the Solver Add-In check box and click OK.

Even if it appears that nothing has changed, a quick check of the Data tab shows that the Solver button and its group have been removed from your Ribbon.

If you want to remove a .COM add-in, Step 3 is slightly different: Select the .COM add-in to be removed, and then click the Remove button. After the add-in has been removed, click the OK button.

Searching for Additional Add-Ins Online

Now that you know which add-ins come with Excel, take a look at some of the other add-ins that are available to you online. Some are available directly from Microsoft; others, you need to find on the Web.

Watch Your Step

The add-ins you installed during the previous exercises are free add-ins that Microsoft provides when you purchase Excel. Not all add-ins are free, however, nor are all add-ins "good" add-ins. Before you install one that you find on the Web, do your research. Make sure that the developer is reliable, reputable, and competent.

Finding add-ins on Office Online

The best way to find add-ins that Microsoft has developed is to go to Office Online (www.office.microsoft.com/excel) and search for **Excel add-ins**. This action shows you a page of results with a mix of Excel add-ins developed by Microsoft and those that are linked to from the Microsoft site.

Microsoft add-ins are marked as such in the search results. Non-Microsoft add-ins state that they are available from the Office Marketplace, and a link to the Marketplace page is included.

Add-ins developed by Microsoft are usually free. Add-ins advertised on the Office Marketplace (a special area of the Office Online site for vendors to use to advertise their items) may or may not be free. Be aware: Just because an add-in is available in the Marketplace doesn't mean that Microsoft has sanctioned it to do what you want it to do. The add-in may cost you, and it may or may not be what you need.

Finding add-ins other places

In addition to finding add-ins from the Microsoft site, you can search the Web for add-ins created by other Excel users. To find those add-ins, go to your favorite search engine and enter the search phrase **Excel add-ins**. You will get thousands of hits. Some of your results will work with Excel 2007, and some won't. To find the ones that will work with Excel 2007, search for **Excel 2007 add-ins**. You will get fewer results and should be able to investigate them more thoroughly.

Determining which kinds of add-ins are out there

Over the years, developers have produced a wide range of add-ins. Most of them are in one of these three categories:

Computational: This type of add-in has been developed to add functions and equation solving to Excel. Some offer you a better interface for selecting cells on which to base your computations. Others combine existing functions with code to come up with computations targeted to specific types of data.

Information Kiosk

If you are in the healthcare industry, a whole series of available add-ins can help you with computations such as bed days for certain illnesses, recovery rates for various conditions, and much more.

Analysis: Analysis add-ins expand what you can learn from your data. For example, some add-ins use stock market data to help you make decisions about what the stock market will do in the future. Another common use of an analysis add-in is to work with the data from a database to build complex pivot tables, data cubes, and pivot charts.

Charting: Add-ins in this large category offer new chart designs, new chart formatting options, and extensions of the Excel charting functionality. Some even render data into 3-D charts, which seem to float in the air when displayed.

Search the Web to see which add-ins you can find that match your needs. I am sure you will find a few.

add-in: A macro that has been changed so that it can be accessed from any open Excel file.

automate: To cause to happen automatically or with limited user intervention.

macro: A piece of software that has been created to automate a task (or series of tasks) so that you do not need to perform them manually every time.

record: To tell Excel which steps you want your macro to perform and the order in which you want them performed.

trust settings: Settings within Office that allow you to tell it that certain content or programs are from a safe source and can be run as desired.

Last Stop

Practice Exam

1. Macros and add-ins allow you to _____ a series of steps so that you don't need to perform each one manually.

_____

2. Which of the following is true?

a. After installation, add-ins are available only from a single file.

b. After installation, macros are available only from a single file.

c. After installation, add-ins are always available, no matter which file is opened.

d. After installation, macros are always available, no matter which file is opened.

3. True or False: Add-ins are always installed by using the Excel interface.

4. Name four basic types of add-ins that you can install.

_____

_____

5. Which of the following cannot be installed by using the Office Button menu?

a. VBA add-ins

b. .COM add-ins

c. Smart tags

d. All add-ins are installed from outside the Excel interface.

6. How do you add a document inspector?

a. Inspect a document for changes.

b. Use XML.

c. Use the add-in options available from the Office Button menu.

d. You can't add document inspectors; you can only disable them.

7. True or False: Uninstalling an add-in always changes the Excel interface.

8. All add-ins found by using Office Online

    a. are from Microsoft.

    b. can be trusted.

    c. are free.

    d. None of the above.

Programming Excel: An Introduction to VBA and Macros

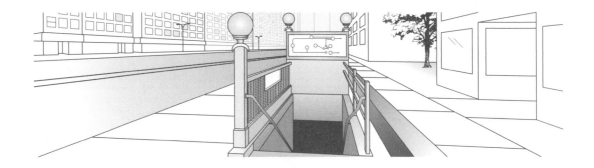

Enter the Station

Questions

1. Why do you need to enable macros?

2. Which format should you use when saving Excel files with macros in them?

3. Why would you turn on the Developer tab?

4. Why would you want a macro to contain an `If...Then` statement?

5. Why would you want a macro to contain a loop?

6. Where do you debug macros?

7. What is the difference between a syntax error and a scope error?

8. Why should you trap errors?

9. How do you add a macro to the QAT (Quick Access Toolbar)?

10. What is a trusted source?

Express Line

If you already know how to create basic macros in Excel, you can skip ahead to the next chapter to learn how to convert a macro into an add-in. However, if you are new to Excel 2007, you may want to read the sections in this chapter about the Developer tab and trusted sources before skipping ahead.

You are about to enter the world of the computer geek. As you have become more familiar with Excel, you have probably already found many tasks that you perform over and over. These processes are ripe for automation. To automate a process in Excel, your first step is to create a *macro* that performs the process once. After you do that, you can adapt the macro to do even more operations, to do them in different areas of your sheets, or to do them without your intervention.

You start on your journey of learning by building several simple macros. Although this chapter is an introduction to using Visual Basic for Applications (VBA) to create macros, this course is not about programming. If you want to learn more about VBA, programming, and automating your processes, check out *Excel 2007 Power Programming with VBA,* by John Walkenbach (Wiley).

In this chapter, you learn what you need to know to create, run, debug, and adapt macros. You will create a basic macro and then expand and adapt it as you progress through the chapter.

 ### Watch Your Step

To create the macros in this chapter, you must activate the Developer tab on the Ribbon (as described in the section "Working with the Developer Tab"). If you attempt to activate the tab and it does not appear, contact your IT department to get permission to create macros for yourself.

Macros: Making It Easier to Do Your Work

To start you off in working with macros, look at one of the most basic but time-consuming and human-intensive computations in mathematics: progression. In progression, you might, for example, find the sum of two numbers. The sum then becomes the third number in the series. The fourth number is the sum of the second and third numbers. The series can continue forever.

To create a spreadsheet to perform the progression, your first step is to enter the first and second numbers into two cells of your sheet. You then create a formula for the third cell that adds the first and second numbers. In the third step (creating the progression), you drag the formula so that it autofills the other numbers in the series.

Rather than create the progression by hand, you can create a simple macro that creates the formula for you and uses the new formula to populate a cell. The code to create the sequence is shown here:

```
Sub progression1()
'
' This macro takes two numbers from consecutive cells in
' column C and finds the next 10 numbers in the progressive
' series
'
    For I = 3 To 13
        nextvalue = "c" & I
        Range(nextvalue).Select
        ActiveCell.FormulaR1C1 = "=R[-2]C+R[-1]C"
    Next I
End Sub
```

Look at what that code really says:

- The first line defines the name of the macro: `progression1`. You use this name to tell Excel which macro to run.

- The lines that begin with single quotation marks are *comments*. They tell someone reading the code what the code does.

- The next five lines are the macro itself. The `For` line says that you want Excel to perform all lines up to the word `Next`, once for each value of `I`. This *loop* is a basic concept of automation. You use loops to tell the computer to perform tasks a certain number of times so that you don't have to repeat the process manually.

    In this example, the loop you want Excel to perform uses the value of `I` to figure out the next cell reference, to select that cell, and to put the next number in the series into that cell.

From this basic start, you can expand this macro so that you tell it which column you want to contain the progression and how many times you want the progression to happen. Follow these steps to run the expanded macro:

1. **Open the `Ch15Progression.xlsm` file.**

A security warning appears below the Ribbon, as shown in Figure 15-1.

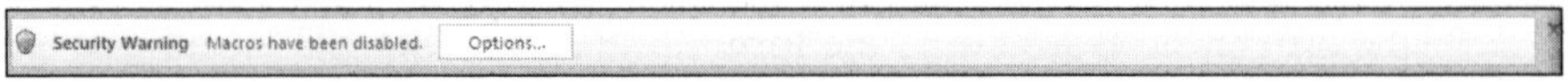

Figure 15-1: A security warning about macros.

This warning appears because the file you just opened contains macro code. Before Excel runs the code, it needs to know whether you trust the code in this file.

2. Click the Options button.

The Microsoft Security Options dialog box opens, as shown in Figure 15-2.

Figure 15-2: The Security Options dialog box.

From this dialog box, you can enable the macro. Perform this step only if you trust the source of the macro.

3. Select the Enable This Content radio button and click OK.

The dialog box closes, and you can run the macro.

4. From your keyboard, press Ctrl+Shift+M to run the macro.

This sequence initiates an expanded version of the macro that was introduced at the beginning of this section. In this case, the macro prompts you for several values and then computes the progression.

5. Answer each prompt as requested. You are asked to supply the two numbers (for example, 1 and 1), the column for the results (for example, A), and the number of times to iterate (for example, 15). After you type each answer, click the OK button.

After you respond to the last prompt, the results of your progression are displayed in the column you specified. If you used the answers in the example in this section, your sheet should look like the one shown in Figure 15-3.

The progression shown in these steps is a special progression known as *Fibonacci numbers*. This series goes on as long as you want. Play around with it to see the results you can create with other starting numbers.

You have successfully run your first macro and are ready to build your first macro on your own.

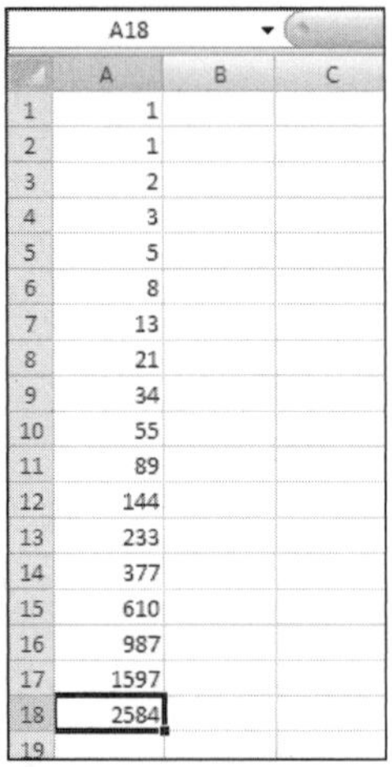

Figure 15-3: The results from the expanded progression macro.

Repeating a Series of Steps with a Macro

The fairly complicated macro you just ran asked you for a series of values and then used those values to loop through the same steps a number of times. As you learn to use macros, you will be creating macros that are not nearly that complicated.

Most macros in Excel are written to automate either of these elements:

- A series of steps you perform regularly and want to do quickly

- A process that you do only once in awhile and need to be able to repeat exactly each time you do it

In the exercises in the remainder of this chapter, you have an existing set of data that summarizes the number of complaints received at stores in a chain. You receive this data only once a year, and it needs to be formatted the same way each year when you are done with it. Follow these steps to create a simple macro that adds the row and column headers to this data:

1. Open the file Ch15Complaints.xlsx.

This file contains the complaint data for one year.

To add the headers manually to this data, you would need to type each value by hand each time. Instead, you will perform the steps once while Excel watches and records what you do. *Recording* the macro is the process of having Excel watch what you do and remember the steps. You can more quickly record the macro the first time you create the headers and then apply the macro to the complaint data as you need it each year.

2. Choose View → Macros → Macros → Record Macro.

The Record Macro dialog box appears, as shown in Figure 15-4.

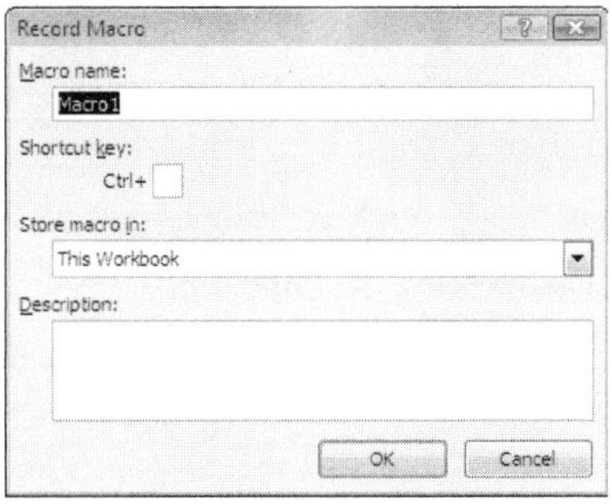

![Record Macro dialog box with Macro name field showing Macro1, Shortcut key Ctrl+ field, Store macro in dropdown showing This Workbook, Description field, and OK and Cancel buttons]

Figure 15-4: Enter the name for the macro and begin recording.

You use this dialog box to name and describe your macro. You also set up a shortcut key that you can use later to initiate the macro.

3. **Replace the name Macro1 with** AddHeaders. **In the Description box, type this chunk of text:** This macro adds the month and store names to the basic complaint data for a year.

Always give your macros a descriptive name and a full description. Although you may find this step tedious at times, it will turn out to be worthwhile when you later need to remember what the macro does and don't have time to look at the code.

Watch Your Step

Macro names can be made up of a set of letters, numbers, and underscores but cannot contain embedded spaces or many special characters. To see the complete list of invalid characters, search for **recording macros** in the Help system.

4. **Enter** m **as the shortcut key for this macro.**

You will start this macro by selecting it from the macro list or using a shortcut key.

Watch Your Step

Only letters can serve as shortcut keys. You cannot use numbers or special characters. In addition, if you use a capital letter when you create the shortcut key, you have to press Ctrl+Shift to execute the macro.

5. **Click the OK button to begin recording your macro.**

You do not see a visible indication that you are recording your macro. You just have to remember that you are recording and stop the recording when you finish.

6. **In this step, you add headers to the table. Add the 12 months in order in cells A3 through A14. Then, in cells B2 through F2, enter the following values:** Highland, Jonestown, Jefferson, Parkstown, **and** Marshall.

After you fill in all the cells, you're ready to stop recording the macro.

7. **Choose View → Macros → Macros → Stop Recording.**

Again, it appears that nothing has happened. However, you have completed the recording of your first macro. Now you'll run the macro again on a second set of data.

8. **Select cell Sheet2!A1.**

This sheet contains a second copy of the table. Next, you'll run your macro on this data so that you can see whether it works.

9. **From your keyboard, press Ctrl+m.**

As you watch, your data is selected, changed, and formatted. The result is shown in Figure 15-5.

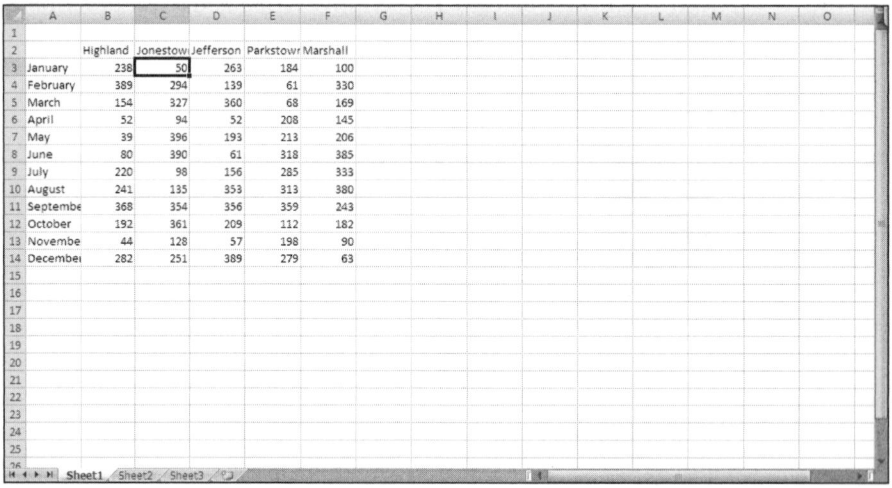

	A	B	C	D	E	F
1						
2		Highland	Jonestown	Jefferson	Parkstown	Marshall
3	January	238	50	263	184	100
4	February	389	294	139	61	330
5	March	154	327	360	68	169
6	April	52	94	52	208	145
7	May	39	396	193	213	206
8	June	80	390	61	318	385
9	July	220	98	156	285	333
10	August	241	135	353	313	380
11	Septembe	368	354	356	359	243
12	October	192	361	209	112	182
13	Novembe	44	128	57	198	90
14	Decembe	282	251	389	279	63

Figure 15-5: The result of running your new macro.

Now that you have run the macro, it's time to look at the code you created.

10. **Choose View → Macros → Macros → View Macros.**

The Macro dialog box appears, with your new macro on the list, as shown in Figure 15-6.

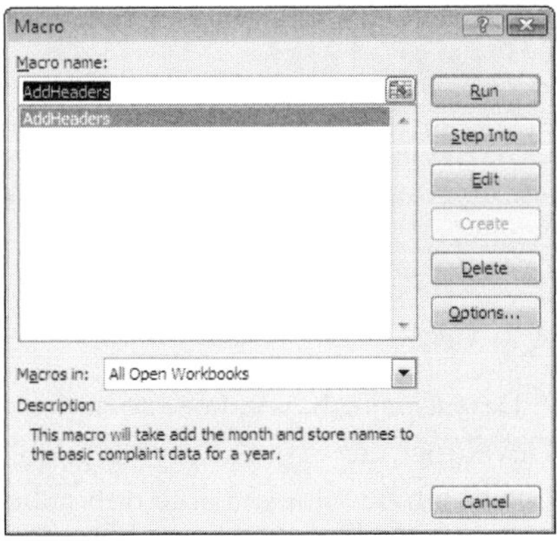

Figure 15-6: Your list of macros appears in the Macro dialog box.

Your new macro name is selected in the Macro Name list box, and the macro description you entered appears at the bottom of the dialog box.

From this dialog box, you can run your macro from beginning to end without stopping, step through the macro one line at a time, edit the macro, or delete the macro. Click the Options button to change the name, description, or shortcut key for the selected macro.

11. **Close the Macro dialog box.**

Before you go much further, save your work.

12. **Click the Office Button and choose Save As and save your file with the `.xlsm` extension. (XLSM is the macro-enabled file format.)**

Remember: If you don't change the file extension, you cannot save the code with the macro. Excel reminds you about it and gives you a chance to change the file format before it discards your macro code.

13. **Open the file you just saved and run the macro again on an empty sheet.**

Running the macro should add your headers to the specified cells without changing anything else on the sheet.

Watch Your Step

If you open your file and attempt to run the macro without resetting the macro security options, you won't get any results. If you try to run the macro by using the keyboard, you will probably hear a "bing" from your computer. This is Excel's way of telling you that it doesn't know what to do with the keystrokes you entered. If you try it by using the Macros button, you can't run the macro.

That isn't all you'll find. After you open the Macros dialog box and return to looking at your data, you'll notice that the security warning is gone. The easiest way to restore it so that you can enable macros is to close the file, reopen it, and enable the macros right away.

Working with the Developer Tab

You can create macros in one of two ways. The short method is to use the Macros button, as described in the preceding section. However, a better way to create macros is to use the buttons on the Developer tab.

Activating the Developer tab

Before you can use the buttons on the Developer tab, you need to activate it. Unlike the other tabs on the Excel Ribbon, the Developer tab is not always available, although it is not a contextual tab, either. This special tab becomes visible only when you activate it. Follow these steps to do so:

1. **Click the Office Button, and then click the Excel Options button.**

The Popular group of options appears in the Excel Options window, as shown in Figure 15-7.

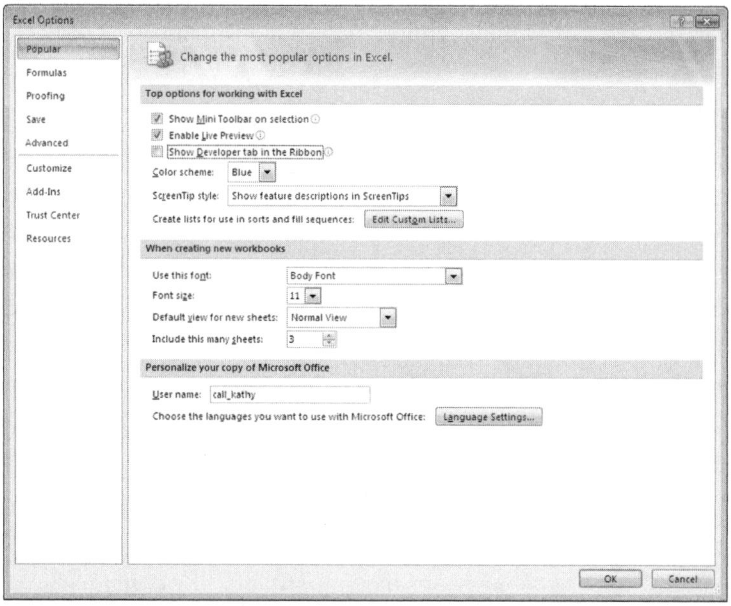

Figure 15-7: Popular Excel options.

2. **Select the Show Developer Tab in the Ribbon check box and then click OK.**

The Developer tab appears on the Ribbon, to the immediate right of the View tab, as shown in Figure 15-8.

3. Click the Developer tab.

The buttons and groups on the Developer tab appear, as shown in Figure 15-8.

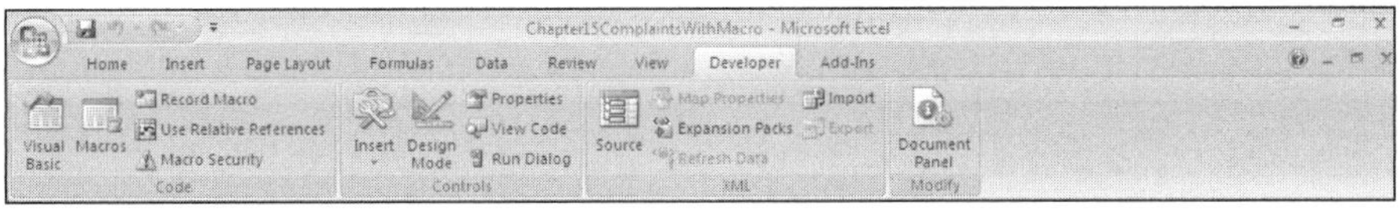

Figure 15-8: Buttons on the Developer tab.

Four groups of buttons are on the Developer tab. These groups, which are described in the following list, let you work with code and development items:

- *Code:* This group is an expanded view of the Macros button on the View tab.

- *Controls:* This group lets you add interaction items to your work. These items include dialog boxes, radio buttons, check boxes, drop-down lists, and much more.

- *XML:* You use the buttons on the XML tab to map the XML in your file to source definition files that you have created elsewhere, and vice versa.

- *Modify:* Use the buttons in the Modify group to change which document properties must be verified before a document can be saved.

Viewing your code in the Visual Basic window

The next step in learning about macros is to use the Visual Basic button to take a peek at the code you created when you recorded your basic macro:

1. Open the file Ch15Complaints.xlsm.

2. Choose Developer → Code → Visual Basic.

The Visual Basic window appears, as shown in Figure 15-9.

The Visual Basic interface can be split into four areas. Across the top are the menus you use to work with your code. The left side is split into two windows. The top window shows you the active items, or project elements, in the open Excel file. The highlighted element is the current active item. (In this case, the active item is Sheet3 of the workbook.) Below the list of project elements, you find the list of properties for the current active item.

To see the properties for your macro, you'll expand the list of modules and select your macro.

3. Click the plus sign next to the word *Modules* to expand the list of modules.

Any modules in this project are shown. Your list may have one module or two.

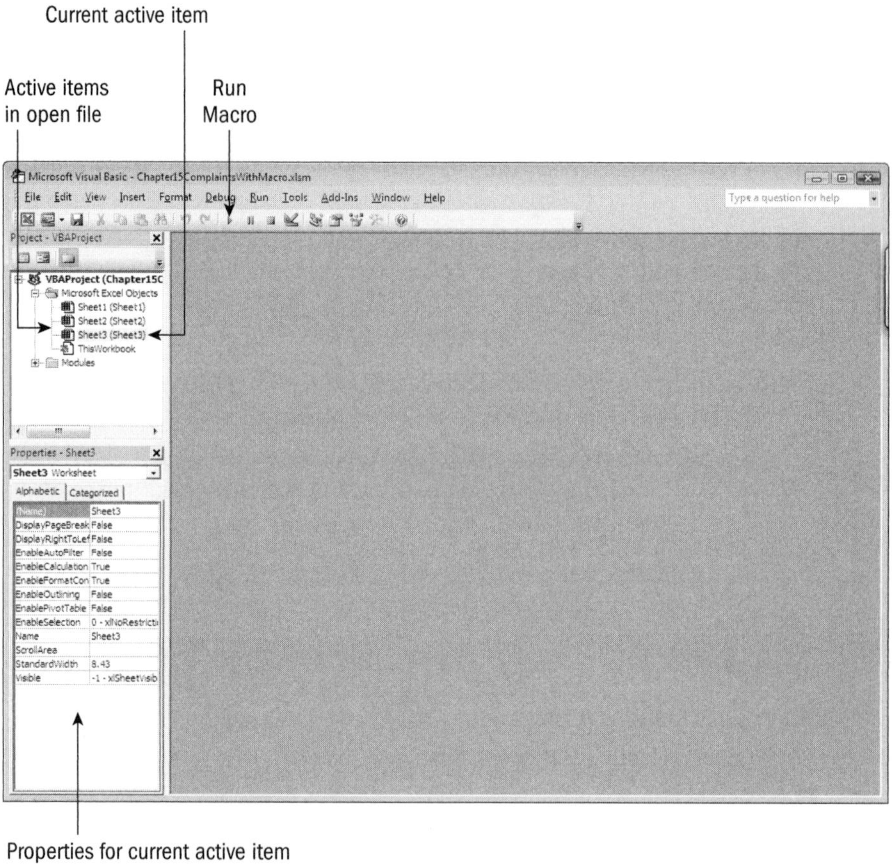

Current active item

Active items
in open file

Run
Macro

Properties for current active item

Figure 15-9: An empty Visual Basic window.

4. **Double-click each available module in turn until a window opens to the right that contains code.**

When you double-click a module that contains live code, the code appears in a new window (see Figure 15-10) on the right side of the interface.

The code in this macro is shown in pairs of lines:

- The first line of each pair selects the cell.

- The second line of each pair assigns the cell the value you designated.

You can move around in the code just as you move around any other text document. If you make changes to the code, the results of the macro will change the next time you run it. For some quick practice, in the next step you'll change one of the town names and run the macro again.

Assigns the designated value to the cell

Selects the cell

```
(General)                                        ▼  AddHeaders                                     ▼
Sub AddHeaders()
'
' AddHeaders Macro
' This macro will take add the month and store names to the basic complaint data for a year.
'
' Keyboard Shortcut: Ctrl+m
'
    Range("A3").Select
    ActiveCell.FormulaR1C1 = "January"
    Range("A4").Select
    ActiveCell.FormulaR1C1 = "February"
    Range("A5").Select
    ActiveCell.FormulaR1C1 = "March"
    Range("A6").Select
    ActiveCell.FormulaR1C1 = "April"
    Range("A7").Select
    ActiveCell.FormulaR1C1 = "May"
    Range("A8").Select
    ActiveCell.FormulaR1C1 = "June"
    Range("A9").Select
    ActiveCell.FormulaR1C1 = "July"
    Range("A10").Select
    ActiveCell.FormulaR1C1 = "August"
    Range("A11").Select
    ActiveCell.FormulaR1C1 = "September"
    Range("A12").Select
    ActiveCell.FormulaR1C1 = "October"
    Range("A13").Select
    ActiveCell.FormulaR1C1 = "November"
    Range("A14").Select
    ActiveCell.FormulaR1C1 = "December"
    Range("B2").Select
    ActiveCell.FormulaR1C1 = "Highland"
    Range("C2").Select
    ActiveCell.FormulaR1C1 = "Jonestown"
    Range("D2").Select
    ActiveCell.FormulaR1C1 = "Jefferson"
```

Figure 15-10: The `AddHeaders` code listing.

5. **Find the line in your code that changes the value for cell E2. Change the word *Parkstown* to the word** TempTown.

You are ready to run the code to see whether your change works.

6. **On the toolbar, find the Run Macro button (refer to Figure 15-9). Click the button to run the macro.**

Even though it looks like nothing has happened, your macro has been run. To verify it, you'll switch back to Excel to see the change to the active sheet.

7. **Click the taskbar button for your current Excel document.**

Verify that cell E2 contains the text TempTown.

8. **Click the Microsoft Visual Basic taskbar button.**

You return to the Visual Basic window.

9. **To close the Visual Basic window, either click the red X in the upper-right corner or choose File → Close.**

10. **Close Excel and save your work.**

Congratulations — you have created and adapted your first macro!

Debugging Macros: The VBE (Visual Basic Editor) Experience

It would be nice if every macro you created worked as well as the one in the preceding section. Unfortunately, that doesn't usually happen. When you create any kind of code, you should expect it to have problems.

Those problems, or *bugs,* happen for a wide variety of reasons. Code can have three basic types of errors:

- **Syntax:** Excel does not understand what you are trying to say. This type of error includes typographical errors, misformatted command errors, and unknown command errors.

- **Logic:** Excel cannot make sense of what you told it to do. Making this type of error is similar to specifying to use salt rather than sugar in a cake recipe — Excel makes the cake, but you won't like the result.

- **Scope:** The code works, but it ends up doing something in the wrong place or to more or less data than you expected. Making this type of error is like asking someone with a compact car to transport the whole football team: It can be done, but you cannot get the whole team there in one trip.

In the following three exercises, you look at code that has these kinds of errors and learn how to fix them.

Identifying and fixing syntax errors

To start debugging a macro, follow these steps:

1. Open the file named `Chapter15SyntaxError.xlsm`.

The file that opens looks just like the complaints file you have been working with. The new macro it contains, BoldMarch, has a deliberate syntax error. Next, you'll find and fix that error.

2. Click the Options button next to the security warning. Select the Enable This Content radio button and click OK.

Next, you'll need to enable access to the BoldMarch macro before trying to run or edit it.

3. Choose Developer → Code → Macros.

The Macro dialog box appears, with the current macro highlighted.

4. Click Run to start the BoldMarch macro.

The view changes to the Visual Basic Editor. The macro code is shown with one line highlighted. In front of the code is an error message, as shown in Figure 15-11.

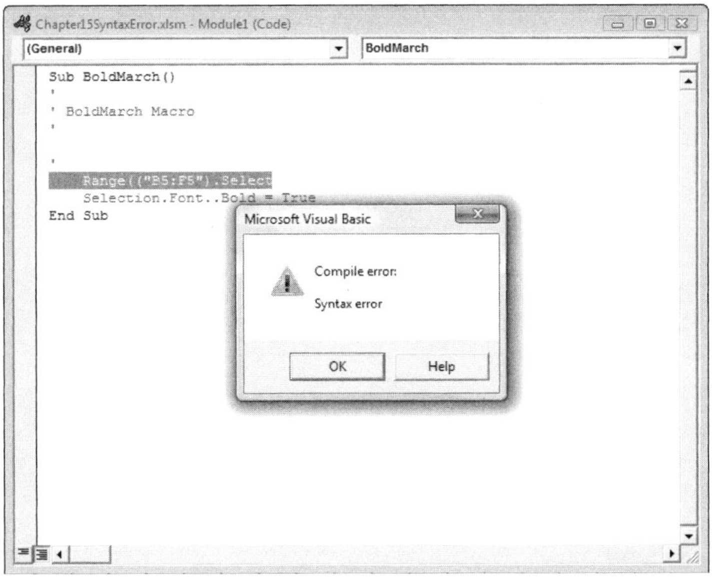

Figure 15-11: A syntax error message.

The message notifies you of two distinct problems:

- An error occurred at compile-time. Code is *compiled* to change English-like text, which you provide, into code that your machine's CPU can understand and run.

- The specific compile-time error was a syntax error.

5. **Click OK to clear the message from your screen.**

Now that the error message is not obscuring the code, you can see that the first line is highlighted in yellow and the first line of executable code is highlighted in blue, as shown in Figure 15-12.

The yellow highlight shows how much of the macro was run. Because the syntax error is in the first line of code, none of the code has run, and the start of the routine is the current line.

The blue highlight shows the line with the syntax error. VBA does not tell you exactly what the error is — only *where* the error is. It is your job to find the error in the line.

In this case, the error is a single extra character in the code. Two parentheses (rather than a single parenthesis) appear before the definition of the range. Next, you'll remove one of the parentheses and fix the error.

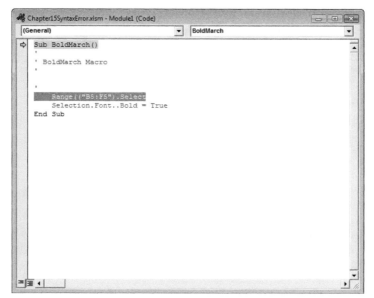

Figure 15-12: Viewing your code after Excel finds a syntax error.

 Watch Your Step

When your code has a syntax error, it may not be on the line where VBA shows it to be. When you compile the code, VBA works through the code from the top down and marks a line as having an error when the data you have entered is proven to not make sense.

In this case, the compiler has marked the extra parenthesis. It knows that the code has one parenthesis too many. Although the compiler doesn't know whether the error is in this line, it knows that it cannot proceed because of the parenthesis. The real problem may be on this line, or it may be several lines above the one with the parenthesis. You have to check carefully in some cases to find where the error occurred.

6. Use the mouse or arrow keys to move to the first parenthesis and then delete it.

You can move around in your code by using either the mouse or the arrow keys. However, you cannot move around by using the scroll wheel on your mouse.

Notice that when you remove the extra parenthesis, the blue highlight disappears, indicating that you changed the line. The disappearance of the blue highlight doesn't say that you have made the *right* change — just that you have made *a* change. (In this case, you made the right change, so you can continue running the code.)

Now you have a number of options. You can tell VBA to continue running the code, assuming that the code has no other errors. Or you can close the VBA window, end the macro, and go back to Excel. In both cases, Excel attempts to compile the code again and tells you if any other errors occur.

The best thing to do now is to attempt to compile the code from the Visual Basic Editor to check for other syntax errors.

7. **To compile your code, choose Debug → Compile VBA Project.**

You receive another compile error message.

8. **Click OK to clear the message from your screen.**

The next line of code is highlighted in blue.

9. **Fix the error by removing the extra period.**

When you are working with macros that you have typed, you are unlikely to have made only one syntax error. A programming rule of life is that if you have one error, you are likely to also have *more than one.*

10. **Choose Debug → Compile VBA project to compile your code again.**

This time, nothing seems to happen when you compile. This is the VBA way of telling you that it did not find any other compile errors and that the code is ready to continue running.

11. **Press F5 on your keyboard.**

This step continues running your code. Again, it appears as though nothing happened, because the changes occur in the Excel spreadsheet — not in the code.

12. **Press Alt+Q on your keyboard to close VBA and return to Excel.**

The March entries are all in bold type now. Because the syntax errors were fixed, your code ran and changed the March entries by applying bold to them.

Not all errors are as obvious or as easy to fix as the syntax errors you just found. However, the process for debugging is the same: Run the macro, find the bug, fix the bug, run the macro, and continue until all bugs are fixed.

Information Kiosk

You hear people who create a lot of code talk about *programmer's optimism,* which is the belief that the bug you just found is the last remaining bug in your code. If it weren't for programmer's optimism, many coders would give up and abandon programming.

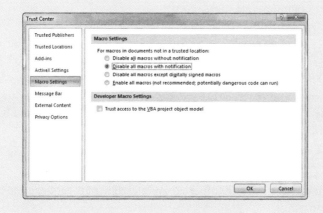
Tackling more complicated problems

Now that you have found and fixed a couple of simple bugs in a simple routine, you can work with a more complicated macro that has bigger problems:

1. **Open the file named Chapter15OtherErrors.xlsm.**

   This file has the BoldMarch macro in it as well as the ChangeToTable macro, which changes rows and columns into a table and adds totals for each row and each column. Notice that the table is in a slightly different spot on the sheet than it was in the previous sample files.

2. **Choose Developer → Code → Macros.**

   The Macro dialog box appears, with the first macro highlighted.

3. **Click ChangeToTable to select that macro, and then click Run to run the macro.**

Almost immediately, an error message appears, as shown in Figure 15-13.

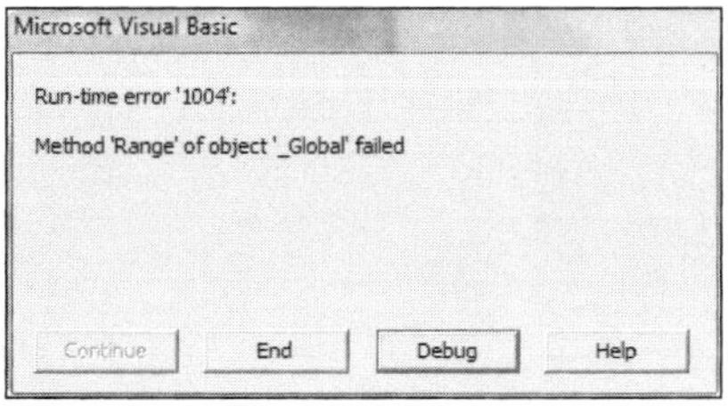

Figure 15-13: A macro error message.

This macro is set up to assume that the table to be converted is in a specific spot on the sheet. Because the table isn't in that spot, an error occurs.

At this point, you have a several choices:

- Ask for help with the error. The Help information doesn't help much, but you may find it worth looking at sometimes.

- End the macro and live with the results you received.

- Use the Debug button to find out what happened and what to do about it. This is the method you'll use for this exercise.

4. **Click Debug.**

The view changes to the Visual Basic Editor, and the last line of the macro is highlighted, to indicate that the error occurred there.

In this case, it appears that the error occurred when the correct cell could not be selected. Although this is true, it isn't the only error.

5. **Press Alt+Q on your keyboard to return to Excel. Click OK when prompted to stop the debugger.**

The real error is that the table isn't where it is supposed to be on the sheet, so the entire macro produced unusual results, as shown in Figure 15-14.

As you can see, Excel tried to format the data the way you wanted but just couldn't figure out how. This type of error, an input error, is common. You write or record your macro assuming that the data is always in the same location, but this time the data is in a different place.

You have to fix a number of problems in the macro:

- You need to figure out a way to end the macro more gracefully if the table isn't where you need it to be.

- After the macro ends, you must decide whether you want to record a macro to move the table from where it is to where you want it to be, or just move it manually before you run the macro again.

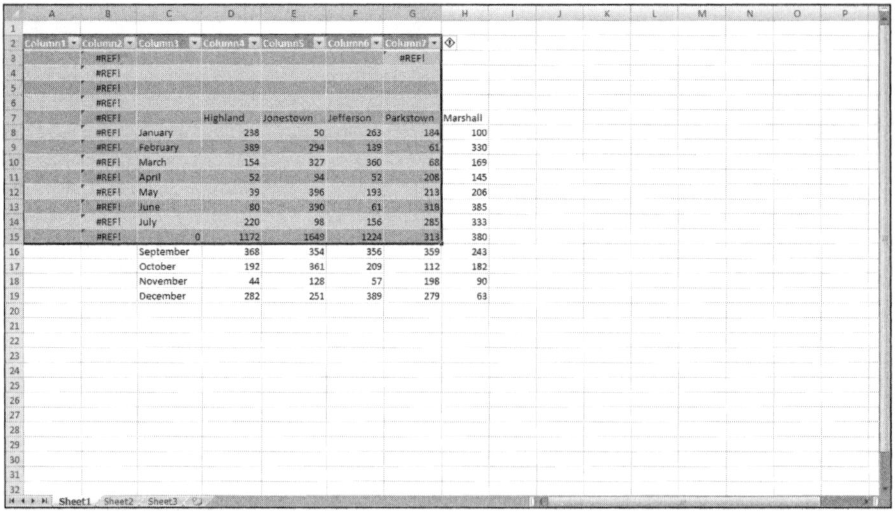

Figure 15-14: This table is in the wrong place.

For this exercise, you'll write an error routine that traps general errors and ends gracefully and then traps the specific error of the table not being where you want it and ends gracefully.

6. **Close your file without saving the changes. Reopen the file**
   Chapter15OtherErrors.xlsm.

You need to close the file without saving it because you need to start with a copy of the worksheet without the added table. This sheet is set up to allow the macro to run correctly.

7. **Choose Developer → Code → Visual Basic.**

You return to the Visual Basic Editor with the macro code as the active window. Your next task is to add code at the beginning of the macro that checks for the first value in the table. If the value isn't where it should be, the code pops up a message so that you can cancel the macro.

8. **Add a blank line to your macro before this line:**

```
Range("A2:G15").Select.
```

9. **Type the following lines of code onto the blank line you just created:**

```
If Range("B2") <> "Highland" Then
    Reply = MsgBox("Table isn't where it should be.
        Move it so that the Highland data is in
        column 2.", vbCritical)
    Else
```

10. Type the following line of code just before the **End Sub** line in your macro:

```
End If
```

By adding the code in Steps 8 and 9, you add a conditional branch to your code. You tell Excel: "Check to see whether cell B2 contains the word *Highland*. If it doesn't, display an error message. If it does, process the table."

If statements are made up of three parts:

- The condition (does cell B2 contain the value Highland?)

- The code to run if it is true (display the error message)

- The code to run if it is false (the regular processing)

The MsgBox command allows you to ask the user for input and store the result in a variable. Using a MsgBox instead of an InputBox allows you more flexibility in creating targeted code.

11. To compile your code, choose Debug → Compile VBA Project.

Make sure that you did not type anything wrong when you added the conditional processing. If you see any compilation errors, fix them and compile again. When you finish fixing compilation errors, continue to the next step.

12. Close the Visual Basic Editor and run your macro on Sheet1.

To run your macro, click the Macros button in the Code group on the Developer tab. Click ChangeToTable to select that macro, and then click Run.

Notice that the error message pops up when you try to run the macro, as shown in Figure 15-15.

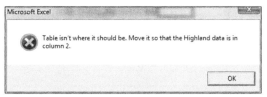

Figure 15-15: This error message reports a problem with the table location.

13. Click OK to clear the message.

14. To make sure that the main part of your macro still runs, change to Sheet2 and run the macro again.

You should not see an error message, and the table should be formatted the way you want. If you don't get these results, go back to your code and make sure that you typed the changes correctly.

Finding and fixing an error in logic

You have seen two of the three most common kinds of errors. The third kind, an error in logic, is a little harder to find and fix. In the following steps, you work with the same data and macros but fix a hidden error in the code:

1. Open the file named `Chapter15OtherErrorsIfStatementAdded.xlsm`.

This file is set up the same way as the file in the preceding section. The only difference is that the fixes you made earlier to the code have been incorporated. You could continue with the file you have been working with, but the changes you already made to the data will prevent you from receiving the expected results during the exercise.

Next, you will use the new file to run the macro more than once to find the hidden logic error in the code.

2. Select the data on Sheet1 and move it so that the word *Highland* is in cell Sheet1!B2.

3. Run the ChangeToTable macro on Sheet1.

The data is formatted, and the totals are added.

4. Change to Sheet2 and run the ChangeToTable macro on the table there.

You receive the error message shown in Figure 15-16.

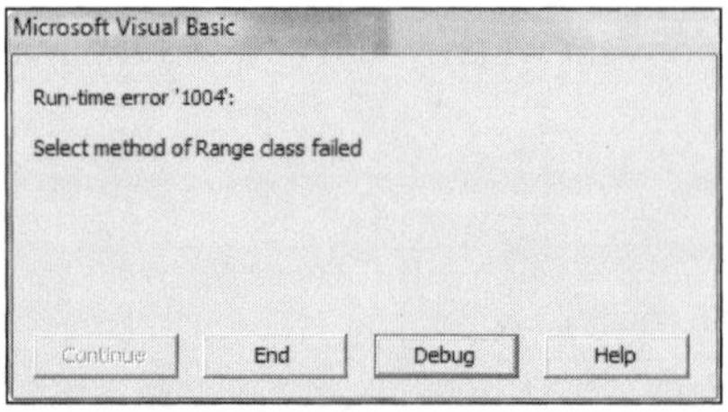

Figure 15-16: A runtime error message.

The message is unclear — it is saying that it could not do something that your code wants done. To find out where the error occurred, you'll need to look at the code itself.

5. Click Debug.

The view changes to the code, with the problem line highlighted in yellow, as shown in Figure 15-17.

This line is telling Excel to select the table named Table1. But the error occurred when you ran the preceding line. The preceding line tried to name the range A2 through G15 as Table1. Unfortunately, because Table1 is already defined, Excel displays an error message. Your next task is to change the code so that no error occurs.

```
Chapter15OtherErrorsIfStatementAdded.xlsm - Module2 (Code)
(General)                                    ▼   ChangeToTable                              ▼

'  ChangeToTable Macro


'
If Range("B2") <> "Highland" Then
    Reply = MsgBox("Table isn't where it should be. Move it so that the Highland data is in column 2
    Else

    Range("A2:G15").Select
    ActiveSheet.ListObjects.Add(xlSrcRange, Range("$A$2:$G$15"), , xlYes).Name = _
        "Table1"
⇨   Range("Table1[#All]").Select
    Range("B15").Activate
    ActiveCell.FormulaR1C1 = "=SUM(R[-12]C:R[-1]C)"
    Range("Table1[#All]").Select
    Range("C15").Activate
    ActiveCell.FormulaR1C1 = "=SUM(R[-12]C:R[-1]C)"
    Range("Table1[#All]").Select
    Range("D15").Activate
    ActiveCell.FormulaR1C1 = "=SUM(R[-12]C:R[-1]C)"
    Range("Table1[#All]").Select
    Range("E15").Activate
    ActiveCell.FormulaR1C1 = "=SUM(R[-12]C:R[-1]C)"
    Range("Table1[#All]").Select
    Range("F15").Activate
    ActiveCell.FormulaR1C1 = "=SUM(R[-12]C:R[-1]C)"
```

Figure 15-17: The problem line is highlighted.

6. **Before you can make changes to the code, stop the current execution of the code by choosing Run → Reset.**

Information Kiosk

You can make changes to your code while you are in Debug mode. However, the changes you can make are limited. Get in the habit of ending Debug mode if you want to make any changes other than the most basic changes to your code.

7. **After the line of code that reads `Else`, add this line:**

```
NameTheTable = "Table" & InputBox("What year does this
data cover?")
```

This line uses an input box to ask the user for a string that will be the unique part of the table name. When you provide the year, Excel concatenates the word *Table* and the entered year and assigns both values to the variable `NameTheTable`. You can then use this variable anywhere you would use the string `Table1`.

Next you'll tell Excel that you want to use the variable `NameTheTable` to represent the table name rather than the string.

8. **Choose Edit → Replace.**

The Replace dialog box appears.

9. **In the Find What box, type** Table1**. In the Replace With box, type** NameTheTable**. Click Replace All.**

You use the built-in find-and-replace feature to change the table name from a static string to a variable name. Eight changes should be made.

10. **Close the dialog box.**

11. Choose Debug → Compile VBA Project to compile your project and make sure that you made no errors.

12. Close the Visual Basic Editor and run the macro on Sheet2. Use the year 2006.

If you are not sure whether the macro worked, look at the name for the table. It is not Table2006 — it is NameTheTable. You still have an error to fix.

13. Return to the Visual Basic Editor.

Take a look at how you are referencing the variable NameTheTable. When the Replace All command is done, the string Table1 is replaced with NameTheTable. But the quotes around Table1 stayed around the references for NameTheTable. Now the code works the first time, by naming the table NameTheTable; after that, however, you are in the same situation again. You need to finish making the change by making sure that Excel uses the value of NameTheTable rather than the string NameTheTable, as outlined in the next step.

14. Locate the first instance where **NameTheTable** is used (which is in the **ActiveSheet** line) and then delete the quotes around it.

15. Change all other **Range** statements to reference **NameTheTable** rather than **"NameTheTable[#All]"**.

16. Delete the last line of code, which reads:

```
"Range("Table1[[Highland]:[Column2]]").Select
```

When you complete these steps, your code should look like this:

```
Sub ChangeToTable()
'
' ChangeToTable Macro
'

'
If Range("B2") <> "Highland" Then
    Reply = MsgBox("Table isn't where it should be. Move it so that the Highland
        data is in column 2", vbCritical)
    Else
    NameTheTable = "Table" & InputBox("What year does this data cover?")
    Range("A2:G15").Select
    ActiveSheet.ListObjects.Add(xlSrcRange, Range("$A$2:$G$15"), , xlYes).Name =
        _ NameTheTable
    Range(NameTheTable).Select
    Range("B15").Activate
    ActiveCell.FormulaR1C1 = "=SUM(R[-12]C:R[-1]C)"
    Range(NameTheTable).Select
    Range("C15").Activate
    ActiveCell.FormulaR1C1 = "=SUM(R[-12]C:R[-1]C)"
    Range(NameTheTable).Select
```

```
      Range("D15").Activate
      ActiveCell.FormulaR1C1 = "=SUM(R[-12]C:R[-1]C)"
      Range(NameTheTable).Select
      Range("E15").Activate
      ActiveCell.FormulaR1C1 = "=SUM(R[-12]C:R[-1]C)"
      Range(NameTheTable).Select
      Range("F15").Activate
      ActiveCell.FormulaR1C1 = "=SUM(R[-12]C:R[-1]C)"
      Range(NameTheTable).Select
      Range("G3").Activate
      ActiveCell.FormulaR1C1 = "=SUM(RC[-5]:RC[-1])"
End If
End Sub
```

You have fixed your code so that you are using your new variable rather than a static string to define the table. You can run this code on any unformatted set of data that meets the criteria, and you will get a new table with a new name every time.

Watch Your Step

The code still has an error in it. You cannot redefine a table by using code that is already defined as a table. To test your code, copy and paste the table contents from either Sheet1 or Sheet2 as values to a new sheet. Ensure that cell B2 of your new sheet contains the word *Highland*. Run the macro there. If you want to learn more about coding with Excel tables, read about it in the Excel Help system.

Adapting a Macro for Flexibility

When you are using a macro, you can control what the macro does in a number of ways. You have already read about asking the user for input and letting that input determine what the macro does. You also have learned that you can base the path through the macro on a condition.

Another common way to control what a macro does is to place the processing in a loop and repeat the steps to be performed. By adding loops, you can control how many times the steps in a macro are run. By following the steps in this exercise, you will learn how the various looping mechanisms in VBA work.

You will also learn how to add good comments to your code to help yourself and others be able to better understand the macro later on. Although it may seem silly to add comments to macros, studies have shown that code is read several times for each time it is modified. By improving your comments, you make your macros easier to adapt in the future.

In the exercises in this section, you improve the progression macro that you ran at the beginning of this chapter by adding good comments and by creating loops that control the code:

1. Open the file named **Ch15Progression.xlsm.**

2. Choose **Developer → Code → Visual Basic.**

   The code for this routine appears, as shown in Figure 15-18. As you learn what this macro does, you'll comment it so that you can remember what it does.

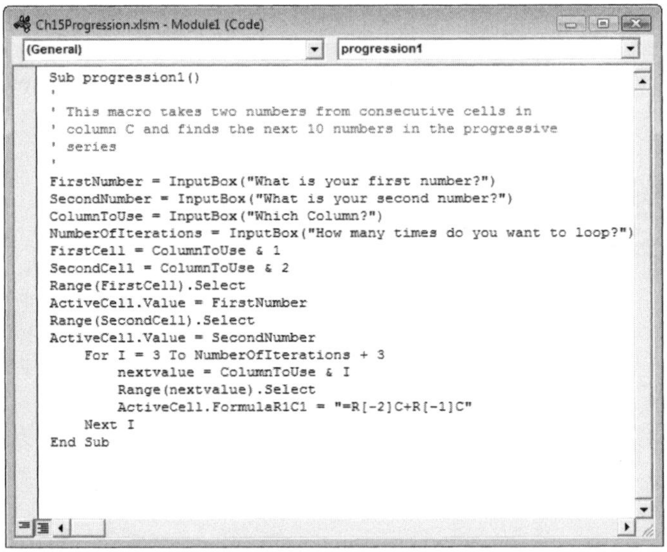

Figure 15-18: Sample code for a progression macro.

The first line of this macro (`Sub progression1()`) assigns the macro its name. Following that line, five lines start with single quote marks. These *comments* tell the person reading the program what the program is doing. The *comment indicator,* a single quote at the beginning of the line, tells VBA to skip this line.

3. **Start a new line before the first real line of code. On the new line, type this comment:**

```
' FirstNumber is going to contain the starting number
for the progression. It can be any number, integer or
decimal.
```

This is the first line of comments that you'll add to this code. Unlike the general comments that describe the overall processing of the macro, these comments work through the macro step by step to explain what is happening. In addition, comments are a good way to tell users what limits and conditions might exist on the use of the macro code.

4. Add a second comment line to continue the comments for the input box:

```
' SecondNumber is the next number in the sequence. It
too can be any number, integer or decimal.
```

5. Add a third comment line to continue the comments for the input box:

```
' ColumnToUse is the column where the results should be
displayed.
```

You cannot just use the word *column* as a variable name because it is a reserved word. *Reserved* words mean something specific to VBA and cannot be used as variable names.

6. Move down to just before the line that defines **NumberOfIterations**. Add another comment line to continue the comments for the input boxes:

```
' NumberOfIterations contains the number of loops the
progression makes. It needs to be an integer, or whole,
number.
```

You are done adding comments for the moment. Now you'll need to add a piece of functionality to the macro. If the number that is entered is greater than 1600, the numbers that are generated will be too large for Excel to handle. The program will continue to run, but it will put an error value in the cells rather than a number. To avoid this problem, you'll add a check for the size of the number of iterations and keep asking for one until a valid entry is provided.

7. Add the following code and comments to your macro after the line that asks for the number of iterations:

```
While NumberOfIterations > 1600
    ' Ask for replacement number
    NumberOfIterations = InputBox("That number was too
        large. Excel can only handle up to 1600 iterations
        before the resulting number is bigger than Excel
        can handle. How many times do you want to loop?")
Wend
```

You have just added your first loop to a piece of code. You can use the `While...Wend` construct to check the value in a variable and then loop until that value is valid. In this case, you tell Excel to repeatedly ask for a new number of iterations until the number is small enough to provide valid results.

8. Close the Visual Basic Editor, and run the macro by pressing **Ctrl+Shift+M**.

If the macro runs successfully, you are ready to test it. If it has errors, open the Visual Basic Editor and fix the errors before you continue. Testing is an important step in creating any macro. As your macros grow in complexity, you have to do more testing. Test to make sure not only that the code runs but also that you have handled errors and unusual circumstances. When you test, use regular numbers for basic tests and extremely large and small values for other tests. When you use extreme values, or *edge tests,* you ensure that your code does not stop running when a number is too big or too small for the value provided.

9. **Run the macro several more times, using exceedingly large and small numbers for each value.**

10. **As your last test for this section, use a number rather than a letter for the column name.**

When you use a number, Excel accepts the number but returns the error message shown in Figure 15-19.

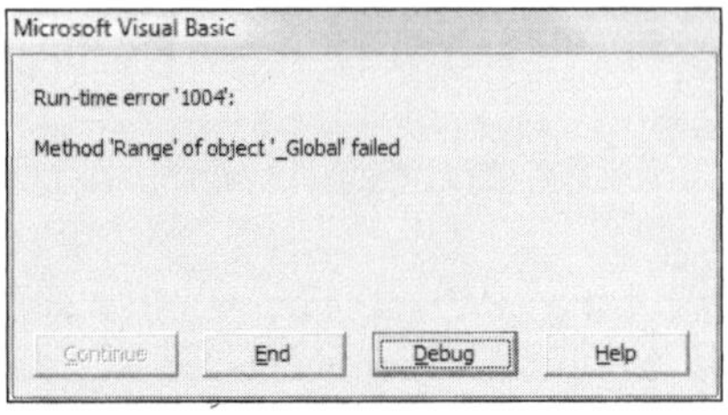

Figure 15-19: The '1004' runtime error message.

11. **Click the Debug button.**

The view changes to the Visual Basic Editor, with the error line highlighted, as shown in Figure 15-20.

Excel tries to use your number as a column name. Because column names are letters, Excel does not know what to do with your input and tells you so — in a rather nasty way. A better method is to catch and handle the error on input rather than when Excel tries to use the value. The solution is easy: Adapt the input message for ColumnToUse and then check to ensure that the value the user entered is legal.

12. **Choose Run → Reset.**

To test your change, you have to run the code again from scratch. In this case, the best way to do that is to stop the execution now and run the macro again after you've made your changes.

13. **Change the input box string for ColumnToUse from Which Column? to** Enter the letter (or letters) for the column to contain the results**.**

Now, rather than rely on users to know that they need to enter a letter as the value, you explicitly state that the entry should be either a single letter or a group of letters indicating which column to use.

The code still has an error in it. If a user enters a value that isn't within the defined range for the input, your code still ends with an Excel-generated error message. If you want to add code to check for an error, add another While...Wend structure to ensure that the information provided is correct.

```
Ch15Progression.xlsm - Module1 (Code)

(General)                                    progression1

Sub progression1()
'
' This macro takes two numbers from consecutive cells in
' column C and finds the next 10 numbers in the progressive
' series
'
' FirstNumber is going to contain the starting number for the progre
' SecondNumber is the next number in the sequence. It too can be any
' ColumnToUse is the column where the results should be displayed.
FirstNumber = InputBox("What is your first number?")
SecondNumber = InputBox("What is your second number?")
ColumnToUse = InputBox("Which Column?")
' NumberOfIterations contains the number of loops the progression ma
NumberOfIterations = InputBox("How many times do you want to loop?")
While NumberOfIterations > 1600
    ' Ask for replacement number
    NumberOfIterations = InputBox("That number was too large. Excel
Wend

FirstCell = ColumnToUse & 1
SecondCell = ColumnToUse & 2
Range(FirstCell).Select
ActiveCell.Value = FirstNumber
Range(SecondCell).Select
ActiveCell.Value = SecondNumber
    For I = 3 To NumberOfIterations + 3
        nextvalue = ColumnToUse & I
        Range(nextvalue).Select
        ActiveCell.FormulaR1C1 = "=R[-2]C+R[-1]C"
    Next I
End Sub
```

Figure 15-20: The error line is highlighted.

14. Add a new line before the **FirstCell** line. Add the following comment on that line:

```
'   These two lines create the cell references for the
first two cells in the progression.
```

Comments should always indicate not only what the code is doing but also *why* it is being done. The comment "Sets FirstCell to the entered column's first cell" is true, but it doesn't tell the user much. Instead, the comment you added indicates which new variables are being created and why.

15. After the line **Range(FirstCell).Select**, add a new line with the following comment:

```
' Select each of the first two cells and give them the
progression values entered by the user.
```

The Range(...).Select statement allows you to select a cell or range of cells in a spreadsheet and lets Excel know that you want to work with that range for the next few statements. Until you select another one to use, this range can be referenced by using ActiveCell, which is the VBA way of saying "the current cell."

After you select the range, you need to tell Excel what to do with that range. In this case, you are setting the value for that range to the value stored in the variable FirstNumber. You can work with attributes other than just the value for the current range. For more on that topic, see *Excel 2007 Power Programming with VBA,* by John Walkenbach (Wiley).

After the code selects and sets the first cell, it then does the same thing for the second cell in the series. Your next step is to comment the loop.

16. Add a new line before the line that begins with `For I`. Add the following comment on the new line:

```
' Once for every iteration of the progression, find
the next cell down and store in it the next value in
the progression. When you have gone through the number
of iterations requested, stop.
```

You now see the loop that does the bulk of the processing for this macro. Each time through the loop, Excel finds the reference for the next cell down and gives it a value equal to the sum of the two above it.

This loop is different from the `While...Wend` loop. A `While` loop checks to see whether a value meets the stated test and then executes the loop. A `For... Next` loop completes the loop and then checks to see whether the value is out of range.

By combining these two loops with the `If` statements you learned about earlier in this chapter, you can adapt any piece of processing to repeat or run whenever you want it to — and only when you want it to.

17. Close the Visual Basic Editor, and run the macro to test whether you made any errors when adding the comments.

If you typed everything correctly and remembered to add comment indicators, the macro should work. If it doesn't, return to the macro to find and fix your errors, and then test it again.

 ## Information Kiosk

The Visual Basic Help information in Excel is better than you might expect. You can search the Help system for a command to learn how to use it, find out which options you have with that command, and even get sample code that uses the command.

Many VBA users learn about the Object Model for Excel this way. They create macros by recording them and then use the Help information to adapt the tasks they complete to meet other needs.

Adding Your Macro to the QAT (Quick Access Toolbar)

The macros you have created in this chapter are initiated by either pressing a shortcut key or choosing the macro from the macro list. You can also add your macro to the QAT and access it from there, as detailed in these steps:

1. Open the file named **Ch15ProgressionFinished.xlsm.**
2. Click the Office Button and then click the Excel Options button.
3. In the Excel Options window, select Customize.

The Ch15ProgressionFinished.xlsm file contains the final version of the Progression1 macro. You'll add the macro to the QAT for only this file.

4. From the Choose Commands From drop-down list, select Macros.

The left column shows the separator option and the macro (progression1) in this file. The right column shows your current QAT settings, as shown in Figure 15-21.

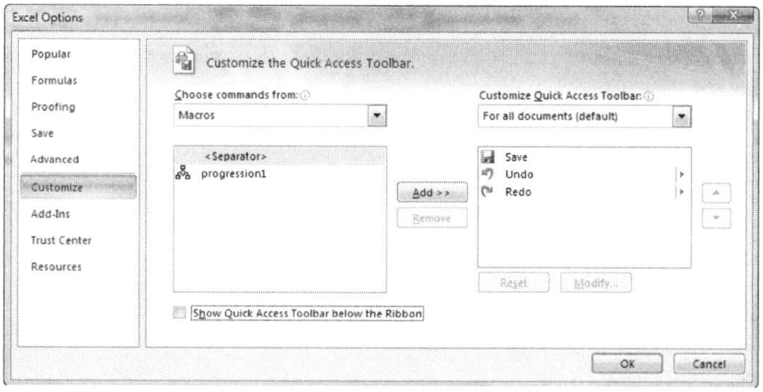

![Excel Options window showing Customize the Quick Access Toolbar with Macros selected in Choose commands from, listing Separator and progression1 in the left column, and Save, Undo, Redo in the right column.]

Figure 15-21: Customize the QAT to add macros.

5. From the Customize Quick Access Toolbar drop-down list, select the For Ch15ProgressionFinished.xlsm option.

You'll make changes that apply to only this file. You do not want to show these changes in other files because they don't have access to the code.

6. Click the Add button to add a separator to the QAT. Select the progression1 macro and then click the Add button to add the macro to the QAT. Click OK to apply the changes.

The right side of the QAT now shows the separator and an icon for the macro, as shown in Figure 15-22.

Separator   Macro icon

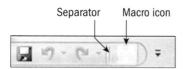

Figure 15-22: The customized QAT shows a separator and a macro icon.

If you hover your mouse pointer over the macro icon, you see a ToolTip that contains the name of the macro.

7. **Close the file and don't save the changes. Then reopen the file.**

Because you did not save the changes to your QAT for this file, the QAT reverts to its original state.

8. **Repeat Steps 2 through 5 in this exercise. Close and save the file. Reopen the file.**

This time the changes to your QAT were retained because you saved the changes to your file. Just like any other changes to an individual file, QAT files for a specific file must be saved in order to be retained.

Finding Out What Else Macros Can Do

Macros can be created to do just about anything that you can do in Excel. In fact, you are likely to find that you can record more Excel functionality as a macro than you would expect.

Charts

If you follow a complicated process for creating charts from your data, record the process with the macro recorder and then make changes with the macro rather than to each individual chart. You are then guaranteed that if the data is in the right place and named the same way as it was in the chart you first created, your other charts will look just the same.

If you don't know where the data will be for your chart, use the input statements you learned about in this chapter to define the range of cells to be used for the chart. Voilà! The result is a chart maker that you can use to define what you want every time, no matter where the data is or how big of a block it is.

If you want to transform a chart from one type to another, record the process. Apply the macro to existing charts, and then you don't have to remember which information changes from one chart to another — the macro does it for you. This statement is true for both chart formatting and the chart type itself.

Computations

If you have to perform a complicated computation that crosses multiple sheets or multiple files, create a macro to do it rather than do it by hand. You spend a little more time creating the macro than you would spend doing the computation the first time, but from that point on, the computation is ready to go at the click of a mouse.

Suppose that you want to change only one part of the computation. One advantage of using a macro is that you can copy the macro code to create a new macro, make your change, and then know that you haven't affected anything other than the changes you applied. You may recall the sum calculation on the table macro from earlier in this chapter. You can change that macro to an average macro by using the Replace All command to replace Sum with Average.

Formatting

If you need to ensure that cells in heading rows and columns always look the same, set up the macro once and record it. You now have the formatting ready to go at the click of a button. If one of the column headings changes, you can edit the macro to show the new name, and you don't have to remember to do it by hand the next time.

Suppose that your company is making a global font change. Set up a macro to change all the text from the old font to the new font. The process is quick, easy, and complete. You can make the format changes with the Format Painter feature, but the chance of making errors is less when you use a macro than when you do it by hand. Another advantage to making formatting changes with a macro is that the person running the macro doesn't need to know as much about the tool. You can give the macro to people who don't know as much about using Excel as you do, add it to their QATs, and let them run the macro. You then know that those people will make the formatting changes you want every time.

Data entry

As you get better at creating macros, you'll find that some spreadsheets are easier to create with a macro than by using simple data entry. By asking for the input in a more formal way, you can tell users exactly which data you want, specify the ranges for that data, and warn users when they enter something outside of what you expect. Better data entry means better results.

If you want to go a step further, record a macro for opening a text or CSV file. You may be amazed at what the macro lets you do to clean up repetitions of the process.

Step Into the Real World

If you will be creating full applications for Excel, you may want to investigate a programming language and environment other than VBA. You can create Office-specific macros and programs by using the Visual Studio Tools for Office (VSTO). VSTO allows you to create programs in other languages, such as C++, and a more visual programming environment, such as .Net. These development tools and languages are available at additional cost. They are not included with Excel or Office.

If you are looking for more information, check out the Office 2007 Developer Center at `http://msdn2.microsoft.com/en-us/office/default.aspx`.

Full applications

You can take your VBA knowledge to another level and use only VBA macros to write applications that run on top of Excel. Users can then load up spreadsheets with data without having to know everything there is to know about Excel.

Introducing Trusted Locations and Trusted Sources

Sometimes, you'll want to run a macro or add-in without worrying whether your current security settings allow you to run macros. To facilitate that process, Microsoft has added a pair of features to Office 2007: trusted locations and trusted sources.

Taking a look at trusted locations

Trusted locations are special locations on your hard drive or network that are designed to contain code that can be trusted no matter who creates the files. Any Excel file placed in one of these locations can contain code that runs without asking you for permission, no matter how your current security settings are configured.

When you install Excel 2007, several locations are set as trusted locations by default, including the ones in this list:

- The default template locations for the current user (for both system-wide and user-created templates)

- The default user startup folders for Excel (for system startup items, Office startup items, and user startup items)

- The default add-ins location for Excel

You can remove any of these defined locations and add your own by using the Trust Center.

Adding a trusted location

Follow these steps to access the Trust Center and add a trusted location:

1. **Click the Office button, and from the pop-up menu, click Excel Options.**

2. **In the Excel Options window, select Trust Center.**

The Trust Center appears on the right side of the options list, as shown in Figure 15-23.

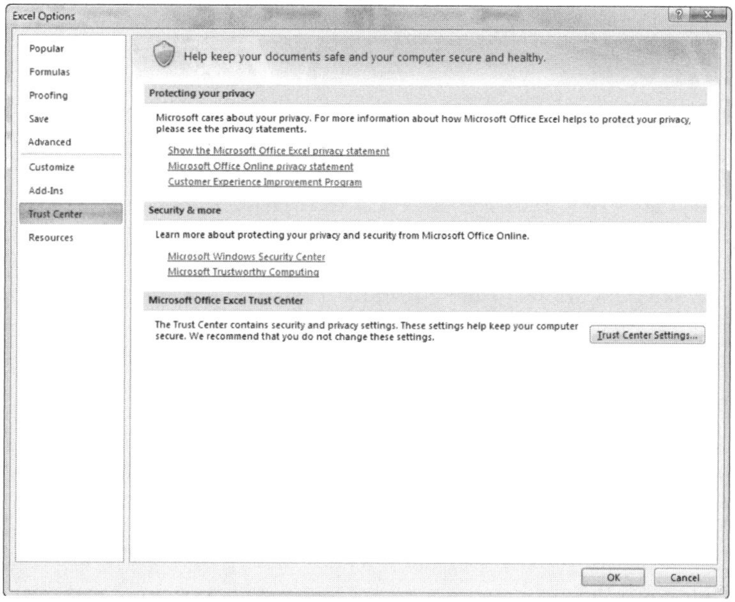

Figure 15-23: The Trust Center options list.

i   Information Kiosk

You can also access the Trust Center from the Developer tab. Choose Developer → Code → Macro Security to activate the Trust Center. The only difference is that the default page displays the Macro Settings list rather than the Trusted Locations list.

Use the top two sections of the Trust Center to learn about Microsoft Office privacy statements, the Windows Trustworthy Computing initiative, and other interesting topics.

3. Click the **Trust Center Settings** button.

The detailed Trust Center appears.

4. Select **Trusted Locations.**

The Trusted Locations list appears, as shown in Figure 15-24.

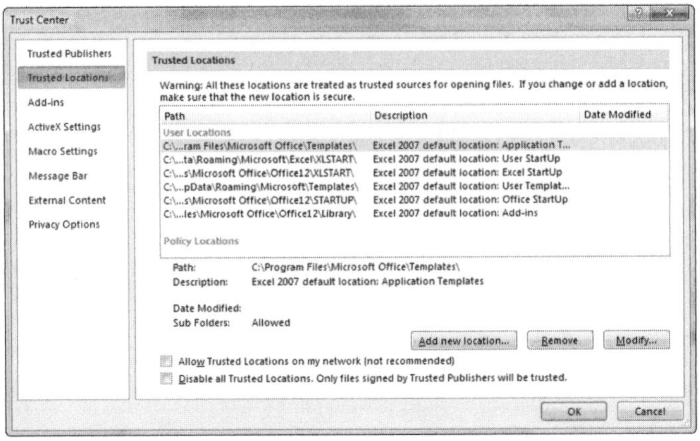

Figure 15-24: The Trusted Locations list.

The exact locations of the currently trusted folders on your computer are shown. You use the buttons and check boxes at the bottom of the list to change trusted locations.

Because you don't want to mess with the default Trusted Locations list, you'll add a new trusted location in this exercise and then remove it. If you want to add one for your own use, you can add it when you finish the exercise.

5. Click **Add New Location.**

The Microsoft Office Trusted Location dialog box appears, as shown in Figure 15-25.

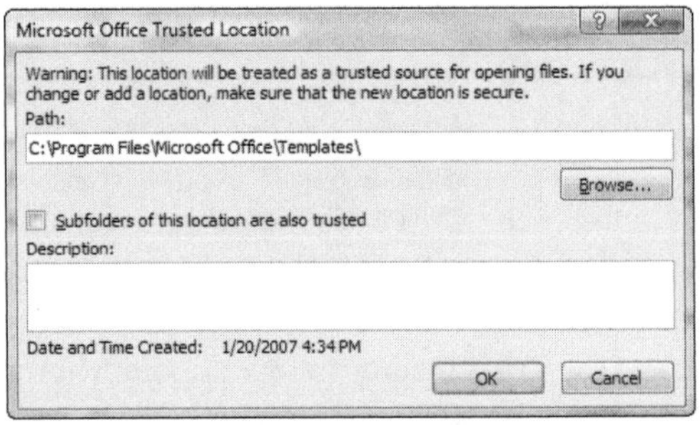

Figure 15-25: The Trusted Location dialog box.

As the warning says, if you were adding this location for real use, you would need to be sure that it is in a location on your hard drive that is not accessible by other users and over which you have total control. Do not add any public folders as trusted locations unless access to those folders is secured.

6. **Click the Browse button. Navigate to your desktop and create a new folder named** ExcelTrustedTestFolder**. Click OK to add this new folder to the trusted list.**

By creating a new folder on your desktop, you know that the new location is not accessible by anyone other than you. Clicking OK returns you to the Trusted Locations dialog box.

7. **Add this description for the folder:** Temporary Trusted Location for testing**.**

8. **Select the Subfolders of This Location Are Also Trusted check box.**

You decide whether to trust subfolders in general. Microsoft recommends that you add only individual folders to your Trusted Locations list. In this case, you can trust the subfolders because you are not creating any.

You are ready to trust this new folder.

9. **Click the OK button to close the dialog box.**

After you add a new folder, you should see it at the top of your list, as shown in Figure 15-26.

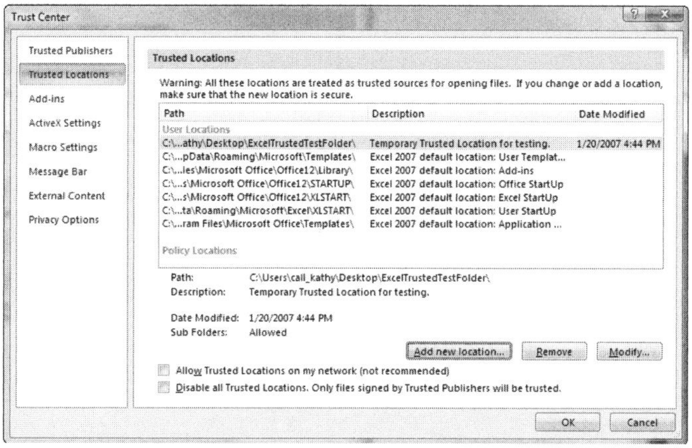

Figure 15-26: Trusted locations with a new folder added.

Notice that this folder not only has a location and a description but also has just been modified.

If you want to change the description of this folder or select a different folder to trust with this same description, click the Modify button. The Trusted Location dialog box reappears, and you can modify any part of the location definition.

Step Into the Real World

In the Trust Center, you find a link to the Customer Experience Improvement Program (CEIP). Check it out when you have time. By participating in the CEIP, you help Microsoft understand how you normally use Excel. You are not telling Microsoft anything about the documents you are creating; instead, you tell it which features you use and whether you had difficulty finding them.

Participating in the CIEP has always been a good idea, but it is an even better idea in Office 2007. In the new interface, users make clear to Microsoft which parts of the Ribbon are working well and which ones aren't. By participating in the CIEP, you help improve the next version of Excel.

Now that you have defined a trusted location, using it is simple. Any file placed in that folder is trusted by the Office security settings. No matter which security settings are enabled, the code in files in those folders runs without prompts.

10. **Click OK twice to return to the Excel sheet you were working on. Close Excel and open Windows Explorer.**

11. **Copy one of the files you have created that contains a macro. Paste the file into the new trusted folder you just created.**

12. **Reopen Excel and open the document you just created.**

Notice that the file opens with no security warnings or messages. To prove that you can now open a file that contains macros without warnings, set the security settings to disable macros and then close and reopen the file. Although you should still not receive any security warnings, you should be able to execute the macro.

If you want to stop trusting a location, you can delete it from the list, as described in the next two steps.

13. **Return to the Trust Center. Select the new folder from the list and then click Remove.**

Notice that the folder name is removed from the list.

14. **Click the OK button twice to return to Excel.**

To confirm that the settings have changed, reopen the file you placed in the trusted location, and notice that the warnings return.

Exploring additional Trusted Locations options

At the bottom of the Trusted Locations list are check boxes to allow you to trust locations on a network and to disable all trusted locations.

If you know that you can trust all users on your network, you can create a common trusted location on your network and select the All Trusted Locations on My Network check box to enable it. Doing this can open a hole in your security system, so think carefully before enabling trusted locations on a network.

If you are traveling and your PC will be connected to an unsecured network, consider disabling the network locations.

If you don't want to have any macros run except those that are signed, select the Disable All Trusted Locations check box. That way, you don't expose your machine to the possibility of code being added to one of your trusted locations by software running on another machine.

Understanding trusted sources

Another Trust Center feature that affects your system when you work with code is the Trusted Publishers feature.

When code is developed for deployment to the general public, the company doing the development can buy a certificate that verifies that the company is who it says it is. This certificate, which is issued after a background check, lets you know that you can trust the code that is developed and signed with this certificate. Certificates issued to trusted publishers are similar to the certificates you see on secure Web sites.

If you install code written by someone who has a full certificate, information about the publisher or distributor of the code appears on the list of trusted publishers in the Trust Center.

Step Into the Real World

If you are running Office 2007 in a corporate environment, you likely cannot add your own trusted locations. Your corporate IT department may have set up trusted locations according to a corporate security policy and set up your machine to follow that policy when Office 2007 was installed. In this case, you are likely to have a few local trusted locations as well as one trusted location on a network drive that is controlled and secured by your IT department.

automate: To make a computer perform a series of steps with less user intervention than would be required if the steps were performed by hand.

bug: An unintended error in your program that causes events to happen that you do not want to happen or that causes events not to happen that you want to happen. Some features are bugs.

code: The set of programming steps you create to tell the computer what to do when it is running your macro.

comments: Lines of code that are added to a program to help users understand what the code is trying to do. (Comments are non-executable code.)

debug: To remove bugs from a program. (You are always "almost done debugging" or "on your last bug.")

executable code: Lines of code that tell the computer what needs to be done and how to do it.

features: The defined set of tasks that your program or macro performs.

For...Next: The programming statement that loops through the statements between the `For` and `Next` statements, repeating the process at least once. The variable defined in the `For` part of the statement is incremented each time through the loop.

increment: To change a variable by steps in a controlled way. Variables can be incremented positively or negatively (in other words, by growing larger or smaller), but most people increment only up, not down.

Object Model: The set of rules that must be followed when developing the statements that make up your code. The Object Model defines what processing can and cannot be done from VBA. The Object Model encompasses the properties of objects and which commands can be performed by VBA.

record a macro: To have Excel watch what you do and remember it so that you can repeat the steps later.

runtime error: An error that occurs while your macro is running through the steps you defined.

statement: An individual line of code.

syntax error: A type of error caused by incorrectly entering a step in a macro's process. Syntax errors are generally caught during compile-time.

trap an error: To capture an error as it happens and end the macro gracefully. If you don't trap errors, users see generic error messages when errors occur. Generic messages are not helpful. In addition, when you do not trap errors, your code can end in the middle of processing and leave the spreadsheet in an undesired state.

Visual Basic Editor (VBE): The program you use to create, navigate, compile, and debug programs written in Visual Basic. In this book, Visual Basic Editor refers to the specific version of the program that comes with Office products and is designed to handle code developed in Visual Basic for Applications.

Visual Basic for Applications (VBA): The language used to translate human-readable information and steps in a process into information that the computer can understand and process. (Also referred to as Visual Basic.)

Last Stop

Practice Exam

1. True or False: All macros are enabled automatically.

2. Name the two tabs that contain buttons that let you record macros.

_____

_____

3. True or False: All Excel functionality can be recorded into a macro.

4. Which of the following is a valid macro name?

    a. Count Numbers

    b. CountNumbers

    c. Count/Numbers

    d. Count

5. True or False: The shortcut key M initiates the same macro as the shortcut m.

6. What commands does Excel record after you start recording a macro?

    a. All tasks you perform on your computer until you click the Stop Recording button.

    b. Only the next command that is executed.

    c. Most of the tasks you perform in Excel until you click the Stop Recording button.

    d. Nothing. You cannot record macros in Excel 2007.

7. True or False: Activating the Developer tab in Excel affects other Office programs.

8. True or False: After you record a macro, you cannot change it.

9. Which of the following is not a valid way to create a macro:

    a. Copy the code from another application or file and paste it in.

    b. Record it.

    c. Type it from scratch.

    d. All these methods are valid ways to create a macro.

10. If you add an extra parenthesis in macro code, Excel

    a. displays an error message when you type the parenthesis.

    b. displays an error message when you close the Visual Basic Editor.

    c. displays an error message when the code is run.

    d. always removes the error.

11. Describe how you know which line Excel thinks caused the error when a running macro encounters an error.

_____

12. Name a circumstance in which you would enable all macros.

_____

_____

13. Give an example of a conditional statement.

_____

_____

14. `For` loops and `While` loops are different in which of the following ways?

    a. Code in a `For` loop always executes once. Code in a `While` loop may not execute at all.

    b. Code in a `While` loop always executes once. Code in a `For` loop may not execute at all.

    c. Code in both types of loops always runs at least once, but a `For` loop does the incrementing for you.

    d. Code in both types of loops always runs at least once, but a `While` loop does the incrementing for you.

15. True or False: The MsgBox and InputBox commands in VBA do the same thing.

16. Name two ways to initiate a macro.

_____

_____

17. True or False: Macros in files stored in the templates folders are automatically trusted when Excel is installed on most machines.

18. Who can add trusted locations to your installation of Excel?

    a. Anyone with a user ID for the computer.

    b. The person who installed Office on your computer.

    c. You.

    d. All of the above.

19. Folders are to trusted locations as certificates are to trusted _____.

Building Your Own Excel Add-Ins

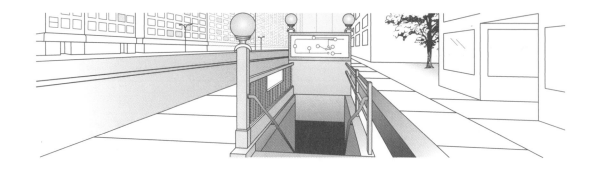

 # Enter the Station

Questions

1. How do you make a snippet of code run every time you open Excel?

2. How do you make a snippet of code run every time you close Excel?

3. How do you access code in PERSONAL.XLSB?

4. Why would you not want to design a macro directly in PERSONAL.XLSB?

5. Why would you want to share a macro with other users?

6. What does the Visual Basic statement On Error allow you to do?

7. Where are Excel add-ins stored by default?

8. How can you access code in an add-in?

9. What do you need to be careful about when you deliver code to other users?

So far, you have used other people's add-ins and developed your own macros. In this chapter, you will combine the two ideas and create your own add-in.

You have three main reasons to convert a macro that you created into an add-in. Each of these reasons has its own special rules and processing attached to it:

You want to use the macro in files beyond the one that originally held the macro. Although in these cases you can call the macro from other files, it is a better idea to turn the macro into an add-in. If that is all you want to do, you can save the Excel file with the same name and the `.xla` extension. If you install the add-in as you have already learned to do, you will be less open to errors and unexpected results.

You want your macro to always run when you open or close Excel. Macros in this category are put in a special Excel file with unique macro names and are considered add-ins. These add-ins need some special testing to ensure that you don't mess up any files on the system when you open the file.

Other users want the functionality your macro provides, so you convert the macro to an add-in. When you create this type of add-in, you must ensure that the macros in the add-in don't depend on something that exists only on your system. You also must ensure that you trap errors in a more formal way to ensure that you don't cause damage to other people's files.

Creating Open and Close Macros

There are two special names for add-ins that can be used to target when the code is run. These two macros are stored in a special file named PERSONAL.XLSB. This file is saved on your hard drive in a location attached to your user ID. The file is hidden by default and is created the first time you create one of the two automatically run macros. These special macros are described in the following list:

Auto_Open: Always runs whenever you open Excel. Use this macro for code that you want to run every time you start Excel, no matter which files you're working with. You can use Auto_Open to load macros that will be available in all Excel files or to specify which cell or sheet is selected when you open Excel.

Auto_Close: Always runs whenever you close Excel. In previous versions of Excel, this macro was used to store code that cleaned up toolbars, for example. Now you can use this macro to unload other macros that are loaded with Auto_Open, to do other cleanup work, or to delete temporary files that were created while Excel was open.

Watch Your Step

The PERSONAL.XLSB file is stored in a location that is by default a trusted location. Auto_Open and Auto_Close routines therefore do not need to be enabled unless security on the computer is set to the highest level.

Creating and testing two simple macros

The process for creating and editing these two macros requires you to outthink Excel and be a little tricky. In the next exercise, you create one of each of the two special macros and test whether they run. The test macros you create display a message saying that they are running. To find out about more complicated macros, check out *Excel 2007 Power Programming with VBA,* by John Walkenbach (Wiley).

Follow these steps to create two simple macros that run whenever you open and close Excel:

1. Open a new blank document. Choose Developer ➔ Code ➔ Record Macro.

The only way to create the first automatic macro is to record a temporary macro. You cannot create it by just giving it a name until after Excel has created the file that will hold the special macros.

2. Fill out the Record Macro dialog box as follows:

- *Macro Name:* Name the new macro **Auto_Open**.

- *Store Macro In:* Select Personal Macro Workbook from this drop-down list. By selecting this option, the macro will be available whenever you use Excel.

- *Description:* Enter the following description: **Create a simple macro to be run anytime Excel is run.**

Your Record Macro dialog box should now look like Figure 16-1.

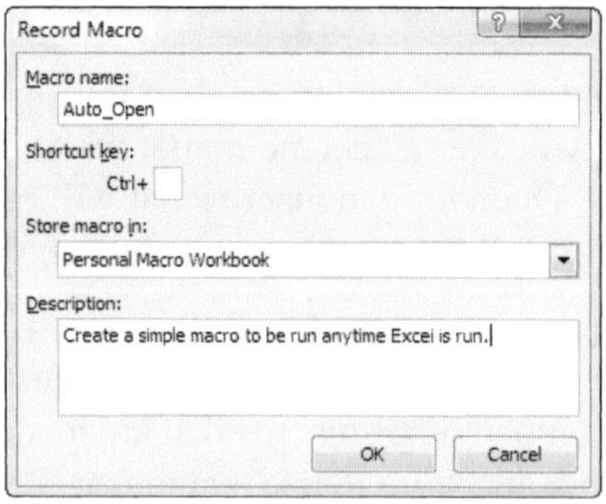

Figure 16-1: The Record Macro dialog box is ready for recording the Auto_Open routine.

3. Click OK to close the dialog box and start recording your macro.

4. In cell A1, type the word anything. Choose Developer → Code → Stop Recording.

5. Click the Macros button to open the Macro dialog box, which displays the list of macros.

The list of macros contains your new macro, as shown in Figure 16-2.

Figure 16-2: The macro list with the newly created Auto_Open routine.

Now that your macro shell is created, you have to edit it so that it does what you really want it to do. You could have recorded steps for this macro; however, experience will show that you seldom create an Auto_Open macro by recording it. Usually, you create the macro in a specific Excel file and then copy the code into the Auto_Open macro after it has been debugged and is ready for general use.

You should also test the macro on a variety of files before you commit to running it every time Excel opens or closes.

The macros in PERSONAL.XLSB are hidden macros, so you can't edit them as you normally do. Instead, you have to step into the macro, stop the debugger, and then edit the macro, as outlined in the following steps.

6. Click Step Into to edit the macro.

The view changes to the Visual Basic Editor, and the new macro looks like the one shown in Figure 16-3.

Your code may look slightly different from the code shown in Figure 16-3. For example, if you didn't explicitly select cell A1, you won't have the Range("A1").Select line. The differences don't really matter — you are going to delete the code and replace it with real code in two steps.

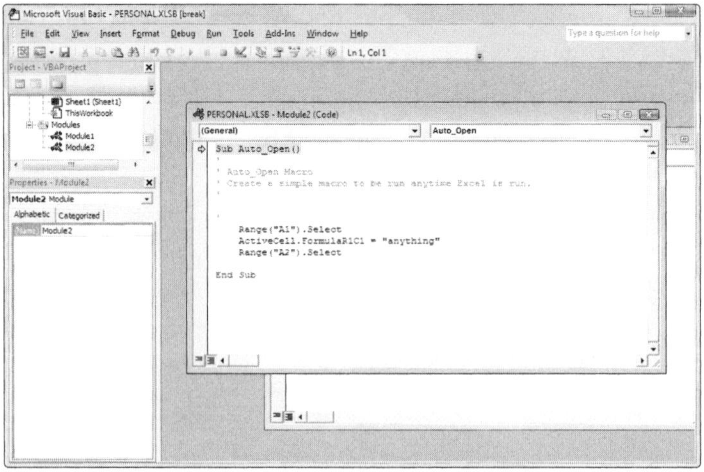

Figure 16-3: Recorded code in Visual Basic Editor view.

You are now ready to stop the debugger and edit your code.

7. Choose Run → Reset.

This command stops the execution of the current macro so that you can edit it. Next, you will replace the recorded code with the code you want to run.

8. Select the three lines of code between the comments and the End Sub line.

9. Replace the three lines you just selected with this single line:

```
MsgBox("Starting Auto_Open routine.")
```

10. Select the entire macro, press Ctrl+C to copy it, and then press Ctrl+V to paste it on a new line just after the End Sub line.

11. Change the word *Open* to *Close* in every place that it exists in the new routine.

When you complete the edit, you have two new routines: one that runs whenever you *open* Excel and one that runs whenever you *close* Excel. The code should look like Figure 16-4.

Notice that Excel added a line between the two routines when you pasted in the second copy. This visual clue helps you know where one routine ends and the other begins.

Information Kiosk

If you were creating a real Auto_Open or Auto_Close routine, you would select the code from the macro list of the Excel file that contains your actual code, copy the code, and then paste it into the appropriate routine.

12. Choose File → Close to close the Visual Basic Editor, save your changes, and return to Microsoft Excel. Save your changes if you are prompted to do so.

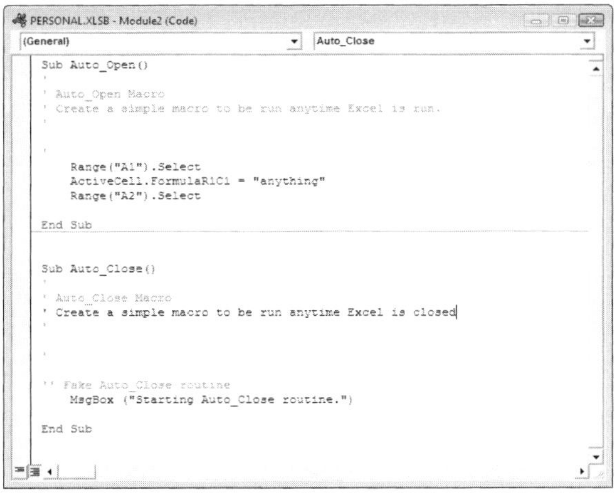

Figure 16-4: Edited Auto_Open and Auto_Close routines.

13. Display the list of macros again.

Your list of macros now contains the two macros you just created, as shown in Figure 16-5.

Figure 16-5: The Macro list with the Auto_Open and Auto_Close macros.

14. Close the Macro dialog box and then close the file without saving the changes to the Excel file you just created. Close Excel.

You have now saved a new copy of PERSONAL.XLSB, but not the blank Excel file you were using to create it. When you close Excel, you should see a message box with an informational message generated by the Auto_Close routine, as shown in Figure 16-6.

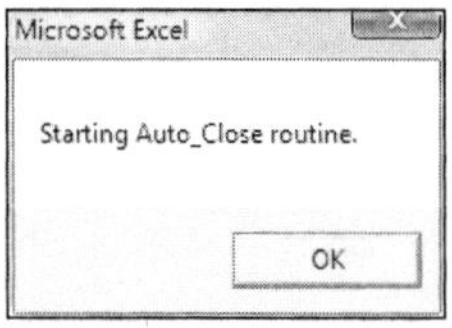

Microsoft Excel

Starting Auto_Close routine.

OK

Figure 16-6: An informational message generated by the Auto_Close routine.

 ## Watch Your Step

If you don't see the informational message, you likely mistyped something in the macro. The most likely error is forgetting to include the underscore between Auto and Close. Don't worry: After you reopen Excel, you can go back and reedit the macro by following Steps 5 and 6 in this step list to access the code a second time.

15. Click OK.

The informational message from your Auto_Open routine appears, asking whether you want to save the changes to your Personal Macro Workbook, as shown in Figure 16-7.

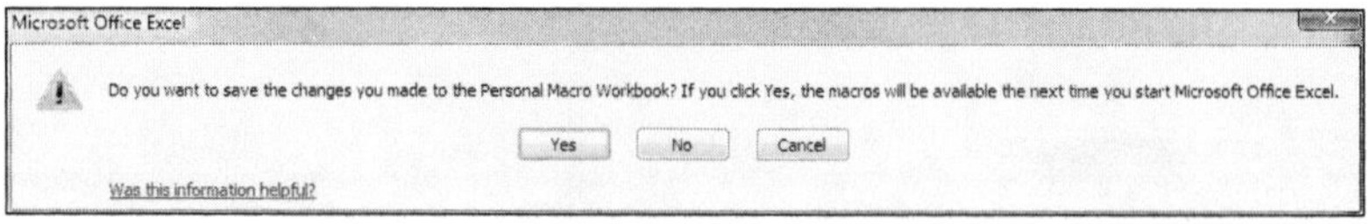

Microsoft Office Excel

⚠ Do you want to save the changes you made to the Personal Macro Workbook? If you click Yes, the macros will be available the next time you start Microsoft Office Excel.

Yes   No   Cancel

Was this information helpful?

Figure 16-7: Excel prompts you to save your changes.

16. Click Yes to save the changes.

Excel closes.

17. Reopen Excel.

A second message box should appear, as shown in Figure 16-8.

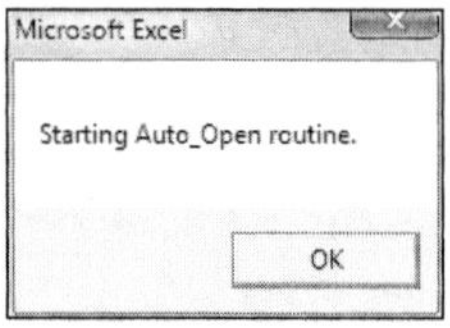

Microsoft Excel

Starting Auto_Open routine.

OK

Figure 16-8: An informational message from the Auto_Open routine.

18. Click OK.

Excel opens a blank spreadsheet as usual.

You have now created a pair of simple macros that run whenever you open and close Excel. In addition, you have created a place to put macros that you want available at all times when you are running Excel.

Making a different macro always available

After Excel creates the PERSONAL.XLSB file, you can store a macro directly in that file by selecting the file from the list of locations in either the Macro dialog box or the Record Macro dialog box. Chances are fairly good that when you start putting macros in this file, you will find that you want other ones there too.

Watch Your Step

Even though you can create a macro directly in the PERSONAL. XLSB file, after you save the macro the first time, you cannot edit it without stepping into it. The same statement applies to deleting a macro: You can delete a macro from PERSONAL.XLSB only by stepping into it and deleting it from within the Visual Basic Editor.

Converting Your Macro to an Add-In

If you plan to share a macro with other Excel users, don't store it in your PERSONAL. XLSB file. Instead, create an add-in that contains the macro code.

You can save the file containing the macro as an XLSM file — which is the quickest way to convert it to an add-in — but it's not the safest way to do it. When you share a macro with other users, you must ensure that the add-in you have created doesn't take over their machines or cause unexpected changes to their Excel files.

When you deliver code as an add-in, you need to make the following changes:

- Give users a better way to start the routine than by using shortcut keys. Although you know which shortcut keys you use on your machine, a key that is free for use on your machine is unlikely to also be available on every other machine.

- If you're asking for any kind of input from users, ensure that the input boxes clearly specify what data the code needs in order to run.

- Have an error-handling mechanism in place to handle unexpected errors gracefully and close down the add-in without corrupting users' documents.

The macro you work with in the rest of this chapter helps you find the winner in a monthly guess-the-number contest. In the contest, a number of items, from 40 to 4,000, are placed in a jar, and customers try to guess the number of items in the jar in order to win a store gift certificate. At the end of each month, after you receive a stack of entries, you enter the entry numbers and the guesses into an Excel spreadsheet.

After all the numbers are entered, you need to find the correct guess, or the one that is closest to correct without going over. (Yes, you can sort the data to find this number, but this chapter explains how to work with add-ins, not with tables.)

In this section, you convert this macro to an add-in. After you make the conversion, you need to test the macro to ensure that it has a minimal unexpected effect on other machines.

Converting the macro

To convert the guess-the-number contest macro to an add-in, follow these steps:

1. Open the file `Ch16GuessMacro.xlsm`. If your macro security level is not set to allow code to be run, activate the macro.

Transfer

If you want a refresher on how to change your macro security level, refer to Chapter 15.

The file you opened has a large number of entries. First, you'll run the macro so that you know what it does before you convert it to an add-in.

2. Press Ctrl+Shift+G to run the macro. Answer the prompt. In the message that shows up after you click OK, notice the answer that is given. Make sure that the answer shown in the second message box is the correct one.

The macro should ask you for a number between 40 and 4,000, verify that you specified a valid number, and then provide a message box that tells you the winning answer and the row where it was found. At the end of the macro, the selected cell will be in row 4500.

Your next step is to make sure that errors in the code are handled gracefully. Although you can easily work with a macro stored in one of your files, editing a macro in an add-in can be a hassle. You should instead make sure that at least the minimum level of error handling is included before you change the file type.

3. Choose Developer ➜ Code ➜ Macros.

4. Select the macro FindTarget and then click Edit.

The Visual Basic Editor opens. You see the current macro in the frontmost window. Behind it, you are likely to see the macros for your Auto_Open and Auto_Close routines, which you created earlier in the chapter. For this exercise, you will work with the FindTarget macro.

5. Just after the first group of comments, type the following line of code:

```
On Error GoTo FindTargetErr
```

The first part of the code should now look like this:

```
Sub FindTarget()
'
' FindTarget Macro
' Find the number closest to the target supplied by the
user
'
On Error GoTo FindTargetErr
```

The `On Error` statement lets you easily trap any error that may have occurred. While the `On Error` statement is placed at the top of your code, it traps any error in the routine. In this case, the `On Error` command tells Excel that if an error occurs, processing should jump to the defined error routine and let it end the macro gracefully.

When you're working with code that other users will run, use `On Error` commands to redirect the path of the code when errors occur. You can then end things cleanly and without users realizing that anything went wrong.

You are now halfway done with the error processing. Next, you need to tell Excel what to do when an error occurs.

6. Just before the **End Sub** line of your macro, type the following lines of code:

```
Exit Sub

FindTargetErr:
MsgBox("An Error Occurred. Please try again")
```

When you press Enter after the second line, it adjusts itself out to the left margin.

The `Exit Sub` line tells Excel to exit the subroutine rather than execute the next line. The line that reads `FindTargetErr` is a label. The `On Error` line you just added tells Excel that if an error occurs, you want it to go directly to this label and run the code there. In this example, the code is an error message, followed by the end of the macro.

When you finish, the code should look like the code shown here:

```
Sub FindTarget()
'
' FindTarget Macro
' Find the number closest to the target supplied by the user
'
On Error GoTo FindTargetErr

' Get the number of items for this month from the user
    Range("B1").Select
    CorrectAnswer% = 0
    While CorrectAnswer% < 40 Or CorrectAnswer% > 4000
        CorrectAnswer% = InputBox("How many in the jar this month?(40 to 4000)")
    Wend

'Set up variables that will hold the closest answer
    NearestSoFar = 0
    RowForNearest = 0

'Loop through the entries and find the answer that is closest without going over
    For I = 2 To 4500

'Select the next cell and get its value
        Range("B" & I).Activate
        CurrentGuess = ActiveCell.Value

        ' If the current value is greater than the correct answer, then skip it
        If CurrentGuess < CorrectAnswer% Then

        ' Now, if the current answer is bigger
        ' than the best previous guess - make it the new guess
            If CurrentGuess > NearestSoFar Then
                NearestSoFar = CurrentGuess

                'RowForNearest is the entry number that has the best guess so
                    far
                RowForNearest = I
            End If
        End If
    Next I

        'Now tell the user what you found
        MsgBox ("Nearest Guess is " & NearestSoFar & " and row for nearest is "
            & RowForNearest)
    Exit Sub

FindTargetErr:
    MsgBox ("An Error Occurred. Please try again")
    End Sub
```

You are now ready to test whether this chunk of code works.

7. Compile the code by choosing Debug ➔ Compile VBAProject. If errors occur, fix them before continuing.

After the code compiles, you will run a few quick error checks on the code.

8. Close the Visual Basic Editor to return to the main Excel interface.

9. Press Ctrl+Shift+G to run the code.

10. When the input box appears, type the letter Q as the answer and then click OK.

A new informational message appears, as shown in Figure 16-9.

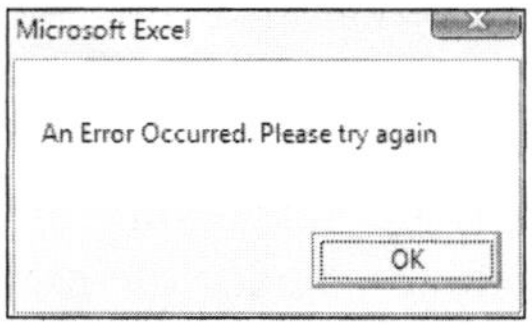

Figure 16-9: This informational error message proves that the error was handled gracefully.

11. Click OK. Run the test again with a valid number to make sure that the error message is not displayed.

12. Select the data in columns A and B and then delete the data.

Because this is an add-in, the file should contain just code, not data.

13. Click the Office Button and choose Save As.

14. In the Save as Type drop-down list, select Excel 97-2003 Add-In to change the file type to xla.

When you change the file type, the file location should change to the area where Excel stores your add-ins, as shown in Figure 16-10.

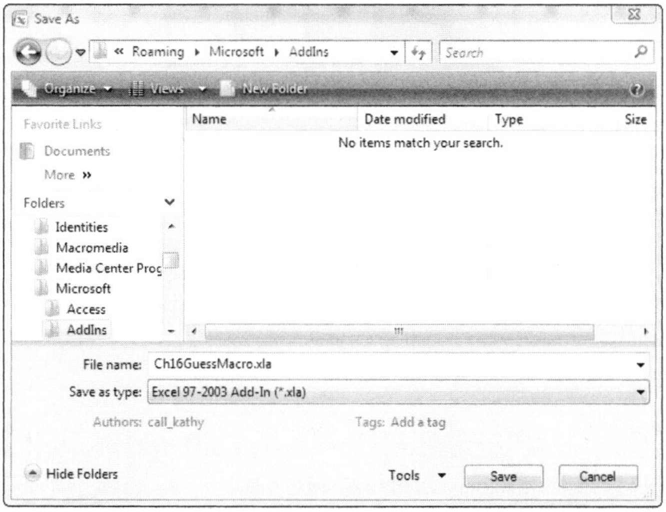

Figure 16-10: The Save As dialog box shows where Excel changes your add-in location.

15. **Change the filename to** FindTarget. **Click Save.**

You have saved the file as an Excel add-in. Now you are ready to close Excel, reopen it, and install the add-in.

16. **Close Excel.**

If the informational message from the Auto_Close routine appears, click OK.

17. **If you are prompted to save your changes to the `.xlm` file, don't save them.**

If you save the changes, you will wipe out the original version of the macro. Because you will work with the add-in file from now on, you do not have to save your changes to the macro file.

18. **Reopen Excel.**

You again receive the original informational message. This is not a problem. If you find it annoying, open the Visual Basic Editor and comment out the messages in the Auto_Open and Auto_Close routines. Next, you install the add-in.

19. **Click the Office Button and then click Excel Options. Select Add-Ins from the left column.**

20. **Click the Go button next to the Manage drop-down list.**

The Add-Ins dialog box appears, but your add-in may not be listed yet.

21. **Click Browse.**

A Browse window appears, which points to the Add-Ins folder on your hard drive. Next, you will select your add-in and install it.

22. **Ensure that FindTarget.xla is selected and then click OK.**

If you see a warning message that the add-in is already listed, click Yes to add it again. It may have been in the list, but it was probably not yet loaded. When you return to the Add-Ins dialog box, your add-in's check box is selected, as shown in Figure 16-11.

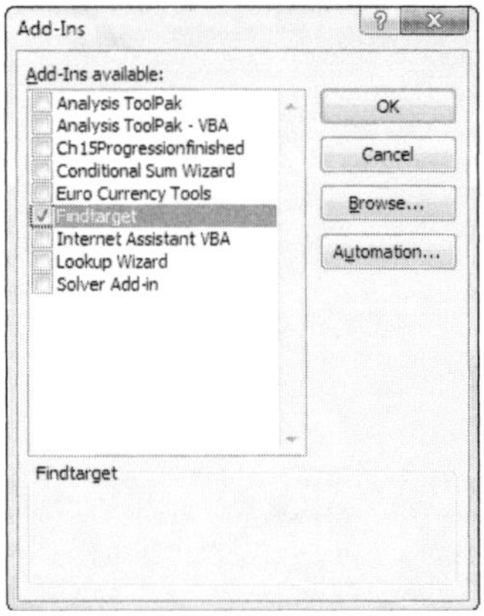

Figure 16-11: The Add-Ins list includes your new add-in.

23. Click OK to complete the installation, but don't close Excel.

Your add-in is installed and ready to be used. If you want to initiate your add-in from a button on the Add-Ins tab, check out *Excel 2007 Power Programming with VBA* by John Walkenbach (Wiley).

Adding your add-in to the Quick Access Toolbar (QAT)

To make it easy to run your new add-in, follow these steps to add your add-in to the QAT:

1. Click the Office Button and then click Excel Options. Select Customize from the left column.

2. From the Choose Commands From drop-down list, select Macros. Make sure that the Customize Quick Access Toolbar drop-down list shows For All Documents (Default). Click FindTarget and then click the Add button.

The macro name now appears at the end of the list of buttons on the QAT.

3. Click OK to apply the change to your QAT.

You now have one-button access to your macro any time you run Excel on your machine. However, if you remove the add-in, you have to go back to the Customize section of Excel Options window and ensure that the button also has been removed from the QAT.

Your add-in has now been installed and can be run. The next step is to test it as an add-in on your machine and on other machines.

Making Sure That Your Add-In Works

Now that your add-in is installed, you have to test it. First, you'll test it on your machine to see whether it still runs the way you want. In the process of testing it, you will undoubtedly find some things you want to improve. Write them down, and work on them in your spare time.

To start testing your add-in, follow these steps:

1. Initiate the macro you just created by pressing Ctrl+Shift+G. Answer the prompt and note the response you see.

This first test runs the macro on an empty spreadsheet. You should see the informational message with the result shown in Figure 16-12.

Because you had no data for comparison, your add-in found no match and no row containing the match. You can go back into your add-in and add an error check for a nonresult. Then you can provide a clearer error message for the case when no match occurs.

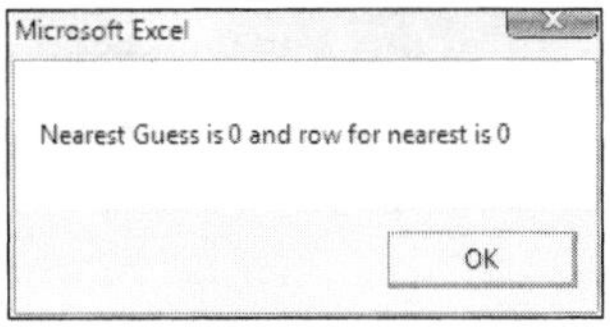

Figure 16-12: No results were found.

2. Add test data to your spreadsheet by hand or by copying it from the original file (`Ch16GuessMacro.xlsm`).

3. Click the button you added to the QAT to check whether your macro can be started from the QAT.

You should see the message requesting your input, and then the macro should run just as it does by starting it from the keyboard. Make sure you get the right results.

4. Perform a series of tests to prove that the macro is working and catching errors.

After you prove that your add-in works the way you want, you have to decide whether you want other people to use this add-in as well.

When you decide to deliver an add-in to other people, first answer these questions:

- **Have you tested the code thoroughly to be certain that you will not adversely affect someone else's computer?** If you aren't sure, find a test environment, install your add-in there, and run it for a while.

- **Have you provided a way for someone using your add-in to run it without your having to be physically present when they run it?** You cannot assume that someone else will be able to use the same keyboard shortcut that you use on your machine. If someone else has already assigned that shortcut to another macro, you cause problems for that person.

- **Are you sure that you want to take on the security issues involved in deploying an add-in to other people?** When you install code on other users' machines, you must be willing to talk to them and document the potential dangers of running someone else's code. It is a good idea to explain in your documentation all the steps involved in setting up the appropriate level of security on their systems so that your code can run. You should also document that decreasing their level of security to accommodate your code can expose their machines to other code being run too.

- **Have you verified that your comments are clear and specific?** If they aren't, when you come back later to improve the code, the comments may not help.

- **Do you want to add a cleaner, more consistent way to run the code?** If so, investigate using Ribbon X to add the button to the Add-Ins tab rather than adding it by using methods shown in this chapter.

Information Kiosk

To learn more about Ribbon X and working with the Office 2007 interface, check out Patrick Schmid's blog, on the Web at `http://pschmid.net/index.php`. Patrick offers information on how to work with the entire interface by using code and his toolset to improve how you work with Office 2007.

close gracefully: To handle an error in a way that provides information about what caused the situation or error.

hidden macro: A macro stored in a hidden file. In this chapter, hidden macros are stored in the `PERSONAL.XLSB` file.

label: A line of code that you use in other places in the code to reference that line. You can use labels to "jump over" code without executing it. In this chapter, you use the label to set an exit point for macros using the `On Error` statement.

On Error: A Visual Basic command that allows Excel to trap errors and close your macro gracefully.

PERSONAL.XLSB: A hidden file that Excel creates automatically to hold your Auto_Open and Auto_Close modules. This file can also hold any piece of code you want to have available at all times when you are running Excel.

prompt: To request input from the user.

reset: To stop the execution of a macro and set it up so that it can be started from the beginning the next time it is run.

share code: To provide users with a file that contains a macro that they can use on their own machines. When you share code, you eliminate repetitive work, but you also make yourself responsible for supporting the code and any side effects it may cause.

shell: A macro with no executable code. Used as a starting point for creating macros that are typed in instead of recorded.

step into: To execute the first line of code in a macro and then stop. You can step into a hidden macro to edit it when you would not otherwise be able to access it. In addition, you can step into a macro when you are debugging code to watch the progression of steps through the macro.

Practice Exam

1. **Which of the following statements is not true?**

   a. Code in the Auto_Open routine runs every time Excel opens.

   b. Code in the Auto_Close routine runs every time Excel closes.

   c. Code in the PERSONAL.XLSB file runs every time you use Excel.

   d. Code in the PERSONAL.XLSB file is always trusted.

2. **True or False: You can use the Edit button in the Macros dialog box to access the Auto_Open and Auto_Close routines for editing.**

3. **True or False: Code in the Auto_Close routine runs whenever an Excel file is closed.**

4. **Which of the following may not be a good way to initiate a macro that you are delivering as an add-in?**

   a. A keyboard shortcut.

   b. A button on the Add-Ins tab.

   c. A button on the QAT.

   d. All of the above are good, safe ways to allow people to start your add-ins.

5. On Error **is used to** _____ **errors so that your code can end gracefully.**

6. **What is the difference between** Exit Sub **and** End Sub**?**

   a. Exit Sub can be used anywhere in a macro, and End Sub can be used only at the end of the macro.

   b. End Sub can be used anywhere in a macro, and Exit Sub can be used only at the end of the macro.

   c. There is no difference; they are interchangeable.

   d. You can use only one of them in any given macro.

7. True or False: You cannot edit code in an Excel 2007 add-in.

8. True or False: After you record a macro, you cannot change it.

9. True or False: Storing an add-in in the default location automatically installs it.

10. When testing an add-in, you should

    a. trust that it works and just deliver it after you save it.

    b. run it on your machine, verify that it works, and then hand it over to users.

    c. run it once on another machine, verify that it works, and then hand it over to users.

    d. run the macro in every possible way on another machine, verify that it works, and then hand it over to users.

APPENDIX

A

Exam Answer Appendix

In this appendix, you find the answers for the Practice Exam at the end of each chapter.

Chapter 1

1. Before Excel 2007 was released, the number of rows that spreadsheets allowed was

   a. smaller than the number of columns now allowed.

   b. fixed.

   c. 26.

   d. There was no limit, just as there is none now.

   Answer: a. smaller than the number of columns now allowed.

2. You use the _____ Button to perform tasks such as opening and saving files.

   Answer: Office

3. The Ribbon is made up of which of the following:

   a. Tabs

   b. Groups

   c. Buttons

   d. All of the above

   Answer: d. All of the above

4. Which tab contains the commands for adding content to your worksheet?

   Answer: The Insert tab

5. True or False: You can collapse the Ribbon by double-clicking a tab.

   Answer: True

6. If you look for the Table Tools tab and it isn't showing, what should you check first?

   Answer: Because the Table Tools tab is contextual, it is shown only if the current cell is in a table. The first thing you should check, therefore, is whether the current cell is in a table.

7. XLSX files

   a. are compressed XML and formatting files.

   b. are binary files.

   c. are files in a proprietary format.

   d. can be opened only by Excel.

   Answer: a. are compressed XML and formatting files.

8. True or False: XLSX files can contain macro code.

   Answer: False. XLSM files can contain macro code, but the code is removed when a file is saved in XLSX format.

9. True or False: Splitting the file format for Excel files into a macro-enabled format and non-macro-enabled format was done to allow greater security and protection against viruses.

   Answer: True.

10. Which of these file formats can Excel open?

   a. XLSX

   b. XLS

   c. XLSB

   d. All of the above

   Answer: d. All of the above

11. True or False: All of the Help information for Excel 2007 is stored locally on your computer.

Answer: False. Much of the Excel 2007 Help information is gathered from the Web, so you need an Internet connection to access that information.

Chapter 2

1. Name two elements of a worksheet that are used to reference a cell.

Answer: Cell, row, column, worksheet, filename

2. When cell G55 is selected, which of the following cells can always be reached in one keystroke?

a. Cell A1

b. The first cell with data in column G

c. Cell H56

d. Cell XFD55

Answer: c. Cell H56. All other cells may be reached in one keystroke sometimes, but it depends on the contents of the cells next to G55.

3. If you are in cell Q999, what is the quickest way to get to cell B6?

Answer: Click in the cell reference box, type **B6**, and then press Enter.

4. If cell A16 on Sheet1 is selected, which cell will be selected when you move to Sheet2?

Answer: The last cell selected in Sheet2.

5. What is the quickest way to select all cells in a single row?

Answer: Click the row number.

6. Name three advantages to using templates.

Answer: Templates save you time, ensure consistency, have predefined formatting, and have pre-defined formulas.

7. How do you edit the text in a cell from the Formula Bar?

Answer: Select the cell. Click the Formula Bar, and use your keyboard to edit the text.

8. When sharing files with people who are using other versions of Excel, you will need to:

a. Send them the XLSX file, which they will be able to open.

b. Send them a printout of the file, and tell them to mark it up and you will edit it.

c. Save your file as an XLS file, which they will be able to open.

d. You cannot share files with people using older versions of Excel.

Answer: c. Save your file as an XLS file, which they will be able to open. Those with Excel 2002 and Excel 2003 may be able to open your XLSX files, but to be safe, it is best to use Save As and save your file as an XLS file when sharing with users running an older version of Excel.

Chapter 3

1. List two circumstances in which you would need to adjust the size of the column or row for a cell.

Answer: When the contents of the cell are too wide, you need to widen the column. When the contents of a cell extend to multiple lines, you need to increase the height of the column. If you want to see more data on the screen, shorten the rows and narrow the columns.

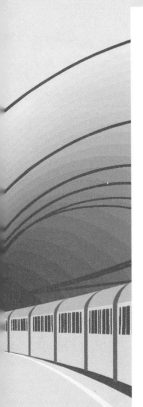

2. **After you follow these steps, how many times will the data be pasted?**

1. Select three cells.

2. Copy the cells.

3. Move to the left three cells.

4. Paste.

5. Move to the left three more cells.

6. Type **Excel 2007**.

7. Paste.

Answer: One time.

3. **Name three advantages of grouping data into tables.**

Answer: The data can be formatted quickly and consistently. Total rows and columns can be added easily. You can name a table and reference it as a single item.

4. **True or False: You can make the Table Tools tab appear at any time, regardless of whether you are working in a table.**

Answer: False. The Table Tools tab is a contextual tab and is available only when you are working with a table.

5. **What are the steps to apply the stop sign conditional formatting to a series of cells?**

Answer: Select the cells. Choose Home ➜ Styles ➜ Conditional Formatting. Select Icon Sets from the list, and then select the set you want.

6. **Which tab is used to change how your worksheet will look when you print it?**

Answer: The Page Layout tab.

7. **How can you tell if a word in a cell is misspelled?**

Answer: It has a squiggly red underline.

8. **List the steps to print your worksheet.**

Answer: Choose Office ➜ Print. Accept the default print options, click the OK button, and print your document.

Chapter 4

1. **Name three ways to add the Sum function to your document.**

Answer: Use the Sum button on the Home tab, type it in by hand, use the formula directly from the Formulas tab.

2. **Which of the following is a relative address?**

a. $C16

b. C$16

c. C16

d. $C$16

Answer: d. $C$16

3. **When you create a formula that produces the result #Div, what do you need to change to fix the error?**

Answer: Fix the formula so that you are no longer pointing to an empty cell or a cell that does not contain a value.

4. True or False: When you use the Insert Function button, you need to know the exact function you want to use.

Answer: False. If you don't know the exact function name, you can use the Search option to find it. For fun, type **junk** as the function to find, and then click Go.

5. What is one danger of adding formulas to cells on multiple worksheets at once?

Answer: The data in all the cells may not be the same. You may also be wiping out data that exists in cells on the other sheets.

6. Open the `MarketResearch6.xlsx` file that you used in the exercises in this chapter. Describe how you would use a logical function to determine whether more than 80 percent of the needed respondents were used in this survey.

Answer: Click in cell I3, and add the logical function `IF` to it. The logical test is `H3/H2 > 0.8`. Make the True string `"Enough Responses Received"`. Make the False string `"More Responses Needed"`. The result is shown in the Function Arguments dialog box.

7. In this chapter, you learned about Date and Time functions. How can those functions prevent an AutoFill problem caused by adding years to a series of cells?

Answer: They prevent the date and time from being miscalculated.

8. What is an advantage to naming cells and ranges to be used in formulas?

Answer: It ensures that the right data is being used, even if the data is moved. It ensures that future users of the file will be able to understand where the data comes from.

9. Which of the following is not a valid name for a range?

a. HappySheetResult

b. Excel!6

c. Date_Of_Ground_Breaking

d. YesOrNo

Answer: b. Excel!6. This name contains a reserved word in the name of the cell.

Chapter 5

1. Which of the following elements is the only one you should never make invisible?

a. Title

b. Grid lines

c. Values

d. Legend

Answer: c. Values

2. True or False: To change from one chart type to another, you must rebuild the chart from scratch.

Answer: False. You generally just select the new chart type while the old chart is selected, and the change happens.

3. To move a chart to its own sheet, use the _____ button in the _____ group on the _____ tab.

Answer: Move Chart, Location, Chart Tools Design.

4. Bar charts are to column charts as horizontal is to _____.

Answer: Vertical.

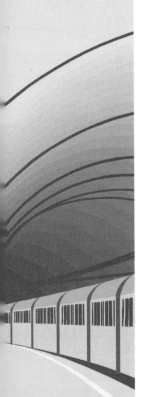

5. When you need to see percentages of a whole, the best kind of chart to use is

a. pie chart.

b. bar chart.

c. line chart.

d. bubble chart.

Answer: a. pie chart.

6. How many series of data are charted with a pie chart?

Answer: One.

7. True or False: The order of data in the legend is fixed and cannot be changed.

Answer: True.

8. Name one situation in which you would use a line chart with two axes.

Answer: When you want to show a relationship between two series where the data has radically different scales

9. True or False: Markers on line charts are always boxes.

Answer: False. Triangles and some other shapes are allowed.

10. Trendlines can be used with which type of chart?

a. Bar chart

b. Scatter chart

c. Pie chart

d. Area chart

Answer: b. Scatter chart

11. What happens when you click the Default Rotation button while formatting the perspective and rotation of a 3-D area chart?

Answer: The current rotation and perspective are set as the new defaults for future 3-D area charts.

Chapter 6

1. True or False: Everything you can do with a PivotTable, you can also do by hand.

Answer: True

2. Which of the following is not an advantage of using PivotTables?

a. Speed

b. Additional understanding of the data

c. Colors in tables that are not available anywhere else in Excel

d. Flexibility

Answer: c. Colors in tables that are not available anywhere else in Excel. Formatting for PivotTables is the same as that for regular tables. No additional colors or combinations of colors are available for PivotTables.

3. True or False: PivotTables can help you analyze inventory data.

Answer: True. By allowing you to look at the data in a wider combination of ways, PivotTables help you understand how inventory has flowed in and out through a store.

4. Which of the following is required for the creation of a PivotTable?

    a. Blank lines within the data

    b. A header row for the data

    c. A connection to an SQL server

    d. A minimum of 100 rows of data

    Answer: b. A header row for the data

5. True or False: In the field definitions for a PivotTable, Q1 and Quarter 1 are the same.

    Answer: False. They might mean the same to you, but unless they are identical, they are split into different categories by Excel when creating the PivotTable.

6. Which of the following cannot be automatically determined with a PivotTable?

    a. The number of times a name appears in a table

    b. The sum of the years in a table

    c. The minimum number of items sold in a month

    d. The longest customer name in the data

    Answer: d. The longest customer name in the data

7. You can change the visibility of the data in a PivotTable in which of these ways:

    a. Click the minus sign for a cell in the first column of the table.

    b. Click the minus sign for the first row of the table.

    c. Change the formula for the value cells.

    d. Right-click a value cell.

    Answer: b. Click the minus sign for the first row of the table.

8. True or False: Data in a PivotTable cannot be formatted.

    Answer: False. As you saw in the exercises, the data might not be formatted by default, but you can use the Value Field Settings dialog box to change the formatting.

9. Describe one case where you would change the settings of the Show Values As tab in the Value Field Settings dialog box.

    Answer: To see the difference between the data in two columns in the same PivotTable

10. Changing the visible data for a PivotChart affects

    a. only the visible data on that PivotChart.

    b. the visible data on all PivotCharts.

    c. the visible data for the current PivotChart and the PivotTable it is based on.

    d. the visible data for the current PivotTable and all PivotCharts based on that table.

    Answer: d. the visible data for the current PivotTable and all PivotCharts based on that table.

11. Give one reason why you would limit the detail level on a PivotChart.

    Answer: To make the PivotChart more understandable or readable

12. Which of the following charts cannot be based on a PivotTable?

    a. Line chart

    b. Pie chart

    c. Bubble chart

    d. None. Any chart type can be created from a PivotTable.

    Answer: c. Bubble chart

Chapter 7

1. Which of the following is not an advantage of importing data into Excel?

    a. Importing data removes errors placed there originally.

    b. Importing data is faster than retyping it.

    c. Importing data eliminates the addition of new typing errors.

    d. b and c

    Answer: a. Importing data removes errors placed there originally.

2. Name one advantage to working with data in Excel rather than in Word.

    Answer: In Excel, formulas are easier to work with, and charts are easier to create.

3. True or False: A comma is the only delimiter that Excel knows how to handle.

    Answer: False. It can use tabs, spaces, and many other characters.

4. Survey questions with a limit of 256 characters per answer are an example of _____ data.

    Answer: Fixed-length

5. When you import data from a CSV file, extra commas

    a. are ignored.

    b. create new columns.

    c. divide large numbers.

    d. tell Excel that the data is a paragraph.

    Answer: b. create new columns.

6. True or False: You can change the length of the fields in a non-delimited file.

    Answer: True. You can do it, but you shouldn't because it may affect how the data is imported into the Excel file.

7. Data grabbed from the Web

    a. cannot be refreshed.

    b. cannot be stored locally.

    c. must be grabbed from the entire Web page or not at all.

    d. can be of any type.

    Answer: d. can be of any type.

8. Name one situation where you would link to data rather than import it.

    Answer: When you want to maintain only one copy of the data. You would also link the data if you always want the data in the Excel file to be up to date.

9. True or False: Access is the only database program that Excel can talk to.

    Answer: False. Excel can talk to any ODBC-compliant database and to most SQL databases.

10. One reason that Excel can now handle larger amounts of data is the prevalence of data being imported from _____.

    Answer: Databases and OLAP cubes

Chapter 8

1. True or False: Interactive worksheets can only be designed for use on the computer.

    Answer: False. Sheets can be laid out to make them easy to use both on the computer and when they are printed.

2. **Name two advantages to working in Page Layout view when you first begin creating a worksheet.**
   Answer: You can see exactly which data will and will not print. You can also add headers and footers in a more natural manner.

3. **Why would you turn on gridlines when viewing a worksheet, but turn them off when printing it?**
   Answer: So that the printed copy looks clean and clear

4. **What is one possible consequence of not setting a print area for a large worksheet?**
   Answer: A large number of blank (or partially blank) sheets will be printed.

5. **Describe two ways to add a background to your worksheet.**
   Answer: Use the Background button on the Page Layout tab. Use the Fill Color options for selected cells.

6. **True or False: Adding a background to your worksheet covers the entire printed page.**
   Answer: True.

7. **Name three elements of an Excel file that are affected by changing the theme for the file.**
   Answer: Table layout, header layout, cell colors, chart colors

8. **Name one print scenario where you are usually likely to print your worksheet and one where you are not likely to print your worksheet.**
   Answer: If you are creating an Excel spreadsheet where the only element to be shared is charted data, you don't have to worry about printing the data itself. However, if the data itself will be printed (for example, data for an annual report), you want to ensure that the data is formatted for print as well as for work.

Chapter 9

1. **What is the difference between the three different CSV file formats Excel can create?**
   Answer: One is for the Mac exclusively; one is for older PC files; and one is for any version of Excel.

2. **True or False: You can save two sheets of data in the same CSV file.**
   Answer: False. You can have only one sheet of data per CSV file.

3. **Name two advantages to linking Excel data when pasting into another application.**
   Answer: Data is kept only in one place. Data is updated once, and the update is shown in both places.

4. **In which of the following cases can you not create a single mail merge from your Excel document?**
   a. Data from the Excel spreadsheet is in multiple sheets.
   b. Column names for the data in the spreadsheet don't match the predefined names in the mail merge.
   c. The Excel sheet contains more columns of data than you want to use in the mail merge.
   d. The Excel sheet contains more rows of data than you want to use in the mail merge.
   Answer: a. Data from the Excel spreadsheet is in multiple sheets.

5. **Name one reason that you should check more than one record when preparing for a mail merge.**
   Answer: The first record can be a header record. The first record can be information about the contents of the file.

6. **True or False: By default, a chart pasted into a PowerPoint presentation is linked and editable.**
   Answer: Yes.

7. **Give a reason why you might choose SharePoint over Office Live or vice versa.**
   Answer: The size of your company

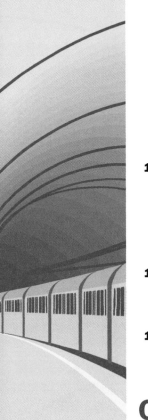

8. Which of the following is needed to create a document library?

    a. A user name

    b. A password

    c. A URL for the site

    d. All of the above

    Answer: d. All of the above

9. True or False: You must have permission to create libraries in order to store documents in them.

    Answer: False. Library creation is controlled by a different set of rules than the creation of items in the library.

10. Which of the following is not possible from Excel?

    a. Upload a document.

    b. Check in a document.

    c. Create a library on SharePoint.

    d. Discard the check-in of a document.

    Answer: c. Create a library on SharePoint.

11. Name the main difference between retrieving a document and checking it out.

    Answer: You can check changes back in only to a document that has been checked out. If you retrieve a document without checking it out, you risk making changes to a copy that is different from the current copy.

12. Explain why version history is important.

    Answer: Version history tells others which information has changed, when it was changed, and why the changes were made.

Chapter 10

1. Name one situation where you would sort your data and one where you would filter your data.

    Answer: Sort: When you want to see the top or bottom elements. Filter: When you only want to see the data that matches the stated criteria.

2. Name one way to define the sort criteria for your data.

    Answer: Use the column title, or click the Sort button on the Data tab.

3. Name two ways that you can find the count of rows in a range of data.

    Answer: Check the bottom of the Excel window; set the total value to Count rather than to Sum; count the rows by hand.

4. Describe a situation where using conditional formatting with sorting improves your productivity as well as the understandability of your data.

    Answer: When your data has errors in it, using conditional formatting to mark the erroneous data allows you to sort the bad data to the bottom and then work with just the valid data.

5. You can't complete which of the following tasks from the Custom List dialog box?

    a. View any custom lists.

    b. Delete a custom list.

    c. Name a custom list.

    d. Edit a custom list.

    Answer: c. Name a custom list.

6. **Name the biggest advantage to filtering your data.**

Answer: It enables you to hide unwanted data and leave behind only the data that you're interested in working with.

7. **To clear the filters in use in your document, use the _____ button in the _____ group on the _____ tab.**

Answer: Clear; Sort and Filter; Data

8. **True or False: You can filter only on numeric data.**

Answer: False. You can filter on any type of data that Excel understands.

9. **Which addressing method is used when you create an advanced filter: relative addressing or absolute addressing?**

Answer: Absolute addressing

10. **Which of the following does not prevent Excel from grouping and outlining your data? (More than one answer is possible.)**

a. No labels are defined for the data set.

b. Empty cells are in the data set.

c. You have empty rows of data.

d. Text data is within the data set.

Answer: d. Text data is within your data set.

Chapter 11

1. **Which one of these examples has duplicate cell content?**

a. Jenny and jenny

b. 99.00 and 99

c. 1/1/2006 and 1-Jan-06

d. sixty and 60

Answer: c. 1/1/2006 and 1-Jan-06

2. **Describe a situation where you would use the Remove Duplicates feature on cells in a single column.**

Answer: The Remove Duplicates feature is used on a single column when the data in the columns of the spreadsheet are not related to each other.

3. **Describe a situation where you would use the Remove Duplicates feature on cells in multiple columns at once.**

Answer: The Remove Duplicates feature is used on multiple columns when the data in the columns is related to each other

4. **True or False: All columns in a sheet must be checked for duplicates at the same time.**

Answer: False.

5. **True or False: Duplicate data can be valid data.**

Answer: True.

6. **Name the three parts of a validation rule.**

Answer: The allowed data (the data to be placed in the cell), the type of the data (the definition of what the data can look like), the range of the data

7. Error circles
   a. can be applied to more than one sheet at a time.
   b. stay active when a file is closed.
   c. disappear when the error is fixed.
   d. can be different colors at different times.
   Answer: c. disappear when the error is fixed.

8. Input messages can be set to be shown
   a. to the left of the cell.
   b. only when a cell is selected.
   c. whenever a cell is blank.
   d. always, no matter whether the cell is selected.
   Answer: b. only when a cell is selected.

9. Name the two buttons that appear on an informational error message.
   Answer: Ignore and Cancel

10. True or False: Data lists for a validation rule can be on a different sheet from the data.
   Answer: False. All data and all list entries must be on the same sheet.

11. True or False: Text data can be consolidated.
   Answer: False. There is nothing to be consolidated with text. Only numerical data can be consolidated.

12. When are consolidation results refreshed?
   a. When the consolidation is linked to the data and the data changes
   b. Whenever the file is opened
   c. Whenever the data used for the consolidation is changed
   d. When the consolidation sheet is copied
   Answer: a. When the consolidation is linked to the data and the data changes

13. True or False: Consolidation results can be nested.
   Answer: True.

Chapter 12

1. Which of the following statements is true?
   a. When you're using Goal Seek, the results can be stored in a range of cells.
   b. Cells in multiple sheets can be changed during the creation of a single scenario.
   c. Formulas can be used to define the change to a cell when creating a scenario.
   d. Cells containing formulas can be used as the *by changing cell* of a goal.
   Answer: a. When you're using Goal Seek, the results can be stored in a range of cells.

2. What does the Show button in the Scenario Manager do when a scenario is selected?
   Answer: It changes the data in the actual sheet to show the result of running the manager.

3. True or False: Only five cells can be used to create a single scenario.
   Answer: False. You must have at least five cells, but you can have more.

4. Name one difference between the target cell and the *by changing cell* when goal seeking.
   Answer: The target cell is the cell that contains the answer you're seeking. The *by changing cell* is the cell where the change will be made.

5. True or False: Goal Seek always finds an answer.

Answer: False. You can ask it to make an impossible calculation.

6. True or False: All answers found by Goal Seek are valid.

Answer: False. For example, you cannot have someone work a negative number of hours to reach a payroll goal.

7. Suppose that cell R5 contains the number of employees and cell B17 contains the profit. Using Goal Seek, which of the two cells would you change and which one would Excel change?

Answer: You change B17, and Excel changes R5.

8. Which of the following situations prevents you from being able to create an exponential trendline?

a. Too many data points are in the series.

b. Negative data points are in the series.

c. Too few data points are in the series.

d. Too much of a difference exists between data points in the series.

Answer: c. Too few data points are in the series.

9. By default, how far in the future does a Linear Forecast Trendline reach?

Answer: Two months

Chapter 13

1. True or False: Excel 2007 makes it easy for any user to add buttons to any tab.

Answer: False. You can add buttons to a tab only if you understand XML or have a special tool.

2. What is the QAT?

a. Quick Access Toolbar

b. Quick Action Toolbar

c. Quietly Accessible Tools

d. Quality Assurance Tools

Answer: Quick Access Toolbar

3. Name the three buttons that are on the QAT by default.

Answer: Save, Undo, Redo

4. Which of the following actions does not hide the Ribbon?

a. Right-clicking a tab on the Ribbon.

b. Double-clicking a tab on the Ribbon.

c. Pressing Alt+H on the keyboard.

d. Selecting the More Commands option on the Customize Quick Access Toolbar menu.

Answer: c. Pressing Alt+H on the keyboard.

5. True or False: You can put the QAT anywhere you want.

Answer: False. You can place it only above and below the Ribbon.

6. True or False: You can have only 50 buttons on the QAT.

Answer: False. You can have as many buttons as you want.

7. QAT changes

    a. can be applied to all Excel documents on the computer.

    b. go away when the current Excel session is closed.

    c. can be applied to only the current document.

    d. A and C

    Answer: d. A and C

8. Buttons are added to the QAT

    a. from right to left and cannot be moved around.

    b. from left to right and cannot be moved around.

    c. from right to left and can be moved around.

    d. from left to right and can be moved around.

    Answer: d. from left to right and can be moved around.

9. True or False: Buttons on the QAT can be moved by dragging.

    Answer: False. They can be added or moved only by using the customization interface.

10. True or False: All buttons that can be added to the QAT are found elsewhere on the Ribbon.

    Answer: False. Some buttons that can be added to the QAT were not implemented on the Ribbon.

11. To change the default location of your AutoRecover files, which category of options do you need to access from the Excel Options window?

    a. Popular

    b. Advanced

    c. Resources

    d. Save

    Answer: d. Save

12. To find out whether you need to add any updates to your copy of Excel, which category of options do you need to access from the Excel Options window?

    a. Popular

    b. Advanced

    c. Resources

    d. Save

    Answer: c. Resources

Chapter 14

1. Macros and add-ins allow you to _____ a series of steps so that you don't need to perform each one manually.

    Answer: Automate or repeat

2. Which of the following is true?

    a. After installation, add-ins are available only from a single file.

    b. After installation, macros are available only from a single file.

    c. After installation, add-ins are always available, no matter which file is opened.

    d. After installation, macros are always available, no matter which file is opened.

    Answer: c. After installation, add-ins are always available, no matter which file is opened.

3. True or False: Add-ins are always installed by using the Excel interface.

Answer: False. Some add-ins are installed by external install routines.

4. Name four basic types of add-ins that you can install.

Answer: Excel add-ins or VBA add-ins, .COM add-ins, smart tags, and XML expansion packs

5. Which of the following cannot be installed by using the Office Button menu?

a. VBA add-ins

b. .COM add-ins

c. Smart tags

d. All add-ins are installed from outside the Excel interface.

Answer: c. Smart tags

6. How do you add a document inspector?

a. Inspect a document for changes.

b. Use XML.

c. Use the add-in options available from the Office Button menu.

d. You can't add document inspectors; you can only disable them.

Answer: a. Inspect a document for changes.

7. True or False: Uninstalling an add-in always changes the Excel interface.

Answer: False. Some add-ins do not change the interface at all.

8. All add-ins found by using Office Online

a. are from Microsoft.

b. can be trusted.

c. are free.

d. None of the above.

Answer: d. None of the above.

Chapter 15

1. True or False: All macros are enabled automatically.

Answer: False. To run most macros, you must click the Options button next to the security warning and then select the Enable This Content radio button in the Microsoft Office Security Options dialog box.

2. Name the two tabs that contain buttons that let you record macros.

Answer: The View tab and the Developer tab.

3. True or False: All Excel functionality can be recorded into a macro.

Answer: False. Although most functionality can be recorded, you may find some Excel functions that cannot be recorded. As you find out more about VBA, you'll learn to search the Object Model to find out how to do virtually any task that Excel can do.

4. Which of the following is a valid macro name?

a. Count Numbers

b. CountNumbers

c. Count/Numbers

d. Count

Answer: b. CountNumbers. Macro names cannot contain spaces, special characters, or reserved words.

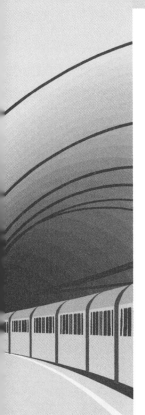

5. True or False: The shortcut key M initiates the same macro as the shortcut m.

Answer: False. The capital letter *M* and the small letter *m* are not considered the same letter in terms of initiating macros so that more macros can be controlled by using the keyboard.

6. What commands does Excel record after you start recording a macro?

a. All tasks you perform on your computer until you click the Stop Recording button

b. Only the next command that is executed

c. Most of the tasks you perform in Excel until you click the Stop Recording button

d. Nothing. You cannot record macros in Excel 2007.

Answer: c. Most of the tasks you perform in Excel until you click the Stop Recording button. Excel records all Excel-related functionality that it can record until you click the Stop Recording button. If you do something while recording that cannot be recorded, Excel just skips those keystrokes and continues at the next point possible, which can cause some unusual results in your recorded macros.

7. True or False: Activating the Developer tab in Excel affects other Office programs.

Answer: True. Turning on the Developer tab in Excel, Word, or PowerPoint turns it on for the other two applications too.

8. True or False: After you record a macro, you cannot change it.

Answer: False. Using the Visual Basic Editor, you can adjust the macro in many different ways.

9. Which of the following is not a valid way to create a macro:

a. Copy the code from another application or file and paste it in.

b. Record it.

c. Type it from scratch.

d. All these methods are valid ways to create a macro.

Answer: d. All these methods are valid ways to create a macro.

10. If you add an extra parenthesis in macro code, Excel

a. displays an error message when you type the parenthesis.

b. displays an error message when you close the Visual Basic Editor.

c. displays an error message when the code is run.

d. always removes the error.

Answer: c. Displays an error message when the code is run. When you compile or run the code, you see the message that an error occurred.

11. Describe how you know which line Excel thinks caused the error when a running macro encounters an error.

Answer: The line that was being compiled when Excel found the error is highlighted in blue.

12. Name a circumstance in which you would enable all macros.

Answer: If you are working on debugging a complicated macro and you need to open and close your file regularly, enable macros while you do the debugging. Be sure to return the security level to a more restrictive setting when you finish debugging the macro.

13. Give an example of a conditional statement.

Answer: `IF...Then...Else, While...End While,` and `For...Next`. Conditional statements control the processing order of lines of code.

14. `For` loops and `While` loops are different in which of the following ways?

   a. Code in a `For` loop always executes once. Code in a `While` loop may not execute at all.

   b. Code in a `While` loop always executes once. Code in a `For` loop may not execute at all.

   c. Code in both types of loops always runs at least once, but a `For` loop does the incrementing for you.

   d. Code in both types of loops always runs at least once, but a `While` loop does the incrementing for you

   Answer: a. Code in a `For` loop always executes once. Code in a `While` loop may not execute at all. A `For` loop is always run at least once. A `While` loop executes only the first time if the condition for the `While` loop is true when the loop is started.

15. True or False: The MsgBox and InputBox commands in VBA do the same thing.

   Answer: False. You use MsgBox to tell the user something. You use InputBox to tell them something and ask for a value in return.

16. Name two ways to initiate a macro.

   Answer: Three different methods are mentioned in this chapter: Use a Control character sequence, the Macro dialog box, or the QAT (Quick Access Toolbar).

17. True or False: Macros in files stored in the templates folders are automatically trusted when Excel is installed on most machines.

   Answer: True. However, you or your IT department can make the templates folders nontrusted locations if you want.

18. Who can add trusted locations to your installation of Excel?

   a. Anyone with a user ID for the computer

   b. The person who installed Office on your computer

   c. You

   d. All of the above

   Answer: d. Anyone with a user ID can change the trusted locations. This is one reason to be sure that you know who has access to your computer if you enable a new trusted location.

19. Folders are to trusted locations as certificates are to trusted _____.

   Answer: Publishers or sources

Chapter 16

1. Which of the following statements is not true?

   a. Code in the Auto_Open routine runs every time Excel opens.

   b. Code in the Auto_Close routine runs every time Excel closes.

   c. Code in the `PERSONAL.XLSB` file runs every time you use Excel.

   d. Code in the `PERSONAL.XLSB` file is always trusted.

   Answer: c. Code in the `PERSONAL.XLSB` file runs every time you use Excel. Although code in the Auto_Open and Auto_Close routines runs every time you use Excel, it may or may not run if you have other code there.

2. True or False: You can use the Edit button in the Macros dialog box to access the Auto_Open and Auto_Close routines for editing.

Answer: False. To edit the code in these (or any other routines) in `PERSONAL.XLSB`, you must step into the routine and then edit it.

3. True or False: Code in the Auto_Close routine runs whenever an Excel file is closed.

Answer: True.

4. Which of the following may not be a good way to initiate a macro that you are delivering as an add-in?

a. A keyboard shortcut

b. A button on the Add-Ins tab

c. A button on the QAT

d. All of the above are good, safe ways to allow people to start your add-ins.

Answer: a. A keyboard shortcut. You should not use a keyboard shortcut to initiate a macro delivered as an add-in because that key may be mapped to another application.

5. `On Error` is used to _____ errors so that your code can end gracefully.

Answer: trap or capture

6. What is the difference between `Exit Sub` and `End Sub`?

a. `Exit Sub` can be used anywhere in a macro, and `End Sub` can be used only at the end of the macro.

b. `End Sub` can be used anywhere in a macro, and `Exit Sub` can be used only at the end of the macro.

c. There is no difference; they are interchangeable.

d. You can use only one of them in any given macro.

Answer: a. `Exit Sub` can be used anywhere in a macro, and `End Sub` can be used only at the end of the macro.

7. True or False: You cannot edit code in an Excel 2007 add-in.

Answer: False. You can edit code in an Excel add-in if you directly open the add-in file.

8. True or False: After you record a macro, you cannot change it.

Answer: False. You can edit any macro whose code you can see.

9. True or False: Storing an add-in in the default location automatically installs it.

Answer: False. Placing the add-in in the default folder makes it available for installation, but does not make it available to run.

10. When testing an add-in, you should

a. trust that it works and just deliver it after you save it.

b. run it on your machine, verify that it works, and then hand it over to users.

c. run it once on another machine, verify that it works, and then hand it over to users.

d. run the macro in every possible way on another machine, verify that it works, and then hand it over to users.

Answer: d. run the macro in every possible way on another machine, verify that it works, and then hand it over to users.

B

Getting Help with Excel

You've finished this book and are ready to get out there and use Excel! As you work with Excel, however, you will learn things that you want to share with other users, and you will want to learn more about various areas of Excel. You will also find special circumstances where something doesn't work quite right in Excel.

That's when you should check out this appendix. It lists sites that are useful for finding help when you're stuck on an Excel problem. This appendix is split into three sections:

Microsoft online communities for Excel: Sites with information that is covered in each of the seven Excel communities that Microsoft hosts on its site. The communities offer peer-to-peer support from volunteer users across the Microsoft communities. You can reach these sites by using the Microsoft site links, Google Groups, or a newsgroup reader, such as Outlook Express (in Windows XP) or Windows Mail (in Windows Vista).

Other online communities for Excel: The online groups that I trust the most. They aren't the *only* ones I trust — just the ones that I am most comfortable using. These communities include online forums and e-mail lists. Like the Microsoft communities, these sites are run by Excel users who want to ensure that others can find the Excel help they need.

Web sites and blogs supported by the Microsoft MVPs in Excel: Sites that are run by the best of the best in the Excel world. I owe major debts to many of the content providers listed in this section. When I get stuck, they are there to help me. These sites can be of great help to you, too.

Watch Your Step

Before you start using these online resources, please take a moment to verify that the URLs for the sites haven't changed. The Web is a dynamic place, but this book is static. If the sites move, the addresses aren't updated in the printed book. If a link mentioned in this appendix (or anywhere else) doesn't take you to the site that you think it should, search for the site at Google.com to find out whether it has moved.

Posting Etiquette

The volunteers at the resources in this appendix are your peers — they answer questions because they want to, not because they have to. Before you ask questions at any of the sites, read the rules of etiquette for using them:

If you join a group, be a good member. Know whether you are signing up for an e-mail group or a group where you need to check a Web site to find your answers. Realize that other people on the group are asking and answering questions. Don't get upset if it takes a little time to get an answer. Don't get upset if you receive answers that aren't related to your issue.

- **Check back for your answers.** If you don't get a response, don't assume that someone doesn't like you. The site's personnel may be busy or just not know the answer.

- **Provide as much information about the problem or situation as you can.** Remember that the person on the other end can't see your computer and doesn't know exactly what is happening. If you receive an error message, provide its exact wording. If you have an unusual setup, say so.

- **Talk about not only the problem you are having at the moment but also the task you are trying to perform.** You may run across a better way to do what you need to do. If your posts mention only the exact problem you encounter, no one can help you solve bigger problems.

- **Always specify your version of Excel and your operating system, and mention whether you have any add-ins installed.** If you have recently made changes to your system, say so — even if you don't think that the changes could possibly make a difference.

- **Be polite.** The people who are trying to help you are doing it because they want to. Saying "please" and "thank you" goes a long way with volunteers.

Microsoft Online Communities for Excel

For many years, Microsoft has hosted an excellent resource known as newsgroups, where you can ask questions of other Excel users on a wide variety of topics ranging from basic questions to detailed coding questions. The Excel Communities have these seven groups:

- **Excel General Questions:** The catchall area for any Excel-related question. If your question doesn't fit well in one of the other areas, if you aren't sure which area to check for an answer, or if you need to post a question and don't know where to post it, use this group.

- **Excel New Users:** If you're new to Excel and don't know how to start a project or what you can do in Excel, check out this group.

- **Excel Application Errors:** If Excel is crashing on you or you're receiving an error message that you don't understand and the Help system doesn't make it clear, search this area to see whether anyone else has had the same problem. If you don't find a resolution, post your question.

- **Excel Charts:** This group covers everything you ever wanted to ask about simple or complicated Excel charts.

Excel Setup: You may be having a problem installing Excel, or it may be trying to reinstall when you open another part of Office. Chances are good that the people answering questions in this group know what to do about the problem.

Excel Programming: If you're having VBA problems, your solution is here! This community is where the extreme Excel code gurus hang out. If they can't give you an answer off the top of their heads, give them a little time to help you work it out. If you're posting a question about a specific code problem, always post the relevant snippet of code.

Excel Worksheet Functions: If you're not getting the results you expect from an equation, check out this community area. These folks know functions. They can tell you how to compute almost anything. (If someone in this group can't compute something, it probably can't be computed with Excel.)

To get to the communities, either go to the Microsoft Office Online Excel page and follow the Communities link, or go directly to the Office Communities Home page and click the appropriate Excel link. Both sites are listed here:

Office Online Excel page: `http://office.microsoft.com/excel`

Office Communities list: `www.microsoft.com/office/community`

If you don't speak English, don't worry. When you go to the Communities pages, you're always sent to the page for your part of the world. If Excel communities in your language exist, the Communities page for your country links to them rather than to the U.S. community.

Other Online Communities for Excel

In addition to being able to visit the Microsoft Communities, you can check out several other sites for help from people who use Excel and Office. The communities listed here are simply the ones I like the best:

Microsoft Office Freelist Group (MSO) (`www.freelists.org/webpage/mso`): MSO is an e-mail-based, peer-to-peer group maintained by Linda Johnson, who runs the popular Office site Linda's Computer Stop (`http://personal-computer-tutor.com/index.htm`). This group regularly answers questions about all Office products. Look into it, and you may even see a post or two by yours truly.

The Office Experts Forum (`www.theofficeexperts.com/forum/`): If you don't want to get e-mail or you prefer a forum-style interface over an e-mail or newsgroup style, check out the Office Experts Forum. Run by part of the MrExcel team, the forum is staffed by several Office MVPs.

MrExcel Message Board (www.mrexcel.com/board2/): Another of the MrExcel Web forums, this one is dedicated to Excel and Excel solutions. Staffed by the Excel gurus whom MrExcel knows, this site is a forum for every Excel user, from novice to expert.

Excel MVP Web Sites

The goal of Microsoft's Most Valuable Professional program is to recognize experts across the company's product line. MVPs are not Microsoft employees — they are users who started where you are and then became product experts. MVPs donate time to the online community in a variety of ways and specialize in Microsoft products ranging from the Xbox to servers and everything in between.

The sites listed in this section are hosted by Excel MVPs whom I know personally and whose sites are among the best known in the world. Most of the 73 Excel MVPs from around the world have sites that are just as good as the ones listed here. If you need to learn something about Excel and you cannot find it on one of the following five sites, search the sites for other Microsoft Excel MVPs:

Bill Jelen (www.mrexcel.com/): Bill, also known as MrExcel, has a site full of tips and ideas for all Excel users. He was the first person to create a program to push data successfully from Excel to OneNote by using VBA.

Tushar Mehta (www.tushar-mehta.com/excel/): Tushar is the creator of many Excel and PowerPoint add-ins. You can find him online at www.tushar-mehta.com/.

Jon Peltier (www.peltiertech.com/index.html): If you have an Excel charting question, Jon is your source for answers. If he doesn't know how to make a chart do what you need it to do, chances are that it cannot be done. His site contains more than 500 pages of great information.

Andy Pope (www.andypope.info/index.htm): Andy is another Excel guru who seems to know almost everything. Even though I can't even begin to classify the range of content on his site, I can tell you that if you want to stretch your belief in what Excel can do, check out his Fun and Funky page at www.andypope.info/fun.htm.

John Walkenbach (http://j-walk.com/ss/): If you need to find an Excel resource to take you to the next level, John has probably written just the book to take you there, no matter where "there" is. Amazon.com lists more than 60 books written by John, with more being published all the time. (His site lists only 32 books, but his Excel and Office 2007 books aren't on the site yet.)

If you need more online Excel resources, check out the MVPs.Org Excel links at www.mvps.org/links.html#Excel. Although this site is run by current and former Microsoft MVPs, it isn't connected to Microsoft. The site is full of links and resources offered by Microsoft MVPs from every area. The site itself is a fun place to spend an afternoon. The breadth of knowledge covered in the sites hosted and linked to from here will amaze you.

Index

exam, 422–423
testing, 408–412, 419–420
built-in cell styles, 70
buttons
    about, 9
    adding to QAT, 330–332
    Close, 6
    Command, 5
    Debug, 379
    Developer tab, 371
    Enable All Macros, 378
    Enable This Content, 365
    Excel Options, 337, 370
    finding location, 335–337
    Help, 17
    Macro Security, 378
    Minimize, 6
    Office, 5, 20
    Options, 14, 365
    Paste Button options, 56–57
    rearranging, 332–335
    Refresh All, 187
    Resize Table, 61
    Restore, 6
    Run, 15
    System Info, 341
    Table Name, 61
    Table Style Options, 62
    Table Styles, 62
    View Macros, 409
    X, 12

C

calculations
    about, 109
    iterative, 93
    options, formulas, 92–93

categorizing data, pie charts, 124–130
cells
    about, 26
    alignment, 64
    borders, 208–211
    to cell moving, 27–28
    fill color, 64
    formatting, 63–66
    formulas in, 87–89
    references, 27
    referencing in formulas, 89–91, 93–94
    selecting, 30
    selecting column, 31
    selecting small group, 30
    styles, 70
Change Chart Type dialog box, 120
changing
    cell alignment, 64
    cell fill color, 64
    Excel settings, 337–341
    files from library, SharePoint,
        241–243
    numeric format, 65
    QAT location, 329–330
chapter 1 exam
    answers, 426–427
    questions, 21–22
chapter 2 exam
    answers, 427
    questions, 46–47
chapter 3 exam
    answers, 427–428
    questions, 81–82
chapter 4 exam
    answers, 428–429
    questions, 110–111
chapter 5 exam
    answers, 429–430
    questions, 146–147

F

features, 400
Fibonacci numbers progression, 365
field, 171
field layout, 171
file extensions
    CSV, 17, 178–179, 196
    PDF, 17
    TSV, 181
    TXT, 17
    XLS, 11, 16, 44, 225
    XLSB, 16
    XLSM, 13–16, 369
    XLSX, 11–13
    XLTM, 17
    XLTX, 17
    XML, 11, 350
file formats
    about, 11–17
    macro-enabled file format, 369
    text files, 178–179
filenames, 26
files
    changing from library, SharePoint,
      241–243
    consolidating data across, 295
    CSV, 17, 178–179, 196
    delimited text, 178–179
    Excel, 26
    fixed data, 184–185
    fixed text, 179
    flat, 171
    importing, 183–184
    importing delimited text, 180–183
    PDF, 17
    saving Excel data as CSV, 223–225
    sharing, 44

tab-delimited, 181
template, 17
text, 178–179
TSV, 181
TXT, 17
XLS, 11, 16, 44, 225
XLSB, 16
XLSM, 13–16, 369
XLSX, 11–13
XLTM, 17
XLTX, 17
XML, 11, 350
fill color, cell, 64
filling in series of entries, AutoFill,
  40–43
filters
    about, 79, 249, 259
    advanced, 263–264
    custom, 59
    exam, 270–271
    number, 59
    PivotChart Filter Pane task pane, 164
    quick, 261–263
    single criterion, 259–261
    table data, 59–60
    text, 59
Find, Word, 186
Find and Replace dialog box, 10, 11
finding
    location of buttons, QAT, 335–337
    templates on computer, 33–35
fixed data files, 184–185
fixed text files, 179
fixing
    errors, 378–381
    logic errors, 382–385
    syntax errors, 374–378
flat files, 171

cells in formulas, 89–91, 93–94
data, 190–191
refining styles, 71–72
Refresh All button, 187
relative addresses
about, 109
formulas, 89–91
removing
add-ins, 356
duplicates from columns in table,
277–279
duplicates from select columns in
table, 280
removing duplicate data
about, 275–280
cells from single column, 276–277
from columns in table, 277–279
repeating series of steps, macros, 366–369
Replace, Word, 186
Replace dialog box, 383
reports, using Excel data, 225–227
Research task pane, 74–75
reset, 421
Resize Table button, 61
resizing
columns, 51–52
rows, 51–52
Restore button, 6
retrieving documents from library,
SharePoint, 239–241
Review tab, 7
Ribbon
about, 4–5, 20
check boxes, 370
Developer tab, 363
Office Button, 5
QAT, 6
tabs, 6–9

rows
about, 26
height, 80
limits, 27
resizing, 51–52
rules
Top/Bottom Rules, 67
validation, data, 281–284, 298
Run button, 15
runtime error, 400

S

Save As dialog box, 417
Save dialog box, 10
saving
Excel data as CSV file, 223–225
Excel data as workbook format, 225
worksheets, 43–44
XLS files, 44
scales, Color Scales format, 67
scatter plot charts, 135–138
scenario, 321
Scenario Manager, 303, 305–309
scope
bugs, 374
debugging macros, 374
screen capture program, SnagIt, 348
secondary axes, 132
Security Options dialog box, 365
Security Warning dialog box, 15
security warning macros, 364, 369
segment, 145
Select Data Source dialog box, 128
selecting
cells in a row, 30
cells in a column, 31

summary sheet, 321
surface charts, 142
syntax
    debugging macros, 374
    errors, 374–378, 401
System Info button, 341

T

tab-delimited files, 181
table data
    filtering, 59–60
    sorting, 59–60
Table Name button, 61
Table Style Options button, 62
Table Styles button, 62
Table Tools Design tab, 61–62
tables
    about, 57, 80
    customizing, 61–63
    fit on single page, printing, 75–76
    grouping data in, 57–63
tabs
    about, 20
    activating Developer, 370–371
    Add-Ins, 8
    Advanced, 339
    contextual, 8
    Data, 7
    Developer, 363
    Formulas, 7
    Home, 6
    Insert, 6
    Page Layout, 6
    PivotChart Tools Analyze, 167
    Review, 7
    Ribbon, 6–9
    Table Tools Design, 61–62
    View, 7
tags, smart, 353–355
target cell, 321
target value, 321
task panes
    about, 9–10, 20
    Clip Art, 10
    PivotChart Filter Pane, 164
    PivotTable Field List, 156
    Proofing, 74
    Research, 74–75
    Thesaurus, 74
TechSmith, 348
templates
    about, 45
    Billing Statement, 35–38
    creating worksheets from, 33–38
    files, 17
    finding on computer, 33–35
testing building add-ins, 408–412,
    419–420
text
    filters, 59
    functions, 102–103
    strings manipulation, 102–103
text files
    about, 178, 197
    delimited, 178–179
    fixed, 179
    importing, 180–183
    moving data from, 178–185
themes
    about, 70–71
    applying, 215–216
    Use Destination Theme option, 55

Thesaurus, 74
Thesaurus task pane, 74
3-D area charts, 170
3-D charts, 144
3-D Clustered Column charts, 120
time functions, 104
titles, chart, 116, 145
tools
    analysis, 350
    PivotChart Tools Analyze tab, 167
    Table Tools Design tab, 61–62
    Visual Studio Tools for Office, 394
Top/Bottom Rules format, 67
transpose, 80
Transpose option, 56
trap an error, 401
trendlines
    about, 321
    what-if analysis, 304, 315–320
trends
    about, 145
    scatter plot charts, 135–138
Trust Center
    about, 378
    Trusted Publishers feature, 399
trust settings, 358
Trusted Location dialog box, 396
Trusted Locations list
    about, 396
    check boxes, 399
trusted locations macros, 394–399
Trusted Publishers feature, Trust Center,
    399
trusted sources macros, 399
TSV files, 181
2-D charts, 144
TXT file extension, 17

U

upload, 244
uploading
    Excel files with Excel, 238
    Excel files with SharePoint, 236–237
URLs, 244
Use Destination Theme option, 55

V

validating data
    about, 275, 281, 298
    exam, 299–300
    invalid data messages, 285–287
    list of items, 287–289
    messages, 284–285
    rules, 281–284
validation rules, 281–284, 298
Value Field Settings dialog box, 160–161
values
    chart, 116, 145
    target, 321
Values and Number Formatting option, 55
Values and Source Formatting option, 55
Values Only option, 55
VBA Project Object Model check box, 378
VBA (Visual Basic for Applications),
    347, 363, 401
VBE (Visual Basic Editor)
    about, 401
    debugging macros, 374–385
version
    about, 244
    history, 244
view
    data view, printing worksheets, 79
    Page Layout, 208–211

X

X button, 12
XLS files, 11, 16, 44, 225
XLSB files, 16
XLSM files, 13–16, 369

XLSX files, 11–13
XLTM files, 17
XLTX files, 17
XML expansion packs add-ins, 350
XML files, 11

Elevate your
education.

The L Line puts learning on the express line. Each book gives you a crash course in the skills you need to master concepts and technologies that will advance your career or enhance your options. Discover how quickly you can reach your destination on The Express Line to Learning.

What you'll find on *The L Line*

- Pre-reading questions to help you identify your level of knowledge
- Real-world case studies and applications
- Complete tutorial coverage with plenty of illustrations and examples
- Easy-to-follow directions
- Practice exams that let you evaluate your progress
- Terminology overviews to clarify technical jargon
- Additional online resources

Give more at the Office.

Master the skills you need to make yourself indispensable in the business world.

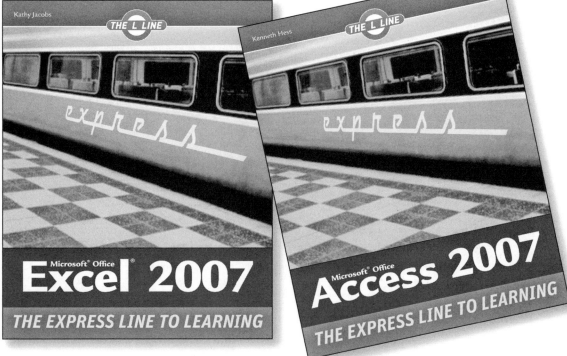

Excel is the second most-used Microsoft Office application. Conquer the newest version of the world's most popular spreadsheet program with *The L Line*, focusing on common practices and skill sets that professionals need.

ISBN-10: 0-470-10788-X
ISBN-13: 978-0-470-10788-1

Proficiency in Access 2007, the Microsoft Office database application, is increasingly in demand. Gain the skills you need with *The L Line*, including plenty of practical examples that prepare you for the real world.

ISBN-10: 0-470-10790-1
ISBN-13: 978-0-470-10790-4

WILEY
Now you know.

The more you know, the farther you'll go.

Jump aboard *The L Line*, the direct route to sharper skills and better opportunities.